A Volume of Friendship

A Volume of Friendship

The Letters of Eleanor Roosevelt
and Isabella Greenway
1904–1953

Edited by
Kristie Miller and Robert H. McGinnis

Preface by Blanche Wiesen Cook

THE ARIZONA HISTORICAL SOCIETY
TUCSON

For
T. L. Hawkins
and
Carol McGinnis

THE ARIZONA HISTORICAL SOCIETY
949 E. Second Street
Tucson, Arizona 85719

Copyright © 2009, The Arizona Historical Society
Library of Congress Cataloging-in-Publication Data

Roosevelt, Eleanor, 1884–1962.
A volume of friendship : the letters of Eleanor Roosevelt and Isabella Greenway, 1904–1953 /
edited by Kristie Miller and Robert H. McGinnis ; preface by Blanche Wiesen Cook.
p. cm.
Includes bibliographical references.
ISBN 978-0-910037-50-1
1. Roosevelt, Eleanor, 1884–1962—Correspondence. 2. King, Isabella Greenway,
1886–1953—Correspondence. 3. Presidents' spouses—United States—Correspondence.
I. King, Isabella Greenway, 1886-1953. II. Miller, Kristie, 1944– III. McGinnis, Robert H.
IV. Arizona Historical Society. V. Title.
E807.1.R48A4 2009
973.917092—dc22
2009007650

Book design: David Alcorn, Alcorn Publication Design

Contents

Abbreviations

IG – Isabella Selmes Ferguson Greenway King.
ER – Eleanor Roosevelt.
FDR – Franklin Delano Roosevelt.
RHMF – Robert Harry Munro Ferguson.
TR – Theodore Roosevelt.

Preface

*E*leanor Roosevelt Roosevelt[1] and Isabella Selmes Ferguson Greenway King met when they were teenagers (sixteen and eighteen), before that word entered our language. New York debutantes, connected by an immediate sense of joy in each other's company as well as labyrinthian family friendships, they both married in 1905. Isabella was one of ER's bridesmaids, and they spent some part of their European honeymoon travels together. Their remarkable friendship survived long geographic distances, profound political differences, and remained to the end marked by vast admiration, trust, and integrity. Their children were friends, and Isabella's Arizona homes provided them a riding and camping sanctuary, a life-long healing center, during upsets and troubles.

During the 1920s and 1930s, Isabella Greenway was one of ER's most important friends: a guide when it came to raising children, a profound ally when it came to political visions and actions. Indeed, during the first White House years, Isabella was ER's closest confidante among her political allies. A woman of spontaneity, warmth, and bold determination, Isabella Greenway was on an airplane within thirty minutes when ER called for advice during a campaign stop. After she was elected to Congress, Greenway brought a welcome flamboyance to ER's circle. All New Deal efforts for women and workers were enhanced by their "air our minds" bi-weekly luncheons— a convergence of the "four of hearts": ER, Greenway, Mary Harriman Rumsey, Frances Perkins, and occasionally others, notably Caroline O'Day and Lady Lindsay (Elizabeth Lindsay, married to Sir Ronald Lindsay, Britain's ambassador to the United States). ER wrote about these luncheons in *My Day*: "Four of us, all intimately connected to public life for many years . . . [meet] to unburden our souls. Each time we do it, I think what a safeguard it is to have anyone anywhere in the world whom you feel you can talk to with absolute sincerity and with no danger of having the rest of the world knowing

1. Eleanor Roosevelt married Franklin D. Roosevelt, and thus was a double Roosevelt.

ix

anything about it, or of any misunderstanding arising between you individually. . . . We laugh together a great deal, but I often come away with the feeling that back of the laughter something serious was really on our minds and all the better for being off our minds."[2]

By 1938 political differences intruded upon their friendship. Greenway decided not to run again for Congress, and returned to Arizona. Then, in 1940, their friendship was profoundly challenged by Isabella Greenway's opposition to FDR's third-term race—and her decision to support Wendell Willkie. Not only did Isabella Greenway fear the dictatorial implications of a third-term presidency in time of war, she opposed FDR's retreat from New Deal efforts on behalf of still-struggling unemployed Americans. She wrote ER: "Here comes another chapter & one I don't like the experience of—I haven't a doubt that some of the publicity . . . has reached you about my support of Willkie—& that you have wondered why you have not heard from me—For too many reasons to inflict on you—I made up my mind before the Democratic convention that I couldn't endorse a third term. . . . In addition to that you know my overwhelming conviction that more and different programs could & should be followed thro about employment."

Isabella Greenway met with Willkie in Colorado Springs, and was persuaded that he would pursue a bold program regarding "re-employment" far more hopeful than any the "various departments of Government . . . including Commerce" contemplated. Evidently Isabella Greenway's meetings with Harry Hopkins and others had left her "entirely disheartened." Willkie restored her political enthusiasm. She knew ER would understand: "How I love & admire you—you know—There was enough to read between the lines of your convention speech to convince me that you were not instrumental in initiating the third term policy—& your statement (a while ago) that to date 'we have bought the time to think'—is I believe one of the great truths of this period. It is in the hope that further constructive efforts can be forced thro that I am going to join those Democrats working for Willkie. . . . You would I know do what I am doing if you felt as I do. I feel very confident that my participation will be kept to impersonal issues & that our lifelong family relations will be safeguarded to the best of my ability. . . . A heart full of love always—& an understanding that surpasses all words—& will survive in spite of everything. Devotedly, Isabella."[3]

2. Cook, *Eleanor Roosevelt*, 2: especially 73 and 313-14 (quote).
3. IG to ER, August 19, 1940.

ER did understand. But she did not approve. It was the first she had heard of Isabella's defection, and she wrote: "I am, of course, sorry to have you openly on the other side, but I realize that you have to do whatever you think is right. It is a little difficult, however, for me to understand, with your knowledge of Congress, why you think that Mr. Willkie can accomplish the things which he promises. Also it is hard for me to believe that knowing his record . . . as a utility head, how you can feel safe in his future attitude toward labor and social reform. . . . I am afraid that I would watch with considerable apprehension for fascist tendencies in him and in the group which nominated him. I felt I had to say this to you so you would understand what my feeling is, but of course, as far as I am concerned political differences never make any differences in one's own personal feelings. . . ."[4]

It is astonishing to report, for ER and Isabella Greenway, that remained true. Their friendship survived, and again during the war they were allied in work and perspective. With the publication of these letters, their enduring fifty-year friendship will now live forever.

Blanche Wiesen Cook
24 May 2008

4. ER to IG, August 22, 1940.

Editors' Note

The letters that follow are copious but incomplete. The editors combed the archives of the Arizona Historical Society in Tucson, and the Franklin D. Roosevelt Library at Hyde Park, New York, and came up with 139 letters of Eleanor Roosevelt to Isabella Greenway and 85 letters of Isabella Greenway to Eleanor Roosevelt. Isabella's family recently discovered three more of Eleanor's letters in an old trunk. But there are obviously still some missing letters.

Except where otherwise noted, the letters of Eleanor Roosevelt are in the Arizona Historical Society, and the letters of Isabella Greenway are in the Franklin Delano Roosevelt Library.

The reader will notice many misspellings. These are in the originals; Eleanor was apt to misspell even family names. Some long paragraphs have been divided into shorter paragraphs for greater readability.

Where the meaning is unclear, explanatory text is supplied in brackets.

When the meaning of a word varies today from the way Eleanor and Isabella used it, the historical meaning is supplied from the 1923 Merriam Webster Dictionary.

For verification of internet citations used in this book go to www.kristiemiller.com.

Introduction

*E*leanor Roosevelt was distraught. She had returned to the United States after three happy years at boarding school in England. Now Eleanor's socially prominent family—her uncle Theodore Roosevelt was president of the United States—was insisting that she make her debut into society, a prospect the shy and serious young woman was dreading.[1]

The debutante season opened in New York City on December 11, 1902, with a grand Assembly Ball at the Waldorf Astoria Hotel. "I do not think I quite realized beforehand what utter agony it was going to be or I would never have had the courage to go," Eleanor later admitted.[2]

The party should have been a delight. Guests made their way to the hotel, through freezing rain, to find themselves in warm corridors lined with tropical foliage. In the rotunda, bright with crimson velvet and red roses, they were received by society's leading ladies.

Debutantes in billowing white dresses had come to dance and enjoy themselves.[3] But a serious purpose lay behind the merry-making: each girl was supposed to meet and marry a suitable husband.

Eleanor ventured into the vast Waldorf Astoria ballroom, knowing not one man but her uncle Theodore's friend Bob Ferguson. Bob was a dashing Scot, the younger son of a noble family, who had come to America seeking adventure, and had become Roosevelt's ranching partner in the Dakotas. He had also served as one of TR's most outstanding officers in the Rough Riders.

At the ball, Bob danced with Eleanor, and made sure she met plenty of other partners as well. But he realized that Eleanor needed real friends more than casual acquaintances at parties.

1. Eleanor's parents were TR's brother Elliott, and Anna Hall Roosevelt. Anna Eleanor Roosevelt was born on October 11, 1884.
2. Roosevelt, *This is My Story*, 81. Eleanor, a guest at the Assembly Ball, made her own debut at the home of her aunt, Mrs. Valentine Hall, during the last week of December, 1902. *Town Topics*, January 1, 1903.
3. *Chicago Daily Tribune*, December 12, 1902: 5.

Bob, at thirty-five, was old enough to be a suitable chaperone for eighteen-year-old Eleanor. So, in the days that followed, he escorted her around New York, introducing her to interesting people like the distinguished portrait painter, Ellen "Bay" Emmett,[4] and other artists and writers.[5]

One day, Bob called at the gloomy townhouse on West 37th Street, belonging to Eleanor's grandmother, where Eleanor was spending the winter. He brought a new visitor for Eleanor, Isabella Selmes, the daughter of one of Bob's friends who had moved to New York the previous year.

Isabella was only sixteen years old, not yet "out" in society.[6] But she lit up the dark, narrow rooms. Isabella was "one of the loveliest girls I have ever seen," Eleanor later recalled, "already the talk of New York."[7] Isabella would remember that Eleanor was "slender and graceful," with masses of beautiful golden hair. And her blue eyes "crinkled with friendship and a certain humor peculiarly her own."[8]

Many girls form strong relationships as they begin to lead independent lives. But the friendship that sprang up between Eleanor and Isabella was remarkable. The bond between them lasted half a century, ending only with Isabella's death. What is more remarkable, however, is that both Eleanor and Isabella, beginning as debutantes concerned about dresses and dancing partners, went on to achieve political power and prominence on the national scene.

Eleanor Roosevelt became one of the most admired women of the twentieth century. She was America's first lady for an unprecedented twelve years, an inspiration to millions during the Great Depression and World War II. After her husband's death, she was famous as the "first lady of the world" for her work at the United Nations and for international human rights. Isabella Selmes Ferguson Greenway King was an enterprising woman who founded a furniture factory, a commuter airline, and a resort hotel that is still considered one of the best in the world.[9] Her entrepreneurial success led to a leadership role in the Democratic party and eventual election to Congress, where she served two terms, representing the entire state of Arizona.

4. Ellen "Bay" Emmett, 1875–1941, later married to William Rand.
5. Roosevelt, *This is My Story*, 82.
6. Ibid., 85, says they met when Isabella was sixteen. In her memoir, Eleanor was occasionally confused about dates, but Isabella, who was born on March 22, 1886, would have been sixteen in the winter of 1902–3, when Eleanor was making her debut.
7. Ibid.
8. IG to Eugene Lyons, May 12, 1948, GC.
9. The Arizona Inn. Still run by Isabella's family, the Inn was named "one of the top 500 hotels in the world" by *Travel and Leisure* magazine in 2005.

For readers and scholars today, the friendship between Eleanor and Isabella is noteworthy for another reason: it is documented by a profusion of illuminating letters. Although as young women they both resided in New York City, they lived apart for most of the rest of their lives. Their letters kept them connected, and reveal the support women traditionally give each other through childbirth and child rearing, diseases and death. But the letters also show that women in the 1920s and 1930s provided each other with the opportunities traditionally found in "old boys'" networks. The correspondence discloses little-known aspects of Eleanor's personality, such as her playfulness and sense of humor. The record of Isabella's life revealed in the letters demonstrates that while Eleanor Roosevelt was extraordinary, she was not unique; other competent women were participating in public affairs at a high level.

Eleanor's and Isabella's lives intersected because Isabella's parents, Patty[10] and Tilden Selmes, had befriended Theodore Roosevelt during his ranching days in the Dakota badlands. After Tilden's death, Patty moved with Isabella to New York in 1901 to live with Patty's sister and brother-in-law.[11] Theodore, by then president of the United States, and Bob Ferguson, who also knew Patty and Isabella from the Dakotas, introduced the newcomers to Roosevelt friends and family in New York.

When Eleanor and Isabella met, Eleanor was in the middle of her debutante season; Isabella would debut two years later. Even then, each girl had a serious side. Eleanor, "anxious to do something helpful," taught immigrant children on New York's Lower East Side. One afternoon, her cousin Franklin Roosevelt accompanied her to the tenement home of one of her students. The experience shocked him deeply: he "simply could not believe human beings lived that way." Eleanor believed that visit affected Franklin for the rest of his life.[12]

Both Eleanor and Isabella were early members of the Junior League, founded in 1900 by elite young women interested in social reform. Isabella was also influenced by Eleanor's cousin Corinne Robinson. When they drove together to balls, Corinne would read aloud to Isabella books by Jack London, because she worried they might be in danger of forgetting about the less fortunate. Corinne's mother foresaw the benefit of their social work, declaring

10. Martha Flandrau Selmes was always known as "Patty."
11. Sarah ("Sally") and Frank Cutcheon. The Cutcheons had no children. Frank, a successful attorney, gladly assumed the role of father, calling Isabella his "ready-made daughter." Frank Cutcheon to Isabella Selmes, July 7, 1902, FC.
12. Cook, *Eleanor Roosevelt*, I, 138.

that it was important for the girls to feel "absolutely at home in all sets." She predicted great success for Isabella, who had the added advantage of beauty.[13]

For women of their social class, the debutante season—whom they met at the glittering parties and whom they married—decided a girl's fate. But they could not seem desperate. And, as Isabella later observed, "no matter how serious-minded we were, we realized that to appear to be having fun was a part you played."[14] For Eleanor, once the ordeal of the Assembly Ball was behind her, this was not such a difficult task. Franklin Roosevelt, her charming distant cousin, had begun paying her a great deal of attention. They danced together, nearly matched in height. They talked, they laughed, they read poetry together. As the season wore on, they attended the same house parties, and Eleanor was invited to Franklin's home by his formidable mother, Sara Roosevelt. When Franklin returned to Harvard, they wrote each other almost every day.[15] By late 1903, Franklin and Eleanor were engaged. Because custom dictated that the marriage ceremony follow within six months of an announced engagement, the couple had to keep their plans secret for another year.[16]

13. Miller, *Isabella Greenway*, 31–32.
14. IG to Eugene Lyons, May 12, 1948, GC.
15. Cook, *Eleanor Roosevelt*, I, 132–33; 138–39.
16. Pottker, *Sara and Eleanor*, 101.

A Volume of Friendship

Part One
Girlhood and Early Marriage

On October 11, 1904, Eleanor's twentieth birthday, Franklin presented her with an engagement ring from Tiffany's. Although Eleanor would wait until November to tell the extended family, she could not resist telling Isabella beforehand. During a weekend visit to the home of her aunt Corinne Robinson,[1] Eleanor confided her hopes and fears about the coming marriage. In her first letter to Isabella, Eleanor thanks the younger girl for her sympathy and understanding.

"Overlook" Orange, NJ[2]   [October 24, 1904]
Monday night 12:30 PM[3]
Dearest Isabella,

This is only a line to thank you many times for your kindness & patience of last night. You were very, very sweet to me & I only hope that someday I may have the chance to help you dear, as much as you helped me.

The others have just gone to bed, after a long & exhaustive discussion in here of next winter's terrors![4] I've tried to make it seem less dreadful but I fear quite unsuccessfully!

I hope you will have a wonderful time in St. Louis[5] with your Mother! I want you to give her my best love.

1. Corinne Roosevelt Robinson was the sister of Elliott and Theodore Roosevelt. She and her husband, Douglas Robinson, were the parents of Eleanor's first cousin, also named Corinne.
2. A seventy-two acre estate owned by Eleanor's aunt Corinne Roosevelt Robinson and her husband Douglas Robinson. Caroli, *The Roosevelt Women*, 146.
3. Eleanor probably means A.M. here, or half-past midnight on Monday night.
4. "The others" were probably other debutantes who were coming out at the same time as Isabella. Eleanor may have been trying to reassure them that the debutante season would not be as bad as they imagined. Geoffrey Ward to the editors, March 6, 2007.
5. Isabella's mother, Patty Selmes, planned to take her daughter to the St. Louis World's Fair. Formally known as the Louisiana Purchase Exposition, it ran from April 30–December 1, 1904. The exposition, delayed by one year, marked the centennial celebration of the Louisiana Purchase. It covered two square miles, and included two hundred buildings.

I'm feeling quite sane again so you need worry no more about me!

Dear love to you Isabella & please believe that I feel much which I cannot express & so shall not even try.

Always devotedly,

Eleanor

Isabella was soon to make her own debut. Patty wrote to her aunt, Julia Dinsmore, that she hoped their trip to St. Louis would provide "a few quiet times with Isabella . . . before she begins the New York rush . . . it is all a great lottery and I want her to start as level-headed as possible."[6]

At Thanksgiving, Franklin and Eleanor disclosed their engagement to their families. Isabella wrote to encourage Eleanor.

28 E. 75th Street [NYC]   Sunday Nov. 27 [1904]

My very sweetest Eleanor,

It is a selfish reason that makes me write you. I want you to know how constantly I am thinking of you these days and of all the best prayers and wishes I make for your happiness. Be as happy as you are good and sweet and true and I couldn't wish anything more. I'll see you very soon. As soon as you have a moment to spare and I shall look forward to it but I just wanted to write you how delighted I am that it is going to be announced so soon. Goodbye with a big hug and kiss 'til I see you[,] and love me [a] little [in return].

Affectionately,

Isabella

I hope Mr. Roosevelt[7] is better.

Eleanor's engagement was formally announced in the *New York Times* on December 3. Indeed, on the same page,[8] the *Times* also announced that Mrs. Henry Parish,[9] Eleanor's godmother, to whom she was very close, and with

> The hamburger, the ice cream cone, and iced tea all became popular there. Trager, *The People's Chronology*, 658–59; http://www.lib.udel.edu/ud/spec/exhibits/fairs/louis.htm

6. Patty Selmes to Julia Dinsmore, October 25, 1904, DC.
7. Franklin D. Roosevelt. In that more formal time, Isabella would not have called him by his first name. Franklin's father was deceased.
8. "What is Doing in Society," *New York Times*, December 3, 1904: 19.
9. Susan Ludlow ("Cousin Susie") Parish was a first cousin of Eleanor Roosevelt's mother, Anna Hall Roosevelt. Alycia J. Vivona, archivist, Franklin D. Roosevelt Library, to the

whom she was then living, would give a tea at her home[10] for "Miss Isabel Selmes." This was Isabella's introduction into society.

Isabella became an instant belle. She was so popular at the debutante balls, Patty wrote her mother-in-law, that the girl had dined at home only once in five weeks.[11]

If the debutante season was a lottery, the prize was a husband. Isabella's widowed mother invested her meager savings in Isabella's ball gowns, hoping that her daughter would marry someone who could provide financial security. Eleanor's friendship was one of the few things Isabella could already count on.

Tivoli on Hudson[12]   December 27 [1904]
My dearest sweetest Isabella,

Cousin Susie [Parish] has sent me your [Christmas] card & she tells me there's a book awaiting me from you. Many many thanks for the latter, which I know I shall love, but even more thanks for your card and remembrance of me. I think you know dear, how very, very fond I am of you but I wonder if you do know how much your affection means to me. There are very, very few people dear on whom I count as I do on you & there are few people for whom I wish as much this New Year. May it bring you only joy dear & all the happiness which you deserve.

I'm looking forward to seeing you Friday morning & giving you a kiss.
     Always devotedly,
          Eleanor

The Roosevelts were married on March 17, 1905, a date chosen to suit the convenience of President Theodore Roosevelt, who was to give away his niece in marriage, but who was also scheduled to participate in a St. Patrick's Day parade. Isabella Selmes was one of the six bridesmaids; all but one of the others were Roosevelt cousins. The week before the wedding, Isabella helped Eleanor write thank-you notes for some of the 340 presents

editors, March 13, 2007. "Cousin Susie was a very tall, very proper woman, who in motion reminded the younger people of 'a full-rigged ship.' [Quoting an interview with Margaret Cutter.] She was strait-laced and opinionated and refused to have anything to do with people who were outside Society. Nevertheless, she was very kind to Eleanor." Lash, *Eleanor and Franklin*, 147–48.

10. 8 E. 76th Street, New York City.

11. Patty Selmes to Sarah B. Selmes, December 28, 1904, DC.

12. Tivoli on Hudson was the home of Eleanor's maternal grandmother, Mary Livingston Ludlow Hall, with whom Eleanor lived after the death of her parents.

she had already received. At one point, Isabella became so immersed in her task that she signed her own name instead of Eleanor's.[13] After the wedding, the guests flocked around Theodore Roosevelt, all but ignoring the bride and groom. On the way to the train to spend their wedding night at Hyde Park,[14] Eleanor and Franklin stopped off to visit Bob Ferguson, who was laid up with a recurrent fever that had plagued him ever since the Spanish-American War.

Because Franklin was studying law at Columbia University, the Roosevelts postponed their three-month European honeymoon until the summer.[15] Meanwhile, unbeknownst to them, Bob Ferguson was furiously courting Isabella.[16] Bob was almost twice Isabella's age, thirty-six to her nineteen, but Isabella, after agonizing over leaving her mother ("I'm all she has"), and protesting that Bob ought to be completely well before they wed, gave in to his urgings. They were married on July 12 at her uncle's farm on Long Island. Theodore Roosevelt and his sons rode over on horseback from neighboring Sagamore Hill. Then Bob whisked Isabella off to Scotland. The newlyweds stayed with Bob's elder brother, Ronald Ferguson, Lord of Novar, a highland estate of some 20,000 acres that had been in their family for generations.[17]

The telegram announcing Bob and Isabella's marriage surprised Eleanor, who was also honeymooning in Europe. She and Franklin joined the Fergusons in Scotland. Eleanor already had become friends with Bob's sisters, Alice and Edith (Edie), when she was at school in England.

Eleanor's visit to Novar marked a turning point in her life. Ronald's wife, Lady Helen, surprised Eleanor with a "devastating question," asking her to explain the difference between national and state government. Mortified that she could not answer, Eleanor vowed on the spot to learn more about her country's political structure.[18]

The two young couples returned to New York, and moved into similar small brownstone houses that they referred to as "the band-boxes."[19] The

13. Roosevelt, *This is My Story*, 98.
14. FDR's childhood home, "Springwood" or "Hyde Park on the Hudson," was frequently referred to simply as Hyde Park. Sara Roosevelt lived there.
15. Cook, *Eleanor Roosevelt*, I, 170 ff.
16. Bob had sworn Isabella to secrecy.
17. The Novar estate belonged to the Fergusons. Bob's mother's family, the Munros, owned another estate, Assynt, in the Northern Highlands, in the far northwest of Scotland. Bob Munro-Ferguson and his siblings thus inherited two estates.
18. Roosevelt, *This is My Story*, 107.
19. A bandbox was a box for storing hats or other small articles.

following year, Eleanor and Isabella endured their first pregnancies together. Isabella was godmother to Anna Roosevelt, born in May 1906.

That summer, the Roosevelts joined Franklin's mother at her summer home on Campobello Island[20] in the Bay of Fundy, New Brunswick, Canada, where they stayed in an adjacent cottage.[21] Eleanor's brother, Hall, visited, too. While Eleanor was enjoying the cool sea breezes, Isabella, who was expecting her first baby in September, sweltered at her aunt and uncle's farm on Long Island.

Campobello Island   [Aug. 6, 1906]
Dearest Isabella,

I'm thinking about you so much these days that I must send you [a] line even though it is an uninteresting one. Oh! How I wish you & Bob could be here to enjoy the long sails and walks. It has been such lovely weather that just to be alive was all one wanted & Hall is with us now so we are really having a very pleasant time.

Your goddaughter is looking very well & now weighs 14 lbs. If she keeps on I'm sure you won't know her in September! In another week or two we will put her in short clothes[22] (that is to say, we will, *if* the flannel petticoats which I am now making her are finished) & then I will have to take some Kodaks & send them to you.

I suppose you are more & more thankful every day that you have very few people in town to bother you, but I wish very often that I were near enough to go to see you. I do hope Bob is well & please give him my love & Mrs. Selmes also when you see her.

Franklin sends love to you both, he & Hall are just going out to play golf.

Please don't answer this as I know it is hard to write & I only wanted you to know dear Isabella that you were never far from my thoughts or my heart either.

> Ever devotedly,
> Eleanor

20. Sara Delano Roosevelt's late husband, James, had purchased the house in 1883.
21. Franklin and Eleanor also lived next door to Sara Roosevelt in Manhattan.
22. At that time, little babies wore long full gowns. Around five months of age, a baby went into "short clothes," that ended above the ankle, so they could more easily crawl and walk. These garments were usually made of soft materials like linen or flannel. http://www.history.rochester.edu/godeys/readers/kh/db-1850/index.htm.

In the fall of 1906, Franklin passed the bar and joined the law firm of Carter, Ledyard and Millburn as a junior clerk.[23] Bob Ferguson, meanwhile, became a trustee for the Astor estate,[24] as well as for his wife's cousin, Isabella Breckinridge, a daughter of tire magnate B. F. Goodrich.[25]

Martha Ferguson was born in early September 1906. The two families continued to grow: James Roosevelt was born in December 1907, and Robert Munro Ferguson (called "Robbie" or "Buzz" when he was very little, "Bobbie" when he was older) was born in March 1908. Eleanor referred to her children, and sometimes to Isabella's offspring, as "chicks."

Eleanor and Isabella, living near each other in New York City, had little occasion to write. They met often, at lunch or at meetings of the Three Arts Club[26] or the Junior League,[27] of which both were early members. However, the two women were about to enter a stormy period that would separate them for most of the rest of their lives.

The Fergusons received calamitous news on November 18, 1908, when Bob was diagnosed with tuberculosis.[28] Before the discovery of antibiotics in the 1940s, a diagnosis of TB was a very serious matter. In 1900, TB was the second leading cause of death in the United States, after influenza.[29]

23. Ward, *A First-Class Temperament*, 70 ff.
24. TR had recommended Bob Ferguson for the position with the Astor Trust Company, on whose board sat "many of the best known financiers of the United States." *New York Times,* December 1, 1912: 2. "I learn his name has been suggested in connection with the vacancy among the trustees of your estate. As you know he is an intimate personal friend whom I have known from the time he was a boy. He was my partner in my ranch out West and the godfather of one of my children [Kermit]. I would trust him with anything I had in the world, not merely with my fortune, but with my honor . . . There is no service of trust and responsibility needing resolution, tact, and high minded integrity for which I do not think Ferguson well fitted." TR to John Jacob Astor, November 9, 1900, FC.
25. Isabella Selmes Ferguson was the great-granddaughter of James Dinsmore. Isabella Goodrich Breckinridge was the granddaughter of James Dinsmore's sister, Susannah Dinsmore Goodrich. B. F. Goodrich was Susannah's son. Cathy Collopy, education coordinator, Dinsmore Homestead, to the editors, January 9, 2008.
26. *New York Times*, May 15, 1904, described The Three Arts Club as having been founded "a few months ago." The club was created to provide safe, comfortable lodging for young female artists, musicians, and actresses who flocked to New York to study.
27. The Junior League for the Promotion of Settlement Movements, founded by Mary Harriman in 1901. Eleanor Roosevelt joined in 1903.
28. Bob had tuberculosis not only of the lungs, but also at the site of a hemorrhoid operation two years earlier. This caused the wound to heal slowly. TB can affect not only the lungs but also the central nervous system, lymphatic system, circulatory system, genitourinary system, bones, and joints.
29. http://www.cdc.gov/women/owh/firstlady/roosevelt.htm.

Dismay, even depression, was the common reaction, even as late as the 1950s.[30] The disease was highly contagious; patients with TB had to be segregated. Not only did they require separate sleeping quarters, food utensils, and bath rooms, but even hugging and kissing were forbidden in order to protect loved ones from a similar fate. The fact that Bob and Isabella had no more children suggests that sexual contact between the couple ceased.

To a man married only three short years, with a lovely young wife and small children, this must have been heartbreaking. Gallant soldier that he was, Bob took the news "in the pluckiest sort of way," Frank Cutcheon informed Ronald Ferguson. Bob's future was "impossible to prophesy," he added darkly.[31]

Bob and Isabella went at once to the Trudeau Sanatorium in Saranac, New York.[32] At first, the children stayed behind with their grandmother, Patty Selmes, and the Cutcheons. They were also cared for by Julia Loving, known in the family as "Mammy."[33]

Isabella would not return to live in New York City for nearly thirty years. During that time, she and Eleanor would correspond faithfully. Eleanor, trying to cheer her friend, supplied Isabella with news about their mutual friends; Isabella painted word portraits for Eleanor about the Fergusons' new life.

Dec. 13 [1908]

Dearest Isabella,

You and Bob have been constantly in my thoughts but I did not write before as I knew how busy you would be unpacking & getting settled.

I telephoned Mrs. Cutcheon on Friday & heard good news of you all & I hope this week to see Martha & Robbie who seem to be finely from all accounts.

30. See Leah Latimer, "Quarantined: How a Daughter was Robbed of Her Mother's Affection," *Washington Post Magazine*, December 11, 2006.
31. Frank Cutcheon to Ronald Ferguson, November 21, 1908, FC.
32. Cold mountains and dry deserts were thought to be most beneficial for curing TB. Established in 1885, the Edward L. Trudeau Tuberculosis Sanatorium, located at Saranac Lake in the Adirondack Mountains of New York, was the first tuberculosis sanatorium in the United States. Robert Louis Stevenson was one of the first patients in 1887–88. Cartoonist Garretson "Garry" Trudeau is a modern descendent of the founder.
33. Julia Loving was an African American woman whose family had come to Kentucky with Julia Dinsmore's parents. She went with Patty to the Dakota Territory as a nanny for the infant Isabella. The *New York Times* was said to have reported that Julia Loving cared for TR during an illness while he was in the Dakota badlands. He invited her to visit him in the White House in 1902, when he was president. *Arizona Daily Star*, December 19, 1953.

We are just back from Roslyn where we went yesterday afternoon to the Mortimers'. The Biddle children were christened & Mr. & Mrs. Goodrich & Charlie Draper were on the train & I hear the chicks were good as gold but when I went to see them this morning Pete was suffering from too much after celebration![34] The baby is too sweet & has so much hair that it actually *curls* to the top of her head which made me green with envy.

We had a hectic week with the Ledyard[35] ball in the middle which nearly finished us both! It was such a pretty sight though & all the clothes looked so picturesque. Mr. Ledyard seemed to enjoy it & ended by dancing himself.

Brother Rosy[36] is supposed to have gone South today & as it is snowy & horrid I think he may have gone & Helen[37] told me Friday he felt better! We are going to supper with Auntie Corinne[38] so I must run & dress. Ever & ever so much love to you & Bob & write me when you have nothing to do.

> Ever devotedly,
> Eleanor

Franklin sends love.

Bob faced an uncertain future. Preparing for the worst, Frank Cutcheon and Bob's brother Ronald each contributed to a trust fund for Isabella and the children. When Ronald suggested Franklin Roosevelt as one of the trustees, Frank responded, "For some reason Isabella does not like the idea." Perhaps it was because Franklin, in his youth, was considered an intellectual lightweight (his contemporaries joked that F. D. stood for "Feather Duster"). Or, she may have wanted to keep their relationship purely social.[39]

34. Possibly a Biddle child who ate too much.

35. Lewis Cass Ledyard was an old business associate of James Roosevelt, and FDR's boss. Ward to editors, March 6, 2007. Ledyard was also a colleague of Bob Ferguson's on the Astor Trust.

36. James Roosevelt Roosevelt, known as "Rosy" (1854–1927), was the eldest son of James Roosevelt and his first wife, Rebecca Howland. Rosy was FDR's elder half-brother. He served as First Secretary of the U.S. Legation at Vienna and as chargé d' affaires at the U.S. Embassy at London. Ward, *A First-Class Temperament*, 7, 86–87; Caroli, *The Roosevelt Women*, 86.

37. Rosy Roosevelt's daughter Helen married Theodore (Teddy) Robinson on June 18, 1904.

38. TR's younger sister, Corinne Roosevelt Robinson. Corinne and her husband, Douglas Robinson, were the parents of ER's cousin Theodore (Teddy) Robinson (1883–1934).

39. When Geoffrey Ward was writing *A First-Class Temperament*, he interviewed Isabella's son John S. Greenway. "My impression from her son was that Isabella always distrusted FDR." Ward to editors, March 6, 2007.

At the Trudeau Sanatorium, patients were encouraged to sleep on porches, where the cold, dry air might help heal tubercular lungs. One night the temperature dropped to minus 20 degrees, freezing Isabella's eyelashes. The Fergusons relied on Patty and Mammy's reports of the children's Christmas: Martha was rendered speechless by her pile of presents, and Bobbie received a set of wee bagpipes.

December 28 [1908]

Dearest Isabella,

Anna's slippers are a great joy to her & you & Bob were too dear to think of her. Franklin & I love the photograph too & it is splendid of the children.

Robbie came to our Xmas tree & was too sweet for words. It was great fun seeing all the children together though they are still too young to enjoy it much themselves! I went to Helen [Roosevelt Robinson]'s tree on Xmas eve & also to Pauline [Merrill]'s[40] but did not take Anna so I know I am considered a fussy Mother but I feel sure Anna was better without more excitement.

I am going tomorrow to lunch with your family & hope to see Mr. Ronald & hear the latest news of you & Bob.

By the way we went to see Mrs. James A.[41] [Roosevelt] on Xmas day & she showed us your sketch & was so much touched at your remembering her & I think both your ears must have burnt.

Our chicks are very well. I hope soon Martha will be able to come & join them on the roof occasionally.[42]

We are chaperoning a children's theatre party tonight so I must run & dress!

Much love to you both from us all.

Ever devotedly,

Eleanor

Theodore Roosevelt chose not to run for a third term, and Secretary of War William Howard Taft was elected president in 1908. Because Inauguration Day was held in March, TR was still in office when Franklin and Eleanor

40. Pauline Dresser Merrill, youngest sister of Edith Dresser Vanderbilt and wife of the Rev. George Grenville Merrill, lived in Tuxedo Park, N.Y.
41. Probably Mrs. James Archibald Roosevelt. Ward to editors, March 6, 2007.
42. Then as now, children in crowded New York City often had play places on the roofs of buildings.

attended a diplomatic reception at the White House in January 1909. Eleanor, who was expecting her third child in March, would, as custom demanded, "cease going out" in public until after the baby's birth.

When she was in the nation's capital, Eleanor often visited her Aunt Anna ("Auntie Bye"),[43] whose home was a political salon.

From Washington, Eleanor provided Isabella, isolated at Saranac, with news of the wider world.

The White House, Washington   January 8 [1909]
Dearest Isabella,

I meant to write & answer your letter[44] before but as usual New York life was too much for me & I had to wait for the quiet of a morning down here!

I am so glad you had a happy Xmas & find all comfortable in your house. I adore the sketch of you getting out of a few warm clothes & I think it must be wonderfully healthy for you as well as Bob. Of course his improvement will be slow to show but I am delighted the doctors think his wound[45] is healing so well.

I met Martha & Mammy on the street the other day & I see a great improvement in Martha and as for Robbie he is more wonderful every time I see him!

We came down here last night for the diplomatic reception & it was such a pretty & picturesque sight. Some of the foreign ladies were most marvellous & the Cuban lady had a tower on her head which made her at least a foot taller than she would ordinarily have been.

Mr. & Mrs. Bayard Cutting[46] came down by the same train & are with Auntie Bye. I haven't really seen Auntie Bye yet but hope to go there for tea

---

43. TR's older sister Anna (Auntie Bye or Bamie) Roosevelt Cowles (1855–1931) was ER's aunt. In 1895, at age forty, Bye married William Sheffield Cowles, a U.S. naval officer and, eventually, admiral. Their son William Sheffield Cowles, Jr., called Sheffield, was born in 1898. Before Bye's marriage, she had a close friendship with Bob Ferguson and also with James "Rosy" Roosevelt. Her home in Washington, D.C., became a haven for ER when FDR was assistant secretary of the Navy. She and her husband also had a home in Connecticut. Stacy Cordery, "Alice Roosevelt Longworth," *ER Encyclopedia*, 115–6.

44. Missing.

45. The tubercular hemorrhoid wound.

46. William Bayard Cutting and Olivia Murray Cutting were part of what Louis Auchincloss described as New York's "brownstone aristocracy." Bayard Cutting made a fortune in railroads and mercantile activities, and became a philanthropist and civic reformer. Lowitt, *Bronson M. Cutting*, 2–6. The Cuttings were very close friends of Isabella and Bob Ferguson, as well as Eleanor and Franklin Roosevelt.

this afternoon. All the White House family seem well & Ethel [Roosevelt][47] is having a very good time I think & not being spoiled by it, at least not as far as I can see & not along Alice[48] [Roosevelt]'s lines at all! Alice was here only a short time last night as she had a cold & headache etc. but she looks lovely & very well & so quiet!

Anna & Brother[49] are very well but Cousin Susie [Parish] tells me if I keep them up on the roof so much I will ruin all their chances for growing up with any imagination & so I have bought Brother a carriage & he & Anna will spend occasional afternoons in the park to "cultivate their imaginations & see other children." It strikes me as a little ludicrous to worry so young about these things but I suppose that is because I am so "matter of fact."

We go home on Sunday night & I intend to cease going out after this final splurge!

Much love to you & Bob.
> Devotedly always,
> Eleanor

Eleanor wrote frequently at this time, trying to help Isabella feel less isolated, and to cheer her up.

49 E. 65th Street [New York, N.Y.]   January 28 [1909]
Dearest Isabella,

I really have no news but must write just a line so you & Bob won't think we're quite lost.

The concert for the 3 Arts Club was given this morning & it was lovely & looked to me crowded so I hope they made a good deal.

I hear splendid reports of your babies & Robbie's weight fills me with envy & though both our chicks are quite well I fear James will never catch up with Robbie!

I lunched with Helen [Robinson] on Wednesday but except for that one glimpse have seen very little of her as they are going out madly now & she

---

47. Ethel, seventeen years old at this time, was Theodore Roosevelt's fourth child and second daughter.

48. Alice was TR's first child, daughter of his first wife, Alice Lee Roosevelt, who died on February 14, 1884, two days after giving birth to her namesake. Young Alice had a well-deserved reputation for wild behavior. In 1906 she married Ohio congressman Nicholas Longworth in an extravagant White House wedding. Cordery, *Alice Roosevelt Longworth*.

49. James, the Franklin Roosevelts' second child and first son.

has worked very hard over the 3 Arts Club concert. Mr. [David] Bispham[50] gave them some trouble by announcing that he only sang to an Everett piano which of course was not the piano provided at the Waldorf! After much persuasion he consented to sing without his special piano if they would put a note on the programmes stating that he always sang to an Everett as he could not be responsible for his singing when accompanied by anything else! You can think with what amusement the note was printed.

It's getting very late & must close. So much love from us both dear to both of you.

> Ever devotedly,
> Eleanor

The Fergusons' many friends also inundated Bob and Isabella with encouraging letters. Olivia Cutting wrote Isabella every week.[51] At nineteen, Olivia was not yet burdened with as many responsibilities as Eleanor had to bear, and her constancy carried Isabella over what she later called "black periods of discovery"[52] during the early days of Bob's invalidism.[53] Friends also came to visit. Helen and Teddy Robinson[54] were among the first to find their way to Saranac.

As her pregnancy progressed, Eleanor laughed about her increasing size. Franklin had once said that "his lonely childhood had created a great desire to have a large brood of children, six at least." [55] Franklin and Eleanor eventually had six children. At this point, in the middle of her childbearing years, Eleanor's letters are full of news about other people's children as well.

50. David Scull Bispham was the leading American baritone of his day. Born in Philadelphia in 1857, his love of music was long opposed by his mother, who attempted "to warn him against the temptations of opera," but who later relented. He died in 1921 in New York. "David Bispham Dies in His 65th Year," *New York Times*, October 3, 1921: 10.
51. Olivia Bayard Cutting, the daughter of William and Olivia Murray Cutting, was six years younger than Isabella. Nevertheless, the two young women were extremely close.
52. IG to Olivia Cutting, undated [autumn 1921], GC.
53. "You'll know yourself one of these days, how undeserving I've always been of all you've given," Isabella wrote Olivia. "But along with it, perhaps you'll like to think what a happiness you've been to a certain bandbox family. . . . I've known the truest of joys in you that can ever come. . . . Just once in a while, when everything's quiet, I find it's a good thing to have confidential times with a few thoughts and sentiments. How about you?" IG to Olivia Cutting, April 7, 1909, FC.
54. Theodore Douglas Robinson (1883–1934), the son of Douglas and Corinne Roosevelt Robinson.
55. Cook, *Eleanor Roosevelt*, I, 134, quoting Ward.

E. 65ᵗʰ Street [New York, N.Y.]   Feb. 19ᵗʰ [1909]
Dearest Isabella,

It was too lovely to get your long letter[56] & also to hear of you from Helen & Teddy [Robinson]. They all seem to think Bob looks better than they have ever seen him & though of course I know the constant up & downs & the pain must be hard for him & for you still it is wonderful that he goes on steadily getting better & you must take care of yourself & not get tired etc.

I should think we did have a wild bit of the highlands in our midst. I have not seen the dancing[57] but the accounts of those who have are somewhat lurid & the virtuous elderly matrons are quite too scandalized for words! I did hear it would *have* to stop soon so I suppose she is making the most of her time now & accumulating large sums of money, so the take goes for that school in Scotland where poor boys are to be taught first of all to dance.

You asked about Ellen & I am glad to say she has been wonderfully well & bright & plucky. It was a great sorrow but fortunately she can look forward to another baby cheerfully & she is crazy to have one at once & Dr. Ely[58] says there is no reason for things to go wrong now. Did you know Muriel [Martineau][59] expected another the middle of June? She is enchanted & writes she is so well.

Pauline [Merrill] lunched here yesterday & I never saw anyone look better or seem to feel better. Of course she is sylph-like compared to me but I feel fine & active as possible.

Both chicks are well & Anna went to a Valentine party at Pauline's the other day which was too funny. Each child played alone or tried for a brief moment to wrest the other child's toy away & tricky Emmet was on the verge of tears all the time & little Pauline spent her time with her arms about his neck.

I must stop now but will write soon again. More love than I can say to you both.

> Devotedly,
> Eleanor

56. Missing.
57. Lady Constance Stewart Richardson danced on February 15 at a musicale given by Edoardo Bosco in Emil Fuch's studio at the Beaux Arts. Lady Constance wore a brilliant green satin gown and danced "one of her wonderful pas seuls" in her bare feet. *New York Times*, February 16, 1909: 9.
58. Albert Ely, gynecologist who also attended ER. Ward to editors, March 6, 2007.
59. Muriel Robbins Martineau was a cousin of Franklin, the sister of Warren Robbins, and the wife of Cyril Edgar Martineau (1871–1918). Cyril also suffered from TB.

Franklin, Jr. was born on March 18, 1909, the day after the Roosevelts' fourth wedding anniversary. At 11 pounds, he was "the biggest and most beautiful" of all her children, Eleanor thought. In the meantime, Martha Ferguson joined her parents at Saranac, while Bobbie stayed in New York City for a little while longer.

49 E. 65th Street [New York, N.Y.]   [April 14, 1909]
Dearest Isabella,

I've been wanting to write [to] thank you & Bob for your telegram[60] for nearly a week but there have been so many interruptions that letter writing has been out of the question! I am feeling quite well again & have been out but am not yet allowed stairs so that I can't go to see Pauline [Merrill]'s baby which of course I am longing to do! My own babe is very flourishing but I've already stopped nursing him so I don't expect him to gain much for a little while though the food agreed with him finely.

Your Mother & Robbie came to see me on Sunday & I was glad to hear Martha & Bob were both so well. It must be a joy to have Martha with you again & Robbie looked to me quite himself again & I do hope your worries about the children are over.

Helen & Teddy [Robinson] have been to Burlington for the past two weeks staying with the Perkins & they only got back yesterday so I haven't seen Helen for some time but I hear that they expect another baby this summer. Cousin Susie [Parish] told me this so you probably know it already but I have no news so you must forgive me if I tell you what you already know!

Much love dear to you & Bob & I will write again when I have seen Pauline.

     Devotedly,
        Eleanor

Although Eleanor now had three small children, she also had nannies, which enabled her and Franklin to plan a trip to visit the Fergusons in Saranac.

                                Tuesday [May 19, 1909]
Dearest Isabella

Unless you & Bob cannot see us we are going to spend next Sunday at Saranac. I am longing for a glimpse of you but Franklin cannot get off for

60. Missing.

long now so we will go up Saturday night & have Sunday with you, coming down that night. Please don't feel us on your mind at all as we can go to the Hotel for meals & we just want to see all we can of you without tiring Bob. Of course let me know if for any reason you would rather not have us now as we can go up later.

> Lovingly,
> Eleanor

Eleanor would later write that, for a decade, she was "always just getting over having a baby or about to have one, and so my occupations were considerably restricted."[61] Most of her friends were in the same situation; newly married, and without ready access to birth control, they were all having babies. The men folk, like Eleanor's uncle Theodore and her cousin Kermit,[62] were leading far more adventurous lives.

Despite her responsibilities as a mother, Eleanor made a considerable effort to keep up her network of friends and family. After visiting the Fergusons, she and Franklin went to Boston to see her brother Hall graduate from Groton, and then visited her cousin Susie Parish in New Jersey.

Llewellyn Park, Orange N.J.   June 9 [1909]
Dearest Isabella,

I have just let the days slip by & am half ashamed to write so late & tell you how much Franklin & I enjoyed our day with you. We loved every minute of it & only a multitude of busy days have kept me from writing before. You don't know dear, how much I miss you & how much it meant for me to really see you again as well as Bob & the children. I thought Bob looked so well & I do hope all your cares are going to grow lighter now that you can really rest both mind & body.

Franklin & I came out here yesterday afternoon to stay till Friday. Cousin Susie [Parish] & Cousin Henry[63] both look well & are looking forward to seeing you this summer. We were to go to Tuxedo today & lunch with Pauline [Merrill] but it is pouring & I think Pauline is really thankful not to have us as she had to go to town yesterday in search of a cook!

61. Roosevelt, *This is My Story*, 127.
62. Kermit Roosevelt (1889–1943) was the third of TR's children, his second with Edith. Kermit was Bob Ferguson's godson.
63. Henry was Susie Parish's husband.

Our three days in Groton were very delightful & Hall did very well & the Rector said very nice things about him but Van Webb took most of the prizes & stood highest in the form. Mr. Choate[64] spoke but though it was a charming light speech, I don't think it was quite the serious affair the Rector & most of the other people seemed to expect.

I suppose you know Lily Lee had a son? Also did you hear that Alice Draper had twins? One weighed 3 lbs 13 oz. & the other 4 lbs 2 oz & they were kept in an incubator but are doing wonderfully well I am told. I am afraid she will find two such small babies a tremendous care & she has of course very little money which makes it harder.

Helen [Robinson] is not out here today as she has taken little Helen in town to have the red mark over her eye removed. Auntie Corinne said they had telephoned out that it had been done successfully & Helen expects to come out tomorrow.

Aunt Edith[65] is staying with Auntie Corinne now. She looks very tired & seems still to have fearful headaches. She said she had heard from Uncle Ted & that he & Kermit were both enjoying it[66] & objected only to the ticks!

Give Mrs. Selmes my love & a great deal also to Bob, the chicks & yourself.

>   Ever devotedly,
>   Eleanor

Franklin and Eleanor joined Sara Roosevelt at Campobello Island, where she had bought the young couple a thirty-four-room house on five acres of land.[67] Eleanor enjoyed having this space of her own, where she could entertain her friends.[68]

Sometimes Eleanor's news to Isabella about mutual friends verged on gossip.

64. Possibly Judge William G. Choate or Joseph Choate.
65. Edith Kermit Roosevelt, TR's wife.
66. Theodore ("Uncle Ted") Roosevelt and his son Kermit had departed for an African safari, sponsored by the Smithsonian Institution and the National Geographic Society, in March 1909.
67. She paid $5,000 for it. Ward to editors, March 6, 2007.
68. Pottker, *Sara and Eleanor*, 143.

Campobello, Eastport, Maine[69]   Aug. 10 [1909]

Dearest Isabella,

Since Auntie Bye & Sheffield[70] have been staying with mama [Sara] I have just been feeling that the only thing wanting to make this perfect was to have you & Bob & the children staying here. How I wish you could be here! Franklin & I love our house, the view is too lovely, the sailing glorious & the weather deliciously cool but of course, people, there simply are none!

I had not seen Sheffield in a long time & I think he is such a fine little chap & he seems quite strong & independent. He is sweet to Auntie Bye & it is wonderful to see how very much of a companion she is to him. I only hope I shall be half as successful.

We had quite a houseful last week as Hall brought some friends. Julia Newbold[71] was one of the party & she told me something you may be interested to hear. It appears that Bayard Cutting had to give up his post in Tangier because his wife could not find a house there which she cared to live in! Have you ever heard anything so enraging & yet ludicrous.

Franklin has had to go back to work now but will be back on the 27th. Hall seems to be so busy that I doubt if he succeeds in doing more than coming to Boston to meet me when I leave here so that we can furnish his room together.[72]

The children are all well but James has done wonders & for the first time looks really sturdy. He can walk all over & fight Anna which is a great relief.

How are Martha & Robbie? I often wonder if you have any heat & how Bob stands it [whether it's hot in Saranac and if that is hard on Bob]. Do write sometime just how you all are. Do you see a great deal of Cousin Susie [Parish]? She seems to have had a great many people staying with her & she wrote me that she was now going to begin a rest cure.

Much love to Bob & the chicks & more than I can say to you dear from

　　Your devoted

　　　Eleanor

69. The nearest town to Campobello with a post office.
70. Auntie Bye's son, Sheffield, born in 1898, was about eleven years old at this time. Anna suffered all her life from curvature of the spine and arthritis. Eleanor admired how well her Auntie Bye kept up with her young son.
71. The Newbolds were the Roosevelts' neighbors in Hyde Park.
72. Hall was about to enter Harvard.

By the fall of 1909, the Fergusons realized they would not be returning to New York City any time soon, and decided to rent out their home to provide more income, since Bob was no longer able to work. Isabella made several trips to New York City over the summer to get the Ferguson house ready to rent, and find places for the family's belongings. Although Bob, as well as her uncle and her mother, cautioned her not to overdo, Isabella believed that the more work she could spare Bob, the better his chances for recovery.[73]

News that Eleanor's cousin, Corinne Robinson, was to be married to Joseph Alsop[74] would have interested Isabella because the bride's mother, Corinne Roosevelt Robinson, was Patty Selmes's closest friend.

Hyde Park on the Hudson   Oct. 25, 1909
Dearest Isabella,

I found your letter[75] when I arrived Saturday & you can't think how delighted I was & the Kodak is too sweet. The children look adorable & so well & strong & from your description of Bobby & the pussy I should imagine he was as strong as he looks!

I am so glad to hear that you feel Bob is going steadily ahead & Mr. Aspinwall[76] whom I saw the other day said Bob looked so well.

It must have been hard getting the bandbox ready to rent but your things will be far better taken care of in Mrs. Cutcheon's and Cousin Susie [Parish]'s houses than in storage for I know from experience that is ruin! If I had only known you were to be in town I would have arranged to see you & perhaps I could have helped you but just at that time I was getting new nurses & therefore spending all the time up here. We are nearly settled now both here & in town & I expect Auntie Bye, Uncle Will & Sheffield to stay with us for Corinne's wedding.[77] I went down to Orange for a day last week to see Helen [Robinson] & the baby, Betsy Mary, who is very cunning.[78] I think

---

73. Miller, *Isabella Greenway*, 51.
74. Corinne Douglas Robinson was the daughter of Corinne Roosevelt and her husband, Douglas Robinson, and a niece of TR. Like her cousin ER, she had attended Allenswood Academy in England under the tutelage of Mlle. Marie Souvestre. She was a bridesmaid in Franklin and Eleanor's wedding. Corinne and Joe Alsop became the parents of syndicated columnists Joseph Alsop and Stewart Alsop.
75. Missing.
76. Franklin's uncle John Aspinwall?
77. Corinne Robinson married Joseph Alsop on November 5, 1909.
78. A hundred years ago, the meaning of "cunning" was more positive than in the early twenty-first century. It could mean "learned, skillful, delightful." *Webster's New International Dictionary*. Here, it has the modern meaning of "cute."

the little mark on her nose & forehead will fade & it is nothing like as bad as Helen seems to think. I saw Auntie Corinne [Robinson] & I really think for the first time her thoughts are being distracted & she is thinking of pleasant things. They say Corinne is radiant but I have not seen her as she was still at Farmington.[79] I don't know Jse. Alsop well but everyone who does says the nicest things about him. I will write you all about the wedding & perhaps before long we can run up & see you again.

Anna & James are very well but baby Franklin is not as fine as I would like however I hope he will improve in the next few months.

Pauline [Merrill] lunched with me the other day & looks very well but she was much upset about a cook & she was too funny about it. It will be hard for her really however when Margaret is married & she does take domestic trials very hard![80]

Much love dear to you & Bob & the chicks.

> Ever devotedly,
> Eleanor

Baby Franklin did not improve. Along with the other Roosevelt children, he came down with influenza. His heart was affected and he died on November 1. He was just over seven months old.

Eleanor was devastated. The fact that in those days one out of five children died before the age of five did not absolve her of what she saw as a failure to be a good mother. All her life she would remember baby Franklin's funeral and "how cruel it seemed to leave him out there alone in the cold."[81]

Isabella was on hand to comfort her grieving friend. Sorrow for Eleanor, coupled with work and worry, had worn down the resilient Isabella. Even as she wept on her Uncle Frank's shoulder, she tried her best to comfort Eleanor.

Hyde Park   Nov. 12 [1909]
My dearest Isabella,

I have wanted to write ever since I saw you but one thing & another has prevented. You do not know what a comfort it was just to get that glimpse of

79. Farmington refers to the home of Anna ("Bye") Roosevelt Cowles and her husband, Admiral William Sheffield Cowles, at 148 Main Street, Farmington, Conn. Also known as the Zenas Cowles House, it was built in 1788. It was sometimes referred to as "Oldgate."

80. Perhaps Margaret is a housekeeper and ER is saying that when she leaves to get married, Pauline will really have domestic difficulties.

81. Roosevelt, *This is My Story*, 128.

you. Sometimes I think it is a little help over our own sad places to know that our lives are a help to others so I wanted to tell you dear that your unselfish, cheerful example in all your anxiety & sorrow has helped me these past weeks more than you will ever know. I am oh! so happy that Bob is better & may God bless you both & give you the reward which you deserve.

Sometimes I think I cannot bear the heartache which one little life has left behind but then I realize that we have much to be grateful for still & that it was meant for us to understand & sympathize more deeply with all life's sorrows.

Anna & James are very sweet & we take them home on Monday. Love to Martha & Robbie from them & I wish they could play together!

Much love to Bob & your dear self.

> Ever devotedly,
> Eleanor

Although her occupations were "considerably restricted during this period" because of the children, Eleanor "rather intermittently" took lessons to keep up her French, German, and Italian. She also did a great deal of embroidery and knitting, and tried to learn how to cook.

49 E. 65th St.   [November 18, 1909]
Dearest Isabella,

Thank you so much for both letters[82] but above all for the picture of Bob. It does me good to see him look so well & the thought of you both being here around Christmastime makes me very happy but I still hope to run up to you for a day before that!

We are all settled & have just completed a sandbox on the roof which seems to fill Anna & James with joy. Pauline [Merrill] tells me Elizabeth's house in 64th St. is so nice & I am hoping to go there in a day or two & beg for Pete's company on the roof. I think a few children her own age or older will do Anna good as she has taken to copying James & behaving like a baby. Cousin Susie [Parish] took her out in her motor [car] yesterday P. M. & we are going there to dine on Saturday. I am sure her house will look quite changed with all your lovely things but I know I shan't like it for I feel as though no one had a right to those things except the dear people who chose them & loved them.

82. Missing.

20

Corinne & Joe [Alsop] are back & I hear all is "couleur de rose" & Corinne's one interest is tobacco![83]

Pauline & I have enrolled our names at "Teachers College" for cooking lessons, twice a week, but it looks as though we would miss most of the lessons for she is going to Boston today for the Yale-Harvard game & I will be at Hyde Park for Thanksgiving thereby missing Friday of next week also.

Dearest Isabella, I wish you could be nearer together but you know my thoughts are *often often* in the Adirondacks & it is good to feel that yours are with us also.

With love to Bob & the chicks in which Franklin joins.

   Ever your devoted
    Eleanor

Eleanor was occupied with the logistics of constantly moving her growing family between their brownstone in New York, the country home at Hyde Park where they lived with Franklin's mother, and summers in Campobello.

49 East 65th St.   Dec. 29 [1909]

Dearest Isabella,

How did you ever think of anything as enchanting as the pack full of toys. It was like another stocking & Anna adored it. I never have had any warm slippers before & expect to revel in such lovely ones which are just the right size. You gave us much too much thought & time dear, besides all the rest but if you could have seen the pleasure which you gave I know you would have been pleased. The Kodak of the chicks I love better than anything & they do look *so* healthy.

I meant to answer your dear letter[84] long ago but was very busy shopping before Christmas & am equally busy now trying to tell everyone who has been good to us what a lot of pleasure they have given.

Everyone at Hyde Park thought & talked so much of you & I wish you could have seen Douglas [Robinson] & Anna playing in the snow. It was far too deep to move except where the snow ploughs had made a path but both chicks dug hard & enjoyed the sleighing very much.

We go up again for New Year & then we will all settle down again in town & I hope soon to go up & see you for a day.

83. Alsop owned a tobacco farm.
84. Missing.

With many thanks again to you & Bob & so many good wishes for the New Year.

> Ever devotedly,
> Eleanor

Eleanor became pregnant again about a month after Franklin, Jr.'s death. She was depressed for most of the next year, but hid her emotions from Isabella. Nor did Isabella always confide in Eleanor to the extent that she confided in Olivia Cutting, although we cannot be sure, because so many of Isabella's letters are evidently missing. Isabella and Eleanor each tried, by her example of cheerfulness, to hearten the other.

49 East 65th Street, New York, NY   Jan 29 [1910]
Dearest Isabella

It was nice to get your note[85] the other day & I do want to see you & Bob so much that I am much tempted to go up with Mrs. Selmes. However I could not leave all my family for more than two nights & Franklin cannot make up his mind to forego a chance of Sunday in [illegible] boating & he wants to go up & see you also, so you see[,] with all the many complications I do not think we stand much chance of getting to you just yet.

What have you heard from Ronald's election?[86] The flood in Paris seems most alarming & the two little Collier girls[87] are there with Mlle. Mathieu so we all feel rather worried. Muriel & Cyril [Martineau] are now at Monte Carlo & she writes it is doing Cyril good as the cold & damp in England had affected his spirits very much. They want to come over in the spring for a year & I wonder if you can tell me what some of the homes near you rent for? Warren Robbins[88] is engaged to a lady in Buenos Aires! Her father is a Belgian & she is lovely he writes & I do hope he will be happy for he is a dear boy.

85. Missing. Eleanor evidently did not keep as much of their early correspondence as Isabella did; some of Isabella's letters referred to by Eleanor are missing.
86. Ronald Ferguson was elected as a member of the British Parliament, representing Leith Burghs, the port area of Edinburgh, from 1886–1914. He must have done well, for he was appointed Governor General of Australia in 1914. *Australian Dictionary of Biography Online*, http://www.adb.online.anu.edu.au/biogs/A100605b.html.
87. The daughters of Sara Roosevelt's sister Katherine and the writer Price Collier.
88. Warren Delano Robbins, Muriel Robbins Martineau's brother, was FDR's cousin, a groomsman in the Roosevelts' wedding, and later State Department chief of protocol. Cook, *Eleanor Roosevelt*, I, 490.

Pauline [Merrill] dined here last night & looked so pretty & was most amusing. Helen & Teddy [Robinson] were here on Thursday too & Teddy is becoming a great farmer in his Father's absence & starting a milk powder industry at Henderson[89] & [will] astonish the family on their return! I went in for a minute to say goodbye to Corinne [Robinson Alsop] yesterday & she looked so well & happy it just did one good to see her.

We are all fine here & Hall is at home for the midyears which always adds to the excitement in the house!

With love to you all from us all.

     Devotedly,

       Eleanor

In March 1910, Isabella went to New York City to have a gynecological operation. While there, she attended a party at the Parishes in honor of the Roosevelts' fifth wedding anniversary. She reported to Bob that "Eleanor looks as always . . . ever so sweet and tall and slim in her black [mourning clothes for Franklin Jr.]." But, after the party, Eleanor "went all to pieces . . . and is spending today [the day after her and Franklin's anniversary] at Hyde Park near her Baby Franklin on his birthday."[90]

Isabella also informed Bob that women in New York City did not "take the slightest interest in [partisan] politics . . . anti-vivisection, suffrage and Christian Science being the three topics of the women folk. Even clothes and babies are forgotten." Evidently, she would have liked to discuss politics with her women friends. Neither Isabella nor Eleanor, however, indicated any support for woman suffrage at this time.[91]

While Isabella was in New York, Bob's favorite sister, Edith [Edie], had come to stay with him in Saranac. She also had been in poor health, and the Ferguson family hoped the bracing climate would revive her.

Eleanor, herself, was feeling poorly. She was pregnant again, and still depressed over the death of baby Franklin.

89. Henderson House, in Herkimer County, N.Y., summer home of Douglas and Corinne Roosevelt Robinson. Teddy was their son, Helen was Teddy's wife.
90. IG to Robert Munro Ferguson, March 18, 1910, FC.
91. Ibid., March 20, 1910.

49 East 65th Street, New York, NY,   Jun 10 [1910]

Dearest Isabella

From what I hear I think perhaps you & Bob & Edie will be in town for Ted's wedding[92] so won't you all lunch here at 1:30 & dress here if you care to? A. Bye will be with us & I will try to get Helen & Teddy [Robinson]. I am so glad you are both to have a holiday & give my love & congratulations to Bob.

Ever your devoted
Eleanor

92. Ted Roosevelt, TR's eldest son, married his childhood sweetheart, Eleanor Butler, on June 20, 1910. They would have four children: Grace, Quentin, Theodore Roosevelt III, and Cornelius.

Part Two
A Southwestern Homestead and New York Politics

After Isabella returned from New York City, Bob's health declined; he began to lose weight and to cough more. The doctors at Saranac told him that his only hope of surviving was to move to the dry climate of the Southwest. Isabella immediately rose to meet this new crisis, writing her mother, "the struggle . . . for life must have gotten us down to a Bed Rock of real foundation." It would be sad for her to leave New York, her home and all her friends and relations, but she reasoned that happy people always built their real homes "in their hearts or the hearts of others!" She concluded gaily: "Here's to life in a pueblo, sitting in Navajo blankets!"[1]

The Fergusons' friend Bronson Cutting,[2] another tuberculosis patient, had moved to Albuquerque, New Mexico, where he was thriving. Bob's fellow Rough Rider and good friend John Greenway lived in Bisbee, Arizona, where he was general manager of the Calumet and Arizona Copper Company. Greenway urged the Fergusons to locate near him.

Bob and Isabella chose to settle half way between Albuquerque and Bisbee, in a place called Cat Cañon, near Silver City, in the southwest corner of New Mexico. Doctors at the famous Cottage Sanatorium nearby could give Bob the treatment he needed.[3] The family moved in mid-November 1910.

The Fergusons made a little settlement in the desert, living in half a dozen Adirondack tents. These semi-permanent structures had wooden floors, and screen siding, to admit the fresh air thought so beneficial to TB patients; canvas could be rolled down over the screens in cold or windy weather. The "tents" were quite substantial, the functional equivalent of pre-fab houses of the late-twentieth century. The Fergusons would live in their Adirondack tents for four years.

1. IG to Patty, undated, probably July 1910, GC.
2. Son of William and Olivia Murray Cutting, brother of Olivia. He later became U.S. Senator from New Mexico and served with Isabella Greenway in Congress during the New Deal.
3. The Cottage Sanatorium was run by Dr. E. S. Bullock, who claimed a tuberculosis cure rate significantly higher than sanatoria in New York State.

Isabella's mother, Patty, and Julia Loving ("Mammy") went along to help their girl in this difficult new situation. Mammy grumbled to Julia Dinsmore, "I like living under a roof with other people, not in a tent. When the winds blow (which is quite often) one is frightened to death for fear of being carried away."[4] The Fergusons hired local women—Delia and Maggie—to help them cope with the primitive living. New Mexico was not yet a state, and Isabella laughingly referred to her family as "Mexicans." She tells Eleanor of the arrival of a man who knows a mutual friend of theirs. Her comments about this man show that she has already adopted the traditional Western attitude toward effete Eastern dudes.

The Roosevelts also were experiencing big changes. On September 23, 1910, Eleanor gave birth to another son, Elliott. Her first two babies had weighed in at over 10 pounds, and baby Franklin had weighed 11 pounds at birth. Elliott weighed an amazing 11 pounds, 14 ounces. Eleanor stayed in New York City over a month, recovering.

A week after Elliott's birth, Franklin began campaigning for his first elective office, the New York state senate. Reform Democrats, looking for "new faces," had recruited twenty-eight-year-old Franklin Roosevelt to run from the 26th district (near Hyde Park). Although FDR had voted for Theodore Roosevelt, his wife's uncle, in 1904, Franklin's father and elder brother were Democrats, and he followed their tradition. FDR's victory in November was the first Democratic win for his district since his neighbor, Thomas Jefferson Newbold, had held the seat in 1878. The state legislature met in Albany.

Cat Cañon, Silver City, New Mexico   Nov. 21, 1910

How you would laugh Eleanor dearest were you to drive up Cat's Cañon to find us wild Mexicans—basking in the sun along with the drying towels & sponges—while Delia sweeps the dining room porch! Maggie does the family wash in two quarts of scarce water! Mammy hustles in her tent house—and Mother Buzz & Martha rattle down the cañon after[5] the dinner and the family milk—to be found on a neighbor's fence post halfway to town.[6] Bob on the porch of the living room looks far off over hills. Pink & blue far hills & sandy near ones with scrubby dwarf evergreens that break the desert sweep.

4. Julia Loving to Julia Dinsmore, December 30, 1910, DC.
5. "After" means to obtain.
6. Apparently, the Fergusons had arranged for a neighbor to leave out a meal and a container of milk for them to pick up.

The air is marvelous & still—sunshine, indeed, too good to be true. So I hope we'll have plenty [of] good results to write you before a great while.

Bob loves it all and it certainly seems just what we were looking for. A few more tent houses will let us spread more comfortably. (Just now Bob & I are living in the sitting room!)

Already a handful of neighbors have cropped up. Of amusing variety certainly. While we're not too isolated, we're not on the beaten track which has its advantages.

You & Franklin must come & see for yourselves one day. Much love to him from us.

Such a deal[7] to you dearest. Always. How I wish you could look in on our 6 o'clock evening meal—off an oilcloth table cover[,] a kerosene lamp for a center piece & Martha & Buzz stuffing silently anything they are given. And we're all sleeping peacefully by 8:30 or at latest, nine. The great daily excitement being twenty some ponies that come tearing up the cañon just after sundown to pasture up behind us. Pasture being a rocky knoll that nothing less than a pick ax makes any impression on—and a few cactus here & there.

We're thinking of your move to Albany and longing to hear all about it & the kind of house you might possibly get & all that comes along—but I know you'll write us—when you have the time.

> Hugs and kiss[es] Eleanor from us one & all—
> Yr Isabella

The tale runs that Redmond Cross's[8] millionaire friend Dr. Cochrane [illegible] went to the shoemaker in his shop & slapping him on the back said "I say, if you'll move out of your house today and let me move in tomorrow I'll give you $15,000.00 dollars"

"Go to hell" was all the shoemaker had to say. He's made a great stir since he arrived a week ago and is generally considered "dippy" because he came in a private [railroad] car[9] & with a Doctor as [illegible] caretaker.

In Albany, the Roosevelts moved into a large sunny house, fully furnished for the three months a session typically lasted. Looking forward to a fresh

---

7. "Such a deal" means "(I'm sending) such a great deal of love (to you)."
8. Redmond Cross, later author, with Kermit Roosevelt, of *Hunting Trails on Three Continents*. New York: The Derrydale Press, 1933.
9. Wealthy Americans owned their own private railroad cars, often luxuriously appointed. These could be attached to a train when they wanted to travel.

start in new surroundings, Eleanor shook off the previous year's depression and entered wholeheartedly into her husband's new life. She was nervous, but eager.

49 E. 65th Street   Nov. 26 [1910]

Dearest Isabella,

I was so glad to get your letter & you were a dear to write—for my thoughts are very constantly with you all & if wishing can get me out to see you I will surely descend upon you before long!

Franklin & I spent yesterday in Albany & you don't know how I am looking forward to the winter there. It is all so quiet, no crowd, no rush, just stately houses overlooking a broad street with occasional passers by, really, I feel one might have time to live there & it is such an effort here to reach that end! We have practically decided on a square brown stone house on State Street only two blocks from the Capital [*sic*] so Franklin can be home for lunch. It is quite a big house with a piazza[10] & big yard at the back & built more like a country house. We will have two nice spare rooms & I am looking forward to getting Cousin Susie [Parish] & Henry to come up & rest. The only thing which appals me is the elaborate food! We lunched with a Mrs. Van Rensselaer & had 6 courses, I thought we would never get through! I am sure I can never live up to their standards!

Mrs. Cutcheon left me some things of Martha's which I am delighted to have & you can think of baby Elliot in the warm coat & Scotch stockings all winter. I am sending out a little Xmas parcel rather early but as the papers threaten another express strike before Xmas I thought I had better get things off early. Please do not open it in any case till Xmas!

Ever so much love to all the family in which Franklin joins & my dearest to you.

      Devotedly,

        Eleanor

Isabella was learning the ways of the arid West, hauling water—she insisted to her mother that a "well-applied quart" could go a long way—raising chickens, and riding a horse to visit a neighbor woman 25 miles away.

Eleanor, meanwhile, was learning to run a household without being able to depend on her mother-in-law or cousin Susie Parish for advice, an experience

---

10. A colonnaded porch.

she found exhilarating. Realizing that she "craved to be an individual,"[11] Eleanor quickly learned to entertain her husband's diverse political associates, however unpromising they may have seemed at first.

Both women were taking on new challenges, and each served as an inspiration to the other.

Hyde Park on the Hudson NY   [Thursday, Dec. 29, 1910]
Dearest Isabella,

I can't tell you how much I love the lovely embroidery & it is just what I need in Albany to help cover up the many hideous things in the drawing room! Anna's bracelet is too pretty & she adores it & would like to wear it all the time. You wonderful person to think of us when you were barely settled yourself.

Your letter was a delight[12] & I am glad the children are so well & it is good to know Bob is even a little more comfortable. I wonder if you realize what a wonderful influence your sweet & cheerful spirit always is to me dear but you never can know how I love & admire both you & Bob. If it is possible, I should love to go & see you both before the next year is out but if I can't you know dear that anything I can do for you in this part of the world would be a pleasure for me.

We had a very nice Xmas here & though I could only bring Anna up [with me], I went to Albany Sunday to start getting settled yesterday & [to arrange things for] Baby Elliott [so he could be] moved up, but the house is still at sixes and sevens & I am trusting to Providence that it will be more settled by the time we go up from here Saturday. Mama goes with us & on Monday as many of Franklin's constituents as come up for the Inauguration are to lunch with us, about 200 I believe! After that I hope we will have a quiet week to find our bearings a little! Some of the people are so funny I just wish you & Bob could see them! One, a Mr. Hoyt Assemblyman from Fishkill[13] is little but oh! so large in importance. He called upon us Tuesday evening & sat on an unopened express box & told me he understood "there was quite a high class society in Albany" & he "hopes I'd like it" & he would bring Mrs. Hoyt up on Sunday so she could call that afternoon & "get acquainted" before

11. Roosevelt, *This is My Story*, 133.

12. Missing.

13. Most likely Ferdinand Hoyt, elected at the same time as FDR. His older brother, Morgan, was chairman of the Fishkill Democratic Committee. Morgan introduced FDR eight times in Fishkill where his first campaign began. Ward to editors, March 6, 2007.

the reception Monday. I believe she is rather awful at least I gather so from Franklin's extreme reticence about her, however, I am sure we will get on beautifully.

My love to Mrs. Selmes, Bob the chicks & you & many thanks again for our enchanting & beautiful gifts.

Devotedly,

Eleanor

When Franklin and Eleanor began a new life together in Albany in 1911, it was the start of the twentieth century's most remarkable political partnership.

On January 1, the day after she arrived, Eleanor entertained a house full of friends and constituents. When the legislative session began, Eleanor could often be found in the gallery, listening to the speeches. At first she attended out of a sense of duty, or so she claimed; it quickly became clear that she was captivated, first by the larger-than-life personalities of the politicians, and later by the issues.[14] She ventured out to meet Franklin's constituents, his colleagues, and their wives.[15]

During his first year in office, FDR led a group opposed to the Tammany machine.[16] The New York state legislature's first challenge was to pick the Democratic nominee to the U. S. Senate.[17] Tammany favored "Blue-eyed Billy" Sheehan, while FDR and the insurgents wanted Brooklyn mayor Edward Shepard. FDR garnered press attention for his opposition to Sheehan. Later, Eleanor, like her husband, made friends with Tammanyites who were interested in reform causes.[18]

Eleanor was more active in reform causes than FDR, but he came out for woman suffrage in 1911, before Eleanor had given the matter any real consideration.[19] In this letter, Eleanor assumes that Bob, not Isabella, would have

14. Roosevelt, *This is My Story*, 133.

15. Cook, *Eleanor Roosevelt*, I, 190.

16. "Tammany Hall" was the designated term for the Democratic Party political machine that played a major role in New York City politics from the 1790s to the 1960s. http://www.albany.edu/~dkw42/tweed.html.

17. The U.S. Constitution provided for state legislatures to elect senators. In 1913, the 17th Amendment was ratified by the states, allowing for direct election of senators. Nineteen fourteen was the first year "all senatorial elections were held by popular vote." http://www.senate.gov/artandhistory/history/common/briefing/Direct_Election_Senators.htm.

18. Cook, *Eleanor Roosevelt*, I, 191–92.

19. Lash, *Eleanor Roosevelt*, 238–39.

wanted to hear the legislative debates. For the first time, Eleanor displays growing enthusiasm for the political game; it would not be long before Isabella began to show similar interest. Their letters still reflect their traditional roles as wives and mothers—here Eleanor expresses reluctance to leave her children too often—but from now on there will be more and more glimpses of the politicians they would become.

248 State Street, Albany, NY   Jan 11th [1911]
Dearest Isabella,

Your letter of the 2nd[20] came two days ago & I am so glad you like the photograph & I surely will send one to Edie [Ferguson] as soon as I get some more but just now we have given them all away.

I am so sorry Bob has such a bad time with a tooth & hope there were no ill effects & that he is up again now. How nice the Cooleys[21] are to be near you, especially if you like her. How is your Mother? I haven't heard a word of her in so long.

Muriel [Martineau] writes very cheerfully but I don't think her news is really encouraging. They have been 9 months at Davos[22] & Cyril has been in bed all the time & much of the time in great pain. Dr. Spengler thinks he is improving & the pain is due to an abscess as the "tuberculosis bugs" are nearly all gone.

I do hope he will be OK soon for it must be so discouraging to Muriel not to *see* any improvement—her two children are quite adorable & the baby very well & strong & little Cyril far stronger than when he went up.

We are quite settled here now & the house is very attractive though there are some fearful things in it such as cream satin panels in the drawing room & a modern tapestry of wonderful colors. We had 250 constituents to lunch on Inauguration day & went to a dance that night at the Governor's.[23] Since

20. Missing.
21. Alford W. Cooley married Susan Dexter Dalton in 1904. In 1899, when Alford Cooley was twenty-six, he was elected to the New York state assembly. There he became a "stanch friend" of Governor Theodore Roosevelt. Theodore Roosevelt, *Autobiography*, 326. After TR became president, Cooley was appointed to the Civil Service Commission. He went on to serve as Assistant Attorney General of the United States, and Justice of the New Mexico Supreme Court, having moved to Silver City when he contracted tuberculosis. *New York Times*, October 8, 1904: 9; July 21, 1913: 7.
22. Davos is a city in the high valley of eastern Switzerland, famous for winter sports and as a healthful resort for lung disease patients. Thomas Mann's "Magic Mountain" is set in a sanatorium there.
23. John Alden Dix, a Democrat.

then I have met so many people that I feel quite bewildered & I pay calls in every spare moment![24] Friday we are going to New York as Franklin has a democratic dinner but after that I don't think I shall go away much as I don't like leaving the chicks.

We went to the opening of the Senate & Bob would have enjoyed hearing a dreadful Senator Newcomb[25] attack the Governor's message & then Senator Grady,[26] who is a reprehensible character but a delightful speaker, get up and defend it. I thought they would come to blows & it certainly was not a dignified argument but Grady had the whole room laughing before he had been speaking five minutes & one could not help being sorry for anyone who tried to oppose him!

The excitement now is great about the U.S. Senatorship & She[e]han men & Shephard men are gathering rapidly.

Much love from us all to all of you.

> Ever devotedly,
> Eleanor

Soon, Eleanor dropped all pretense of simply doing her duty, and reveled in the frank enjoyment of political combat.

248 State Street, Albany NY, Jan. 30 [1911]
Dearest Isabella,

I have a photograph now of baby Elliott & myself all ready to go to Edie [Ferguson] & I have lost the address which I thought I had carefully kept! Will you send it to me again?

24. By the beginning of the nineteenth century, the etiquette of calling was a firmly established ritual in society. A lady would start making calls as soon as she arrived in town. She would usually remain in her carriage while her groom took her card to the door and handed it to a servant. The card was conveyed to the mistress of the house, who would then decide whether or not to receive the caller. Calls were to be made to people only on their At Home days. Days and times for these were engraved on visiting cards. A newcomer waited until she received cards from neighbors. It was then good manners to call on those neighbors who left cards. http://www.literary-liaisons.com/article026.html.
25. Josiah T. Newcomb (b. 1868), Republican senator from New York City.
26. Thomas Grady (b. 1853) represented the 14th Senate District, in New York City. A Democrat, he was "associated with Tammany" but also an "ardent" reformer. Cook, *Eleanor Roosevelt*, I, 193. Later he would oppose woman suffrage in New York State. ER admired his eloquent speeches. Once he wrote Eleanor to decline a dinner invitation, and "worded it so charmingly," Eleanor said, that she kept the note for years. Roosevelt, *This is My Story*, 133.

You have probably seen by the papers what excitement we have had here over the election of a U.S. Senator. We talk & think of nothing else but we don't seem any further than we were at the beginning & as the governor won't say anything it looks as though there would never be a decision. Franklin had a nice letter today from Uncle Ted[27] which cheered him somewhat but the game of politics has so far not had any written rules so it can be played rather unfairly which is rather trying to anyone new at the game!

Helen & Teddy [Robinson] spent two nights with Beatrice Pruy last week & they dined with us & went to the Senate with me to hear a lively & diverting contest of tongues! Brackett,[28] the republican leader, is delicious and so is Grady & both know the game so well it is most amusing to watch them & I think Teddy & Helen enjoyed it.

I had a long letter from Muriel [Martineau] the other day. She says Cyril [Martineau] looks better but this getting well does take a long time & he has been in bed nearly ten months.

Mama is coming to spend this Sunday with us & Cousin Henry & Cousin Susie [Parish] the next so we feel quite gay! The chicks are very well here & the baby is getting quite big & weighs 16 ½ lbs already!

My love to Bob & the children & Mrs. Selmes & your dear self.

> Ever devotedly,
>
> Eleanor

Meanwhile, the Fergusons' friends followed them out to the frontier. Most were Bob's buddies. TR's son Kermit was Bob's godson.[29] Isabella's cousin, Dave Goodrich,[30] and John Greenway were among Roosevelt's favorite Rough Riders, along with Bob Ferguson. Olivia Cutting came down from Albuquerque, where she had been visiting her brother, Bronson. Edith Roosevelt and her daughter Ethel also dropped by.

In spite of all the company, or perhaps because of the work that it entailed, by the end of June Bob thought his young wife deserved a break and urged

---

27. Theodore Roosevelt.
28. Edgar Truman Brackett (b. 1853), Republican state senator from Saratoga County. He was the Republican leader for the 1911–1912 session, selected by the Republican caucus as permanent chairman. *New York Times*, September 27, 1912, p. 2.
29. Kermit was "the most sensitive" of TR's children, and prone to occasional moodiness. But he was, like Bob, also an intellectual and a doughty fighter. http://www.theodoreroosevelt.org/life/familytree/kermit.htm. Kermit was then twenty-one years old.
30. David Goodrich was the brother of Isabella Goodrich Breckinridge. See first paragraph of introduction to letter of December 13, 1908.

her to accept John Greenway's invitation to visit him in Bisbee, 200 miles away. John, a thirty-nine-year-old bachelor, was a successful mining engineer and executive; his house, to someone living in tents, seemed almost palatial. Greenway's aunt and uncle were staying with him, making Isabella's visit perfectly respectable. Isabella's letter to Eleanor, describing her two-week visit, includes her first, almost casual, reference to John Greenway.

This letter also marks another milestone: Isabella's growing interest in politics. She clearly understood that Eleanor's work was of vital importance to Franklin's career. In turn, she describes territorial politics for Eleanor. She also foreshadows the coming border trouble with Mexico.

Meanwhile, Isabella's hands were full with her two children, now three years old and almost five. She dwells on the positive aspects of her situation, chiefly the beauties of nature, but also the eccentricities of some of her fellow Westerners.

August 1st, 1911

Dearest Eleanor,

If only you were alongside [us] this warm but pleasant New Mexican summer afternoon and Franklin too[. A]nd surely Anna & James and Eliot would like feeding chickens and building rock houses and going [on] a most cautious barefoot stroll on the paths between tents.

Bob and Kermit have gone to town. It's been such a joy to find Kerm the same dear. He walked in yesterday and has settled so simply to the Cañon's routine, reading to Bob & playing with Martha & Buzz. Surely it's very refreshing to see a young person who remains so unchanged, at heart, never mind how life & time has crowded in between glimpses. And wasn't it like him to have come so far and in spite of Bob's firmly writing not to (thinking it far too expensive unless he could take in a bear hunt or something worth while later when Dave[31] & Alec Lambert[32] propose coming out for one.)

Well again I say I wish very often we weren't quite at such ends of the earth from each other. I can't say how I miss you blessed Eleanor or how ever constantly you and Franklin are in our minds. We've had the pleasure of following Franklin's work this winter [—] that you can imagine—and like to think of the big share that's been yours. Spring must have seen you both rather tired & we'll be glad of some news of a real holiday & rest. Mrs. Lambkins' was the

31. Probably David Goodrich, one of Isabella's cousins and a favorite of TR in the Rough Riders.
32. A Dr. Alec Lambert was a close friend of TR. http://www.doctorzebra.com/prez/dr_lambert.htm. This may be his son.

last news, after her visit at Hyde Park. We realize our lack of first hand news is well deserved.

The practical odds & ends of every day, living as we do, keep one's hands so full. Indeed you'd find it hard to believe till you'd see for yourself. The simplicity of life you'd hardly picture but it's largely the reason its so healthy. Living in scattered tents—fetching & eating food a large part of the day—Running a garden patch that keep[s] us fairly well supplied with vegetables & some profusion of flowers—nearly 200 chickens & now a horse—& no man!! My horsemanship is rather disappointing. One day he ran away with me & the next succeeded in getting my too casual knot undone & in careering round the corral & smashing buggy & harness to many pieces. I think I might be more successful with a cow & a motor & may try them next. You see the real frontier spirit creeps in & we've still much to learn.

Mrs. Parish[33] tells me she gave you all our news just after Dave & Fletcher Harper[34] were one of us for six weeks. Bob was better then than at all [better then than he was before or since]—and we did so enjoy having them in and about. Frolicking like boys over anything or nothing—and apparently getting some real health out of this queer life. Fletcher was amusing as could be having had little experience out of New York & Long Island. He took to currying [grooming] his pony & blacking his shoes[35] in the most friendly manner & gained pounds.[36]

It's all of it rather a lark while Bob goes ahead [makes progress in getting well]. And I believe there's real progress on the whole. You know what a tedious business it is at best. Slow and with setbacks. Bob shows great contentment in the life & that's always a part [of] the battle & is ever so good about the infinite patience necessary.

We hope Olivia & Mrs. Cutting[37] may come down shortly from Santa Fe. Olivia to stop on[38] for a while. There are some such [very] pleasant neighbors. Only [However,] one grows to consider anyone within two or three hundred

33. Eleanor's "Cousin Susie" Parish, one of Patty Selmes's best friends, would have heard the Fergusons' news from Patty and passed it on to Eleanor.

34. Possibly a grandson of Fletcher Harper, one of the founding brothers of Harpers Brothers Publishing, the forerunner of HarperCollins.

35. Probably oiling his horse's hooves to condition them in dry weather.

36. Before antibiotics were available to cure infectious diseases, it was thought prudent to carry some extra weight to withstand a long siege of illness.

37. Isabella's letters to Olivia in the Arizona Historical Society present a frank portrayal of the Fergusons' circumstances in New Mexico.

38. At that time, "stop" also had the meaning of "stay."

miles as neighbors. & to think nothing of a 24 hour jaunt. Nearby mines bring all sorts here from time to time. Among them some of Bob's Rough Rider friends.

While [For example,] John Greenway has been the best of friends in coming up 200 miles (from Bisbee Arizona) quite often. I wish you had been along on my two day visit to him in July!! It grew to two weeks and every moment was interesting to a degree. [My] First [experience] in the life of a booming young Western mining town of that type. The most substantial Fifth Avenue buildings apparently thrown down the copper color cañons & the residences perched on "Young Blood Hill up behind Brewery Gulch" or "Bright Angel Trail that leads from Quality Hill."[39] Our surrounding country [is] more beautiful in vast desert plains & mountains than anything I had ever dreamed of.

We went over [to] the scene of recent battle at Aqua [Agua] Prieta[40] (just over the border from Douglas). It was hard to picture 60 men killed, and the fighting that had riddled the whole place with bullet holes. So peaceful was it as we saw it.

Then Cananea[41] (in old Mexico) [which] was particularly picturesque & [I met] a trio of Princeton people Dr. [Louis David] Ricketts[,] his mother & sister[,] a most delightful surprise in parts so remote. Perhaps you knew

39. Isabella is saying that buildings as big as those found in New York City were perched on the edge of canyons, and residential areas as yet had no real street names, just general designations.

40. On April 13, 1911, Mexican revolutionaries attacked federal troops in the northern Mexican border town of Agua Prieta. Shots from the battle crossed the border into the adjacent town of Douglas, Arizona, killing and injuring Americans. A sixteen-year old girl was sitting in her father's house when a federal bullet passed through her arm. U.S. forces went into Mexico and quelled the fighting. "Our Soldiers Stop a Fight in Mexico," *New York Times*, April 14, 1911: 1. The attack by the revolutionaries at Agua Prieta and numerous other attacks by multiple revolutionary groups ultimately led to the forced resignation, on May 25, 1911, of Mexico's long-time dictator, Porfirio Diaz.

41. On May 13, 1911, the rebel army of Juan Cabral forced the surrender, without an actual battle, of local federal troops in Cananea, Mexico, thereby seizing the town. "Cananea is Taken; Nogales in Danger," *New York Times*, May 14, 1911: 3. At the time, Cananea was the site of one of the largest copper producing mines in the world, with a copper belt estimated to be five miles in length and between 1,000 to 2,000 feet in width. "The Cananea Camp: Destined to Become World's Largest Copper Producer," *Wall Street Journal*, August 26, 1904: 2. Some of the Americans living in Cananea were evacuated by U.S. border town residents who drove automobiles into Mexico to retrieve people and return them to the safety of the United States. "No excitement attended the exodus, the women appearing to enjoy the adventure." "Cananea is Taken."

them. They've been in and about New York & are great friends of the Osborn family. Mrs. R. aged 84 is a famous character. For diversion she runs koyotes [coyotes] down across the plains by motor[car] & during the excitement at Cananea had carpets & chairs taken to the cellar so they could be comfortable during the shooting.

I'm very anxious that Bob go down [to visit Greenway] when autumn's cool makes travelling more possible. John's work is remarkably interesting (what I could understand of it). One day it was 106 in the shade when we were looking at smelters & yet not very uncomfortable.

Then of course one hears the astonishing home politics of this most frightfully corrupt territory from the Cutting family who live in Santa Fe. It's quite true that no one is a proved politician till he's been shot at a certain number of times in the Public Plaza! The points of view on many sides are certainly astonishing to us—who doubtless astonish them in our turn. There's a young crude life & enthusiasm about most of it that is invigorating & simple. One can't help feeling that young Americans should know parts of this country as a part of their education.

Here's a warm hug Eleanor and a heart full of love. Kisses to Anna from Martha & me & Bob's love with mine to Franklin. Yr loving Isabella.

Hope you can read this. I can't. Edie [Ferguson]'s been having a grand lark in London. Please give my love to Mrs. Roosevelt. Some Kodaks will follow—better explaining M & B's wild selves. They become very companionable & full of problems—having a most intimate & casual relation with creation in general & God in particular.

Eleanor continued to assume that it would be Bob who was interested in the Roosevelts' political news, even though she wrote to Isabella.

Hyde Park on the Hudson, NY   Dec. 30 [1911]
Dearest Isabella,

You & Bob always send the most adorable presents, but to have a letter from Bob was the nicest of all. Thank him many times & tell him that I am going to answer it from Albany as I think there may be some more amusing things to tell him by that time for the winter promises to be interesting I think.

And now to thank [you] for my lovely green "reboso."[42] I simply love it & it will be so useful. Anna & James were much excited over the saddle blanket

42. Reboso (rebozo), a traditional Mexican shawl used as a baby sling

for their pony & send their love & many thanks to Martha & Buzz. We are a little sad because it will not snow or get cold enough for skating & it is hard not to use new sleds & skates! I have never seen it so mild as late as this.

We had a very happy Xmas with the chicks & went to New York on Sunday to have a family dinner at Mama's home for Hall & Margaret.[43] I was very sad Auntie Bye could not be there but Uncle Ted was splendid & told us stories of his European trip until eleven o'clock! Cousin Susie [Parish] had a dinner for them Thursday which was great fun & they went yesterday to Oyster Bay to see Aunt Edith [Mrs. Theodore Roosevelt] as she was not well enough to dine with us. We expect them up tonight for New Years & all go to the Rogers' party which is to be chiefly Anne's friends however so I expect we shall feel very ancient!

Did you know Teddy [Robinson] & Helen had a house only two blocks from us in Albany?[44] Poor Teddy has been bored to death there so far & he has not been able to stand it for more than two days at a time but when the session begins I hope he will be as much interested as he expects to be.

I saw Corinne [Alsop] yesterday & she looks very well & I hope she & Joe are coming to us in Albany about the 17th. You know of course that she expects a baby in March?

Franklin went on to Buffalo last week to speak to the Saturn Club[45] & stirred up all kinds of trouble & Mr. McCabe,[46] the Albany democratic boss has been calling him every conceivable name ever since! So many thanks again & love to you all.

> Devotedly,
> Eleanor

Our address in Albany this winter is 4 Elk Street & we go up on the 8th.

In 1912, Theodore Roosevelt, disappointed with his chosen successor, the very conservative William Howard Taft, decided to challenge President Taft for the Republican nomination. This gave Eleanor and Isabella a common political topic, as Bob Ferguson was intensely interested in his old colonel's prospects.

43. Margaret Richardson, a woman Hall had met while at school.
44. Theodore (Teddy) Douglas Robinson was a member of the New York state assembly.
45. A men's club in Buffalo, N.Y., founded in 1885. Motto: "Where the women cease from troubling and the wicked are at rest." http://www.waymarking.com/waymarks/WM1HFR
46. Patrick E. "Packy" McCabe, chairman of the Democratic County Committee (Albany), ca. 1900–1919.

As part of her promise to educate herself about her country's government, Eleanor read a number of civics books. The first volume she mentioned to Isabella was William C. Hudson's *Random Recollections of an Old Political Reporter*.[47] Woven through Hudson's narrative are specific tips and clues for political success that may have influenced Eleanor's evolution into a public woman. Her ambition to learn something about politics may be gauged by her willingness to curl up on a cold night with a political memoir.

4 Elk Street, Albany, New York   Jan 29 [1912]
Dearest Isabella

At last I have time for a little chat with you! We are having a blizzard & Franklin has gone to the Monday evening session but I could not make up my mind to go out & so have had a lovely evening finishing such an amazing book "Random Recollections of an old Political Reporter"[48] quite an eye opener as to political methods & chances & of course that is all we talk of now! How do they feel out your way about Uncle Ted & do you think any other Republican could carry the West against a democrat, say Harmon?[49]

How are you & the children & Bob? I do hope all goes well and please give your mother my dearest love & beg her to stop with us on her way back. I do long for a glimpse of you all & think I shall have to take a flying trip[50] alone in the spring if Franklin won't take the time off.

Helen [Robinson] is still waiting for her baby & she seems very well. Roger Poor is here & they come to supper every Sunday night. Teddy [Robinson] is broadening wonderfully & I think really likes his work.

47. William C. Hudson, *Random Recollections of an Old Political Reporter*. New York: Cupples & Leon Company, 1911.

48. Hudson presents a vivid portrait of an early female political figure, Kate Chase, the daughter of U.S. Supreme Court chief justice Salmon Chase. Hudson describes Miss Chase "in the flush of beautiful womanhood, tall and elegant, with exquisite tact, with brains of almost masculine fiber, trained in the political arts by her father...." (18). Hudson also stresses the importance of political networks. He cites the example of the 1876 Democratic nominee, Samuel J. Tilden: "Little that was political occurred in any part of the United States of which he did not have the earliest and fullest information" (42). He notes that Theodore Roosevelt, from the very beginning of his political life, exhibited "a strong personality, abundant vigor, great energy of mind, a combative positiveness, whether right or wrong, and intense interest in all that concerned humanity" (144).

49. Judson Harmon, Ohio governor (1909–1913).

50. A quick trip. Nine years after the Wright brothers flew at Kitty Hawk, commercial airline travel was still in the future.

Joe Choate[51] was up here today & [had] lunch with us & I suppose you know that Cora [Cora Oliver Choate] is expecting No 4 any day soon?[52] I do hope it will be a boy. Also, Muriel [Martineau] writes me Caroline Philips[53] is in the family way again & I do hope she will be granted her heart's desire this time.

Lilian Lord & her husband spent Saturday night with us & I think she found Albany very odd! It is so amusing to see what an interest so many young men are beginning to take in politics & some of them really do good work!

We are going to Buffalo on Saturday & Franklin is speaking there that night & then on Monday we dine in New York to meet some political lights! Hall & Margaret [Richardson] come to us to-morrow as the mid years are beginning. I think they will be married the end of June & go abroad for the summer. I feel as though one of my children were starting out in life & they do seem very young but one must hope that all will go well!

Ever so much love from us all to Bob & the children & your dear self.

Devotedly,
Eleanor

Eleanor was drawn away from politics by losses that befell her family and friends. Her cousins Helen and Teddy Robinson lost their baby to whooping cough,[54] reminding Eleanor of her own baby's death. On March 1, the Roosevelts' and Fergusons' old friend Bayard Cutting died, leaving Isabella a legacy of $20,000. Bayard and his wife had always considered Isabella "like a daughter," Mrs. Cutting wrote.[55]

Still, Eleanor was cheered by her uncle Theodore's leadership of the growing Progressive movement.[56] Taft had fired Gifford Pinchot, founder of the

51. Joseph Choate, Jr. His father was an American lawyer and diplomat, and Ambassador to the Court of Saint James in Great Britain 1899–1905, as well as a good friend of FDR's mother, Sara Roosevelt. *New York Times*, May 22, 1917. FDR would name his old friend director of the Federal Alcohol Control Administration in 1934. Ibid., May 1, 1934: 46.
52. Joseph H. Choate III.
53. Caroline and William Phillips were among Eleanor and Franklin's "closest shared friends," according to FDR biographer Geoffrey Ward. They were part of "a small circle of slightly older officials" who included the Roosevelts. William was an Assistant Secretary of State. His wife, Caroline, an Astor, was a close friend of Eleanor's. Ward, *A First-Class Temperament*, 215. Later FDR would name Phillips ambassador to Rome. Ibid., fn 258.
54. "Whooping cough," or pertussis, along with typhoid and diphtheria, has been virtually eliminated in the United States through the DPT shots children receive in infancy.
55. Olivia [Mrs. Bayard] Cutting to IG, March 1, 1912, FC.
56. The Progressive Era was a period of reform, beginning around 1890 and extending until

U.S. Forest Service, who had served under Presidents Cleveland, McKinley, and Roosevelt, for criticizing administration policies.[57] This rejection of a key part of Theodore Roosevelt's program widened the gulf between Taft and TR. Even though Eleanor felt loyal to her uncle, she recognized that the Democrats had the edge, at least in the East.

Eleanor was also gladdened by the prospect of paying a visit to Isabella and Bob in their new surroundings.

4 Elk Street, Albany, New York   Mar. 7, [1912]
Dearest Isabella

You have probably heard from Cousin Susie [Parish] of the sad time poor Helen & Teddy are going through & it just makes my heart ache. Helen is not strong yet & though her whooping cough is slight still it tires her & the strain of the last few days has been fearful for them both.[58] Of course the poor mite was only a month old & the cough was too much for her. She couldn't eat & at last developed pneumonia. Of course it is not like losing an older child, but no matter how little one's baby is, something of one's self dies with it. I think it leaves an empty place in one's heart which nothing can ever fill again.

Poor Mrs. Cutting too, her sorrows seem too cruel & I know how you & Bob will grieve for her. Oh, well I suppose there is a reason for it all & we can but try to take it in the best way.

Your last letter[59] was a great pleasure as always dear but I was sorry indeed to know you had been anxious about Bob. Slumps must come of course but I hope he has improved steadily since you wrote. Do tell me how things really go for I long so to hear.

It will be splendid if Ronald [Ferguson] comes over in May. Do tell him when you write that we will be in New York then & would love to have him stay with us if he is there any time at all.

Your housekeeping does sound hectic but I hope the cook & child are a success & that Mammy's holiday is now over & has done her a world of good!

1920. Some of the issues targeted by reformers included consumer protection, business consolidation, democratization of the political process, and woman suffrage, causes TR had championed for a long time.

57. Gifford Pinchot (1865–1946) served as chief of the Forest Service from 1905–1910, and was one of the first advocates for conservation. http://www.foresthistory.org/ASPNET/People/Pinchot/Pinchot.aspx.

58. Apparently Helen herself had whooping cough, but, as an adult, was able to survive it.

59. Missing.

Mr. Gifford Pinchot was here for a few nights a short time back & gave a talk on trees in the Assembly Room one evening which was most interesting. He of course is for Uncle Ted.[60] The excitement over nominations is intense & hardly a paper so far has a good word for Uncle Ted but I can't help feeling they will change their attitude before long. The fight is going to be hot & hard even after nominations are secured for if they put up a really good democrat it looks as though there was a good chance, in the East at least, of his winning out.

The legislature closes here March 29th & about the middle of April Franklin & Hall hope to go to Panama.[61] I doubt if I go there with them but I hope to meet them at New Orleans if all goes well. On the way back Franklin & I want to take a short trip from there, but all this is still undecided.

Hall is going to be married on June 17th. They are going abroad for the summer.

I wish I could be a cow girl with you one of these days & your rides sound delightful but I fear I might not enjoy them so much in reality as I haven't ridden but about five times in 6 ½ years!

Our chicks are well & flourishing & send their love to Martha & Buzz. Love to your Mother & Bob from Franklin & a heart full to you Isabella dear.

Devotedly

E.R.

Eleanor hoped to see Isabella during her trip West. The two women had been apart for nearly a year and a half, during which time each had made her own life under very different circumstances.

4 Elk Street, Albany, New York   March 17 [1912]

Dearest Isabella

Would you & Bob care to have us pay you a few days' visit in the first week in May? Please be quite frank because I will understand perfectly if you don't care to be bothered with guests or Bob doesn't feel quite up to it. Franklin is going to Panama April 13th & lands at New Orleans on the return trip April 30th. There, I shall meet him on the 30th or 31st & we thought we would go

---

60. TR's family never called him Teddy.
61. The Panama Canal was under construction. It was begun during Theodore Roosevelt's administration, in 1904, and would be completed in 1914. Hall was an engineering student, and Franklin would model his career on that of his cousin Theodore.

to you for a few days if you wanted us & then return via Chicago. Of course if the children were ill or anything went wrong I couldn't go but as far as we can tell now we will be able to do it & as you know dear, I long to see you & Bob & the chicks.

Pauline & Grenville [Merrill] came up yesterday for Sunday & both look so well. Helen [Robinson] has gone to New York for Sunday & expects to spend the day in Atlantic City trying to induce some hotel keeper to take the family in! She & Teddy [Robinson] are very wonderful & she seems pretty well.

Ever so much love,

Eleanor

Although separated by distance, the two women stayed connected by celebrating each other's milestones. Isabella observed the Roosevelts' seventh wedding anniversary, and Eleanor took an interest in the details of Bobbie's fourth birthday party.

Eleanor also kept track of Bob's extended family, whom she had met during her time in England. She knew that Bob and Isabella were hoping for a visit from Bob's sister Edie.

March 19th [1912]

Dearest Isabella

So many many thanks from us both to you & Bob & your Mother for remembering the wedding day. You are the most wonderful people in your thought of others & you don't half know how much we appreciate it.

Your note & the enclosure for Helen [Robinson] came this morning & as we are walking together at twelve I will give it to her then. She is going to Atlantic City with the children on Thursday for three weeks & Mary Newbold[62] goes with her so I think it will be a rest & pleasure for her. Teddy [Robinson] is to join us for meals whenever he is not otherwise engaged & he only has a week more anyway as he will leave as soon as the session closes on the 29th.

What a nice birthday party Bobbie must have had & how I wish I could have seen it! I am so glad to hear Edie [Ferguson] comes so soon, when does she land & what boat does she take?

62. A mutual friend of Eleanor and Isabella, and FDR's Hyde Park neighbor. Ward to editors, March 6, 2007.

It is good to hear that Bob is better & if he is taking the tuberculosis treatment don't be discouraged by occasional slumps for I know through Muriel
[Martineau] that they occur but she says Cyril [Martineau] is *always* better
afterwards.

Love to you all.

Eleanor

These letters consistently demonstrate the complicated arrangements Eleanor
and Isabella had to make in order to meet. Although the Roosevelts had servants
to help them, Eleanor nonetheless had to coordinate three children, four residences, and a large staff in order to take a trip West. Travel to the territories was
by no means easy, and a threatened train strike could have undone all Eleanor's
plans. Travel to Europe was more precarious still. On April 15, the luxury liner
Titanic went down, with the loss of more than 1,500 lives. One of the victims
was John Jacob Astor, who left Bob Ferguson $10,000 in his will.[63]

47 East Sixty-Fifth Street   April 13th [1912]
Dearest Isabella

Pauline [Merrill] cannot go out [West] with me & I can't very well leave
before the 28th as I have to close the Albany house & move into our house
here as soon as Mrs. Howard leaves[,] for Mama doesn't go to Hyde Park till
May & I want to leave the children near her here.[64] I am therefore going to
follow out my original plan & meet Franklin in New Orleans on April 30th.
As far as we can discover from here we cannot leave until the 1st for El Paso &
then the connections there & in Deming [New Mexico] seem rather close so
I don't know whether we will arrive the 3rd or the 4th but we will telegraph en
route & we may find a quicker way of going when we get nearer! I am so looking forward to seeing you even though it will be for such a little while & I am
already getting excited at the thought of starting! I only hope the engineers
will settle their difficulties before then!

Franklin & Hall are sailing this morning & we are just going down so I
must stop.

63. The income of the average American worker in 1912 was $600 a year. White-collar workers
   might expect to earn $1,200–1,500. Clements, *Presidency of Woodrow Wilson*, 16.
64. Eleanor could not go to New Mexico as early as she had hoped because she had to wait for
   her tenant to leave their New York City house before Eleanor could move her children.
   They would be near Sara Roosevelt, so she could supervise them while Eleanor was out
   West.

Ever so much love & thank Mrs. Selmes for her letter which I will answer soon.

> Devotedly
> Eleanor

For Eleanor, who had never been west of Albany, the trip to New Mexico was an eye-opening experience. The Roosevelts missed their train connection in Deming, and tried to continue in a hired car. The automobile suffered multiple tire punctures on the rough road, and a windstorm sprang up, chilling the travelers in their light spring clothes. By the time a rescue car sent by the Fergusons with hot coffee and warm coats arrived, the Roosevelts had had a taste of the life Isabella was learning to endure.

Eleanor, however, also appreciated the beauties of the new landscape, "marvelling over every cactus and yucca." She was similarly touched by her visit to the Cottage Sanatorium, which, she later wrote, opened a whole new vista to her. The Roosevelts were, Isabella thought, "much stronger and keener in their [social welfare] interests since the Albany experience." She rejoiced that Eleanor also seemed to exhibit a new sense of fun. The two friends talked far into the night.[65]

After her return to New York City, Eleanor, who loved helping people, shopped for Isabella and Patty, since merchandise in the New Mexico territory was limited. She also called on Patty and Isabella's family and friends, to give them first-hand reports of Cat Cañon.

[New York City]   May 11th Saturday [1912]
Isabella dearest,

Here we are home again & I'm thinking of you so much & can't tell you what a joy it was to us both to see you all. I loved every minute we were with you & I have only one regret namely that it makes me realize even more how much I miss you dear people out of my daily life. I am glad to be able to see you all in my thoughts however & I have told the chicks so much about Martha & Buzz that I feel as though they must almost see it all too! Tell Martha that Anna was much impressed with her writing & in a day or two (when I get time to get them) she wants to send them each a post card!

We had a very good trip back, spent the morning in Chicago with the Fred Delanos[66] & reached here yesterday morning at 10 a.m. The children all look

65. Miller, *Isabella Greenway*, 63.
66. Frederic A. Delano was FDR's uncle.

very well & I like my new under nurse very much & so do they & my former under nurse seems to make a very good housemaid so all goes well! I found Leila Delano was in town for just the night so [I] went & lunched with her & then I ordered your shoes & Mrs. Selmes's gloves. I hope the shoes will fit & I think they are just like mine only narrower. This morning I ordered the dresses & they ought to go the end of next week. The children & I also went on a shopping bee together & all of us got our "wedding clothes" as they call their garments for Hall's wedding. I was lucky enough to walk into a dress & hat at—stan's where they are having a sale & nothing has to be done to it so I'm spared all further trouble & thought!

I went to see Pauline [Merrill] this afternoon as little Grenville had his adenoids out this morning & she wanted to hear all about you & said she did wish she could have gone. Incidentally little Grenville was quite well & did not seem to mind it at all.

I telephoned Mrs. Cutcheon last night & she is going to lunch with me if she comes in town Monday or Tuesday. Cousin Susie [Parish] I also called up but the connection was so bad I could only hear that she was quite well but weary from moving & today they went to Mrs. Twimbly for Sunday. Franklin, Anna & I go to her on Wednesday till Saturday & the other two chicks go to Hyde Park Friday. I haven't had time yet[,] tell your mother[,] to go & see Mrs. Lugalls but I will surely go Monday or Tuesday. Give your mother my dearest love & tell her I will write her from Orange when I can tell her more about Cousin Susie.

Franklin joins me in love & so many thanks for all you did for us. You were angels to want us & I hope we did not tire Bob & you can't begin to know dear what it meant to see you & Bob.

Ever devotedly,
E.R.

At the Republican National Convention in Chicago in mid-June, incumbent William Howard Taft captured nearly all the contested delegates from Theodore Roosevelt. TR's supporters, hooting at Taft's "steamroller" tactics, formed a third party, the Progressive, or Bull Moose, party (so called when TR declared he was as fit as a bull moose).

At the end of June, Franklin and Eleanor attended the 1912 Democratic National Convention, their first, in Baltimore. Although Franklin had no real role to play—he was not even a delegate—he made some useful contacts, most notably North Carolina newspaper editor Jospehus Daniels, who later recalled that his first meeting with young Roosevelt was "love at first sight."[67]

New Jersey governor Woodrow Wilson finally won the Democratic nomination on the forty-sixth ballot; Indiana governor Thomas R. Marshall was chosen as his running mate. By then, Eleanor had already left for Campobello. FDR, however, went on to New Jersey for strategy sessions.[68]

Unlike the Republican "Oyster Bay" Roosevelts, FDR was supporting Wilson. He admired the New Jersey governor's progressive record and did not think the Progressive party could win the presidential contest.[69] Loyal to her husband, Eleanor did not speak out in support of her uncle, confiding her thoughts only to Isabella.

As it turned out, Edie Ferguson had to stay in Scotland to nurse Bob's eldest sister, Alice Ferguson Luttrell, who had also contracted pulmonary tuberculosis. However, Bob's elder brother Ronald still proposed to come to America, and Eleanor hoped that he would stay with her and Franklin.

[Campobello]   July 8th [1912]
My dearest Isabella,

I know it is a long time since last I wrote but that does not mean that you are not all of you very frequently in my thoughts. I know your hands are full at present but if you have time do send me a line to tell me how things are going with you all.

I hope the shopping I did for you was satisfactory & that I may be allowed to do some more sometime?

Our moves, as you know have been many of late. On June 17th Hall was married & it was a charming wedding. My little sister-in-law[70] is very sweet & she looked very lovely & I feel very happy about them for I think they are really going to get the right kind of happiness which so many married people seem to miss these days. They sailed on the 20th & are in Paris I think by now.

After settling the children in Fairhaven,[71] Franklin & I went to Baltimore & spent a hot & very interesting week which made me very glad to come up here & settle down for two & a half months. Of course Bob knows all there

---

67. Cook, *Eleanor Roosevelt*, I, 198.
68. Ibid.
69. Ibid., 196.
70. Margaret Richardson.
71. Fairhaven, in southeastern Massachusetts, home to Warren Delano II, FDR's grandfather.

is to tell about Chicago[72] & I was not there but Alice & Nick[73] sat near us in Baltimore & she told me that Uncle Ted's meeting in Chicago was wonderful.[74] Alice looks better & she asked much about you & Bob. Franklin is of course well satisfied with Mr. Wilson's nomination as he has been working hard for him. It seemed to me that the feeling in Baltimore ran very high & the New York delegation was heckled for 5 minutes at one session![75]

I brought my little cousin Mary Hall up with me & she has been quite homesick so I've been quite busy trying to keep her amused!

Franklin comes in two days & Mama in a week but I don't yet know how long Franklin can stay.

Your lovely rug & tea cloth are my daily pride & you don't know how useful they are. Anna & I have lessons on the piazza every morning & I think of Martha & Buzz with Mammy & wish the little classes could be joined.

I have sent a line to Ronald begging him to let us know when he is in New York & to use our house after Sept. 30th, as we expect to be back by then. Has Edie [Ferguson] given up coming?

I forgot to tell you about Nelly Rogers wedding. It was a most beautiful sight but more of a pageant than a wedding! The Huntingtons were there & sent you [said to send you] much love when next I wrote. Nelly had so many & such grand presents that you lost all feeling of individuality & felt you were at Tiffany's! They had sixty guests staying over Sunday, the men sleeping in tents & your little friend Grace Chapin Rodgers distinguishing herself by staying at the dance after the wedding till 1 a.m. & then motoring home to Garrisons alone with Lydia Hoyt! You can imagine the gossip & outraged feelings of some of the neighbors.

I must stop, but how I wish you could all be here with us this summer & sometime you must come for I know you will love the quiet & the lovely view & the sunsets.

72. His Rough Rider friends would have filled him in on TR's doings.
73. Alice Roosevelt married U.S. Representative Nicholas Longworth [R-Ohio] in 1906. He later became Speaker of the House. The Longworth House Office Building is named after him.
74. After TR lost the Republican nomination for president to incumbent William Howard Taft at the Republican National Convention in Chicago, Progressives held a meeting to decide whether to form a new party. The Progressive convention would be held in August, and would nominate Theodore Roosevelt.
75. Tammany boss Charles F. Murphy controlled the New York delegation. To ensure that William Jennings Bryan did not receive the nomination, he was keeping New York's ninety votes in reserve by pledging them to Ohio's Governor Judson Harmon. This action was widely criticized. *New York Times*, June 29, 1912: 3.

Dear love to Bob & the chicks & remember us to all the people who were so kind to us on our brief visit.

> Ever devotedly,
> Eleanor

Evidently, when the Roosevelts visited the Fergusons in Cat Cañon, Bob had shared his concerns about the future of his family estate at Assynt. At the time of the following letter, the financial problems seemed to be under control, at least for the moment.

However, the health of several family members, especially Alice and her sons, also concerned them all.

Bob's other brother, Hector, was captain of the Lovat Scouts, a special corps formed during the Boer War to recruit trackers and game-keepers accustomed to riding, stalking, and shooting in rough mountainous country.

Meanwhile, Bob Ferguson supported his old colonel, Theodore Roosevelt, in the presidential election, as did a number of his fellow Rough Riders, including John Greenway. Isabella, too, was beginning to enjoy the political fray. But when her four-year old son disappeared for a day, it was her role as a mother that mattered most.

Cat Cañon   July 17, 1912

Eleanor dearest,

What has held my pen in this long trance I can't say—unless it's the chores of life these hot days. Those tiresome nothings that eat up all of the lives of the poorly organized. You meantime have given us much food for thought & such pleasure in your news. While your's and Franklin's coming & being actually here is as present as yesterday—& will be for a long time.

At once I must say how altogether satisfactory the shoes & dresses are. My summer wardrobe! In no way could they be improved upon. As no bills have come to me I judge they must have sent them to you—so I enclose two checks—& trust you to say truthfully if the $20.00 covers my delight-ful pink & blue ginghams. It hardly seems possible that it can. The slip [receipt] from Slaters was $13.00 & June 26 (the date on my check) shows how long ago my intentions were first good. It was an awful burden to put upon you—dear—but I am revelling no end in the comfort of both shoes & clo' [clothes].

Then added to all that having Acky[76] to luncheon—Calling on Mother's friend & everything else. Yes it was like you.

Bob was so glad to get your good letter from Oldgate.[77] We haven't sent the [Ronald's] letters on to her [Auntie Bye][78] so far because things have been changing all the time & it seemed better to wait. Things have worked out a good deal better than we expected. There seems to be really no danger now about Assynt & Ronald appears to appreciate the real value of the place for other purposes than sale. About other matters he is arranging to see Uncle[79] about the beginning of Oct & we trust will have a thoroughly open talk with him. It's mighty good of you to think of asking him to come to you & we hope he'll have a chance to go. He'd so love the house too.

So far as we know, for the present, Edie [Ferguson] won't be able to come as Alice must be carefully watched and nobody else [besides Edie] of course can run the House H[old]. . . particularly [the supervision of] a good but hot tempered cook known as "the Marchioness"!

Hector and his scouts had a grand campaign with other forces—down near Glamis[80]—They were soaked daily & nightly with rain & Athole Brose[81] but returned in far better shape than when they started—Lines of mounted regiments charged over moor & mountain [in] the most picturesque & efficient manner—& made successful attacks under cover of fog. The West Highlanders on their shaggy ponies surprised the Southerns by their speed & endurance.[82]

It does seem too bad that "Uncle Theodore" should have to carry such an undue load [have such a struggle]—but, after all, in the end his achievement may become all the more sure and clear [certain]. He might perhaps not have wished to run against Woodrow Wilson & it would have been

76. Isabella's Aunt Sally, Sarah Dinsmore Cutcheon, Uncle Frank's wife.
77. The house of William Sheffield Cowles and Anna ("Auntie Bye") Cowles in Farmington, Conn. Eleanor was visiting and had written to Bob from there.
78. Bob's elder brother Ronald was trying to decide what to do with Assynt, the Munro family estate. Bye had been close to Bob before he married Isabella, and understood the whole situation. She wanted to see Ronald's letters so she could advise Bob.
79. Frank Cutcheon, with whom Ronald had discussed plans to help the Fergusons financially.
80. Glamis Castle—family home of the Earls of Strathmore, a royal residence since 1372. Childhood home of Elizabeth, the Queen Mother. Legendary setting of "Macbeth." http://www.glamis-castle.co.uk.
81. A drink made from water in which oatmeal has been soaked, cream, honey, and Scotch.
82. Isabella explains that her brother-in-law has completed successful military training maneuvers.

easier to step aside & let the break come in the Democratic as in the Republican ranks[83]—but when he puts his hand to any undertaking he never pulls back—or quits until it is finished. He is doing a wonderful work—a great world's work—and he will succeed in the very best way which is his own. It is surprising to read the change in sentiment and public opinion which[,] however much quiet resentment there may have been all over the country against machine methods & their results, yet how very large a share in all this new spirit is due directly to his leadership—and teaching.[84] His wisdom & patience are being as fully appreciated as his fighting crusader qualities.

Rosie's[85] South American move seems good to us without knowing anything about the people he goes with. It seems, to us, a *great* deal more like him than a chemical factory or even rubber works and he will learn much about that great South American continent which a great many more young men of his type should know than do at present.

I wonder if I told you of "Buzz the Outlaw"! He disappeared one morning after a great rage at "the girls" [the hired help] the giggling whispering girls whom he had rocked [threw rocks at]—calling Hazel a Devil. After hours of search over these vast hills we dared not waste daylight & gave the alarm in town. Sheriff[,] 2 deputies & 20 people were here in a few moments! People we'd never seen who had heard of our trouble. & after an hour's more organized stepping & riding over each hill Buzz was found white shaking but not crying in the top of a tree behind the Merry Widow[86]!!!

The Deputy had found return tracks in an arroyo bed where none had been when they started forth. [And] Mammy was sent in to find if he'd returned. The particular tree was search[ed] around so often he must have worked his way home on hearing the excitement. He was very solemn but didn't break down & gave graphic descriptions of all. He'd heard the shouting, seen the

83. Isabella thought that, instead of the break coming between conservative and Progressive Republicans, there might have been a break in the Democratic party between the Southern conservatives and the Wilson progressives. Therefore Wilson had an advantage, because the Democrats would unite behind Wilson, while the Republicans would split between TR and Taft.

84. Isabella credits TR with organizing and directing the general discontent with "corrupt, expensive and clumsy" government. Ayres et. al., *American Passages*, 694.

85. "Rosie" was a nickname of TR's son Kermit Roosevelt (not to be confused with "Rosy" Roosevelt, FDR's elder half-brother, James Roosevelt Roosevelt). After Kermit's graduation from Harvard, he went to work for British Railways in Brazil. Dalton, *Theodore Roosevelt*, 400.

86. A rock formation?

sheriff, etc & when asked why he hadn't answered—explained "Because they was*n't* my friends, Mittie!" [87]

Of course he was locked up all day & treated like one in disgrace with the sole result that at night he said "Well if you don't want me to run away you oughtn't to punish me!"—Old Mr. Dye made a line for the prospect holes two miles back[88] & later rubbed it most mercilessly into the Sheriff. "Oh Robert is a good one—Evades the sheriff & law at four!"

Dearest E, a cable has just come from Assynt & we fear Alice is too weak to stay [live]. Its terribly heart breaking for Bob who is so wonderfully brave— and we sit sadly in the little room looking at the sketches of Assynt. It is as Bob says "Alice has just burnt out in utter unselfishness." She leaves her boys almost on their feet again after such a struggle. There is still faint hope [that she will live].

Eleanor dear this takes a very world of love to you & yours. As you see, Bob's been writing too. We wish we might see all the Campobello family. What a hugging Anna would receive from me.

> Yr very devoted
>
> Isabella

Bob wishes to know really—if you think Hall would care to have a Navajo rug [as a wedding present] for use anywhere. If you do we'll be on the lookout for one. If you don't think he or Margaret would care to have one we'll get something nearer civilization. Perhaps you could suggest something needed knowing what they have. We'd be so pleased if you'd help us out.

We also wonder what the recent reports are of Mrs. Anna. Is she able to have any holiday with Sheffield.[89] We've not heard in ages.

Bob is so pleased with your letter. Do write him when you can spare the time & remember we will understand if you can't spare time often.

Despite all Edie's careful nursing, Alice died. Eleanor hastened to write Isabella and Bob her condolences.

87. Mittie is a Rooseveltian name for mothers. Isabella suggests that Bobbie, originally far from home, snuck back and climbed the tree after it had been searched by the posse.

88. Dye had gone to look for Bobbie in the holes that were dug for minerals, the most dangerous place. When Bobbie was found safely in a tree, Dye teased the sheriff for allowing Bobbie to elude him.

89. Mrs. Anna Cowles, Eleanor's "Auntie Bye," and her son Sheffield.

[Campobello]   July 28 [1912]

My dearest Isabella,

My thoughts have been so much with you & Bob these days for I know you will feel as much as he does this sorrow & it is so hard to see those [whom] our love would like to shield from every pain obliged to suffer. I only hope that Bob is not feeling the heat & that you can see him getting stronger. I should say Bobby was a trifle too independent! What a monkey to give you all such a fright. Elliott will probably do the same for us in a few short years I think, as he already rebels at petticoat rule & tries to follow James everywhere!

Many thanks for the checks which cover everything & for the Kodaks. Anna adored the one of the donkeys. Have you forgotten that you promised to send me the pictures which were in one tent the night we arrived?[90] I want them so much even if they are not finished.

I did not know Kermit was going to South America but I am behind the times not having seen any of the family since Hall's wedding & then only for a short time. I am very glad as I feel sure it will interest him & if I do hear anything about the people he is going with I will write you. South America seems to be the country of the future & so many young men, chiefly engineers, seem to be going to the West coast.

Franklin's mother sails on August 1st so he is waiting in New York to see her off. She will only be gone six weeks but she will be most of the time with Muriel & Cyril Martineau. They came back from Davos this June & are settled in a lovely place in the New Forest[91] & he is improving so much they hope to be able to have Xmas at home & return to Davos only for the three winter months.

I tried to get Pauline & Grenville [Merrill] to come up here but Elizabeth & Pete are staying with them for two weeks & they may go abroad on August 18th so I could not get them. Pauline says she is very tired of Southampton however! I am hoping surely to see her this autumn however before we go away *if* we do go away![92]

Do remember us to the sheriff & the Miss Eccles,[93] we think of them so often. Hugs to the children from me & so much love to you & Bob.

90. Probably sketches Isabella had made.
91. The New Forest is an area of southern England that includes the largest remaining tracts of unenclosed pastureland, heathland, and old-growth forest in the heavily-populated southeast of England; known for its spas.
92. Eleanor may be referring to going to Albany in the case of FDR's re-election.
93. Isabel (Belle) Lancaster Eckles (1877–1971), the state's first female school superintendent and her sister Mary, also a teacher. Belle Eckles taught in the Silver City public schools

Ever devotedly,
            Eleanor
PS this is such a dull letter but I will try to have some news next time & I just felt I must let you know that you were in my thoughts.
            E.R.

The family tried to rally after Alice's death. Eleanor had written to comfort Bob, and Isabella asked her to look after Alice's son, Geoff Luttrell, who was coming to the States for a visit. Bob and Isabella also hoped Edie Ferguson would now be able to come to New Mexico, sailing to America with Isabella's aunt and uncle Cutcheon who were on vacation in Europe. Eleanor's family had also suffered losses, and Isabella tried to take some comfort in reflecting that sorrow brought them all closer together.

With cheerful young children at home, Isabella could not stay sad for long. The fascinating John Greenway was also dropping by to instruct her in her duties as a campaign canvasser, although she protested that only her husband's insistence was responsible for her participation in politics. She unconsciously betrays her growing interest in John Greenway when she describes a close call he had in an automobile.

[Cat Cañon]   August 24, 1912
My beloved Eleanor,
    You have been your usual blessed self in thinking of & for others in so many directions. Edie [Ferguson] writes in full appreciation of your letters & offers to her—& Ronald too.
    We are now hoping that Geoff will step off the steamer [ship from Europe] in good trim so that he may go & have the pleasure of seeing you & Franklin (my mind is hazy as to the laters [latter's] being there).
    To us both, Eleanor it would mean so much to have Geoff know you—& you'll be sure to see the fine fellow he is & have some fun out of him too. If he does go direct to you, will you judge how well he seems & help him in his

for sixteen years, served as superintendent of Grant County schools for two terms, and as New Mexico superintendent of schools for two terms. Then she served as superintendent of Santa Fe schools for ten years. After retiring from education, she "accepted a position with the women's division of the WPA for New Mexico, and was instrumental in founding the museums of Roswell and Silver City." Eckles Papers, PG.

next steps? We'd be glad of a line out here as to how he seems & what you think of the advisability of his going down to Belle Breckenridge's[94] (on the 3rd of Sept or after) Bob feels that *if Geoff is well for travelling and the trip to York Harbor[95] is not too complicated* that he would enjoy it very much & rather hopes he will go (on the underlined conditions) He's [He'd] be sure to find a quiet & homelike life along the most healthy lines at Belle's.

His plans are quite unknown to us and he will doubtless have a time settling on any with the budgets [bundles] of letters & directions awaiting his landing[96]—but will let you know of course first off—& if he does go to you we'd be very grateful for your advise as to his apparent health & the advisability of his going to Belle's.

Private Then too—should he be upset or in anyway, ill, I could go on at once to you or any place—as a member of the family handy. Please don't forget this. Bob joins me in this too. Together we are just *too* disappointed not to be seeing him ourselves—but, while I could go on any moment if need—it's not the opportune time to go jaunting it on pleasure.

Your letter to Bob was so dear. Going direct to his heart as it seemed to come from yours. He was so brave as always but it cut very deep. I look to all sorts of help & joy in Edith's coming as she now proposes. Sailing with Uncle & Acky Sept. 24. She needs a rest & (if easy in her mind) there's every reason she should be able to get it over here while giving us the untold joy of her presence. Eleanor—someday you must realize all she's done this last year—for Alice[,] Alec & those boys[97]—& what this summer meant in peace at last to Alice—who was so terribly tired. Hecker [Hector] is just darling in his letters [of condolence to Bob, for the death of their sister].

We were so distressed to hear of the death of Hall's father in law[98] & think constantly how hard it will be on her [Hall's wife Margaret]. But somehow such big blows bring people so [m]arvelously close together & in such beauty. Will you tell your sister [in-law] how deep is our sympathy.

94. Isabella Goodrich Breckinridge, daughter of B. F. Goodrich, a cousin of Isabella. Her brother Dave was Bob's fellow Rough Rider and close friend. Bob had also been a trustee for her.
95. York Harbor, Maine, was near the Breckinridges's summer home.
96. Presumably letters sent to Geoff might be forwarded to a place like Thomas Cook's or American Express, as was the custom then.
97. Alice Munro Luttrell, Bob's sister, her husband Alexander Luttrell, and their sons Geoff and Ralph.
98. In June 1912 Hall Roosevelt married Margaret Richardson of Boston. Her father, Dr. Maurice H. Richardson, died just a few weeks later.

It must have been a great shock to you all to have Mrs. Hall's death[99] so suddenly after she'd been with you & now Eleanor dear does it mean your caring for the little girl—your goddaughter.[100] Much misery must have slipt [slipped] away in that passing?

One must be more cheerful—indeed one can't help it with Martha & Buzz all excited as we start forth by motor to call on Mrs. & Col Bushnell at Bayard [N. M.] They are to drop off & picnic by a stream while I lunch & pay some long owed calls. They are just too happy.

John Greenway came up for a few days & gave the community a good stir at a progressive meeting out here which was funnier that [than] you would believe. He has done *wonders* & such efficient organization down in Arizona & told us how it should be done up here. Before long we should have our 32000 voters lined up. Bronson Cutting's paper[101] is spreading well & is such a good sheet & strong progressive fighter for the Col.

Returning, John dived into one of our floods & his motor was picked up—like a peanut & tossed down the tearing torrent several hundred yards. It weighs around 5000 lb. so you can imagine what a horrible thing it was—& he pinned under the steering arrangements so that he couldn't possibly have escaped if it had turned over as it threatened to twice!

Bob had a mean little turn 8 weeks ago but is better and *all* interested in this political fight. Pushing me in the most shameless manner. All our love dearest & hugs to Anna & the children. No I've not forgotten [illegible] sketches.

The 1912 presidential campaign was the first time all major political parties had women's divisions. It was still unusual for women to be active in partisan politics; critics argued that political participation made women "mannish." Although Isabella cited Bob's insistence as the motive for her participation,[102] she quickly developed a taste for campaigning.

After accompanying Theodore Roosevelt on a campaign stop in Albuquerque, Isabella was assigned to get out the vote for TR in her area. By August, John Greenway reported, Isabella had signed up forty-five men for a Progressive pledge in "reactionary" Silver City. He thought she must be doing most of

99. Josie Zabriskie Hall, wife of ER's Uncle Eddie, "died after a long illness." Cook, *Eleanor Roosevelt*, I, 202. She was Eleanor's aunt by marriage.
100. The Hall's eldest child, Mary. Roosevelt, *This is My Story*, 145.
101. Santa Fe *New Mexican* and *El Nuevo Mexicano*.
102. Miller, *Isabella Greenway*, 63.

the work for the party in Grant County. "No man seems able to resist her," he wrote Isabella's cousin, Dave Goodrich. John's admiration for Isabella was warming into something deeper. But she was married to his best friend.[103]

Isabella's Uncle Frank Cutcheon addressed his niece as "Lady Boss," but couldn't refrain from asking, "Seriously, if you are going to lead the party, wouldn't it be just as well to have the ballot?"[104] But Isabella, like Eleanor, was not much interested in getting the vote just then.

Cat Cañon   [August 1912]
Eleanor dearest

This is no time for writing is it? I can just picture how busy you are, & I wonder if you know how Bob & I feel about your having Geoff with you now. It should be one of the nicest part[s] of his American trip—& you know what we think of the privilege of knowing you—the sooner that's accomplished in the life of any one—the better off they are for keeps! Geoff must be a great dear himself from all accounts.

If you can spare the time read the enclosed[105] and say if you think it is asking too much.[106] We came to like Mrs. Huneke more & more—& John thinks the boy deserved this second chance. If you'll send me Hall's address on a P. C. I'll send it to V. H[uneke]. & he can call. (The best Navajo's [rugs] don't come in til Nov so we are waiting.)

Susie Cooley & I put in a *most* delightful & interesting day at Albuquerque—where we had a two hour "joy ride" with the Col after his speech. He was more loveable than ever & of you he said so much that warmed my heart. He has brought the best of every New Mexican politician to the fore & personal feuds & greedy ambition seem most genuinely brushed aside as united they stand till Nov. for the Col. Our Spanish race question[107] has never been fairly handled & remains a heavy complication.

103. Ibid, 64.
104. Ibid.
105. Missing.
106. Isabella seems to be saying that a young man, V. Huneke, a friend of John Greenway's, could be helpved by ER's brother Hall, possibly to get back into college. Hall, a brilliant student, Phi Beta Kappa, was a senior prefect at Harvard that year, and would go on to earn an advanced degree in engineering. Cook, *Eleanor Roosevelt*, I, 197. Isabella asked Eleanor how to help the young man contact Hall. While she was thinking of Hall, she mentioned that her wedding gift to him, a Navajo rug, would arrive before long.
107. Isabella regretted that during the debate over statehood for New Mexico, those opposed had resorted to racist allegations about the "Hispano Americans" who lived in the territory. David Holtby to authors, April 10, 2008.

My[,] some of it was amusing. I'd like to tell you no end. Bronson [Cutting] & I had a grand time catching up. He's our only *young* helper & is so respected. He must just hang on to his health while he gets needed Human experience. Bob's of course heart & soul in the fight and pushes me *most* shamelessly in. He's doing finely after a poor summer & we dared not disturb his progress by the trip to Albuquerque.

To be a western progressive one must wear a black felt hat heavily laden with railroad dust. Always be too busy to tie your tie & always be on the verge of washing! Mrs. Cutting has just heard the worst—that Bronson is among the [Progressive] leaders!![108] & looks as tho' he'd been born & grown up among them.

We hear Franklin is doing bully work & heaving to some purpose! What's Grenville [Merrill] doing? Urged on by his energetic wife!!

Your loving

Isabella

Hugs to my Anna bless her. Edie [Ferguson] sails today & M & B gather wood for her. Susie & Alford [Cooley] have had a most disheartening time & the little jaunt did her good & was too brisk to allow time for worry. Our *warm* greetings to Mrs. Roosevelt.

Eleanor had not been able to have Geoff with her in Campobello, and he had apparently visited her Auntie Bye instead. Back in Hyde Park, Eleanor was eager to entertain Geoff herself. She looked forward as well to seeing Bob's brother Ronald, who was visiting New York City, possibly on business. Eleanor was also hoping to greet Bob's sister Edie, who was expected to arrive later with the Cutcheons, and who was planning to go on to see Bob and Isabella in New Mexico.

As the 1912 campaign proceeded, Eleanor responded to Isabella's political news with political news of her own, while seeming to assume that it was Bob who was most interested. But, with three small children, Eleanor still devoted most of her letter to family matters.

108. Even though the Cuttings were progressive Republicans, Mrs. Cutting evidently is horrified that Bronson is becoming one of the uncouth New Mexicans.

Hyde Park on the Hudson   Sept. 24 [1912]
Dearest dear Isabella,

The last weeks at Campo were so busy for me that I never wrote to thank you for your dear letter. We were [d]isappointed too not to have "Geoff" at Campo but he arrived here yesterday to stay until Friday & we are so glad of this chance to know him. Of course the weather is too dreadful, gray skies & rain all the time.[109] Of course he seems very delicate but better than I expected from all I had heard & I think his stay at Farmington must have done him good.

I am so glad Edie [Ferguson] will be here soon & I do hope I shall see her in New York as we will be there on the 1ˢᵗ & I hope that Ronald will dine with us on the 30ᵗʰ as he writes he cannot stay with us.

Anna was delighted with her post card & I was so glad you went to hear Uncle Ted at Albuquerque for I'm sure Bob likes to hear all the news. I am going to try & go to the big mass meeting in New York as I haven't heard him for ages. It looks more to me as though they were going to carry this state. Franklin is running again[110] & so we will be here most of the time till election as he has a strenuous campaign before him.

So far I have missed seeing your mother but I hope she will come back from Henderson to meet Mr. & Mrs. Cutcheon & then I can see her. Cousin Susie [Parish] says they enjoyed all their time together & I think your mother was a great help with Aunt Maggie who is rather a difficult invalid.[111] I never saw Cousin Susie look better & I hope later on to go to Orange for a day or two. Friday I am going up to Cambridge for a night to see Hall & Margaret's house & then on to Portland for a night with Maude[112] getting back to New York Monday morning.

Elliott had his second birthday yesterday & Ellen Adams brought her small son to celebrate & I am ashamed to say that Elliott fought him hard & reduced him to taking refuge in his mother's lap! My youngest is such a rowdy that I don't know what we will ever do with him if he continues as he has begun.

109. Eleanor is expressing one idea in two sentences, namely that the wet weather might have caused Geoff, recovering from a long illness, to seem particularly delicate. People thought that weather influenced health, and so often traveled to places with good climates.

110. State senators were elected for two-year terms.

111. ER's great aunt, Margaret Tonnelé Hall (b. 1840), the sister of her grandfather, Valentine Gill Hall, Jr. Maggie married Edward Philip Livingston Ludlow; their daughter was Susie Parish. Vivona to editors, March 13, 2007.

112. Eleanor's aunt, her mother's youngest sister, Maude Livingston Hall, was married to Larry Waterbury.

Did you know Nathalie Swan had a small daughter born two weeks ago? I am so glad both are well for Lois Lawrence's death must have made her nervous.

Mama got home last week & her trip abroad did her so much good besides giving much pleasure to Muriel [Martineau] & the Collier family. Mr. Collier's[113] German articles begin in the November Scribners[114] but his book won't come out till later. If you think Bob would be interested let me know & I'll send the Scribners out if you don't take it.

Isn't there any shopping you want done now that winter approaches? I am so often in town & could so easily do anything & you can't know how I like to feel that I can do even some little thing for you two dear people.

My love to Bob & the chicks & to you dearest.

> Ever devotedly,
> Eleanor

On their way by boat back to New York from Campobello the Roosevelts brushed their teeth with the water in their stateroom pitchers. It was contaminated, and they fell ill. At first they thought it was merely a "miserable" virus. Franklin was the first to succumb. Although Eleanor admitted she felt "peculiar," she would still dine with Ronald Ferguson as planned. Despite having to take care of Franklin, look after her children, and see friends and family, Eleanor continued to report excitedly on the Progressive campaign. "Franklin, of course, was helping the Wilson campaign," she later wrote, "but that never disturbed Isabella or me!"[115]

Hyde Park On the Hudson   Sept. 28th, 1912
Isabella dearest,

Your letter has gone to Hall & I'm sure he'll do all he can for the boy & be glad of the chance. Their house in Cambridge is 18 Ash Street & I hope to go on this week to see it. Franklin & I expected to go yesterday but he got cold & had a temperature & felt so ill that we gave it up but I hope he'll be fine again tomorrow. His campaign is not yet very active & this last week has been very lazy which perhaps was not very entertaining for Geoff but it gave Franklin a

---

113. Price Collier became the second husband of Kassie Delano, FDR's aunt. Eventually the articles became a book that ER would recommend to Isabella in June of 1913.

114. *Scribner's Magazine* was published monthly, with an annual subscription cost of $3.00. Display Ad, *New York Times*, December 19, 1912: 12.

115. Roosevelt, *This is My Story*, 145–6.

chance to really know him & they had some really nice times together which made his few days here seem all too short.

We expect Ronald to dine with us in town Monday night & Geoff too if he comes in from Mrs. [Bayard] Cutting's that day. I tried to get someone else to meet Ronald but nobody is in town so he will have to put up with our society alone! Franklin goes to Syracuse & Plattsburg Tuesday & I go to Cambridge & then Portland for a night with Maude, getting home Friday!

I'm so glad Bob is doing better again & I'm so sorry Mr. & Mrs. Cooley have had a disheartening time. I am planning to go & hear Uncle Ted & Gov. Johnson[116] too the first time they speak in New York. Uncle Ted's progressive ideas have fired so many of the young men to real work in this state that even if he doesn't win this time I feel a big work will have been accomplished.

I am hoping to see Edie [Ferguson] somehow before she starts for Silver & I am so glad you are going to have her soon.

As far as I know Grenville [Merrill] is doing nothing politically but I have not seen Pauline yet. When I do I will write you all about them!

The chicks are all well & Anna rides daily & is getting quite a grown up little girl. Elliott's going to be a prize fighter and I think has inherited all Uncle Ted's energy, he has James completely subdued & terrified & even Anna is under his thumb.

So much love to Bob & the children & you dear in which Franklin joins.

    Ever your devoted

      Eleanor

Within ten days of Franklin falling ill, Eleanor, too, developed a high temperature. Eventually both were diagnosed with typhoid fever. Eleanor recovered more quickly and was up and around while Franklin was still confined to bed. FDR, fearing that his illness would prevent him from campaigning effectively, turned to Louis Howe, a Democratic strategist, to manage his re-election campaign.[117] In spite of everything, Eleanor lost none of her enthusiasm for the campaign.

Eleanor had not yet been able to see Edie Ferguson, who had arrived in New York City, but was feeling poorly, too fatigued to continue her journey to New Mexico.

116. California governor Hiram Johnson, TR's running mate on the Progressive party ticket.
117. Roosevelt, *This is My Story*, 147–48.

49 East Sixty-Fifth Street   Nov. 2d, 1912

Dearest Bob & Isabella,

You must forgive this pencil scrawl but it is all I'm allowed as yet.[118] Both your dear letters were such a joy[119] & isn't it splendid that Uncle Ted is getting on so well. As election approaches I cannot help hoping he will win but if he doesn't this time he will four years from now.

I am really splendidly & have begun to get up but Franklin after being in bed & out of bed for a month at last had a blood test taken on Wednesday which shows mild typhoid & he is in bed till his temperature has been normal for a time but we hope as he has had it so long that he'll soon be over it particularly as his temperature rarely goes above 101. This really has been rather an unpleasant autumn but such things must [o]ccasionally happen & Mama has worked like a slave over all my household duties & the children have kept splendidly well in the country so we really ought to be grateful! Poor Franklin hasn't done one bit of campaigning so he feels very insecure over his election & I think it has been very hard for him though I still hope he'll get it!

Did I tell you Ronald dined with me the night before he sailed? I was sorry he didn't get to you for I know how you wanted to see him but he said he was coming back in January especially to see you & I do hope that will plan out. Edie seems to have had a horrid time & if she hasn't gone by the end of the week I still hope to see her.

Pauline [Merrill] & Corinne [Alsop] have both been in to see me looking so well & Corinne full of politics![120]

Do write me all your news & I will write again when I have a little more of interest to tell you.

　　　　　Ever your devoted,
　　　　　Eleanor

Franklin was re-elected, but Eleanor's uncle Theodore Roosevelt lost to Woodrow Wilson, whom Franklin was supporting. "During the winter there was some talk of the possibility" of Franklin's being asked to join the Wilson

118. If she is still supposed to be in bed, it would have been awkward to manage an inkstand and dip pen.
119. Missing.
120. Eleanor's first cousin Corinne would become a leader in the Republican party in Connecticut, and would be elected to the state assembly in 1924. She frequently spoke to large crowds and was highly effective and influential due to her stature, position, and intelligence. Although Corinne was a Republican, she and Eleanor always remained close friends.

administration, Eleanor later wrote, but she was "too much taken up with the family to give it much thought."[121] She was also busy helping Isabella weather yet another crisis.

Edie Ferguson, who seemed to be suffering from jaundice, consulted Bob's New York physician, Dr. Walter James. James examined Edie, then wired Isabella to come at once. On December 4, Isabella boarded a train east, crossing paths with her mother, who was heading west to take care of the Ferguson household in Isabella's absence.

Hyde Park on the Hudson, NY   December 10, 1912
Dearest, dear Isabella,

I am so happy to feel that you are so near but so very grieved to hear that Edie is still so ill. I thought of her as being with you in Cat Canon by now & was so surprised when Cousin Susie [Parish] telephoned me yesterday. I was only in town for the day yesterday but we will be down for good on Thursday & then I can go anywhere to see you or meet you anywhere in town or do anything for you if you have any errands you want done.

I hope the Cat Canon news is good so you won't have any worries for them while you are here. Let me know if I can do anything for Edie & I will telephone you on Thursday evening so you won't have to write.

Ever lovingly,
E.R.

Isabella arrived in New York to find Edie "bright yellow" and Dr. James baffled. James called in another doctor. An operation revealed an ovarian tumor that had metastasized to the liver. John Greenway wired Isabella: "my thoughts are constantly with you in your new anxiety."[122] Edie died on December 21. Isabella, exhausted, stayed on in New York through Christmas. When Bob's brother Hector arrived, he and Isabella traveled to New Mexico early in the New Year to comfort Bob and each other as best they could.

Having done all she could to help Isabella while she was in New York, Eleanor tried to cheer her with happy news of mutual friends and droll comments on her own first forays into politics.

121. Roosevelt, *This is My Story*, 148.
122. Miller, *Isabella Greenway*, 67–68; John Greenway to IG, December 20, 1912, FC.

Ten Eyck Hotel, Albany   January 28th, [1913]
Dearest Isabella,

I can hardly realize how long it is since you & Hector started on your journey & I'm glad to know that you arrived safely!

Your wish about Julia & Redmond came true very soon, didn't it?[123] They came to lunch with us on Sunday & she is full of excitement & they were so funny describing how they had told various people & how it had been received! I feel sure it will be happy for them both, don't you? What do you think of Mr. Fletcher Harper's engagement? I knew you would be interested though I hardly know Harriet Wadsworth & he always liked her.

We are really getting quite accustomed to our Albany journey[124] & it seems to agree with Franklin! Next Tuesday instead of coming here we are going to Poughkeepsie for a Charity ball! Can't you see what it will be like & how many Mrs. Snooks & Mrs. Jones I will have to pretend to know when I really never remember seeing them before.

Cousin Susie [Parish] & I went to Cooper Union[125] this morning with Miss Hewitt & had a most interesting time & I felt so ashamed to own that it was my first visit! Somehow there is so little time to see all one would like to see in New York.

I do hope you found Bob & the children well & that you are resting now. Do send me a line when you can dear & give my love to your mother & Bob & the children.

   Ever devotedly,
    Eleanor

Although Isabella admitted to her Grandmother Selmes that Edie Ferguson's death had "wrenched me deeper than I knew," she tried to keep cheerful for the sake of Bob and Hector, who had lost two sisters in one year. The Ferguson household had plenty of company, sometimes ten guests at a time.

123. Redmond Cross married FDR's neighbor Julia Newbold.
124. The Roosevelts decided not to rent a house in Albany that year, but to take rooms at a hotel. Eleanor went up on Monday afternoons and returned on Thursday mornings to the house in New York where the children were staying with nannies, supervised by their grandmother Sara Roosevelt. Roosevelt, *This is My Story*, 148.
125. Cooper Union was a college in New York City founded in 1859 to provide free adult education. No discrimination based on race, religion, or sex was allowed. Abraham Lincoln made an early speech there, Susan B. Anthony had offices there, and the Red Cross and NAACP were organized there.

Isabella tried to think of Edie's death as a blessing, and enjoy what life had to offer. In this letter, Isabella describes a typical morning, with her household staff working side-by-side with Isabella and her mother, who were home-schooling Martha, seven, and Bobbie, almost five.

Cat Cañon   Feb 7, 1913 11 am
Belovedest Eleanor,

The fattest cock has been killed!—by Lupe [a maid]—who is now improv-ing the henhouse—while Virgie [a fourteen-year-old African American maid] shines the Silver[,] Minnie [a maid] repapers the cupboards! The nursery uni-versity is in full morning swing—Buzz writes & illustrates original compo-sition!! Martha & Hazel [a nanny?] take turns at the blackboard. Mother writes for the Post [writes a letter] & Bob takes a day in bed for complete coziness. While a blanket of wet snow settles on us [and] hushes our usual sunny routine!

There you have us on a wet day—and here you have Mittie [myself] in full action [sketch of IF with umbrella].[126] All the [water] tanks are overflow-ing as are our hearts in thankfulness for the many bathes ahead! Tho already we begin to plan economy to see us thro the June drought! What a picture to send to your busy world of things accomplished! Virgie here revived our hectic day! with Bengors[127] food.

Hector missed little that was to be seen & Mother & I wonder what impression he carried off of the West. We motored out the Gila[128] & lunched with the Tom Lyons family. Mrs. Lyons with a brand new red dye on her hair for the approaching wedding of her daughter almost overcame Hector. He completely lost his breathe & afterwards said he'd never dreamed of 3 such square feet of wickedness! Twas a heavenly day—the world was a warm opal with white & other peacocks basking against pink blue hills & he quite loved that spot.

Then we picnic lunched at the turquoise mine looking 300 miles in every direction. [We] scrambled [on] another day over such a quaint & wonderful formation called the "City of Rocks" that I wish you had seen. He mixed with the neighbors—as he pleased—liking Alford Cooley particularly—& calling Susie [Cooley] & Jimmy a "slice & a half" of Boston & *quite* realizing how entirely untransplantable they are. Most Boston folk are as far as I can see.

126. Isabella had taken drawing lessons during her teenaged years in New York City.
127. Bengers Food—a hot milk preparation, like fortified hot chocolate.
128. Wilderness area in southwest New Mexico, now a national forest.

Would that you could have seen him, having an evening meal with a cow puncher friend of ours who sat in flannel shirt[,] black silk handkerchief around his neck—& he [the cow puncher] picked up the bread with a fork and when offered whiskey said, "No ma'am, thank you ma'am—I don't mostly never use it"![129] & spurs bumbing [bumping?] into everything in our limited spaces.

Then Mrs. Walter Douglas arrived in lavendar satin, pearls & her private car & came out to luncheon (Here I must say, for her, that she hadn't intended being so outrageous after a former scolding of mine but had spilt kidney gravy down her country clothes that morning so lunched in her evening ones!) Then we all had tea later on their [private railroad] car—with Mr. Douglas Sr.[130] & Jr.—who had come to start further [mining] developments in the Burro Mountains.

Hector (uninstructed) was somewhat puzzled as to who & why they were! So [he] asked Mr. Douglas "Do you really suppose there is much left in these old mines?" My impression is that he [Hector] fully realizes that for our purposes we couldn't be better situated [with a] Doctor[131] & all—& it should be a solid comfort to him—to have seen for himself. As to his sharing my genuine enthusiasm over the privilege of living & bringing children up out here—that's another question!! He seemed a world better physically & I hope won't return quite so nervous after his hibernating here. He scouted at a great rate with M & B. Martha said "Doesn't Uncle H talk funny? I suppose it's Scotch?"

Twas so hard for them, Bob & H—& the heart of our every day seems so dimmed without Edie. We'll come to realize her as our guardian angel smiling on us more lovingly than ever—but the wrench is constant now. If only Bob & Hector could have seen the beauty of her final sleep. They wouldn't want her back. All we could offer would count as nothing to that eternal peace—to one *so tired* & more & more do I realize that the drifting was just as we'd all

129. The cow-puncher might have been trying to behave in an extra-genteel manner to impress the Scottish nobility.

130. Walter P. Douglas was the son of Dr. James Douglas, the developer of the Copper Queen Mine in Bisbee, Arizona. He attended the Columbia University School of Mines, arrived in Prescott as an engineer in 1890, and in 1901, at age thirty-one, he was appointed General Manager of the Copper Queen Mine, property of Phelps-Dodge Corporation, the dominant mine in the Bisbee area. One of the most powerful men in Arizona, he and his family owned controlling interest in a number of Arizona newspapers, railroads, and banks, as well as mines. http://www.library.arizona.edu/exhibits/bisbee/history/whoswho/walter_douglas.html.

131. Dr. Bullock, see footnote in introduction to November 21, 1910 letter.

want & free from every burden & responsibility. Those last weeks never could have been so quiet & content nearer those she loved *best*.[132]

Dearest Eleanor—you were *everything* to me those weeks—& if I can love you more than before I do now—& I treasure our night at Westbrook[133] with a childish joy—Thank you for it all & bless you forever. May Anna know one friend like you.

Bob's none the worse the Doctor tells me which is all encouraging after such a strain—& now we hope will go up hill again. M & B adore their suitcases. We think we shall have to take them to the coast just to use them! Hector read the books & we are looking forward to doing so. I dread those Albany trips somehow. All love to Franklin.

> Ever devotedly,
>
> Isabella

On March 4, 1913, Woodrow Wilson was inaugurated as president in Washington, D.C. Eleanor and Franklin had arrived three days earlier, so that FDR could lobby for a post in the new administration. Josephus Daniels, who had been named secretary of the Navy, offered him a position as assistant secretary—the same post TR had held under McKinley in the 1890s.[134]

The day before the inauguration, the largest suffrage parade in the nation's history wound through the streets of Washington, nearly upstaging the new president. An estimated five thousand women marched down Pennsylvania Avenue, led by the lovely Inez Milholland[135] on a white horse, the *New York Times* reported in a full page of coverage. Many of the women wore "almost diaphanous" gowns, exposing the women to the chill March winds.

After the inauguration, Eleanor visited Auntie Bye at her home in Connecticut to learn from an expert how to be a political asset to her husband in Washington. Eleanor hoped she and Franklin would be able to live in Bye's small house in Georgetown, where for many years Bye had presided over an important political salon during her brother Theodore's administration.

132. Isabella suggests that if Bob and Hector had been with Edie, she might not have felt free to die peacefully.
133. Isabella was staying with Olivia at Westbrook, and Eleanor visited her there.
134. For FDR's meeting with Daniels, see introduction to July 8, 1912, letter.
135. FDR liked to say he had been persuaded to adopt woman suffrage after Milholland came to lobby him and sat on his desk. Eleanor insisted that he had supported votes for women before that "memorable visit." Ward, *A First-Class Temperament*, 162n.

Already Eleanor was making shrewd observations about the new president and his secretary of state, William Jennings Bryan, a great orator who himself had been three times nominated for the presidency.

[Albany]   March 12 [1913]

Dearest Isabella

We've been so busy lately that I haven't even written thank you for your dear letter which I was so glad to get. I'm thankful Bob's gone on pretty well & though it might have been a help [to him] to be with Edie at the last & realize the perfect rest & peace of her passing[,] still Bob & Hector were spared much of sorrowful detail through your wonderful thoughtfulness & care & it must have made the wrench easier. I realize though what a daily loss it is to you all & how *you* must be working to keep cheerful these days.

I envy Mary & Miss Brice their trip to Cat Canon & wish so often it were possible for me to go. Now however I fear our chances of pleasure trips are small for as you've doubtless seen Franklin is going to be ass. Secretary of the Navy in Mr. Winthrop's[136] place. He is delighted but it means being close to Washington unless he's sent to the Pacific coast any time when of course I'll take my chance of going to see you.

We're not going to take a house in Washington till next autumn but Franklin has to begin work at once so we are going to take an apartment & I am going down every other week. I think we'll try to get A. Bye's house in the autumn.

I know you will be interested to hear that Hall & Margaret have a daughter born yesterday & both Margaret & the baby are very well. I hope to go on to Boston for a day next week to see my niece if all goes well.

We were in Washington for the Inauguration & the crowds were enormous. The suffrage parade was too funny & nice fat ladies with bare legs and feet posed in tableaux[137] on the Treasury steps! Mr. Wilson was very dignified & I think he is going to have an interesting administration as all the Cabinet promise well but socially I think it will be a quiet four years for Washington. The President has none of Uncle Ted's magnetism & really excites little

136. Beekman Winthrop (1874–1940), a New York lawyer and governor of Puerto Rico from 1904 to 1907, was assistant secretary of the Navy under President William Howard Taft, serving for a time as acting secretary.

137. "A representation of some scene by the grouping of persons who remain silent and motionless in appropriate postures." *Webster's Collegiate Dictionary.*

enthusiasm in a crowd so if he becomes popular it will be entirely due to things done. Mr. Bryan is received with far greater manifestations of approval by the populace. Franklin's chief Mr. Daniels seems very nice with a great desire for work & simplicity!

We are in Albany for the last time & I must stop & pack & go & pay some more goodbye calls as we go home tomorrow.

Give my love to Mrs. Selmes, Martha & Buzz & a great deal to you & Bob from

> Your devoted,
> Eleanor

Eleanor's first letter from Washington as the wife of the newly appointed assistant secretary of the Navy is happy and enthusiastic. Although she updates Isabella on all her cousins, she mentions that she again has had a lesson in her new role from Auntie Bye.

These lessons were put to almost immediate use. Eleanor was expected to make literally hundreds of social calls. It was tedious, but Eleanor realized that she had already "come a long way" in the two years she had been in Albany. Before then, she said, "I never could have paid those first calls."[138] Although Eleanor met, and eventually became comfortable with, all sorts of different people, in private letters to Isabella, she wrote what she really thought about them.

The Powhatan, Washington [D.C.]   April 11 [1913]
Dearest Bob & Isabella,

There is so much I want to tell you about that I do not know where to begin! However, first a thousand thanks for your letter & also for Franklin's telegram which pleased him so much.[139] It means so much to have your love & good wishes & you can't think how much I count on the interest which you two dearest of people take in all our doings.

I know you want to hear all about Ethel's wedding[140] & you may have had much news of it already. It was quite perfect I thought, the chancel filled with lovely spring blossoms & Ethel looking so sweet & pretty. They looked most radiantly happy & the villagers cheered them heartily as they came out. There

---

138. Roosevelt, *This is My Story*, 150.

139. Both missing.

140. Ethel Roosevelt, TR's younger daughter and Eleanor's first cousin, married Richard Derby, a surgeon, on April 4, 1913.

was just the right note of dignity & quiet happiness about everything & no fuss. The big room, dining room & piazza were filled with tables & the day was so lovely that one enjoyed being out of doors & I think everyone stayed to see them drive off in an automobile together.

Archie has grown much & both he & Quentin[141] were dear but I was so sorry Kermit could not be there. Alice looked very pretty but Nick was not there. Auntie Bye sat in a chair & everyone was so happy to see her & she seemed so well & in such good spirits but the last cure does not seem to me to have helped her lameness at all. I spent a morning with her in New York & acquired much information as to my duties here. Everyone tells me Mrs. Winthrop did so much & was such a help & popular with everyone. I only hope I shall do half as well!

Last week I spent four days here & I've been here since Tuesday this week but I've only succeeded in paying about 100 calls & I must owe at least 500! I'll be glad when we are settled here in the autumn & there is no [t]raveling back & forth. We can't get A. Bye's house till May 1st, however & that's too late to move the children down so I shall spend every other week here till we go to Campo in July.[142] I fear poor Franklin will spend the summer [in Washington]! Mr. Daniels is a very hard worker & expects the same from all around him. He is a dear however & Franklin likes him very much & Mrs. Daniels is much the nicest of the Cabinet ladies I think, so we are in luck!

I paid my first call on Mrs. Bryan a week ago & it was most amusing. She was much disappointed because Franklin was not with me & at once told me she liked young men & hoped we'd go & call some evening! We've also been received in state by Mrs. Wilson & she seemed a nice, intelligent woman but not overburdened with charm. I haven't seen the girls yet but they seem to be enjoying the gaieties very much & turkey trot quite readily.[143]

Isabella, I went to a lunch at the Marine barracks which made me think of the one you described at the grocer's wife's I think it was. We had candle light & most of the ladies wore evening dresses & the courses went on indefinitely![144]

141. Archie and Quentin Roosevelt were TR's younger sons.
142. The Roosevelt children were in New York City with Sara, their grandmother, and Eleanor thought that moving them to Washington for only six weeks, with their nurses and governesses, would be too much trouble.
143. Mrs. Wilson—Ellen Axson Wilson—wife of President Woodrow Wilson; the girls—the Wilson daughters, Margaret, Jessie, and Eleanor (Nell).
144. Eleanor thinks that candlelight and long dresses are inappropriately formal for lunch, especially in a barracks!

Helen & Teddy [Robinson] are at the Hot Springs[145] just now & I am very glad for Helen as I never saw her look more tired. She has worked like a dog all winter on different progressive committees & everyone says she has helped Teddy tremendously.

How are Buzz & Martha & have they done anything wonderful of late? Anna is getting so grown up & I've just acquired a French nurse for Anna & James. He of course scorned to speak a word but Anna told me she was "trying to learn as it would be such a help in Washington!" Elliott is becoming slightly tamed but there are still dreadful lapses in his manners!

I sat next to Mr. Cleve Dodge at Aunt Maggie's golden wedding party last Monday & he gave me a wonderful account of you all. Mary says she loved every minute of her trip & I never saw her look better.

Dear love to you all from us both.

Ever devotedly,

Eleanor

In addition to her duties as a politician's wife, Eleanor was traveling up to New York City every second week to see the children, who were living with their grandmother.

Isabella was on the move, too. She had told Eleanor she was planning a trip to California, but she may not have revealed everything behind that decision. In March, hoping to recover from coping with Edie's death and all the guests they had in New Mexico afterwards, Isabella, together with two women friends, had gone again to visit John Greenway. This time, Isabella did not get much rest. John was recovering from a poisonous cactus wound and his sister-in-law, who had been keeping house for him, had broken her ankle.[146] Even more overwhelming, when John had recovered enough to leave the house, and they were out of earshot of their chaperones, he confessed that he was in love with Isabella. But Isabella could not confide these developments to Eleanor in a letter, and so Eleanor's next letter makes no mention of John Greenway.

1733 N Street, Washington, DC[147]   May 9th [1913]

Dearest Isabella,

I have been meaning to write for sometime but time does fly these days. First of all I must tell you what you may already know, that Hall & Margaret

145. Probably Hot Springs, Arkansas, now a national park.
146. Miller, *Isabella Greenway*, 69.
147. Anna (Bye)'s house in Washington, D.C.

lost their little 5 weeks old baby girl. I know it is better now than if she had been older but it is very hard & they seem very young to have such a sorrow & to make matters worse Hall was operated on for appendicitis just the week before so he could not be with Margaret which was very hard for them both. However, he has done wonderfully well & I hope they can go off for a short trip soon. I went twice to Boston last week so I feel a little as though the train was my only home these days.

Franklin continues to have to work very hard & Mr. Daniels has been away most of the last two weeks but I think Franklin enjoys every minute of it. Tell Bob that Franklin lunched with Sir Cecil Spring Rice[148] the other day & he talked a great deal about Ronald. His wife has not come yet & so she will be spared the Spring here. The heat has been quite bad for a few days & I find my daily calls rather more wearisome & this is the last week I hope I shall have to do it as I've nearly finished my list. Some 400–500 behind me! I called on the Senate Naval Com[mittee] yesterday & one lady from St. Paul Minn. was most entertaining & we had a grand time talking about the Ames family whom she knew quite well!

I go home to-morrow & on Monday I'm taking Anna & James for four days to Cousin Susie [Parish] at Orange. On Friday, the 16th, the whole family move to Hyde Park & I shall stay there till the 26th to get the children settled & then come here for a week & leave on the 30th for Chicago for Katharine Delano's wedding.

It is so nice being in this house & not in a hotel but I feel all the time as though A. Bye might appear. I hope to go & see her in June.

Did you go with the children to California & are Caroline & Mr. Phillips with you? Also how is Bob & are you & the children well?

Dear love to you all from your devoted
Eleanor

After a hectic spring, Eleanor was looking forward to a rest at Campobello Island, and being reunited with her children. Her letter mentions some tweed

148. Sir Cecil Spring Rice (1859–1918) British ambassador to the U.S. 1912–1917, was a good friend of Theodore Roosevelt and best man at TR's second wedding, to Edith Carow, in 1886. Spring Rice famously remarked about TR: "You must remember that the president is about six [years old]." Morris, *Theodore Rex*, 81; Morris, *Rise of Theodore Roosevelt*, 359; http://janus.lib.cam.ac.uk/db/node.xsp?id=EAD%2FGBR%2F0014%2FCASR. The Spring Rices befriended ER and FDR when they went to Washington in the Wilson administration. Cook, *Eleanor Roosevelt*, I, 206.

material that Isabella had commissioned Hector to buy in Scotland and send to Eleanor. It figures in several subsequent letters.

Meanwhile, Isabella had returned still completely exhausted, from visiting John Greenway. The previous year, Theodore Roosevelt had written his old comrade-in-arms: "Now, Bob, some time I want you to make Isabella go off for two or three weeks to Los Angeles or some other place with a totally different climate. . . . Like myself, you have a wife who will persist in refusing to think of herself—and therefore you and I must think of them. I have always insisted that Mrs. Roosevelt benefitted in no way as much as by a complete holiday from me and the children, in entirely different surroundings . . . in Isabella's case, she should go to the California coast."[149]

Bob, following TR's advice, agreed that Isabella should go with the children and Mammy for a long sojourn by the sea in Santa Barbara, California. They left in May. While she was away, Isabella did not write to Eleanor and Eleanor was getting anxious.

Hyde Park on the Hudson   June 15th [1913]
Dearest, dear Isabella

It seems ages since I had any news of you & yours but I hope no news is good news & that you & the children all enjoyed your trip to the coast & are better for it.

Hector has just written that he is sending me to Campo a plaid for Dr. [David] Ricketts & some blue material & from his letter I cannot make out if the latter is intended for you or for me from you![150] I will let you know when they arrive & forward them to you by the first person who goes in [back to the United States from Campobello] after they arrive.

I have paid my last visit to Washington for this spring & this week we are going to the Harvard-Yale boat race & on the 23rd I go to A. Bye [in Connecticut] for a night & on the 26th we all leave for Campo as Franklin can get off till July 6th. Then he has to return to Washington till Aug. 20th as Secretary Daniels is going on an inspection tour to the Pacific coast! I went to the polo games last week & it was most exciting but I almost wish we had lost the second game for winning by a safety doesn't seem satisfactory. Cousin Susie

149. TR to RHMF, October 29, 1912, AHS.
150. Isabella had asked Hector to send from Scotland blue tweed for Eleanor and a plaid for John Greenway's friend David Ricketts.

[Parish] & A. Corinne [Robinson] were there & Cousin Henry [Parish] even was yelling madly during the game.

Both Corinne [Alsop]'s babies have whooping cough which is hard but I suppose it is better in summer than in winter.

Has Bob yet read Mr. Collier's "Germany & the Germans"[151] & Winston Churchill's last novel?[152] If not I would like to send them out as I think he would enjoy them.

I must go & help Mama entertain about 20 ladies from the village Missionary Society, not a very easy task as the day is very hot & they are not the kind to make one forget one's discomfort!

The children are all well & I'm looking forward to being settled at Campo & being with them all the time again. Maude Waterbury & her two children are to come to us for July. You know I suppose that she has her divorce.

Love to Bob & Martha & Buzz & you from us all.

> Ever devotedly,
> Eleanor

Finally, after receiving several letters from Eleanor, Isabella replied, apologizing for the lapse in her correspondence while she had been traveling. Her trip had been restorative. Isabella had arrived in California exhausted by unremitting work and worry and grief—and possibly by the tumult of her growing feelings for John, feelings she still could not share with Eleanor, especially not in a letter. At first she was so worn out that she collapsed and simply cried for two days, then rested calmly in bed until she felt able to face the world again. Mammy and a cook had accompanied her, and took care of the children while Isabella recovered.[153] Isabella stayed for seven weeks, eating

---

151. Price Collier, *Germany and the Germans: From an American Point of View*. New York: Charles Scribner's Sons, 1913. Collier lamented that in Germany, "There is no association between the cultured classes, and the middle and lower classes." He took pride in America being "much more Democratic" (343, 344). Eleanor was twenty-eight and freshly arrived in Washington when she recommended this book. In later years there would be countless photographs of her walking through slums, climbing down into coal mines, surrounded by every kind of person. If the book did not actually influence her, it reflected preexisting opinions that were displayed in later life.

152. Winston Churchill, *The Inside of the Cup*. New York: The Macmilllan Company, 1913. The American novelist should not be confused with the future prime minister of Great Britain. The book, whose hero is a young preacher influenced by his encounters with corruption, has a fairly overt Christian message. Many of the books mentioned in Eleanor and Isabella's letters address spiritual themes, although there are strikingly few references to God or religion in the letters themselves.

153. IG to RHMF, May 1, 1913, FC.

and sleeping, swimming and gardening and painting, until she could return home strong enough to go back to work.[154]

Shortly after Isabella's return from California in July, Bob was buoyed by a visit from his old colonel. Theodore Roosevelt stopped over for a day and a night, with his teenaged sons Archie and Quentin, on their way to the Grand Canyon. John Greenway met the Roosevelts as they disembarked from the train in Deming, and a number of Rough Riders rode in to greet their former commander. But Roosevelt also made time for private talks with Bob.[155]

Cat Cañon   July 14, 1913
Dearest Eleanor!

How dare I—after so long—Mrs. Lambkin[156] having sent word that you thought I was lost—I take courage—in the fact that you thought [of me] at all—for honestly I should by now have been wiped from your memory forever. It's a great comfort to me to know, somehow, that you will understand my not having written in so long. As I wrote Mother (who has been treated much as you have)—these last months have been rather a nightmarish pulling up & away from a weariness I never before had—& any thoughts of mine on paper would have been a sorry inspiration.

However our jaunt to Santa Barbara was accomplished, the best of results & was a great success. Bob having gained enormously, in being rid of us, & the babes & I are new made over, fat[157] & ready for anything. So don't waste a moments sympathy on us. This detail is only that you may know we are not as apparently blind deaf & dumb to the only things that count as we may seem. Indeed your blessed letters were the greatest comfort—& we know, more keenly than ever, that we depend on them more & more.

We are so distressed about Margaret & Hall's tragedy when Hall was having appendicitis too. I can think how they must both have turned to you—It seems a hard thing to say & a hard thing to understand but somehow such loss gives its strength in bringing an understanding sympathy into the lives of young people that is half the power of living & giving. Oh I am so sorry for them both.

154. Miller, *Isabella Greenway*, 70.
155. Ibid., 71.
156. Evidently a mutual friend of Eleanor's and Isabella's. Mrs. Lambkin was a particular friend of Patty Selmes, with whom she was on a trip to Canada at the time of this letter.
157. In the days before antibiotics, being "fat" was the only buffer against a prolonged illness, and was a source of pride.

I never heard anything to equal your life—of calls & trains. My dear you seem the embodiment of 20th Century activity—& I can hear Anna some-day describing (in a rocking chair on her small-holding[158] front porch) to her children the extraordinary life led by their grandmother! For such a reaction is certainly ahead—& I save every scrap of our writing for her—more graphic understanding!

You will like Sir Cecil Spring Rice's wife (whatever she's called).[159] If she's a bit as she was when first married. A little dynamo of practical energy & sound ambition. Big as a minute & I remember her so well in an apple green tea gown that inspired her husband to call her "Positively magestic"!

So Caroline & William [Phillips] only had ten days after all so [they] post-poned their trip—we hope for some time this summer. Her letter from their Va. plantation was the plainest proof of the good it had done her.[160] It was Caroline at her wittiest—& so encouraging again.

I'm so disappointed Mr. Daniels made the Pacific inspection tour instead of Franklin & pray there may soon be some sufficient disorder to cause another trip—for on such hang our hopes of seeing you both—& if some such plan doesn't bring you I'll pick up my travelling companions & we'll all inspect you & yours. I've my heart set on Anna's & Martha's meeting ere long—[they will be] 8 & 7 years so soon—& that's high time to begin.

Washington must be unspeakable. Judging from the rest of the world. 110 here two days ago in the shade of Bob's porch. But [the higher temperatures were] caused by 3 weeks delay of the rainy season[161] & I'm just thanking all the power[s that be] that Mother is helping revive Mrs. Lambkin in Canada instead of Ky.

Bob would be so glad to have "Germany & the Germans" as you asked & we are *in* Mr. Churchill's last. For some time I have been plodding very thoughtfully thro' Professor Shaler's "Citizen."[162] Essentially a book of ele-ments for a limited intelligence[163] (*not* an accomplished politician like you!)

---

158. A small farm.
159. Florence Lascelles Spring-Rice.
160. Implies that staying on the plantation had done Caroline good.
161. In the southwestern United States, a wind shift in early July brings seasonal rains, which cause cooler weather. In their absence, the weather remained hot.
162. Nathaniel Southgate Shaler, *The Citizen: A Study of the Individual and the Government.* New York: A. S. Barnes & Company, 1904.
163. Isabella is being modest here. *The Citizen* is a comparatively sophisticated analysis of political life in a democracy. The book deals with capital punishment (126); corporate

& to Bob's horror, Buzz is sharing it (including the Darwinian system) & thoroughly enjoying the bigger grasp of universe—! to the complete eclipse of poor old Adam & Eve.[164] His only remark after a thrilling description of the serpents & apple, by Bob, being "Well, Daddie, was it a rattle snake?"—& then later "Daddie did you know your Grandfather was a monkey?"

They are daily dearer—& I can't tell you a half of the fun I had with them at Santa Barbara—where they were like young savages set suddenly in the midst of civilization—but, to my great satisfaction, diving very directly to the heart of things with a kind of self reliant independence that I hope will always stay with them—as the great gain of simple Western life. But their comments on things in general were too funny—Martha summing up the whole on our return said "Just think Mittie we knew 5 families & twenty children & I liked the gardener's children best of all because they was the only ones who *shared*—the others all took our toys away." The gardener's being that kind of dirty swarmy [?] nose running hard to describe but absolutely generous.

Just two or three of the many [people] one met casually—would send me far afield for a second sight. I particularly enjoyed (& count on seeing again) a young couple called Mr. & Mrs. [Austin] Strong. He is grandson of Mrs. R. L. Stevenson[165]—& she [Mrs. Strong]'s a delightful blond New Englander who holds a most well balanced own in the midst of that somewhat erratic

disclosure (133); mob psychology (149); education (173); woman suffrage (213); imperialism (256); the need for civility in politics (281), and numerous other topics. Professor Shaler's conclusions about race relations (222) and on immigration (202) appear questionable, at the very least. But Isabella might very well have agreed with the author's observation that political involvement is rooted in human loneliness.   According to Shaler, human beings remain "strangely apart and lonely in this great universe" and can experience "the supreme evil of isolation….Although the ways in which the loneliness of the individual is lessened are exceedingly varied, the only way in which he can be brought to the station of happiness is by society…. The simplest…of the many institutions of society…the foundation of them all, is the family…But in the great hunger for sympathy there comes a demand for larger associations that are related to the intellectual desires, to the accomplishment of purposes relating to the fate of fellow-men" (294–95).

164. According to Shaler, "The inquiries of naturalists have made it evident that the body and the mind of men came forth from the lower animals. Every bone, muscle, and other part which is found in our frames exists also in the bodies of the lower creatures, such as the chimpanzee and gorilla" (2).

165. The former Fanny Van de Grift Osborne, an American woman who lived in Santa Barbara after the death of Robert Louis Stevenson, she had two children by her first husband. Information later in the letter suggests that Austin Strong was the son of Mrs. Stevenson's daughter.

tribe. They work hard in N.Y. half the year & Eng. the other half. He writes plays—"The Good Little Devil" was his last year.[166]

We'd no end of fun in Mrs. RLS's garden—painting, mending, & developing films of RLS in Samoa. They were having delightful mornings diving into a chest heretofore unopened & containing letters of great interest to him from Meridith,[167] Kipling, H. James, & many others. Mrs. Mary Strong[168] was so like you—& wants to meet you. She's rather frail & almost never goes out.

Then a perfect old dear, Lady Elizabeth Cochrane, sister to Ld. Dundonald[169] of Ladysmith Fame. She was a stolid old maid general herself—stopping with my landlady Margaret Douglas. I don't know when I've enjoyed a "Scotch Study"[170] as much!

Then there was a great & joyful homecoming & a scurrying of tents into order for the Col [TR]'s[,] Archie's, Quentin's & some men's arrival. You can just imagine what it was to Bob—after not seeing him for so long—& wasn't it dear & like him to come to our side track [out of the way place] in his loyal friendly way. He said such fine things of Franklin & you.

We thought he was tired—& naturally after such 18 mos. with no holiday. Archie a dear slender rather delicate & very handsome youth—& such thoughtfulness. Quentin rather dazzlingly alive as to brain—& seeming 19 instead of 15. Dr. Ricketts, a big copper man. Mr. Mills[171] a rough rider & John Greenway livened the gathering & M. & B. said afterward "I think we like the two brothers best because the Col was too fat." Such are the critical eyes of youth!

166. Austin Strong adapted the stage hit "A Good Little Devil," by Rosemonde Gerard and Maurice Rostand, for a 1914 movie starring Mary Pickford.
167. Poet George Meredith (1828–1909).
168. Possibly Austin Strong's mother, since Austin was not named "Stevenson."
169. Lord Dundonald's cavalry won an important victory at Ladysmith (a town in South Africa south of Johannesburg) during the Boer War.
170. Isabella may mean someone who is quintessentially Scottish.
171. Probably Charles E. Mills, superintendent of the Detroit Copper Company at Morenci, Arizona, who had served as a private in the Rough Riders. See Herner, *Arizona Rough Riders.*

Hector is scouting & has written constantly & very courageously. Think Ethel [Roosevelt]& her [husband] Dick[172] are there around now.

Bob sends you worlds of love along with mine which fairly embraces the whole of the solar system—my dearest Eleanor in all the world.

Yr loving

Isabella

Hug the babies so tightly for me. Have they read Kingsley's "Water Babies"?[173] We are revelling in it & are going to take up outdoor geography lessons—some drawing—& poetry learning.

Eleanor wrote the following letter before she had received Isabella's assurance that all was well. Eleanor had her hands full at Campobello, where her aunt Maude, divorced from her husband Larry Waterbury, brought a friend, David Gray,[174] to visit. Sara Roosevelt was not pleased at this irregular arrangement, even though Gray was staying at a hotel. Eleanor, however, enjoyed David's company and was prepared to encourage her aunt's slightly scandalous behavior. Eleanor did not go into the problematic aspects of their visit in her letter to Isabella.

July 18th [1913]

Dearest, dear Isabella

I hope all goes well with you all & that no news is good news for it seems an age since I've heard from you or Bob.

The blue material & plaid are safely here & will you tell me if they are to be sent to you or direct to some other person. I doubt if anyone goes down from here that I can entrust them to until August 10th when Laura Delano is leaving me so you have plenty of time to write me all directions.

I am enjoying every minute here & so far we have had lovely weather & no heat, fires in the evening when it was 90° in New York. Maude Waterbury

---

172. Ethel Roosevelt, TR's younger daughter, and her husband, Dr. Richard Derby, were married in April and may have been on their honeymoon.

173. Charles Kingsley (1819–1875), English curate and author, with a "large and varied" literary output. *The Water Babies* (1863) is Kingsley's humorous children's story about a boy who falls into a river and meets its aquatic denizens. Harvey, ed., *Oxford Companion to English Literature*, 451.

174. David Gray was "an amiable, sensitive man, son of a Buffalo editor, fond of horses and writing short stories about the outdoor life." Maude and David were married in October in a civil ceremony in the Poughkeepsie town hall. In 1940, FDR would appoint Gray as minister (comparable to ambassador) to Ireland. Ward, *A First-Class Temperament*, 203.

& the children [are] with me & on Aug. 1ˢᵗ they move into Hall's house as he gave up coming [to Campobello in order] to take an ass. Professorship at the Summer School & Engineering Camp. I am sorry they couldn't be here but it will be good experience for him.[175]

By the way, Bob will be interested I know to hear that in talking to a man who was just back from Brazil the other day I heard Kermit was doing very well & had got in now with a better firm than before & they apparently think a great deal of him. Isn't it splendid to hear such nice things from strangers? I wonder if you'll see Uncle Ted on his hunting trip in Arizona?[176]

Mr. David Gray is stopping at a boarding house up here & writing so he comes to us for meals very frequently & I just said I was writing you & he is putting in a note.[177]

Jeff Newbold[178] has been staying with us since the day after we arrived & seems quite content with our quiet lives but I don't flatter myself it is our charms alone![179]

Franklin could only stay one week but he writes his office is bearable & the work very interesting & I hope he can get up for one Sunday before he comes back in Aug. for two weeks.

Anna & I have English lessons for an hour every morning & she & James have a half hour of French & really begin to talk quite nicely with the little undernurse. Elliott is improving as to manners but he still has fearful determination! Love from us to Bobby & Martha & Bob & yourself & write when you can.

> Ever devotedly,
> Eleanor

Isabella's boast to Eleanor on returning from California that she was "ready for anything" was immediately challenged when Martha fell ill with her annual stomach complaint.

175. During 1913 Hall studied engineering. By working in the summer, he was able to graduate early, obtaining his ME degree in 1914. Roosevelt, *This is My Story*, 148
176. Described in TR's *A Book Lover's Holiday in the Open*. New York: Scribners, 1916, III, 187.
177. Not included here.
178. Jefferson Newbold, FDR's next door neighbor in Hyde Park, provided financial support for Franklin's 1912 campaign. Ward, *A First-Class Temperament*, 197fn.
179. In a later letter, Eleanor's hunch proves to be true.

Cat Cañon   July 24, 1913
Eleanor dearest,

Our letters must just have crossed. Dear me how welcome yours of last night was. Already read 3 times. Once to myself—next to Bob & finally to Martha—as kind of a reward for taking "Laxol"[180] & when we came to the part about your having "English" in the morning with Anna & James—followed by "French"—she was greatly confused & wished to know if they couldn't talk English.

It's been a bad 5 days for poor Sister[181]—who developed a very acute attack of her old intestinal disorder last Saturday—the temperature was only high one day—& we just all cried for her & the first dose she had to take & be racked with[182]—& since [then] it's been merely a matter of tedious restraint while on starvation diet to be on the safe side—& a more patient, adorable little girl you can't imagine—Eternally thoughtful & gentle & just as full of fun as her weak little self allows—& this morning Buzz joined the hospital while two huge double teeth pushed thro'. I sit between the two on the floor! & only tell you all our details because you'll wonder at my incoherent writing & thoughts. I feel confident that with care a day or two will see them out of the woods & their merry selves as is the rapid recuperating habit of babies.

Our rains came on with such a jerk & sudden jump of fifty degrees—from 100—down—it usually throws the sturdiest grown up out—& we hold it somewhat responsible for these disturbances.

Bob has been greatly diverted meantime by Mr. Ballard ex-Sheriff from Roswell & ranch partner of Dave T's—& docile effeminate appearing little man who has been in untold shooting scraps & holding down a rough community for years. He's been stopping with us while attending a cattle convention.

If my letter has arrived[183] you know by now that the tweed was meant to be a perfect match for your eyes & a substitute for the old tweed—of such dear associations [—] we won't be quiet till we know definitely if there were *duties!!* [184]

180. Remedy for constipation. The cobalt blue glass bottles became collectors' items in the twenty-first century.
181. Her daughter Martha.
182. Probably the Laxol gave her cramps. Evidently the doctor recommended a bowel-cleansing laxative and restricted diet.
183. No letter with this information has come to light. It seems likely that Isabella thought she had mentioned the fabrics but didn't.
184. Import duties or taxes.

The plaid is for Dr. Ricketts. It would be nice (if convenient for you) if we could have it by Sept. 10. He sails Sept 20.

We're looking forward to Miss Ricketts & Mrs. Greenway's[185] coming up for a week soon. The former is very delightful of a quaint old maid turn of mind & much charm (an intimate of Mrs. Fairfield Osborne's!)—Mrs. G is a dear. "Purified by fire" having lost both husband & only child.

I envy you Mr. David Gray—if my memory hasn't played me false. He stood [seemed to be] so worthwhile—Forever touching the simple human side—with no disconcerting (& usually affected) firework turn of mind.

Love no end to Franklin—who'll soon be with you—& hugs to Eleanor from the whole family of us. Bless God[-]daughter [Anna] & her brothers.

> Yr loving
>
> Isabella

PS[186] The tweed is for you dear from us & the plaid we're sorry to bothe r you about but would like to get it forwarded here (for Dr. Ricketts) During my absence there was much confusion & cabling of address' between Bob & Hector. We both want you to know that we count on your *honesty* in telling us if there is duty on them. Hector didn't get the New Brunswick address "for tweeds" till I returned & had likely already sent them.

We do hope the tweeds match your eyes. That was our only direction—

July 26 - At last *Sister seems really better & the trouble has been pronounced "gastritous"* (can't spell) Bob's love too.

The troubles in Mexico had been escalating since Isabella's first mention of unrest in August 1911. Two years later, Mexico was in a full-scale civil war.[187] Franklin had made a speech two weeks after taking office that if fighting broke out in Mexico, he might have to resign, as TR had done during the Spanish-American War, to lead a Rough Rider-style regiment.[188]

[Campobello]   Aug. 5th [1913]

Dearest, dear Isabella,

I wanted to write you a real letter & so the days have slipped by & I haven't even thanked you yet for the tweed[189] which is the most heavenly color. I only

185. Presumably John Greenway's sister-in-law.
186. In her postscript, Isabella repeated some of the information in the body of her letter, evidence that she might have been correct in supposing she was a little incoherent.
187. Meyer et al., *Course of Mexican History*, 505–507.
188. Ward, *A First-Class Temperament*, 206–207.
189. Most likely a bolt of material that Eleanor would have a dressmaker make into a suit.

hope my eyes are as nice & I love it & hope it will go through as many happy times as the old one. Incidentally, I still treasure the old one & joy in it on cold autumn days. Many, many thanks to you & Bob for your thoughtfulness & I will enjoy thoughts of you whenever I wear my blue tweed!

Laura Delano is here & she is taking the plaid on with her & will send it Aug. 18th so you should get it about the 25th I should think. I am so sorry Martha had such a horrid attack & poor Buzz too but I hope they are quite well now. I should think such a fearful drop in temperature would be very hard on everyone. How does Bob get on these days & I hope all your worries have not undone all the good of your holiday.

We have enjoyed your letters so much & Anna & James take such an interest in every scrap of news about Martha & Buzz. I wish you would pick up & come see us but in any case we plan to see you next spring at the latest. If business doesn't take us, pleasure surely will.

Having Maude & her children has been a great pleasure to me & now they have moved into Hall's cottage next door. We still can read together & go off on long picnic and fishing expeditions. The long days out of doors or on the water are a great rest.

Franklin has been busy in Washington but in spite of the heat he has played golf daily & had some interesting times with the President & Sec. of War over the Mexican troubles.[190] He goes to Newport tonight to inspect the fleet & naval station & comes here Saturday morning, leaving Sunday night for Portsmouth. He gets back on the 20th for two weeks however.

"Germany & the Germans" goes to Bob to-morrow. Has he read much of Masefield?[191] We read a good many & are now reading Shakespeare as a contrast!

190. The "Mexican troubles" cited by Eleanor arguably began hundreds of years earlier. They flowed directly, however, from the ouster in May 1911 of the Mexican dictator, Porfirio Diaz. (See footnotes to Isabella's August 1, 1911 letter.) After Leon de la Barra's brief interim presidency, the reformer, Francisco Madero, took office on November 6, 1911. Madero was ousted by one of his own generals, Victoriano Huerta, on February 18, 1913, and was "shot point-blank" three days later. Meyer et al., *Course of Mexican History*, 502, 503. According to President Woodrow Wilson's special envoy to Mexico, Huerta was "an ape-like man.... He may be said to subsist on alcohol.... he is never sober...." Moreover, his government made "unbridled use of political assassination." Ibid., 509–510, 507. Huerta was opposed by many revolutionary leaders, including Venustiano Carranza ("an ardent Madero supporter"), Francisco "Pancho" Villa, and Emiliano Zapata. Ibid., 505–507.

191. The English poet John Masefield (1878–1967), probably most famous for "Sea Fever," a widely anthologized poem about love of the sea.

We've also read for the first time some [delightful books] by Francis Thompson[192] & if you don't know them I'll send them on too.

Cousin Susie [Parish] seems to be taking a good rest at Hot Springs & I hope your Mother is doing the same. I had a postcard from Pauline [Merrill] yesterday from Champery[193] & I was rather surprised as I didn't even know she had gone abroad! It looks lovely & she says she is leading the simple life.

I'm so glad to know something of Lady Spring Rice & I do hope they will both like us for I would like the chicks to play together as I believe they are about the same age. I'm so interested in your Mrs. Strong & wish I could meet her sometime in New York but I don't suppose I will be there long enough even to see my friends this winter.

Hector's letter to me was so brave.[194] I do think he's wonderful the way he's taken up his life.

Mr. David Gray is still here & I like him very much. He likes the simple things of life & is so companionable & gets real pleasure out of playing round with us apparently. Jeff Newbold spent all of July with me but I don't flatter myself I was the attraction as I think he liked a little Boston girl who lives near us very much!

Elliott burnt his hand quite badly the other day in a bonfire they had on the beach but he was very brave & nurse had some wonderful stuff which took the pain out at once so he never lost any sleep & all the chicks are wonderfully well. (In case you don't know about "Unguantine" do keep it in the house it is the best thing for burns I ever saw.)

I was so sorry to see poor Alfred [Alford] Cooley's death[195] & I know you & Bob will feel it. Poor Mrs. Cooley. I wish I knew her well enough to feel I could do something for her.

The mail must go so kiss the chicks for me & so much love to you & Bob.

Ever your devoted

Eleanor

At some point, probably in the summer of 1913, John Greenway confessed to Bob Ferguson his feelings for Isabella. In those days, it would have been

192. English poet (1859–1907). Thompson's most famous poem, "The Hound of Heaven," about God's pursuit of a soul, is said to have influenced J. R. R. Tolkien.
193. A winter sports resort in Switzerland.
194. Hector is still dealing with the heartache of having lost his sisters Alice and Edie.
195. Alford Cooley died on July 19, 1913, of tuberculosis. He had traveled from Silver City to Providence, R.I., to avail himself of a new treatment, injections of turtle vaccine. It proved ineffective. *New York Times,* July 21, 1913.

considered the honorable thing to do. John offered to go to Africa, where there were opportunities for a mining engineer, but Bob simply asked him to promise never to be alone with Isabella. Isabella would never have considered leaving a sick man, the father of her children, nor would John have suggested it.

Isabella became more circumspect about John when writing to Eleanor, but by then Eleanor realized how important Greenway was to her friend. Isabella must have been quietly pleased when Eleanor wrote to say she liked the man Isabella had fallen in love with.[196]

49 East Sixty-Fifth Street   Sept. 23 [1913]
Isabella dearest,

I lunched with Auntie Bye today & Mr. Greenway was there & he told me Martha had not been getting strong as quickly as you would like to have her. Wouldn't it do her good to come East? I believe there is a wonderful man at Johns Hopkins if you cared to bring her or send her to me in Washington & the climate there, not being very cold, might be good for her. If you can get away you know what a joy a visit from you two would be but if that is impossible & you want to send her with a nurse I will take just as much care of her as I would of my own & it would be such a pleasure to have her. Do think it over & just telegraph if you want to come. Dearest Isabella I can't bear you to have this to worry you & I do hope Bob is well as possible.

I am here off & on now getting the house ready to rent & sending things to Washington so you'd best send me word here.

I was so glad to meet Mr. Greenway at last & I like him so much.

Love to Bob & Martha & Buzz.

      Ever your devoted
        Eleanor

Isabella, who had been preoccupied with Martha's illness, apologized for being a poor correspondent. The death of a neighbor girl had reminded Isabella of the precariousness of young life, but Isabella had been cheered by the first visit from her uncle Frank Cutcheon, the man she looked to as a father, and his wife, her aunt Sallie (Patty Selmses's sister). Although her previously giddy descriptions of John Greenway's doings were now muted, still Isabella was delighted that her closest friends had become acquainted.

196. Miller, *Isabella Greenway*, 71–2.

Cat Cañon   Oct. 1st 1913
Beloved Eleanor—

Three of your letters are in front of me—unanswered!! Fancy how deep is my disgrace—& yet somehow I know you'll understand—& forgive—knowing me. Your last letter went direct to our hearts—the one offering to take Martha & care for her as tho she were your own. Because we know you mean every word of it. Bless you—& of course you are *the one* person we would trust her too without a worry—& you know that we'd ask you to take her if it seems best. She has been a very sick little girl.

It began about July 10st [evidently she wrote July 1st, then corrected to July 10]. There were all sorts of worries as to its being subacute appenditis etc. Typhoid was soon given up—We'd a good Dr. from El Paso & *3 local* [doctors] To make a long story short—*Time* has proved it to be a *form* of colitis which many babies hereabouts have had—an unusual no.—on account of the delayed rains & upset seasons. Many have died.

Martha's recovery was very slow—& up till this last week, we have been much bothered by a slight temperature. I had made up my mind to keep her here (while she was evidently gaining a little) until we had had at least a month of *cold* weather to see if that affected her temperature. Just after (a week ago) a very excellent Dr. from El Paso looked her over thoroughly—with Dr. Bullock[197] & quite laughed at me—they said her lungs were grand![198] She was well nourished & in good condition. Her tummy & abdomen quite normal & that, if anything, she was suffering from "over careful nursing."

Ye gods be praised what a good side to have erred on—& now the cold snap has broken her temperature & I shall try letting her be more normal all the time. I've had her day & night, for a month—for my own entire satisfaction. However, if there is the slightest setback or question I am ready to move her any moment. The Dr. said it would be a mistake not to let her present progress here alone[199] & there was no necessity for a change as things are.

I have long had it in my mind that, by hook or crook, I must see you & yours—& if one dares look so far ahead—? You might see us walking into Campobello next summer for a quiet night—& meantime I am praying something will take Franklin to the Pacific Coast this winter or Spring—via Cat Cañon. We'd a trained nurse for Martha during Aunt & Uncle's visit so

197. Dr. E. S. Bullock, director of the Silver City Cottage Sanatorium.
198. She was worried that in spite of all their precautions, the children might contract TB.
199. The doctor thinks they should not move her while she is making progress.

that we could jaunt them about the country. *Nothing ever was so satisfactory to me as their real visit.* I feel 20 years younger.

Bob is having a bit of a reaction after so much heartache over Martha & is taking it easy. Nothing serious—& we can think of nothing but the poor little [Evan] Frazier Campbell family, out in the Burro Mts—who lost their only little girl—after a week's illness. Eleanor, it was the most heartbreaking—& I thought of you so much—all you had told me about the loss of your baby—& the little Mother seemed to get some comfort from what I told her. We had seen a lot of, & become very fond of this couple. He is Scotch & she Kentuckian & he is head engineer for the Phelps Dodge people.

This one little girl was quite *wonderful*—& I don't think I'll ever see anything as touching as her passing—& the way she had the adoration of all that mining camp. Rough Mexicans Storemen Foremen & all crying like children. Nancy (her Mother) was almost terrifying in her control—they have gone to Scotland (he has a shooting[200] in Argyllshire[201]) & we'll miss them awfully—but hope they'll be back in two months.

It was so hard out there away from all family & old friends. I was there before & after & Nancy let me bring the little casket into town & down to Deming—while they prepared hurriedly for Scotland & followed [me] by motor. I did think of you so constantly—the Dr. had been staying with them & everything possible was done. He is just back from Berlin & works periodically under Dr. Cragie in NY. It was he who came on here & saw Martha. In a strange way one does come face to face with life—out here if not the world.

Dear, this is a poor & sad answer to your letter. As a matter of fact we are uproarious, in sound, since M & B are playing together again—& I am a professional runner after running beside the big bronco with a leading rope while they *canter* bareback.[202] Thro this chaotic summer Bob and I have made a fine start on a really worthwhile work—the compiling of Bob's mother's letters for typing (mounting the illustrations)[203] & putting the whole in an adjustable binding—They cover 20 years—& hold their own among any published

---

200. The right to shoot game over a particular area.

201. The second largest Scottish county, covering 115 miles north to south down the west coast of Scotland. http://www.ancestralscotland.com/regions-and-counties/a-ti-ll-satt/argyllshire.

202. At seven and five, the Ferguson children were good equestrians, able to ride a horse bareback when it was going very fast.

203. Before the widespread use of cameras, educated women often learned to draw. Bob's mother may have sent drawings in some of her letters.

letters I ever read—in wit & human description. *They are delightful*—but couldn't be published this generation.

Dear love to you *all* & particularly Eleanor—& Goddaughter. I am so glad you liked John. He's such a *true* friend & had been anxious to meet you for a long time.

PS Woman like [like a typical woman] I find I have forgotten everything of importance—the plaid arrived safely in ample time. Thank you for all the trouble. Bob always enjoys Collier's Books & have either of us thanked you for "Germany & the Germans"? I am dying for "Fortitude"[204]—if you some day have time & I don't ever see when that will be—? & don't send it otherwise or have it on your mind. My dear I just picture the furniture & other moving between NY & Washington!!—& wish I could help.

Please say if the maid has made her winter arrangements yet?[205] For I could almost surely place her in California & will write to ask of any needing a nurse today. I think I know the very woman who has a nurse for her tiny baby & wished very much to get a reliable one for the 3 & 5 year olds. The Santa Barbara climate is *perfect*. I'll write & let you know in case your nurse is still undecided—& let me say *how much* I value your having thought of our possible needs. It's the rarest thing to be amply supplied [with servants] as we are at present & I always say [that you should let me know] if you know of any such—wanting to come[.]

[W]e've a French maid!—with a strange human & humorous side that enables her to sit on this hillside & do the tent work sewing for the children & us. She really is an endless comfort. Lately she has slept in this tent with me & nursed me thro' a beginning of grippe[206][,] caked me with hot oil and flannel jackets & thinks it great fun to "gather wood"—! Paulina is the *worst* about writing—as I told her yesterday. Caroline[,] Olivia[,] E Hoyt[,] & Laulie & Corinne[207] are so good about letters. How did you think Mrs. Anna [Eleanor's Auntie Bye] [was]?

Private[:] Bob has chuckled over some letters of Sir Cecil Spring Rice's[208]—of 15 to 20 years back. Quite too good to be true—tho he might not think so!!

204. See the following letter from ER.
205. Evidently Eleanor had asked if Isabella could use a maid who was leaving the Roosevelts because she needed a better climate. Isabella did not, but suggested friends who might.
206. "Grippe" means "flu."
207. Caroline Astor Phillips, Olivia Cutting, Elizabeth Hoyt, Laura "Laulie" Chanler, and Corinne Robinson were all friends of Isabella's when she was in her teens, and remained her close friends for life.
208. Presumably to Bob's mother.

That fall, Eleanor prepared to move to Washington, D.C., where, she said, her life in politics "really began." Before she went, she consulted yet again with her Auntie Bye. The Roosevelts would live in her Washington house, and they would inherit all of her friends and neighbors, the inner circle of Washington political society.[209]

49 East Sixty-Fifth Street   Oct. 4th [1913]
Dearest Isabella,

I can't help being sorry that we're not to have you & Martha but oh! My dear I am so thankful she is better. What a very anxious time you & Bob have had & here I was thinking Martha was well long ago. Now, Cousin Susie [Parish] tells me she knew all about it but she never wrote me a word about it.

Two days were spent at Orange this week & Cousin Susie looks more rested than ever but is much worried because she [o]ccasionally does not sleep at night, of course I'm not surprised as she dozes for an hour after her breakfast in bed, rests from two to four & again before dinner & goes to bed at ten promptly! I think however she is getting very strong & so perhaps it is all well!

I've seen Auntie Bye almost every day that I've been in town & she has a strange Jew-German scientist doctor that she really believes in. His treatment is very trying but it seems to be helping her & she was much worse when she came down so she was ready to hear anything. She goes home Sunday for two weeks & then returns to him for a time. Of course she is always wonderful & I have loved seeing her. I'm sending you "Fortitude."[210] She thinks it interesting too & the best novel of the moment in spite of its obvious defects. Don't be discouraged by the gloom for the end makes up for it all![211] By the way I met Sir Cecil & Lady Spring Rice at Auntie Bye's one day, but I think I told you didn't I? She is miserable & has to take a rest cure at Dublin for a month.

How wonderful Mrs. Ferguson's letters must be & how I wish sometime I could see some of them. It must be very interesting & absorbing work for you & Bob.

209. Roosevelt, *This is My Story*, 156.
210. Hugh Walpole, *Fortitude*. New York: George H. Doran Company, 1913.
211. What happens at the end? After the hero overcomes countless hardships, "we leave him on his Cornish headland, with the rain and wind beating upon him, this prayer on his lips: 'Make me a man—to be afraid of nothing, to be ready for everything. Love, friendship, success—to take it if it comes—to care nothing if these things are not for me. Make me brave! Make me brave!'" Hildegarde Hawthorne, "Fortitude: Hugh Walpole's Powerful Novel Has A Striking Theme," *New York Times Book Review*, June 8, 1913, 339.

I went last night to the good-bye dinner given to Uncle Ted[212] & it was a most wonderful ovation. It was however "a feast of reason & a flow of soul"[213] for most people got no food! The people came in crowds & put in chairs all around the tables so that the waiters couldn't serve & so they just gave up & retired. Uncle Ted made a splendid speech chiefly on the recall of judicial decisions,[214] absolutely clear & logical & yet very amusing.

All kinds of people were there & there was much enthusiasm. I wished Franklin could have heard him but I was glad he did not hear Mr. Gifford Pinchot who made what I felt was an ill advised & dangerous speech[215] & I like him so much that I felt quite grieved. A Mr. Robbins[216] from Illinois also spoke well & then Sen. Beveridge[217] closed the evening but it was so late that I left before he began. Teddy Robinson seemed to be doing wonderful work in the State & I believe made a splendid speech at Rochester. Helen is a great help & looks so pretty & everyone adores her.

212. Theodore Roosevelt was about to set sail for Brazil, where he would take part in the Roosevelt-Rondon Scientific Expedition to explore the headwaters of the Rio da Duvida, or River of Doubt, later renamed Rio Roosevelt. Kermit, twenty-four, at his mother's urging, was postponing his wedding in order to go with his father. Miller, *River of Doubt*, passim.

213. The phrases "feast of reason" and "flow of soul" come from Alexander Pope's "Satires and Epistles of Horace Imitated," Book 2, Satire 1.

214. Some Progressives favored citizens' right to recall or overturn judicial decisions. Unlike the direct primary and the referendum, which were popular, the idea of recall was very controversial because of the traditional independence of the judiciary, and it was never widely adopted.

215. In his speech, Pinchot attacked what he termed "the magnate system." The *New York Times* quoted Pinchot as saying, "It is not pleasant to realize, but it is true, that our country is governed and controlled for the benefit of a small class.... the one great task which lies before us is to replace the magnate system by a system frankly and effectively directed to make the many prosperous and secure, and not the few rich." "2,000 Bull Moose Speed the Colonel," *New York Times*, October 4, 1913: 1, 2. Although Eleanor worked her entire life to help those at the bottom of society, she nevertheless perceived Pinchot's blunt remarks as "dangerous."

216. Raymond Robins (1873–1954) "was a lawyer, social worker, lecturer and politician...passionately involved in a wide variety of progressive causes." He took part in Progressive party politics, along with his wife, Margaret Dreier Robins, the president of the National Women's Trade Union League, 1907–1922. http://www.nyu.edu/library/bobst/research/fales/coll_mss/robins/erseries4.htm.

217. Sen. Albert Jeremiah Beveridge (1862–1927) served in the U.S. Senate from March 1899 to March 1911, and was chairman of the National Progressive Convention at Chicago in 1912. He was an unsuccessful Progressive party candidate for governor of Indiana in 1912, and for U.S. Senate in 1914. http://bioguide.congress.gov/scripts/biodisplay.pl?index=B000429.

My maid has made no arrangements yet & she's staying on to help me with the house here till Nov. 5th or 8th. So do write me if you hear of a place for her. She is so good & reliable though not brilliant & has had good training with children under nurse. We have thought we might go West to the Pacific in Nov. & I could have taken her out but Franklin arrived to-night & says we are not to go till Spring anyway. In one way I'm glad for I felt we ought to settle down in Washington & begin to really live there as soon as possible but I did want to see you all & we were going to stop. We may go to New Orleans in late Nov. & I'm wondering if there'd be a chance of your meeting us there for a few days, do think it over.

Mr. Greenway had told me about the poor Frazier-Campbells & all you were to them. How much it must have meant to them to have you dear. The older I grow the more I realize that one comes face to face with life, if one lives at all, in the remote spots of the earth as well as in the more crowded ones & you are one of those who live other people's lives as well as your own & that's why we all love & depend on you. Next summer does seem a long way off but of course you know Campo would be entirely blissful if you & Martha & Buzz could come & if only Bob could come too!

I move to Washington for all except weekends on the 15th & the chicks join us on Nov. 8th about. This house is not rented yet but we hope to get it off our hands by the 20th.

Our dearest love to Bob & the two chicks & to you.

> Ever devotedly
> Eleanor

Although Eleanor and Franklin enjoyed contacts with Auntie Bye's friends, Eleanor also had to pay innumerable tedious social calls. However, this enabled her to meet almost everyone in Washington of importance. This networking, as we would call it today, would serve her in good stead in the future. The Roosevelts also entertained a good deal at formal dinners, informal Sunday night suppers for kindred spirits, and lunches to which FDR often brought people at the last minute. Many people admired Eleanor's achievements, but few knew they came at a cost: she suffered from migraine headaches. Meanwhile, she continued her program of self-education, reading books on history, economics, and international affairs.[218]

218. Cook, *Eleanor Roosevelt*, I, 207–11.

In spite of her growing interest in politics, Eleanor still felt that "the whole of my life remained centered in the family."[219]

1733 N Street Washington DC   Jan. 1st [1914]

Dearest Isabella,

Many, many thanks for what promises to be a very interesting book.[220] I'm saving it to read in my lonely evenings when Franklin goes to Haiti, San Domingo & Guantanamo, a 3 weeks trip which is to begin on the 21st! The children & we also are very grateful for the delicious honey & Anna wrote Martha & Bobby.

Our Xmas was spent at Hyde Park. Hall, Margaret & baby Henry were with us & Helen & Teddy [Robinson] & their children next door at Rosey's. Julia [Newbold] Cross & her two at the Newbolds'. So it was quite a gathering. The coasting[221] was splendid & my chicks are too depressed at being back here again! I did wish Martha & Buzz could have joined the coasting party. I suppose you entertained the entire neighborhood & were very busy & I hope very happy.

Are not you coming East soon? Cousin Susie [Parish] told me you were & if you do you will come here for a few days won't you? I can offer you a little 2 x 4 room but oh! Such a warm welcome. I fairly hunger for a sight of you. I would go West to see you while F. is away if you don't come East but Elliott is not really strong yet & the doctors all say this winter will be a critical time so I know I ought to stay home & watch him myself. Perhaps in the Spring I can go.

We stood & shook hands with some 500 hundred people this afternoon at the Daniels until Franklin began introducing me as Mr. Roosevelt! Now he has gone wearily to dine with Siamese minister to meet a Siamese Prince while I am enjoying a peaceful evening at home. On the whole we are fairly gay now & I am horribly busy but it won't last long as Franklin leaves so soon. Love & happy New Year to you all & do write.

  Devotedly

   Eleanor

You know Pauline [Merrill]'s little Wm. was operated for mastoid.[222] He is doing well but we can't feel quite easy til it heals & it breaks my heart to see him with bandaged head.

219. Roosevelt, *This is My Story*, 156.
220. Not known, probably a Christmas present.
221. "Coasting" means sledding.
222. Before the advent of antibiotics, mastoid surgery, an operation to remove disease from the bone behind the ear, was one of the most frequent surgeries performed. http://www.entusa.com/mastoid_surgery.htm.

Although Eleanor dutifully paid the calls that were expected of Washington wives, some women, notably Eleanor's cousin, Alice Roosevelt Longworth, refused to waste time on them.[223] Alice, Eleanor wrote, was "too much interested in the political questions of the day to waste her time calling on women who were, after all, not important." Eleanor was "appalled" by, but probably also a bit envious of, such self-assurance. The calls were extra irksome at this time, because Eleanor was pregnant again and "feeling miserable."[224] To help with her increased duties, Eleanor hired a part-time social secretary, Lucy Page Mercer, a well-educated young gentlewoman of twenty-three in reduced circumstances.[225]

1733 N Street Washington DC   Jan 5th 1914
Isabella dearest

Just a line to tell you the honey arrived & has already filled the children's souls with joy & Franklin & I enjoy it almost as much! Anna wants me to thank you too for her magazine & we are planning to read it together but as she only got back from Hyde Park last night we've not had much time. They had wonderful coasting & F. got some ice boating so the holidays at Hyde Park were entirely successful.

Life goes smoothly with us & I'm beginning to catch up with my calls & to stay at home every week[226] which is a pest!

I'm afraid Mr. Chanler[227] is pretty ill. They have the house almost opposite us & he has a nurse & leads an invalid's life. Cousin Susie [Parish] seems to be quite herself & very busy & your Mother writes she is better & going to you soon. I do hope Bob improves & that you can rest a while for it must have been such work to get in order.

I'll write again soon, this was just to take you both our thanks & love & a happy New Year.

Devotedly
E.R.

223. Alice's husband, Nicholas Longworth, had lost election in 1912. He had been U.S. Representative from Ohio, 1902–1912, but lost his seat during the split in the Republican party. He would be re-elected in 1914, and would serve as Speaker of the House, 1925–1931.
224. Roosevelt, *This is My Story*, 157–58.
225. Pottker, *Sara and Eleanor*, 163.
226. Stay at home to receive calls. See ER to IG, January 11, 1911.
227. Lewis Stuyvesant Chanler, Democratic assemblyman of Barrytown, N.Y. An Astor, Chanler was FDR's distant cousin by marriage. FDR said Chanler was his "ideal of a public man" before 1910. "Eventually they had a falling-out." Ward, *A First-Class Temperament*, 104, 110, 198–99 n. 13.

Ethel [Roosevelt Derby] has been in the hospital but is now getting into the new house.

Isabella, too, was leading a very busy life. In December 1913, Mammy, by then in her mid-fifties, became critically ill and was sent off to Patty, who was then in New York City, to undergo an appendectomy and a hysterectomy. Isabella, without her two mainstays, had full responsibility for nursing Bob and teaching the children. Bob noted that, in addition, she was "Chinese gardener, cook, housemaid, chicken-woman, irrigator, pump-man, chauffeur and store-keeper."[228]

Nevertheless, Isabella still had energy to attend a wedding dance at the Burro Mountain mines, where she "ragged . . . and tangoed and one-stepped" all night, much to Bob's disapproval.[229] It is amusing, therefore, to see Isabella trying to impress her more serious, older friend with how sedate and responsible she is.

Frank Cutcheon, during his visit, had persuaded the Fergusons, who were still living in tents, to build a house, as an investment and as a permanent home for the children. At the end of 1913, Bob and Isabella filed a claim to homestead fifty acres on Burro Mountain, a picturesque site at an elevation of 6,660 feet, beside a creek, surrounded by western pine forest.[230]

By January 1914, Isabella had read *Fortitude,* the book Eleanor mentioned in her October 4, 1913 letter. For Christmas, Eleanor sent new books, including H. G. Wells' *The Passionate Friends.*[231] Isabella's interest in a book about passion and friends—apparently soon after John Greenway's confession that he had fallen in love with her—is understandable. Isabella had regarded John as one of her "pleasant neighbors" in 1911. By January 1914, however, her concept of friendship between a man and a woman had undergone a profound transformation. What might she have thought when she read Wells's observation: "There are no universal laws of affection and desire, but it is manifestly true that for the most of us free talk, intimate association, and any real fellowship between men and women turns with an extreme readiness to love."[232]

228. RHMF to Frank Cutcheon, May 23, 1914, FC.
229. Miller, *Isabella Greenway,* 73.
230. Homesteaders received free land from the U.S. government if they improved it and lived on it for three years.
231. H. G. Wells, *The Passionate Friends.* New York and London: Harper & Brothers, 1913.
232. Ibid., 153.

Eleanor also sent an unnamed book by John Galsworthy[233] and Theodore Roosevelt's *History as Literature and Other Essays*.[234] These, and other volumes, provided Isabella with diversion and education "365 evenings of the year." Isabella's letters gradually became more structured, a change possibly due to the quality of her nighttime reading.

Cat Cañon   [Jan 1914]

Dearest Eleanor,

Bob & I feel you never should have thought of our Cañon Christmas this year at all. For *we* do think constantly of what your days & nights must be. Your letters have been a perfect joy to us & we have read & reread them. Bob was most particularly delighted with the long one you sent him—you dear soul—who helps us defy time, distance absence & all those substantial pasts of friendship.

Thanks to your good thoughtfulness we have many a treat ahead—in these books—which do count more than anything else in camp & on the 365 evenings of the year. We find we are too content setting to them with never a stir of a desire to join the community merry making. Tangoing, turkey trotting etc. They are at it by daylight & after dark—regardless of babies

233. John Galsworthy, English novelist (1867–1933) and author of *The Forsythe Saga* trilogy. The first volume, "The Man of Property," was published in 1906, and the final volume, "The Inn of Tranquility" appeared in 1912. Galsworthy had published four other novels prior to 1914. Harvey, ed., *Oxford Companion to English Literature*, 320.

234. Published by Charles Scribner's Sons in 1913, the book is a compilation of eleven essays and speeches. The *New York Times* listed it as one of the best 100 books of 1913 (two books by TR made the list; the other was his *Autobiography*). "The 100 Best Books of the Year," *New York Times Book Review*, November 30, 1913, 664. *History as Literature* reflects Roosevelt's enormous breadth of interest. A remarkable essay, "The Ancient Irish Sagas," is an analysis of Irish fairy tales, some of which feature young women, including "Emer, the daughter of Forgall the Wily, who was wooed by Cuchulain" and who "had the 'six gifts of a girl'—beauty, and a soft voice, and sweet speech, and wisdom, and needlework, and chastity" (286). There are less demure characters. "Such was the famous warrior-queen, Meave [Maeve], tall and beautiful, with her white face and yellow hair, terrible in her battle chariot when she drove at full speed into the press of fighting men, and 'fought over the ears of the horses.'" Queen Maeve claimed what Roosevelt called "liberty in morals." She demanded of her king "an exact equality of treatment according to her own views and on her own terms; the three essential qualities upon which she insisted being that he should be brave, generous, and completely devoid of jealousy…" (289, 290).

households business & all. It really is amusing. All of it inspired by some N.Y. & Philadelphia rest curers.[235] As Harry Lauder[236] says "It's *maar* velous."

Bob of course is most pleased to have "History as Literature." The others we have been wishing for after the reviews. I always enjoy Galsworthy & this "Passionate Friend" promises most diverting. As all Wells do. Only Eleanor dear *one* book would have given us infinite pleasure & we think you are a bad dear rascal to send all these—but we will enjoy them *endlessly*. I am still enjoying the memory of that *most* unusual & refreshing book Fortitude & thanking you for so many worthwhile hours.

Sister is just tickled with her ball of yarn (having already learned to chain stitch & means to get earnestly to work & reach the prize.

The handkerchiefs are the very loveliest & most satisfactory of all things. The fun of it all is now that Martha & Bobbie genuinely appreciate their treasures & care for them & particularly their limited wardrobe. On the strength of the hankies he got to business at once & straightened his bureau drawer beyond belief!

A year ago was very uppermost in our hearts but no one could be sad thinking of Edie [Ferguson] whose life was radiance & cheer. Evan Frazier Campbell was our only guest—& as brave facing the loss of his only little girl last summer. M & B's joy knew no limit so all was well. This is *no* letter to answer to yours. Just a scrawl from bed before breakfast. We are all confined to the tent to ward off possible colds. I hope soon to have the right teacher for them. We are coming on famously but their lessons get lost in the shuffle of inevitable interruptions to my day. Dear love & much to Franklin & the babes. Yr devoted Isabella

Bob seems very well & we're beginning to get keen about our Mt. home!

One of the best parts of our winter has been the wonderful things about *you* that pour in from every side.

Isabella decided to take the children to New England for the summer of 1914, hoping that cool weather would prevent another attack of Martha's annual illness. Although she was reluctant to leave Bob, Isabella was even more worried about Martha. Uncle Frank rented a summer house in Maine to provide

235. People who came West for their health and brought their Eastern ways with them.
236. Harry Lauder (1870–1950) was one of Scotland's "most famous entertainers, portraying the bekilted, singing Scotsman on stages throughout Britain." http://international.visitscotland.com/library/harrylauder.

a home for Isabella and the children while Patty sailed off to Europe with Eleanor's aunt and uncle, Susie and Henry Parish, to rest at the popular spa at Marienbad.[237] Finally, Isabella was close enough to make the long-hoped-for visit with Eleanor at Campobello. Eleanor, meanwhile, was awaiting the birth of their fifth child.

[Campobello]   June 27th, 1914
Isabella dearest

It was good to get your letter & know that I was to see you sometime at least but I don't feel somehow that your summer will be as entirely easy & restful as I had hoped.

I will have room for you at anytime & want you as much & as often & as long as possible. Franklin is looking up trains & boats to Eastport[238] & will let you know the best ways of coming. I fear you are having a hot trip & I only hope you left Bob feeling & looking better so you are not worrying.

We got here on Thursday & are almost settled. The weather has been cool & lovely & the sunsets glorious & I haven't seen but one old lady to speak to since I came & you can't think how I'm enjoying it! Franklin is getting here the 4th for several days & I shall be relieved to have him out of Washington awhile for the heat there has been terrific.

A heart full of love always dear Isabella.

    Devotedly
        Eleanor

237. In the Carlsbad region of Czechoslovakia. See Miller, *Isabella Greenway*, 74.
238. The town in Maine closest to Campobello.

Part Three
The World War Intrudes

The assassination of Austria's Archduke Franz Ferdinand on June 28, 1914, led to a declaration of war on Serbia by the Austro-Hungarian Empire on July 29. Interlocking treaty obligations quickly escalated the conflict. On August 1, Germany declared war on Russia. On August 2, Germany occupied Luxemburg. On August 3, Germany declared war on France. On August 4, Germany invaded Belgium. Great Britain then joined the Allied Powers, declaring war on Germany.

The outbreak of hostilities caught Patty and the Parishes in central Europe. It took them a month to reach England, where they eventually booked passage on a ship to the United States. Isabella, with no sense of the horrors that were to come, imagined they were having quite an adventure.

[Maine]   August 4, 1914

Eleanor dearest,

I seem to be heaving & pulling in your direction with no evident results! Martha is ever so much better (tho still showing signs of disorder) & Acky [Sally Cutcheon] & Miss V. are ready to take the responsibility & my hope now is start on Friday or Sat. [August 7 or 8]. Uncle upsets us awfully by writing that the war may keep him in NY.[1] How heartless it is—& do you see our beloveds[2] coming home on a warship?

The only news we have is—Mr. Parish's office has had a cable saying [they] have reached London [and hope] to sail as soon as possible—but whether it is without Mrs. P and Mother we don't know. I do feel sure somehow it must be the three of them. Uncle tries to cable [to confirm all three are coming] but is told they won't guarantee to deliver them. I am green with envy of them! Aren't you? Mr. & Mrs. & Mary Newbold were here for a night. I do love

1. The war may have created complications for Cutcheon's law clients that he had to attend to in his New York office.
2. Patty Selmes and the Parishes.

gentle (but so humorous) Mary & marvel always more at such immaturity). They had had to pay $100.00 in order to send their son $50 in England.

Kermit writes that Belle[3] is doing well. You know she is in the N.Y. hospital with typhoid & it does seem too hard. Of course you know Kerm is taking two months course in banking before being in a bank in Rio—a USA bank starting under the new laws. I'm forwarding you 2 pictures of Ronald & Co—that may amuse you. Just get them stuffed by [keep them handy] in case Bob wants them for a scrapbook.

Dearie—this has been an early morning outburst over nothing much. It simply means I grow more impatient to see you—who are ever more vividly with me day & night than any other. Hug Anna & kiss the family round & round.

> Ever yours devotedly
> Isabella

I have all the timetables & your letters of information by me—so don't bother further. I will do whatever seems to give Acky the greatest comfort!

Bob's news satisfactory tho' I know he's to thin. The house [is] practically done.

Isabella went to Campobello alone, possibly because Martha's health was still not robust. She and Eleanor spent several happy days together. The day Isabella departed from Campobello, Franklin returned—just in time, it turned out, as the baby arrived on August 17, earlier than expected. "Never again will I trust her mathematics!" Franklin wrote Isabella afterwards.[4] The couple named the boy Franklin D. Jr., to honor the baby they had lost. Eleanor and Isabella cherished the time they had snatched from family responsibilities to be together.

The day before Franklin arrived at Campobello, he had announced a seemingly impulsive decision to seek the Democratic nomination for the U.S. Senate.[5]

---

3. Kermit had married Belle Willard, the daughter of the American ambassador to Spain, in 1914 after his trip down the Amazon.
4. Ward, *A First-Class Temperament*, 250.
5. Franklin announced his decision to run on August 13, and the primary took place on September 28, 1914. According to an unnamed, inside source, the actual winning of the nomination was "a secondary consideration," while the real goal was to help wrest control of state and county Democratic organizations from party bosses. "Hennessy Launches Anti-Murphy Fight," *New York Times*, August 14, 1914: 12. Franklin was soundly beaten and continued in his position as assistant secretary of the Navy.

Post Office Campobello Island NS   Sept 19 [1914]
Via Eastport Me.

Isabella dearest, I think I haven't written since you were here! I have lived over in thought during these long quiet weeks our talks & seeing you meant so much to me. It was dear of you to come & I know it must have been an effort to come so far & leave the children. I'm so glad Laura[6] & Lorraine got to you & Franklin did so enjoy seeing you.

The baby is doing so well & is such a darling soft bundle with dark hair which is such a phenomenon we can hardly get over it. All the chicks are delighted with him but Elliott has taken him under his protection & calls him "my brother" & tells the others how they should treat him! Anna & James talk much of you & I'm so pleased that you're a real person to them at last & they really feel you're *their* friend.

The lovely pink blanket is much in use & this is such a cold spot now that Miss Spring[7] blesses anyone who made the baby anything warm. Maria[8] is leaving tomorrow taking Anna & James & the rest of us go Oct. 1st but I shall stay in N.Y. at 47 E. 65th St. (Tel. 3437 Plaza) from Oct 2nd to the 7th or 8th so let me know when you are in town. I had another such dear letter from Bob since the baby came. Thank heavens! the Allies seem to be gaining & I only hope peace will come soon. Franklin is campaigning hard & enjoy-ing it!

Ever so much love dearest.

> Devotedly,
> Eleanor

At the end of the summer, Isabella and the children went to New York City to take their furniture out of storage to be shipped to their new house. Isabella's four years of living in tents were coming to a close. She spent time at her aunt and uncle's place on Long Island, and she saw old friends in New York City. She also hoped to see Eleanor when Eleanor returned from Campobello.[9]

6. Probably Laura Astor Chanler (1887–1984), a cousin of the Roosevelts and close friend of Isabella. Laura and Isabella had been debutantes together in 1904–1905. Laura later married M. Lawrence White, the son of noted architect Stanford White. *New York Times,* June 20, 1916: 11. She was a sculptor.
7. Blanche Spring, a trained nurse who took care of the Roosevelt children as babies. She became very close to Eleanor. Cook, *Eleanor Roosevelt,* I, p 178.
8. Probably a servant.
9. Miller, *Isabella Greenway,* 75.

Locust Valley, Long Island   [early autumn 1914]

Eleanor dearest

It's I who have been kicking myself for not having chatted with you on paper from time to time these weeks when I've pictured you on your enchanted island surrounded by the most wonderful family in the world! I've been looking steadily for any children approaching them in interest & attraction & have met none. —& now I pray you are getting in fine shape & ready for your winter training![10] & I am counting on seeing you [in New York City] between the 2nd & 8th [of October]—and have the telephone no. & all tucked carefully away.

I know I told you about Laura [Chanler] & my surprise visit to the Cuttings. Our next excitement was meeting Mother in NY. In the first flush of the excitement she & Mrs. P[arish] looked well, but in Mother's case, one realized afterwards what she has been thro'—for she's very tired after the strain of decisions [that had] to be made etc.[11] & I am tremendously impressed by the *real* things that she came face to face with & that have evidently made a deep mark.

Then we had such a happy family gathering at York [New York?] such as we haven't had since I was married[,] & pleasantly broken by Elizabeth Hoyt & Olivia separately. I feel as tho' I had found them both all over again & it's nothing short of thrilling to realize how almost every friend has taken the *best* out of the years & is marching so vigorously ahead—but all this when we meet.

Then Elizabeth & I did a school girl trick in going down to Beverly hoping to find Caroline home the one night that I could be away—but she alas postponed her return one night! But I wouldn't have missed it for words—Seeing the most adorable pink baby receiving[12] quite alone on a sunlit porch! & then her house is a delirious dream—full of dignity & yet ever so personal—then a few days with Olivia & a general family removal.

Mother M & B & self to Concord Mass for 3 days with 91 year old grandmother [Selmes]—& yesterday to NY & tonight here! & tomorrow I hurl myself into the packing & curtain choosing etc. Stopping at 147 East 36th St.[13] except for Sundays here. Martha is splendid & so is B & Bob's news "all to the good." & its ever so exciting to think of gathering together the material makings of a home.

10. Recover from childbirth and get ready to resume her responsibilities as the wife of the assistant secretary of the Navy.
11. Probably having to plan how to leave Czechoslovakia and get back to the States.
12. Receiving company. Babies were often left to nap on porches to get fresh air.
13. Probably the Cutcheons' house.

Mother saw Hector outside of London & he is splendid. Vigorous & *simple* & hopes to have his men ready for the Continent in 3 weeks.[14] Miss Christie[15] called me yesterday that all was well with Bob's mother after being thrown out of her pony carriage. My love to you—Dearest of all.

>Your devoted
>
>Isabella

I saw a lot of Kermit & admire him as never before. He's had terrible times.[16]

In addition to visiting all her old friends, Isabella saw Eleanor at Hyde Park, but the pair spent less time together than they had hoped for. Isabella also reconnected with Miss Thorpe, the baby nurse who had helped her when the children were born.[17] Isabella was looking for the reassurance of a trained nurse for Martha's recurrent illnesses, as well as help with the children's education, since Mammy had gone back to Kentucky to recuperate from her operation. Miss Thorpe agreed to travel to New Mexico with Isabella and the children. Over the next six months, Miss Thorpe and Isabella would become very dependent on each other for emotional support in that isolated locale. Bob, the only other adult, was increasingly depressed and withdrawn.

The women and children found the new house finished when they arrived in New Mexico on October 19.[18] Although happy with their new home, Bob and Isabella nonetheless were deeply disturbed by war news. Bob's family was in Great Britain and his brother would soon be fighting. The Fergusons often felt frustrated by the apathy of many Americans, and by the country's woeful lack of war preparedness.

Tyrone, Grant County   Dec. 11, 1914
Eleanor dearest

Little did I think that [last meeting] was to be our "Good-bye" for the winter season. You were so miserable with your cold & I so tired I couldn't "think or walk articulately!" & it was so late I didn't dare ask for a peep of the new boy—Well such is N.Y. & if anything could make me more grateful for Campobello than I was—that evening did.

14. Presumably the Lovat Scouts.
15. Evidently a Ferguson servant or family friend with recent news of Bob's mother.
16. Possibly because of his wife's illness.
17. Miss Thorpe's first name is unknown. She was known as "Wawa" by the Fergusons.
18. Miller, *Isabella Greenway*, 75–76, 79.

I don't believe any time ever saw me so ready & inspired to live as after that delightful understanding time with you—at Campo—dearest—& I feel very guilty when I think that it was too near the arrival & you oughtn't to have been bothered. Then I have the picture of you that day at the Belmont [races?] when you looked as though you did at 19!! You see one goes over & over the times that count away off here in our own bit of the moon.

Bob looked awfully tired when I returned but has picked up steadily & so evidently enjoys the house & the fruit trees & planting and all. It is ever so pretty & more homelike every day. The greatest compliment our big room has had was from one Miss Cunningham of Boston who stopped a night & declared we might have been occupying it for generations! It is filled with all possibilities that I could have dreamed of for a home for M. & B. in which to make their start. & I am so satisfied that, for the present it is the right step.

Miss Thorpe is a perfect joy—so very good with M & B who adore her & a real pleasure to live with—in such isolation. The children are tremendously improved in health & behavior! By routine & *home*!! life [home life]—& our lesson[s] progress at quite a pace & soon we are to go to Silver for a few days to be in our class at the Normal School—for stimulation—there you have our small circle in its simple but none the less urgent objects—& at every turn of the day and way do I long for you & look for the day when you will come. You really can rest here—& someday I think the children will get a lot out of it. Yours! Bless them.

Of course the war is our only thought. We talk, dream, & live it. Day & night. Do you feel as convinced as the administration that "we are ready"—or don't you feel there is need to be ready? I hope Franklin may take the bull by the horn & demand & work for an adequate navy in the face of all disapproval as Admiral Fisher[19] did. Fortunately in time & regardless of the disapproving public. The smug complacency of the country at large gets awfully on my ignorant nerves somehow. And we seem to be taking little advantage of the moment's lull & relying too much to the response to a crisis.[20]

Strangely enough (even away out here) the consciousness of a new era is dawning & the instinct for thrift & non indulgence is having its influence. The letters from the women in England are almost more courageous to my mind than the men. Knitting must be a poor occupation with all one's boys at the front. & yet they write as tho' they had more [men] to send! Then I

19. British Admiral of the Fleet John "Jackie" Fisher, 1st Baron Fisher (1841–1920), noted for reform of the Royal Navy.
20. Relying too much on our presumed ability to respond to a crisis.

suppose there is the middle class indifference which must be so discouraging. What a length! & you a busy woman—dear soul—this is that you may know how constantly I am with you—now & for all the years—May Martha ever be so fortunate as to love one good woman as I love you.

Some honey goes to Washington for your & Franklin's breakfasts. Wild alfalfa honey & we wish there had been time to make it ourselves! And I am sending Anna a magazine[21] that enchants Martha—if insipid in part—It just goes to the right spot & has some good stuff in it. Love to Franklin & the babies—their framed photo is ever on my dressing table.

Devotedly,

Isabella

Bob's dearest love—always—Laura [Chanler] wrote of Franklin—I think she's just doing the right thing—unattached—not needed at home & fairly strong—wouldn't you do the same? & she [will] do it splendidly if she's fortunate enough to reach the heart of things.[22] Must Ethel [Roosevelt Derby] come home?

The war placed Eleanor in a difficult position when the Roosevelts returned to Washington that fall; Franklin was part of the Wilson administration, which hoped to avoid war, while Eleanor's uncle Theodore Roosevelt felt that the U.S. should intervene. Franklin did what he could to promote preparedness, but he realized that it might cost him his job if he were too outspoken. Eleanor sympathized with Secretary of State William Jennings Bryan, a pacifist.

1733 N. Street, Washington DC   [Dec. 20, 1914]
Dearest Isabella,

Your dear letter came two days ago & was such a joy. When I think of all you must have done to get Bob rested & still have your big room look "lived in" I am overcome with shame that you should be the first to write. Our extremely utilitarian Xmas gift for use in your bath room (it washes) has not gone as I wanted to send a photograph of the baby & myself with it & they have not yet been sent but I hope to get it off to-morrow. I think we'll be going to San Francisco about March 16th & if you don't join the Phillips' &

21. *John Martin's Book: A Magazine for Little Children*, a monthly children's magazine published by John Martin's House, Inc., Publishers, 5 W. 39th St. New York [and also by] G. Bell & Sons, Ltd., York House, Portugal St., London, WC.
22. Possibly, she was working for the Red Cross.

ourselves there we'll be much disappointed but anyway we'll stop & see you either going or coming!

Our last evening in N.Y. together was certainly not a satisfaction dear but Campo was wonderful & someday we must all be there together for longer. My chicks talk of you often & when they can go & stay with you! Anna is an enterprising lady & this morning begged me to let her go out to Hall & Margaret[23] as they had sent her p.c.'s [post cards] showing the snow & the dog teams & invited her to come if I would allow it!

All except the baby had had a succession of colds since our arrival & I long for any other climate. I really think I'll leave them at Hyde Park till Xmas next year![24] The baby thrives & is adorable but I'm still nursing him which I enjoy except when I try to go out too & then he invariably wakes [on] the night I stay out latest & I return to find an unhappy baby & an infuriated nurse! My calls are being sadly neglected but I hope to catch up later! I'm so glad Miss Thorpe is a success and M & B so well.

Of course war is most in all our thoughts & the horror of it grows. We are most distinctly "not ready" & Franklin tried to make his testimony before Congress very plain & I think brought out his facts clearly without saying anything about the administration policy which would of course be unwise. We fully expect to be bounced anyway however!

I think Laura Chanler is doing just right & wish I could do the same but just now she's having hard luck. She got a holiday for Xmas & came down with chicken pox an hour after arriving here & is now quarantined! Ethel [Roosevelt Derby] I think has to come home as Dick only had 2 months leave.[25] Alice told us also that A. Edith did not enjoy being "turned into a crishe"[26] I hear from the Fred Delano's that Munro[27] is engaged to a Chicago girl & rather a speedy one but haven't heard from the family about it.

---

23. Hall Roosevelt had graduated with a degree in engineering the summer of 1914. That fall, he took "a job with the Guggenheims in the mines near Dawson City in the Yukon." Roosevelt, *This is My Story*, 165.

24. Eleanor may have been joking here—or she may have meant she would like to leave the children in Hyde Park between the family's return from Campobello at the end of the summer and the family gathering in Hyde Park at Christmas.

25. Ethel had become a nurse and served overseas in the same hospital as her husband, Dr. Richard Derby, a surgeon. http://www.theodoreroosevelt.org/life/familytree/Ethel.htm. This sentence may mean Dick had to return to his practice in the States.

26. Possibly she means "crèche," i.e., nursery. The Roosevelts had eight grandchildren, all quite small, who often visited at Sagamore Hill. Morris, *Edith Kermit Roosevelt*, 419.

27. Monroe Douglas Robinson (1887–1944), second son of Douglas and Corinne Robinson, graduated from Harvard College. In World War I, he was a captain in the 77th Division

Helen seems to be having quite a gay time with Teddy [Robinson] in Brazil but I suspect she is getting a good rest in between times & I sincerely hope so. Julia & Redmond [Cross] lunched with us last Sunday & she looks much better.

Hall writes he & Margaret will probably return to civilization in June & then start out on the next step of what looks to me like a hectic life for Margaret!

I'll write again when this busy season is over & in the meantime dear love to Bob & the chicks & to you dearest from Franklin &

Your devoted

Eleanor

It was Isabella's genius to find the fun in any situation. In this letter she gives Eleanor a droll picture of the Fergusons' various houseguests. Even on their "sidetrack," interesting people like Ruth Draper, a celebrated American monologist,[28] came to visit. Sometimes Isabella had to strain to put a positive spin on a difficult situation. Here she says Bob's "isolated" room was "delightful," obscuring the sad truth that he was becoming more and more withdrawn.

Tyrone   [January 1915]

Eleanor darling

First of all your letters are so loved & we feel all cozy & in touch again. We never feel far away but now we're not seeing you thro' the mist of imagination any more.

The photo! I'm quite childish about it dearest! Announcing loudly its the best of our Christmas & you'll find it on our living room table—the center of our family circle. [Charles] Lamb[29] says sentiment is a dish that should be served up hot—or else it is tasteless—so I must stop & wait my chance in person.

and served overseas. He married Dorothy Curtis Jordan, whom he later divorced; the couple had one daughter. http://www.rootsweb.ancestry.com/~nyhchs/legacy.html.

28. Ruth Draper (1884–1956) had been a debutante during the same season as Isabella. Both women were members of the Junior League, and performed together at the League's annual charity play performance. *New York Times*, March 3, 1905. Ruth became a celebrated performer, specializing in character-driven monologues. Among her admirers were European royalty, U.S. presidents, and stage luminaries past and present, including George Bernard Shaw, John Gielgud, and Lily Tomlin. http://www.drapermonologues.com/intro.html.

29. English essayist Charles Lamb (1775–1834).

The result of your last 10 years seems to shine in every line [of the photograph]. So lovely—so well & strong with the dignity of experience—the boy is a beauty—but I *must* stop. The handkerchiefs are in Martha & Bobbie's respective drawers—the lucky ones & they thoroughly appreciate their good fortunes & the fact that Aunt Eleanor is the most thoughtful of our big friends. Buzz here enters with a huge basket of wood! A penny a basket—He's working toward having his playhouse hauled over from Cat Cañon! School is in full swing again or they would write. We chase them *out* every spare moment.

Miss Thorpe is just the dearest most solid comfort & wonderful influence with them. They all ride now! After such sifting & sorting & 3 months constant motion we are settled except for 53 uncleaned windows which must wait the warm weather—& no curtains. I begin to believe with Mr. Choate[30] that windows were meant for air & light—& hesitate to put any [curtains] up.

A stream & rich variety of humans have diverted the domestic routine inside the 4 walls. Several came for the night of the Tyrone [officers'] mess[31] dance—the fast set of Silver! The mother of a young lady was heard to say to her 16 year old daughter "Don't forget Dearie your nighty is in Mr. Ledyard's bag"! Mr. L is the nephew (& [an] insipid Detroit youth) of Mrs. L. C. Ledyard's![32]

My view point is wholly that of a *housemaid* in judging our guests! Some use 6 towels a day. Others none & one rose at 6:30 & washed in the kitchen sink having slept on his coat for fear of mussing the pillow!—& one room was occupied by two successive guests & the wrapper on the soap never opened!! We sat down a merry ten to breakfast in the kitchen—we find that is always cozier in the early morning & I always mean to gather round the range & see the eggs poached. There's a homelike touch that I never before appreciated.

Bob's wing [of the house] is so delightful & isolated & sunny & quiet & he greatly enjoys the people when he feels like it.

Do I understand that we can hope for a glimpse of you in March & will it be at the same time the Phillips may come? Dear, just so long as *you come* that's all we care about. Suit yourself as to time—we could readily put you 4 up in comparative comfort.

30. Possibly Joseph Choate (see ER letter January 29, 1912), or his uncle, Judge William G. Choate, founder of the Choate School for Boys in 1896.
31. "Mess"—soldiers' dining hall. Soldiers had been garrisoned nearby, patrolling the Mexican border.
32. L. C. Ledyard, see ER to IG, December 13, [1908]. Isabella is shocked that a girl would put her nightgown in a man's suitcase—evidence for Eleanor of the uncouth but amusing surroundings in which Isabella lives.

Private: Mummy arrives next Monday & I am deluged with the usual warnings of Mrs. P, Mrs. D. R. etc[33] as to not abusing her! Put delicately to one who might be her cruel stepchild! This time I'm going to keep her for a year & when Mrs. P clamors next summer tell her she's in no condition to racket round—she must stay quietly at home!! How wickedness will come out! Well—[34]

Beside the two tubs are your rugs—of course running hot water in the Burro's is as marvelous to me as wireless telegraphy—& your present [the photo] is the proud *heart* of our home.

Ruth Draper comes for a week on the 17th of Feb. & we're taking the Elks hall for a performance & the *Power House* at Tyrone.[35] I[t] should be lots of fun for the whole community. Thank dear Anna for the letter I so loved. John Martin [the children's magazine] is truck [rubbish] that they don't get much but utter enjoyment out of. But a little of that is as permissible as a day in bed with a novel at our ages when we should be reading Chamberlain or Ferrers.[36] Next time she shall have the Illiad interpreted by Church[37]—Perfect & simple English.

The books you sent M & B are so lovely. We cover a good deal of ground nowadays after lunch and before bed.

A very sunny glistening world of love to you—Laden with pines & junipers & cool breezes off the snowy mt.

> Your loving
> Isabella

Eleanor continued the book chat by asking Isabella if she had read *The Pastor's Wife*.[38] The *New York Times* observed in its review that "*[T]he Pastor's Wife* has portrayed a man's world in which women are adored and revered with the same self-satisfied respect as peasants bestow on pigs."[39]

It was a tribute to the Fergusons' capacity for friendship that so many people made their way—often in wagons through snowdrifts—to their remote

33. Patty Selmes's friends Susie (Mrs. Henry) Parish and Corinne (Mrs. Douglas) Robinson.
34. Isabella resents her mother's friends thinking Isabella does not take care of her mother, especially Susie Parish, who had taken Patty to Europe and gotten her caught in a war.
35. Isabella has arranged venues for her friend to give performances.
36. Possibly British mathematician Norman Macleod Ferrers (1829–1903). The editors have been unable to identify Chamberlain.
37. Alfred J. Church, *The Iliad for Boys and Girls* (1907).
38. *The Pastor's Wife* (Garden City, New York: Doubleday, Page & Company, 1914), by Elizabeth von Arnim, whose many books would include *The Enchanted April*.
39. *New York Times Book Review*, November 22, 1914: 515, 517.

mountaintop. In 1915 they hosted nearly fifty houseguests. But they most eagerly anticipated another visit from Eleanor and Franklin, who planned to stop off on their way back from the San Francisco Exposition.[40]

In spite of her happiness at the prospect of seeing Isabella, Eleanor had not forgotten that Great Britain, where Bob's family lived, was at war.

1733 N Street, Washington, DC   Feb. 18 [1915]

Dearest Isabella,

This is only a line to tell you that I was so glad to get your long unanswered letter & that "John Martin" is a real joy to Anna! We read so much that is "good reading" I think she turns to her own magazine with a sigh of relief! Have you read "The Pastor's Wife" if not, let me know & I'll send it to Bob for it is most entertaining.

Evidently you are to have a stream of visitors this winter for I hear Corinne & Joe [Alsop] are stopping on their return from California & Caroline [Philips] on her way out, if you can bear anymore we plan to stop for a couple of days on our way back, about April 1ˢᵗ or 2ⁿᵈ. Dearest, I know you'll tell me if you find you can't have us for any reason & you can telegraph us in San Francisco after March 18ᵗʰ at the "Fairmont." Will you also tell Ruth Draper who must be with you now that, that is where we are going to stay as I promised to let her know.

I went on to New York on Sat. & will be with Cousin Susie [Parish] & please tell your Mother that she is very well. Uncle Ned was nearly 80 & he suffered much so for him it was a mercy. Of course Eddie[41] is a problem but I can't help feeling that it will solve itself in time.

I'm going to N.Y. again tomorrow for dentist & clothes etc. Then I shall be here till we leave March 14ᵗʰ.

The children are all well & the baby so sweet & I hate to leave him for a day! My love to Martha & Buzz & I'm looking forward to seeing them soon. Love to Bob, I know how anxious he is all the time, so are we all, but one just tries not to think of the horrors. Love to your Mother too.

Dearest love—

Devotedly,

E.R.

40. Officially known as the Panama Pacific International Exposition. See Miller, *Isabella Greenway*, 78.

41. Presumably ER's uncle Edward Hall, her mother's "unpredictable and alcoholic" brother. Cook, *Eleanor Roosevelt*, I, 101

Eleanor and Isabella felt responsible for not only their children but also for relatives of their parents' generation. In Eleanor's preceding letter, and Isabella's letter that follows, they share concern over Susie Parish's well-being.

Tyrone, Grant County   [March 1915]
Eleanor my dearest,

Here am I, sitting in front of [a photograph of] Anna James and Elliot—behind whom are rows of sunlit Chinese lilies. I await my turn at teaching—Miss T[horpe] having them now. Ruth [Draper] tucked away in bed & I pray getting a little rest & relaxation. She needs it woefully & seems to us ruddy m[oun]taineers a bunch of professional nerves. Mother relieved somewhat over Mrs. P's situation by a reassuring telegram from Mrs. Robinson. Bob directing Antonio [a worker?] in the arroya [irrigation ditch?] & there you have us—& our constant wish is that we had you!

Your dear letter is in my hand & we shall wait eagerly for April 1st or any other day you say will bring you—since my glimpses of you have been the best of lifes nourishment over ten years!—I needn't say how *ready* we are & how I shall wait. I've been counting on it ever since last summer but I do so wish you could see your way to stay & snatch a little rest. Couldn't you stop off on your way & join Franklin later or stay on here on your way back? It would be our happiness for many a month to come if we could feel that you had had a little rest here—& there's ample room for two couples if they are simple in their tastes & [two people] can share the same room! Caroline is stopping with us & says she's prepared to sleep in the "parlor safe!"

She comes the 10th & if you & Franklin would care to stop off on your way out it would be just as handy here [convenient for us]. But *do* in any case *stay* a while. Both of you if possible. Surely [at least] you[,] dear! & realize all the while that my heart has been set on seeing you ever since the last sight.

Yes we are reading the "Pastor's Wife" aloud in the evenings[42]—after too much depression over a Russian novel—and find it *very* diverting. I gave Ruth your San Francisco address. She is in the state of hating to have anyone mention her health *Private* but after laryngitis in Colorado Springs, she is a wreck. One is so sorry for her but such determined pluck & enterprise in

---

42. Before the age of electronic media like radio and television, families frequently spent evenings reading aloud to one another. In the Ferguson household, Martha would later recall, Bob read while Isabella and Patty sewed.

her profession (if not overdone) will get her on her feet. She seems patheti-cally [43] glad to be among old friends again.

She touched Silver City as it had never been touched! No simplest ruffian or scoundrel who didn't get the subtlest meaning of her acting—which speaks for its penetrating power. I sat dumbfounded at the progress she had made in the years since I heard her.

Now we're all off for Edith's for supper & then Ruth [Draper] is to enter-tain 250 of the miner's in the store! [warehouse?] It ought to be great fun.

Dear Soul—here is all my love.

As ever yrs

Isabella

Just had a lovely two days with Margaret Douglas—here

Important

If your connections bring you to Deming before 7:30 am on Sunday Wed. or Friday—be sure & come to *Tyrone*. If after 7:30 or, on Monday, Tue—Thur or Sat—come to Silver [City]. It's just as *easy* to meet you at either place.

The Roosevelts were traveling West because Woodrow Wilson had appointed Franklin and his friend, Assistant Secretary of State William Phillips, as fed-eral commissioners to the San Francisco Exposition.[44] Vice President Thomas Marshall, his wife, and several other well-connected Washington friends accompanied the Roosevelts and Phillipses. Although they were "immersed" in "official engagements," Eleanor enjoyed the activities as well as the sights. She was becoming less and less shy every year.[45] Still, Eleanor did not forget her dear friends on the mountaintop, and looked forward to visiting them on her way back East.

Fairmont Hotel, San Francisco   [late March 1915]
Isabella dearest,

I think I can say with a fair amount of certainty that we will get to you Saturday, April 3rd & therefore we will have to go to Silver. We take the night train Friday night from Albuquerque & get to Deming early in the a.m. I'll telegraph any change from Los Angeles on the 31st. If you want to reach me by telegraph send it to San Diego between the 27th & 30th c/o President

43. At that time, "pathetic" did not mean "pitiful," but rather "emotionally moving or stir-ring." *Webster's Dictionary*, 1923.
44. Probably members of a board that organized the Exposition.
45. Roosevelt, *This is My Story*, 166–69.

Davidson[46] or on the 1st to the Grand Canyon.[47] You mustn't think of coming to Silver to meet us. Just ask someone who has a motor to rent to meet us & we'll come over with our bags. I'm afraid we have to leave Monday 4/5 [April 5].

It's such a relief to have Caroline [Phillips] here & we're enjoying it together. You can imagine that it is quite strenuous for us as there are so many official things & we want to see the Fair besides. I'm trying to meet the leader of the Philippines Constabulary Band as I know Mrs. Selmes will want news of him for Mammy.[48] William [Phillips] says your house is too lovely & I'm longing to see it, but even more to see you all.

Devotedly,

E.R.

Eleanor and Franklin enjoyed a good, though brief, visit at the Fergusons' new homestead. Martha and Bobbie were proud and happy to know them at last. Back in Washington, Eleanor made her way amid the movers and shakers of the Wilson administration, while Isabella still struggled to build a life for herself in a remote rural community. Eleanor would later write admiringly, "Isabella was able to create the impression that life was joyous, that the burdens were not heavy, and that anyone who was not living that kind of life was missing something."[49]

Eleanor also noted that the people who worked for Isabella were willing to live in an out-of-the-way place because of their devotion and their "admiration for the gallant fight which she was waging."[50] Miss Thorpe was one such person. In that isolated spot, with Bob becoming more withdrawn, Isabella and Miss Thorpe developed a close mutual dependence. Isabella became distressed when Miss Thorpe came down with a persistent painful medical condition.

46. Exposition president G. Aubrey Davidson.
47. At the time, El Tovar was the only hotel at the Grand Canyon.
48. Soon after the United States took possession of the Philippines following the Spanish-American War in 1898, it organized a military band to perform for official and ceremonial functions of the colonial state. The Philippine Constabulary Band was composed of Filipino musicians who enlisted in the colonial paramilitary police and their African American conductor, (then) Lt. Walter H. Loving, the brother of Julia ("Mammy") Loving. The Philippine Constabulary Band toured many of America's largest cities during its heyday from 1904–1916. http://mtalusan.bol.ucla.edu/research.htm.
49. Roosevelt, *This is My Story*, 170.
50. Ibid.

[Tyrone]   April 7, 1915
Eleanor darling

What that glimpse of you means *no* words can tell—the privilege of seeing (what you so generously allow) into your life has always been the most invigorating inspiration to mine. I am utterly sincere when I say the "most."

Delicious sunshine has followed the snow flurry & the day is like something dazzling seen thro' a crystal ball.

Yesterday Dr. Minor came out *Private* & fears our long patience has been of little avail to Miss T[horpe] & says her patience (& courage) has been unlimited while things point now to some form of stone in the bladder. We pray a slight one.

I am hustling a little to be ready to leave home for a short time in case we have to go to an El Paso Hospital. She is so splendid about it all & we want to get over it as soon as possible & back here before the danger time for Martha. This is only a hug & hurried one & a heart full of love.

    Ever your devoted
        Isabella

M & B are so cunning [cute] over "knowing" Aunt Eleanor & Uncle Franklin. At the moment they are "entrenched" down the arroya having "warfare"![51] Every member of my family & household look ten years younger as a result of your blessed visit. Hugs to Anna & the boys.

Eleanor had been impressed by Isabella's effort to make a home in such an isolated spot. But she also noted that "Bob was no longer his old self, and in spite of the charm which was always his, his illness was taking its toll; and these were sad days for those who loved him and could realize what a burden Isabella was carrying."[52] Eleanor offered to lighten Isabella's load by once again shopping for clothes for the Ferguson family. When Miss Thorpe's condition proved to be very serious, and she had to be evacuated to New York, Eleanor promised to check on her for Isabella.

1733 N. Street, Washington, DC   4/30/15

Dearest, dear Isabella. Here have we been home a week and not a line gone yet to tell you how we loved our days with you. They were joy & rest for us both & for me dear to be with you & see all you do & how you meet life's many problems is always a help.

51. Playing World War I games.
52. Roosevelt, *This is My Story*, 169–70.

I ordered the dresses made for Martha as you wished but instead of blue they will be in a dust colored material, very pretty I thought, the blouse, skirt and bloomers will cost $6, making the three come to $15. I ordered a little green [dress] I especially like as a birthday present from me to Martha & I hope she can use it sometimes & that it will be becoming. I ordered at "de Pinna's"[53] for Bobby 6 dust colored short trousers like James' & they assure me they can climb barb wire fences in them. They cost $3 a piece which I think terrible but their things last better than most! I hope this meets with your approval!

Caroline & William [Phillips] are back also & she says they are rested but Martha Peters says they both seem worn out. I dine there on Sunday & they are bringing the John Saltonstalls to dine on Friday & I've asked them to bring the Higginsons here for lunch.

April 29th—This I thought had gone days ago. I'm *so* sorry. Now I hear Miss Thorpe has come to New York & I feel dreadfully for you & her. I'll try to get her address & see her in New York.

I go to Campo next week & the week after to Hyde Park with the children so I feel quite busy.

My love to all & I hope Martha keeps well.

Devotedly always.

Eleanor

Over the summer, Eleanor was at Campobello and Isabella remained in New Mexico, where she tried hard to stay upbeat while keeping the children quiet and amused, so they wouldn't overexert themselves and become ill. Even in the Burro Mountains, the Fergusons felt the impact of the war on friends and family overseas.

As usual, Isabella's letters jump abruptly from subject to subject as she shares her thoughts with her friend.

Burro Mountain Homestead   [June 1915]
Tyrone, New Mexico

Eleanor dearest I am always so guilty when I add to your list of chores—but you would feel amply repaid could you see our utter satisfaction in the new dresses (*exactly* what we want and sadly needed.) The troussers & that most enchanting little green dress—the latter entirely winning Martha's small feminine heart. It is a delightful apple blossom color and awfully dear on M.

53. A famous New York department store at the time.

The troussers just *suit* & altogether we are *so* grateful to you for solving our summer problem—& we do so realize what it means to find the time in days like yours.

Well here we are sailing toward mid summer & *I* in the one situation that I vowed I would not dare—alone—(without a trained nurse) with Martha. I believe we are doing the right thing tho' in trying a summer at home. The house is delightfully *cool* & the big room blissful—today when its 100 in the sun.

We've bought every game our memories could summon & have a great line of reading planned. Sewing etc. & stop indoors from 11 till 3—& do our riding etc. later—& picnic on the cool days. To say that if it is humanly possible to *prevent* trouble this year I mean to accomplish it—explains the filling of time.[54] It means hourly watchfulness & endlessly happy & companionable times. How heartily I wish we might have been with you—but we shall one of these days.

Miss Thorpe has been to the front indeed and suffered with the bravest. An operation proved far more serious than feared & for days she was in danger. A wire at last tells of her returning strength & we are unspeakably grateful. I've asked her to make her "home" with us regardless of "duties"—the Drs feel she should see real health again & we pray so. Mother has been on a 3 weeks motor trip with her friends the Ballards[55] thro' California & returns much rejuvenated—I hope to stop the summer [I hope she will stay here all summer]!

Bob is daily busier & stronger & the place comes to order & [he has] a promising garden. 150 chicks & turkies & wild flowers in sheets. It's most beautiful. No human comes [during the summer] & we never cross the magic line of our own domain & often it is as though we walked in a 100 year dream. Echoes of the war come trajicly home with mails. Janet [Dana][56] writes most interestingly from Dunkirk.[57]

54. Isabella means she had to amuse the children, to keep them indoors and quiet when it was hot, believing that being overheated made Martha ill.

55. Mr. and Mrs. Thurston Ballard.

56. Janet Dana, later Longcope, a debutante the same season as Isabella; both were board members of the Junior League. Janet was the granddaughter of Charles A. Dana, publisher of the *New York Sun*. She served as a nurse with the French Army in World War I. *New York Times*, June 2, 1974: 63.

57. Dunkirk, a French seaport, was shelled by German planes in the winter of 1914–15. By April 30, 1915, German guns were able to shell the city from twenty-two miles away. "Big German Gun Shells Dunkirk 22 Miles Away," *New York Times*, May 1, 1915: 1. Franklin told ER: "[E]very evening the enemy planes came over the town and bombed it and the entire population was ordered down into the cellars." Roosevelt, *This is My Story*, 193.

A world of love ever goes to you—

I am constantly questioned by M & B "Well now do you love Eleanor more than any friend you have"—more than P & I?[58] & everyone we ever heard of—& still it's E.

In New York, Miss Thorpe was diagnosed with tubercular meningitis.[59] Isabella was distraught at the prospect of losing her friend, and she was also anxious about Martha. Nevertheless, she tried to be philosophical, writing her grandmother: "As so often happens, we find ourselves obliged to mount the thing, of all others, that looked insurmountable."[60] This echoed Eleanor's motto: "You must do the thing you think you cannot do."

The outside world, too, was impinging upon their lives. On May 7, 1915, a German submarine sank a British ship, the *Lusitania*. Almost 1,200 people drowned, including 128 Americans. It would be harder and harder for the U. S. to remain neutral in the world war. On June 8, Secretary of State Bryan resigned because he thought Wilson was favoring the Allies.[61] Eleanor was glad to see him go, but admitted she admired Bryan's pacifist principles.[62]

Hyde Park on the Hudson   June 11, 1915
Isabella dear,

I was glad to hear from you & know the things had arrived & were satisfactory. It took us so long to get anything from De Pinna's that I felt you would be discouraged! I have tried to find out from Cousin Susie [Parish] where Miss Thorpe was but she doesn't know, & at last Ethel [Roosevelt Derby] tells me she is at the Woman's Hospital so I will send her some books or flowers next time I'm in N.Y. I hate to think of you starting the summer without her but I suppose having had her has fitted you better to keep Martha well. I hope all will go well.

I spent three days last week with Cousin Susie who seems remarkably well. I told her quite firmly I considered Mrs. Selmes should stay with you & I think she seems to have made up her mind to it! The trip to California must

58. More than P[a] and I [Martha or Bobbie]. Frances Doar to editors December 18, 2006.
59. Tuberculous meningitis is an infection of the meninges (membranes covering the brain and spinal cord) by the bacteria that causes tuberculosis, Mycobacterium tuberculosis.
60. IG to S. B. Selmes, June 1915, FC.
61. Ward, *A First-Class Temperament*, 297, 305.
62. Cook, *Eleanor Roosevelt*, I, 213.

have been a delightful one. Do ask her from me if Mr. Ballard is still on the Industrial Commission.[63]

We are living among "trunks" at present as the work of building goes on apace.[64] I doubt if we can return in the autumn however so I expect we will go to Fairhaven[65] from Campo. The house ought to be lovely when finished & big enough for any size family! Mama wants me to ask where you got your range [stove] & if it is satisfactory & does it burn a tremendous quantity of coal? She has to get a new one & I thought yours might be the thing for our new "hotel" as Mama calls it!

We are all much excited politically since Mr. Bryan's resignation but I haven't seen Franklin so I don't know what the future developments may be! My new governess has three brothers at the front, one wounded, so we feel the war rather close. I'm thankful to say I like her & the children seem happy all the time. Where is Hector now?

Rosy has been quite ill again & for a time we feared another operation but he looks better & seems quite well again. They are coming to Campo as they cannot go to Scotland.

I haven't been able to get to Auntie Bye but I shall go in the autumn from Fairhaven. Everyone says she is so well & can walk quite a distance now.

I leave for Campo on the 23rd & get there the 25th & I think Margaret & the baby arrive July 10th & Hall a week later. She writes the baby is doing so well & I am delighted for them.

Has Bob seen a book called "Drift & Mastery"?[66] *If* not I'll send it out for we think it very interesting.

Love to you all & as ever dear Isabella a heart full to you.

> Devotedly,
>
> E.R.

63. Thurston Ballard was on the Commission on Industrial Relations created by the U.S. Congress on August 23, 1912. The Commission studied work conditions throughout the industrial United States from 1912–1915. The chairman was Frank Walsh (it was sometimes called the Walsh Commission). "Commission on Industrial Relations, 1912–1915," *Final Report on Commission on Industrial Relations*. 64th Congress, 1st Session. Washington: GPO, 1916, 3.

64. Franklin's mother decided to expand her house at Hyde Park to accommodate the growing number of grandchildren who stayed with her, often for weeks. Pottker, *Sara and Eleanor*, 166–67. Both Franklin and his mother also wanted a house more suited to the needs of a public figure. Ward to editors, March 6, 2007.

65. Franklin's Delano grandfather's home in Fairhaven, Massachusetts.

66. Walter Lippman, *Drift and Mastery: An Attempt to Diagnose the Current Unrest*. New York: Mitchell Kennerly, 1914. Lippman, a prominent writer and a co-founder of the

At the homestead, where few visitors came during the hot summer months, Isabella wrote Eleanor long, chatty letters to create intimacy even though the two friends could not visit in person. As always, sharing books also brought them closer together. Isabella recommended a volume on the Mexican situation, which had by now deteriorated from civil war to "unmitigated anarchy," according to a later historian.[67]

Burro Mountain Homestead   [late June 1915]
Tyrone NM
Eleanor dearest

The very thought of you and the small family at Campo Bello is refreshing—I see you all—& can never cease to be thankful that I reached you last summer.

That is such a good letter you wrote—& I hasten to answer the questions.

Miss Thorpe was pathetically pleased over the flowers & your friendly thought. She has been thro' all one can physically & mentally as I will some day tell you—& has a scrap of life left on which to build—& in a way, begin over again. Her courage is dauntless—A year or more, only, can tell to what extent she may return to health—& she must stay near the big Drs. at present.

Yes, the Ballards are those of the Industrial Commission. He, rather a disgusted member, I judge. I still drag forth Mother's tales of the trip—& his amusing self. It was strenuous but awfully pleasant. Mother and Mrs. Ballard seem to have come to the *end* of their patience (after being kept waiting an endless time outside a shop for him) to enter & find him paying $8.00 for the ear drum of a whale! which he was sure would interest the school children in KY.

In a vague moment of loneliness the other day (we [Isabella and the children] were in town) Mother welcomed a passing tramp to share her tea in the big room—we usually give such a bite in the kitchen—but Mother felt sociable. "Well," said he. "What kind of a summer resort is this anyway?" "It's just our home," explains Mother. "God—It's some home," says he!

New Republic magazine, believed that "to create a minimum standard of life below which no human being can fall is the most elementary duty of the democratic state" (254). However, Lippman thought the primary focus of women should be on the home: "They must go into politics, of course, for no home exists that doesn't touch in a hundred ways upon the government of cities, states and the nation" (224).

67. Meyer et.al., *Course of Mexican History*, 516, 519.

By the way—feeling you really are a Western sympathizer I'm sending "Ruggles of Red Gap"[68]—for reading aloud it is wonderful—and a book that Walter Douglas highly recommends on the Mexican Situation,[69] called "The Political Shame of Mexico."[70] W. D. [Walter Douglas?] *is* so nice—& stops occasionally. They say it's the Sabbath—but I haven't asked "central" yet![71]

M & B at last have their play house—& are making Mr. Mitchell spend the day with them. He dressed in what appears to be black broadcloth for the event. They do keep so well [stay so healthy] & I say it in prayerful gratitude. A strong & beautiful young Texan has taken over the housework & I'm free to care for them.

Hector is shifting about in Eng—Nancy & Evan [Frazier Campbell][72] are in a "stew" if a silent Scotch temperament brooding over a problem can be described this flippantly—& are, poor souls, up against the big moment when they decide to risk their all.[73] His brother is wounded at the front—& with conscription coming I think Evan's impatience is becoming past endurance. We'll miss them more than any—& his going makes it hard for Bob somehow.—

A perfectly wonderful letter from Janet [Dana] just before she was fired out of Dunkirk after the bombardment. Now she's at Dieppe.

We would be so glad to have "Drift & Mastery"—I do turn to you as to what is worthwhile.

A world of love—A hug to the little Alaskan[74] & warmest greetings to his or her? mother.

68. *Ruggles of Red Gap*, by Harry Leon Wilson (1915). Marmaduke Ruggles is an English butler whose employer loses him in a poker game to social-climbing Americans who take him to the West.

69. The "Mexican Situation" referred to by Isabella was steadily deteriorating. In April 1914, the United States Marines captured and occupied Veracruz, Mexico—an important seaport—in order to block a large shipment of arms to Mexican President Victoriano Huerta. This action created immediate and enormous resentment against the United States. Huerta, however, did resign on July 8, 1914. The years following his ouster were "the most chaotic in Mexican revolutionary history." Meyer et. al., *Course of Mexican History*, 516, 519.

70. Edward I. Bell, *The Political Shame of Mexico*. New York: McBride, Nast & Company, 1914. Bell believed that the United States would be compelled to take control of Mexico, which never happened.

71. She was so removed from civilization that she had to call the telephone operator ("central") to find out what day it was.

72. They were the parents of the little girl who had died two years earlier.

73. As Scots, the Frazier-Campbells were debating whether to return to Great Britain.

74. Hall and Margaret Roosevelt's child. The couple had gone to Alaska for Hall's work.

I know no summer life that seems as worthwhile as yours particularly for the children.

Our days drift in writing sewing watering & a little sketching. Tonight a picnic up by the buzzards nest—& we all behave awfully when an outsider breaks in.[75]

Mr. Bryan's loss seems welcomed broadly but certainly, a negative gain in the face [of] our horizon crowding with trouble.[76]

A full blown summer day—here & filled with love & reverence for you. Much love to Franklin & Mrs. R. Hugs to Anna & all.

> Devotedly
> Isabella

160 chicks! Our own garden produce & Bob doing enough to exhaust any 2 well men—full information as to ranges [stoves] follows[77]

Although the war in Europe was growing ever deadlier, Eleanor and Isabella were preoccupied that summer with medical crises.

Franklin suffered an attack of appendicitis and was rushed to the Washington Naval Hospital for an emergency appendectomy. When he had recovered sufficiently to travel, he went to Campobello for five weeks to recuperate.[78]

Miss Thorpe, on her death bed in New York, wrote Isabella a final, unabashed love letter: "I have thought for many years my capacity for loving intensely (man or woman) was gone completely, but you have revived it, and I love you so much it frightens me."[79] Devastated, Isabella suffered indigestion and fainting spells. It helped to be able to pour out her grief to Eleanor.

---

75. She may mean they get overexcited when they do have company.
76. It is unclear what Isabella means here. She may have welcomed the resignation of Bryan, who opposed America joining the Allies (including Great Britain, where Bob's family was). But his removal might also be clearing the way for the U. S. to go to war, which she knows would have negative consequences.
77. Missing.
78. Ward, *A First-Class Temperament*, 307.
79. Miss Thorpe to IG [1915], FC. Young women in the nineteenth century often formed close emotional ties with other women. This language is characteristic of such intense friendships and should not necessarily be taken as evidence of a physical relationship. Carroll Smith-Rosenberg, "The Female World of Love and Ritual," in Cutt and Pleck, eds., *A Heritage of Her Own*, 311ff. With Bob emotionally withdrawn, and John Greenway unavailable, Isabella may have considered Miss Thorpe a safe soul on whom she could lavish her love. We know virtually nothing of Miss Thorpe's situation, and have no basis, beyond this letter, for speculation.

Burro Mountain Homestead, Tyrone   July 15, 1915

Eleanor dearest,

We are so glad of last night's note[80] & the thought that you'll soon have Franklin recuperating at Campo. People make light of apendicitis but its so grave at times & we are wonderfully thankful your crisis is over. Give Franklin our dear love & when his side is better read him "Ruggles of Red Gap"—I think I sent it—If not drop me a P.C. [post card]. It's a grand book to read aloud. & *what* a blessing the kiddies kept well & were settled.[81]

Here we have no heart for anything. Our beloved "Wawa" (Miss Thorpe) lies unconscious. Her family all about her. Acky wires there is no hope—& we are utterly heartbroken. A breathless summer stillness here. Some day I want to tell you how close we touched, how sacred our mutual dependence had grown & she seemed so happy to be one of us. She taught us so much that was beautiful—and I shall always feel her near comradeship & love. We had come to plan everything together.

Her example these last weeks seems only a natural climax to her life of absolute usefulness & self sacrifice. Oh Eleanor it is as tho' one of us were leaving.

This winter [in the health-giving climate of New Mexico] could do little to help her physically for the illness evidently was of long accumulation.

I didn't mean to write so—but, dear, it would put you far away if I didn't.

Margaret & Walter Douglas arrive tomorrow in a [private railroad] car—evidently bent on whisking Bob off for a change. I've *no* idea [if] he can be uprooted—he's *so* interested here [—] but [I] hope heartily he will.

Mrs. Damrosch & 3 daughters arriving July 29 & Dan Barney[82] simulta-neously. Having met Polly D[amrosch]'s charms elsewhere I suspect[83]—& then great hopes for Aunty & Uncs for Aug[ust]—that would be too good to be true.

Martha frightened us on the fourth—but was well in 24 hours & my hopes for a successful summer revive. Ronald wants us all to go to Australia[84]—can't you see us trooping?—& seems to expect Sheffield [Cowles] at any moment!

80. Missing.

81. While Eleanor was in Washington with Franklin at the hospital.

82. Danford Barney, Jr., a young writer whom Isabella met in Maine in 1914.

83. Perhaps Isabella is being coy in pretending Barney is interested in a young woman. Barney had met Isabella in Maine the year before, and was clearly smitten. He would make two long visits to her in New Mexico, and would dedicate to her a published book of poetry.

84. Ronald Ferguson was governor-general of Australia, 1914–1920.

Such a nice letter from him. I'm a weary sight after a fortnight indigestion & fainting. I left a portion of my face on a chair! Two inches the other way & a larger portion would have been removed by the stove! Mother is *sticking* out the wilderness & is such a solid comfort.

A world of love to you & yours. I love to write you when I think you *won't bother* to answer.

Ever your devoted
Isabella

& what are Muriel [Martineau]'s sisters like—are they with you?

Martha was doing better, but now Bob suffered a relapse. Despite his failing health, Bob still yearned to go to England and join his brother Hector in the army. "You cannot think of going abroad . . .," Theodore Roosevelt rebuked him. "They would never let you go to the front or do anything else . . . You would merely die after having been rather a nuisance . . . You must not think of it, Bob." [85]

Post Office Campobello Island, N.S.   July 27 [1915]
Isabella dearest,

Your last letter was a great surprise for I had pictured Miss Thorpe as getting slowly well & I can well imagine how you came to love & depend on her. I think you need a change, indigestion & fainting don't sound very cheering to me & though I realize you can't go till you see the children through the summer I hope you will go East or West just as soon as possible & if it can be managed *without* the children to take charge of constantly!

I have quite a family here but Franklin [her husband, recovering from appendicitis] improves daily & all are well so we are happy. We came up on the "Dolphin" bringing George Marvin with us & he left us yesterday. I don't think you know him but he's one of the editors of the World's Work & we find him a very pleasant guest & companion. [86]

Margaret & baby boy arrived while I was away [in Washington, during Franklin's hospital stay]. He is splendid, fat & placid & pink & white.

Muriel [Martineau]'s little Collier sisters & 2 Fred Delano girls were here also during my absence to entertain a battleship which came up to Eastport

85. TR to RHMF, August 6, 1915, FC.
86. He was also a former master of FDR's at Groton.

for July 4th.[87] The Colliers are dears, very different but delightful to have with one for they enjoy everything & always take the trouble to make others enjoy themselves. The children adore them & we were not missed in consequence!

Hall arrived last Friday. He is full of energy as always & looks splendidly well. The year in Alaska has given them many interesting experiences. Now he is deciding where to try for his next job.

Many thanks for the books. "Ruggles" we have read & enjoyed enormously. I've ordered "Drift & Mastery" & "Bunker Bean"[88] sent you. The last Mr. Lane[89] gave us & we enjoyed almost more than "Ruggles."

Have the Fraser-Campbells gone? It will be hard for Bob.

I saw a "Damrosch" on the way up here at Bar Harbor. I wonder if she is Polly? I fear you are a bit crowded & bothered with so many to care for.

I hope Martha stays well. Anna, James, Elliott & babe all thrive here. This a.m. Anna had her first cooking lesson & shelled all the peas for lunch & made the bread & butter pudding & you can imagine her pride. Cousin Susie [Parish] says I should not take time from cultivating her mind to teach her such things but I wish I'd learned young! Did I tell you that A. & J. & I sleep out on Army cots on the new sleeping porch? I think it is doing James much good.

Much love to you all & a heartful to you dearest.

> Your devoted
>
> Eleanor

Can't you come to us now for a visit in November or early Dec. We'll make room if you'll come.

After Miss Thorpe's death, Isabella was alone at the homestead with her ailing husband and young children. Feeling old [almost thirty] and abandoned, even though friends and family were visiting, she reached out with even more affection than usual to her close friend.

Home schooling resumed in the fall. Isabella took the children to a school in Silver City to be tested. She found that they were on track academically,

---

87. In *This Is My Story*, 163–64, 173, ER writes that Franklin came up to Campobello more than once on Navy ships. Evidently, the ships came into port even when Franklin was not there, but the Roosevelts felt obligated to see they were entertained anyway.

88. Harry Leon Wilson, *Bunker Bean*. Garden City and New York: Doubleday, Page & Company, 1913. The book was dedicated to H. G. Wells.

89. Secretary of Interior Franklin K. Lane was among the Roosevelts' most intimate friends in Washington. Eleanor admired him for his ethics and activism. He liked her, too. Cook, *Eleanor Roosevelt*, I, 208–9.

but that their social development was stunted. She vowed to remedy the situation with more trips to town.

The Homestead, Tyrone N.M.   November 9, 1915

Eleanor darling, I'm with you—100 times a day—& don't know why I don't say so oftener. *You* are the one that almost drives me to the train eastbound. So hungry do I grow for a sight of you, a word with you.

If I weren't thirty—married many moons—& waiting for my grandchildren I'd feel a veritable princess in her 100 year sleep—waiting for her knight. More than a year since we stirred abroad!![90] And stoggy [stodgy] Oh my. An "idea" would swoon at the far end of the cañon from domestic gangrene if it tried to get in edgewise. Olivia [Cutting] says I never feel anything short of the secrets of the German War Office justify a letter—but upon my word—our "news" is not what prompts this—It is a longing to see & hear you dear Eleanor. I've half pictured the late summer & autumn & now wonder if the addition at Hyde Park nears completion & holds you all.

Our summer drifted by. None but the slightest ripples on its serene surface. If you could call 3 *immense* young Damrosch amazons ripples.[91] They were overpowering. A strange product of modernism. Everything mentioned, tasted, seen, or smelt was "perfectly wonderful absolutely"—there was no oxygen left in the big room at all! & we took turns exercising them! but perfect dears in reality & the essence of consideration—prompted by their Mother who was such a treat to us all.

Dan Barney—who fit in surprisingly & proved nicer even than I had remembered—there followed Aunty & Unc for nearly a month. Every moment of their stop was bliss to me—but we were in a state [worried] over their respective heads[,] noses & throats—till Uncle discovered that it was the location of the bed in the left corner of the room that created hay fever. Trading with Acky in the right corner made a vast improvement!

Wasn't it like my beloved Uncs to choose to hibernate here the better part of his short holiday? Then Mother postponed & postponed her leaving—& now she is missed unmercifully—but she needed a change. Bob who was *very dragged* in the summer is as well in appearance as at anytime in years.

90. "Abroad" here means "outside the house, away from one's abode." *Webster's Dictionary,* 1923.

91. The three Damrosch daughters who visited in August.

Hector supposedly is in Subla [Suvla] Bay, Gallipoli.[92] His letters are now very muffled as to news but come regularly.[93] Miss Christie's[94] [letters] are such a buoy—

[And] I'm away over my head in home education but confident I'll swim rather than sink. I sit up nights over modern methods—two days at school in Silver proved us in grades quite with our years. Buzz well ahead physically & in lessons. Martha developed in certain branches & behind in others. We wrestled with every tough in town & B was ever to be seen rolling down some dusty street being pummelled! to rise smiling while the victor would say "He's some huskie but he ain't on to the tricks!" We're going over again to get on to them![95]

Martha was called a girl over Belle [Eckles]'s fence "because you can't curse"—I showed them said M—"I cursed in Mexican, English & Chinese & then they knew whether I was a girl or not"!

Now we're recovering from grippe which swept through our midst sparing no one—& school is suspended till our heads are clearer—& we hunt the Red deer meantime—but with no success. Gene Sawyer saw 5 two Sundays ago—just near us. The usual gatherings [of neighbors] come on Sundays here—miners reunions in every sense.[96] Seldom an outside thought—Buzz wrote Uncle to inquire about the *cost*! of Thatchers [Thacher] school[97] having made up his mind he'd like to go there "because its so near home—!"

Goodnight dear—I love you more every day.

  Devotedly

   Isabella

Hug Anna so tight for me. Martha wrote Uncle Hector begging him not to fight on Xmas. "I think it sinful to murder that day"—but wishing him success every other day.

---

92. The Gallipoli campaign took place on the Turkish peninsula from April 1915 to January 1916. The Allied landing in August 1915 at Suvla Bay on the Aegean coast of the Gallipoli peninsula resulted in severe casualties. By January 1916, the defeated Allies withdrew. http://www.encyclopedia.com/doc/1E1-Gallipol-c.html.

93. Soldiers were forbidden to disclose their whereabouts in wartime.

94. Bob's mother's helper or friend.

95. She means, "We're going back to Silver City so Bobbie can learn the techniques of fighting."

96. Although Isabella would later build a political career on her ability to get along with all classes of people, these were probably not her favorite social companions.

97. The Thacher School, founded in 1889, is a boarding college preparatory high school located 85 miles northwest of Los Angeles, California. Bobbie may also have liked the fact that horseback riding was offered.

One book I have found entrancing will follow unless you have read it "What It Is To Be Educated" by Henderson.[98]

Has Anna found "Little Women"[99] slow or not tried yet? I'm getting it for Martha—Having loved it myself.

Bob's love—& mine to Franklin.

In late July, Woodrow Wilson instructed the Army and the Navy to present to Congress by December plans for "an adequate defense." Franklin, who had sympathized much more with his cousin Theodore's calls for preparedness than with Wilson's careful neutrality, was elated.[100]

1733 N. Street, Washington, DC   Nov. 14 [1915]
Dearest Isabella

Cousin Susie [Parish] mentioned casually in a letter that Martha was ill, is it true? I only hope you are not really worried[,] that it is just a little upset from which she'll soon recover.

I believe Mrs. Selmes is going to be in N.Y. so I may see her as I go up the 26th for Sunday. I long for news of you all but somehow I'm afraid you've had too much on your hands & are not very well, do write me a line sometime & tell me truthfully for you know dear my heart is always with you & yours though my pen I own is poor at showing it.

We're all very flourishing though as I'm expecting another baby in March I fear I am not going to be of much use this winter. We've been celebrating with our friends the Japs[101] the past week but it was quite a relief to have

---

98. C. Hanford Henderson, *What Is It To Be Educated?* Boston and New York: Houghton Mifflin Company, 1914. Isabella might well have agreed with Henderson's observation that "The proper work of education is not to prune and thwart and bend and force. It is to feed and nourish and cheer . . ." (117). She would also have found her methods vindicated in his recommendation that for children younger than fourteen, "we want to throw by far the greater emphasis upon the intimate, institutional knowledge which springs from direct, first-hand experience, that is to say from living; and to leave the symbolic, representative knowledge which results from scientific analysis until the children reach the high school and the college" (433).

99. Louisa May Alcott, *Little Women* (1868).

100. Ward, *A First-Class Temperament*, 308–9.

101. The celebrations were in honor of the coronation of the new Japanese emperor, Yoshihito. "Japanese Ambassador and Viscountess Chinda Entertain a Thousand Guests at Embassy in Honor of Accession to Throne of New Emperor of Japan," *Washington Post*, November 11, 1915: 7.

Mr. Lansing[102] do the speechifying instead of Mr. Bryan for he [Lansing] was not fulsome though quite polite & cordial.

I suppose you know Caroline Phillips is also expecting a baby in Feb? She looks very well but I don't think she ever feels really well & William seems to worry all the time. He has been hard worked of late & looks as though he needed a rest.

I went to see Pauline [Merrill] at her country house this autumn & it is so pretty & attractive & just the place for a real home.

Our chief interest now is discussions over the national Defense bills. F does not think them adequate but the question seems to be "Will Congress give even this?"

Much love to you all & do write soon.

> Devotedly,
> E.R.

Isabella was a little wistful when she learned that Eleanor was expecting another baby, her sixth. TB patients were usually restricted from physical contact, and after Bob was diagnosed, he and Isabella had no more children.

Isabella had little time for regrets, though, as wartime shortages gave rise to dramatic and occasionally dangerous labor strikes. In one of her typically long and dense paragraphs, she discusses Phelps Dodge owner Walter Douglas's attempt to deal with striking miners, including a strike at the copper mine in Morenci, Arizona. The Western Federation of Miners had a history as "the most militant labor organization in America," resorting to violence when strikebreakers were brought in.[103] Isabella gives one woman's account of a narrow escape from such violence—an account that chilled Isabella to the marrow.

She also tells Eleanor about the domestic trials of Margaret (Mrs. Walter) Douglas, adding that she (Isabella) had held Eleanor up as an example of a woman who managed such things easily. Eleanor was gaining confidence in her executive abilities, dealing with five children and a large staff during Franklin's frequent absences: "I was growing accustomed to managing quite a small army on moves from Washington to Hyde Park and to Campobello and back."[104]

102. Robert Lansing (1864–1928), secretary of state, June 1915 - February 1920.
103. Katherine Sutcliffe, http://www.law.umkc.edu/faculty/projects/ftrials/haywood/HAY_WFM.HTM.
104. Roosevelt, *This is My Story*, 171.

Isabella also refers to joining a club, possibly a women's service club, the first organization she has joined in the West.

But ever at the back of Isabella's mind was the war and its effect on their family and friends. Hector, in the field, had to be discreet. Others in England could be more candid, at a time when Britain and France were making few gains, but incurring hundreds of thousands of casualties.[105]

Burro Mountain Homestead, Tyrone   [mid-November 1915]
Eleanor darling—

Our letters must just have crossed. I was so grateful for yours last night—Of course it fills me more than ever with the longing to be near & with you more—tho' I never, somehow, feel far away. but it would be nice to share some of your time these days when you can't be too active [when ER was about to give birth]. Dearie you become just such a woman as my Great Grandmother who lived on the Battery[106] & added an *annual* member to the family. She, tho', had one wet nurse to do for two![107] So the tale goes—& the strange part of it all is I believe I was built for just such a career!—& I envy you your right possibly more than you can think. You who are in the midst of the chaotic results of so many to start right!

I was amused last night (we go for weeks without a peep from the outside world & then suddenly all varieties flock in). Walter Douglas came out with 8 railroad & mine officials & some Scotch "strike breakers"[108]—

By the way, the mob of Western Federation that swept thro' Morenci 2000 strong in search of the managers etc—whom they meant to imprison—but who were meantime slipping quietly out on [railroad] engines without lights tells like a medieval mutiny—or a Galsworthy "strife."[109] The wife of the manager told me the tale & my blood ran cold as she described the distant sound growing stronger & stronger as they swept up her street & then she could hear them shouting "McLean, McLean, down with McLean" (her husband)—& she sat unconcerned while they went thro the house in an orderly

105. http://europeanhistory.about.com/library/weekly/blww1stimeline4.htm.
106. The southern tip of Manhattan, New York City.
107. A wet nurse was a woman who, while nursing her own baby, was hired to breast-feed another woman's baby as well. Without the contraceptive effect provided by nursing, Isabella's great-grandmother was able to have a baby every year. Babies were often nursed for more than a year, so the wet nurse might have been feeding both an extra infant and a toddler.
108. Non-union laborers who would cross a picket line to take jobs ("scabs").
109. "Strife" was a 1909 play by John Galsworthy.

fashion—but before the mob could return & possibly take her—she & her daughter (aged 8) with a suitcase—slipped into the night. This was several months ago & she ended her tale with "and for all I know the electric lights are still burning."

But what amused me, dear, was Walter Douglas describing his & Margaret's start in N.Y.[110]—they have a hugh [huge?] house at Locust Valley with the five children established [living at home]—11 butlers in two months & all told, 31 changes of servants! "But," said Walter, "I have a house keeper now for Margaret so she doesn't have to be bothered!" "It can be done smoothly," said I meekly. "I know one Eleanor Roosevelt who has four children & moves them all 6 times a year—& does everything else besides." He remembers you with admiration & some time I want you to meet Margaret. She goes to town [New York City] 3 or 4 days a week.

Alongside, in the sunny window, sit M & B—studying arithmetic Geography & History preparatory for Monday. Our lessons swing along—& with Martha, it means every thing to be able to turn her out [let her go out] when she needs or [when] the day is fine as one couldn't in school. Painting has come back to me in all its temptations—but we find we have heavenly afternoons on the hills from 2 till 5. Lura (my Texan Hebe)[111] plays with M & B & brews tea. Bob looks a well man most of the time wholly recovered from the midsummer slump.

I had longed to be with you as you suggested for some part of Nov. But we have our second wind[112] & its best not to go when Bob might be snowed in & too isolated. Maybe I'll come on & greet the newcomer![113] & now I must stop talking—Soon I'll have a monologue for you of [describing] the Club in Tyrone to which I belong called "The Helping Hand"—!

Hector's letters are highly colored[114]—tho' no longer filled with information. The letters from Eng—begin to sound more desperate in a certain sense. Optimistic but clutching bitterly at what should have been 18 months ago in organization etc.

My world of love, dearest, is ever yours—I long to *know* Anna—& mean to one of these days—Tell her the other night people dropped in for Sunday supper & I was desperate—having no supper—Martha & Bobbie said "Oh never

---

110. Presumably their situation when he left home.
111. Reference to Greek mythology. Hebe was the cupbearer of the gods.
112. Probably means they are all doing well at the moment.
113. Eleanor's baby, due in March.
114. Full of colorful anecdotes.

mind we'll catch you some" & away they went with the puppy—to return shortly with a squirrel! A big bunch of mistletoe sits behind Anna's photo on my table.

    Devotedly ever
     Isabella

  How nice this is about Janet Dana—A *trump*[115] seems to have discovered her work—& her letters are radiant.

  I'm sorry Caroline [Phillips] isn't feeling better

Eleanor, who had been a friend of the Fergusons before Isabella had met them, was concerned to hear Hector had been hospitalized. Possibly Hector had been wounded at Gallipoli. But Eleanor was even more concerned about the behavior of her first cousin, Alice Roosevelt Longworth, TR's irrepressible eldest child. The two had been close as children. Alice, like Isabella, was a brides-maid at Franklin and Eleanor's wedding. But unconventional and fun-loving Alice was Eleanor's opposite in many ways. Now, in Washington, they were social and political rivals (Alice's husband Nick was a prominent Republican congressman). Up to this point, Eleanor's references to Alice had been kind. In the following letter, however, she begins to be a little more critical.[116]

1733 N Street, Washington, DC   Dec. 21 [1915]
Dearest Isabella,

  Two dear letters from you & only time for a hurried line as I'm hoping it will reach you before Xmas. We will all be thinking of the family in the Burros & wishing them such a happy day. We are all very flourishing & I think our day will be very full as the chicks have learned a new French play for our Xmas gift which is to be given after lunch before the Xmas tree! Mlle[117] is quite an actress which I think makes Mama feel she is on the verge of not being a proper person to be with the young!

  I wish I could tell you about Alice & Nick, having them here is so funny! I went to dine when F. was away the other night & one of the lady guests had a cocktail, 2 glasses of whiskey & soda & liqueurs & 15 cigarettes before I left at 10:15! It was a funny party but I'm glad I'm not quite so fashionable! Alice looks fairly well though & is very nice.

---

115. A good fellow. *Webster's Dictionary*, 1923.
116. Stacy Cordery, "Alice Roosevelt Longworth," *ER Encyclopedia*, 318–19.
117. Mademoiselle—the French governess.

I was sorry to hear from A. Bye Hector was in hospital.

I spent a night with A. Bye & she looks well but she cannot walk any better. I think the old German[118] keeps her about the same but she suffers much. However, as always she was delightful & bright & Cousin Joe [Alsop?] seemed in fine form.

Much much love to you all from all of us.

> Devotedly,
>
> E.R.

Isabella had made new friends in New Mexico, including Isabel (Belle) and Mary Eckles, both teachers. She believed they were people "as fine as any you'd stumble on in any part of the world." [119]

But, as her thirtieth birthday approached, Isabella reflected nostalgically on her long friendship with Eleanor, indulging in fervent expressions of love and gratitude, and longing to share the minutia of her daily life.

Isabella also was showing a growing interest in politics—from the expected participation of women in the war effort, to gossip about Woodrow Wilson's marriage only sixteen months after the death of his first wife, and the prospects of Wilson's reelection.

Although the U. S. was not yet in the war, she was sending food and supplies to aid the allies. Isabella, who probably knew through Bob's family about women in Great Britain volunteering to help the war effort, anticipated a time when some sort of similar organization might be necessary in America.

Burro Mountain Homestead   January 22, 1916
Tyrone, New Mexico
Eleanor—dearest of all—& ever dearer

This [sentimentality] certainly is permissable on the start of another year—& from one old woman on a mt. top. I looked long at you & the baby last night. (Your photograph sits under the lamp on our living room table) & felt a little as tho' I'd seen your twinkling eyes & touched those long slender fingers. Can it be that another wee one is about to start forth on this questionable adventure called "life"—Its gloriously worthwhile tho' & with every one you launch I should think the glory would become greater.

118. Presumably her doctor.
119. IG to Olivia Cutting, November 6, 1911, GC.

I think of you & love you closer every day—& heaven knows why I don't indulge in the joy of writing you oftener. But this is to thank you for our Xmas gifts—which went direct to the right spot & all the time we were saying "But she never should have troubled—" & you know you ought to take advantage of our understanding and not tax yourself about us. But we're doubly appreciative—& can't begin to thank you.

The children's book is delightful & we mean to learn some of the verses by heart. Martha's paper dolls saved the day when she was enduring a cold—none too cheerily—when they were produced—& we've only begun on them. The handkerchiefs with the supply you have given us before are the support of our snub & roman noses & they take such satisfaction in them & have tidied them away just so in their bureau drawers—where they open & pat them periodically.

My whole mode of life has to be reorganized to meet the jacket—the like of which never found its way to wilderness before. Its simply beautiful—& I can't believe its mine!—& from you. The door weight is an invaluable possession promptly snatched from Bob who I know will be snatching it back off my table where it is a photo prop—with Chinese lilies behind it.

Our Xmas was radiantly happy—a big tree in the center of the living room—an expedition to Tyrone on Xmas Eve to sing hymns with the village around their municipal tree. Bobbie's whole heart & frame kept time & many in the crowd asked me if I knew who the little fellow in gray was—who sang so earnestly!

Belle [Eckles,] Mary, their brother & another made us very merry from Dec. 26 till the New year—sliding [sledding] our principal diversion—then came Jack Garrett (Father's nephew)[120] a lovable slow lad of 21. Stopping indefinitely & very nice to have about.

The intervening time has been wholly absorbed in pursuit of furnace men who tore the whole place to piece[s] installing a heating system on this mt. top in order to insure Uncle sounder sleep on Long Island.[121] A broom and an "ugly" temper have been my sole companions since I can remember—only now I am beginning to recover my sunny disposition!! after their exit & a 5 day snow[-]in where all human connection was snapped. Jack who was left for overnight at the hospital (he was thrown from a horse & had a bruised hip) is still there—threatening to walk out!

120. Jack was Isabella's first cousin.
121. Frank had insisted they get a furnace, because Isabella was having to get up in the night to put wood on the fires.

Bob is not well at the moment (he changes so rapidly one never can calculate) & the war is an ever increasing burden to the whole world but particularly here where one hasn't minor diversions. Will you be taking any part as an organizer in our women's defense project—I suppose in time, if well handled, it should get down to local organizations under larger ones & amount to a great deal—? What's *your* honest opinion of the bride & bridegroom of the White House.[122] I'm interested to hear thinking Democrats regretting they can not vote for him. A heart full of love to you & much to Franklin & a very hug & kiss to Anna & her brothers. Yr devoted Isabella

Eleanor took her sixth pregnancy in stride, wryly referring to the impending birth as "entertainment."[123] Times were changing: she no longer felt she had to stay secluded, and she hosted 225 people at an "official navy function" during her eighth month.[124] But motherhood, and even Franklin's persistent throat infection, were less interesting to Eleanor than political news: Lindsey Garrison's resignation from his position as Secretary of War[125] "because the president continued to refuse to advocate universal military training."[126]

1733 N Street, Washington, DC   Feb 24th [1916]
Isabella dear,

I don't think I've even written to thank you for our Xmas presents, or for your last dear letter & I have no excuse except that time seems to slip by without my being able to lay hands on [it]. I love my writing case & shall use it in bed even before I take it travelling! Anna's rug was an inspiration & has given her endless joy as it is put by her bed. You should really not bother about us when you have so much to do.

I am sorry Bob is up & down for I know it always means added care for you but I hope the chicks keep well. Ours have been so well this winter & I pray will stay so till I am well again[127] as there won't be an extra room or bed to share during that entertainment & I don't want to send any to Mama as it would mean no school for the big ones just when they are really working & Mlle can't keep them up in English as she knows none!

122. Edith Bolling Galt married widowed President Woodrow Wilson on December 18, 1915.
123. This is typical Rooseveltian ironic dismissal of bodily discomfort.
124. Pottker, *Sara and Eleanor*, 169.
125. Garrison was replaced by Newton Baker, the reform mayor of Cincinnati.
126. Ward, *A First-Class Temperament*, 310.
127. Eleanor expected to be in bed for a couple of weeks after the delivery, as was the custom at the time.

These have been very exciting times down here & I am sorry to say Franklin has been laid up for three weeks with the nastiest kind of throat but I hope he returns from Atlantic City tomorrow feeling really stronger. One hears so much discussion of the President & congress & Mr. Garrison that really one hardly knows what to think. I do think Mr. G. has always been a bit hot tempered & autocratic but his position was very trying [he was in an awkward situation]. Mr. [Winty-Ward] Chanler blew in from Boston last night & he seems to feel that everything the President has done is hopeless & he and Mr. Henry Adams[128] had decided there was nothing left for the President to do but resign. Alice [Longworth] I gather feels much the same way so that must be Nick's feeling & I suppose Uncle Ted's.

Munro [Monroe Robinson] & his bride came in to tea the other day & I liked her so much. Quiet but lots of character I should think & I only hope she succeeds with Munro. They are going to live in the Orange house next summer. I see very little of Alice for she plays a great deal of bridge & is very gay & we don't play & are rather quiet. She is always interesting & attractive but it must be an empty existence, only one's own pleasure to think about & occasionally an ache or a pain!

Caroline [Phillips] has been waiting nearly 3 weeks for her baby. I only hope it is a boy, for that will make up for everything.[129] I am so glad Kermit has a son.[130] I heard of them from several of the Argentines who were here for the Pan-American Conference & he seemed to be very much liked.

Maude & David Gray come tomorrow to spend Sunday & after that I begin to get things in order for the new baby though I don't expect he or she will arrive till between the 15th & 20th.[131]

Much love to you all. I long to see you & can't help hoping this summer will bring you & the chicks East.

Devotedly,

E.R.

128. Henry Brooks Adams (February 16, 1838 – March 27, 1918) was a writer of history. He was a descendant of two presidents of the United States. Henry Adams's greatest work was *The History of the United States of America* (1889–1891), but he is perhaps best known for *The Education of Henry Adams* (1918). http://www.encyclopedia.com/doc/1G2-3404700049.html.

129. Caroline Phillips's first child had died and Eleanor was "very anxious that everything go well with her." Roosevelt, *This is My Story*, 180.

130. Kermit Roosevelt, Jr. was Kermit and Belle Roosevelt's first child.

131. John Aspinwall Roosevelt was born March 13, 1916.

Early in 1916, Dr. Bullock examined Bob Ferguson and found the tuberculosis in his lungs slowly and relentlessly progressing. Bob had been in bed for weeks and, not surprisingly, he was overwhelmingly depressed. The doctor thought a trip might do him good. Isabella's great-aunt Julia had invited Bob to bring Isabella and the children to Dinsmore Farm. Bob did not feel he could leave the Homestead, but he had never objected to Isabella traveling. In fact, on many occasions, he had insisted on her taking time away.

Isabella wanted Martha and Bobbie to know their great-great-aunt, who was now eighty-three years old. Isabella also wanted to show her children the farm where she had spent much of her own childhood. Patty and Sally and Frank Cutcheon joined them for a family reunion.

While they were at the farm, Isabella and the children made some excursions into Cincinnati, where Isabella visited with Alice Roosevelt Longworth, whose husband, Nick, represented a Cincinnati district in Congress. Much has been made of the rivalry between Alice and Eleanor, but Isabella's letter shows that, at least on occasion, Alice could be generous in recognizing Eleanor's accomplishments.

Although she loved her time away, after so many years of living in rented or impermanent dwellings, Isabella was deeply contented to return to her comfortable homestead.

Back in New Mexico, she discovered that her mother seemed run-down, and possibly depressed. With Bob also sick, Isabella needed help over the summer in case Martha fell ill again. She hoped to send Patty off for a rest cure in the fall.

On March 9, 1916, Pancho Villa had raided the border town of Columbus, New Mexico, only seventy-five miles southwest of Tyrone, killing eighteen Americans.[132] Isabella's letter, however, shows that her chief concern was the raid's economic impact on her neighbors, who were drafted to patrol the border at a mere $15 a month.

---

132. The attack followed President Wilson's extension of diplomatic recognition to the government of Villa's revolutionary rival, Venustiano Carranza. Pancho Villa felt betrayed by President Wilson's decision to support Carranza. Anderson, *Pancho Villa's Revolution by Headlines*, 43. Villa had "courted the United States for years" and "had not even criticized the invasion at Veracruz...." Meyer et al., *Course of Mexican History*, 520. Villa, who "grew up as a sharecropper," later became a "cattle rustler." In the words of an unnamed contemporary observer, Villa "has no fear of physical danger or of the law" and "becomes popular very quickly...." He sought and obtained heavy U.S. press coverage of his exploits. "Admits He's A 'Movie' Star. Villa Delays Ojinaga Attack for Operators' Arrival," *New York Times*, January 8, 1914: 2.

Eleanor hoped for another visit from Isabella. Isabella, who had already taken one trip that year, regretted she could not go to Eleanor.

Eleanor, meanwhile, had had a difficult spring. Her baby, named John Aspinwall, was born on March 13. Two days later, Elliott, who was always "delicate," became ill, and shortly thereafter the older children contracted whooping cough and were sent off to stay with their grandmother.

Burro Mountain Homestead
Tyrone, New Mexico   [late spring 1916]

Eleanor my dearest, How you tempt me. it's hard, ever so hard, to resist— You can't begin to know what it would mean to me to sit at Hyde Park with you & yours for a bit. The need & longing to see you is very upper-most— these days—I am kicking myself for not having written these many weeks. Were I twenty, & not thirty, I'd take the next train—letting expense, children, & a household to organize over the Summer months, go to.[133] But I'm thirty—& more's the pity [regrettably]—faint rumors of a conscience having developed in my system. I know I should not go—having just returned from six weeks in Boone—where we accomplished all I've longed to these many years.

> The attack lasted six hours. The raiders, approximately 500 men, were ultimately repulsed by the 13th U.S. Cavalry garrisoned in Columbus. Eighteen Americans were killed, many were injured, and the town was "burned beyond recognition." Meyer et al., *Course of Mexican History*, 520, 521; Katz, *Secret War in Mexico*, 303.
>
> Some have described the attack on Columbus as simply the "revenge of a reckless desperado," but the real motivation for the raid probably went deeper. "The primary motivation was Villa's firm belief that Woodrow Wilson had concluded an agreement with Carranza that would virtually convert Mexico into a U.S. protectorate." Katz, "Pancho Villa and the Attack on Columbus," 102. By attacking the U.S.—and inviting possible reprisals—Villa hoped to lure the Americans into Mexico in order to create "an insoluble dilemma for Carranza." Villa believed that Carranza would be exposed as a puppet if American troops were allowed to enter Mexico. If Carranza opposed a U.S. invasion, Villa believed U.S. support of his regime would stop and Carranza would be weakened. Katz, *Secret War in Mexico*, 307.
>
> The U.S. did invade Mexico, but only with "a small punitive expedition" of approximately 6,000 troops under the command of Gen. John J. Pershing. Local citizens refused to assist the Americans. After nearly a year of wandering "hot and thirsty through the rough terrain," the Americans gave up and returned. The cost of the expedition was $130 million. Pancho Villa was not caught. Meyer et. al., *Course of Mexican History*, 521, 522. Years later, the Pancho Villa State Park was established in Columbus, New Mexico.

133. i.e., go to the devil.

Great Aunty[134] had *real pleasure* in the presence of the 5th generation—who had enlivened old house & place—& Martha & Bobbie came to know her as she *is*. We took her to the May [music] festival in Cincinnati [every day] for a whole week—very fine but heavy music. The children each went once & Bobbie's description was truly that of a music lover "Dear Daddy, I took Owny to the Festival. It was as big as our house & stables [put together] & lasted two hours"!

Then we'd a pleasant week in Louisville meeting Mother's good friends Mr. & Mrs. [Thurston] Ballard. I was *so* enchanted over one triumph. The dentist told me M & B's teeth were flawless & need not even be cleaned. They had never been to one before & I took them in fear & trembling.

I saw Alice [Longworth] & had as satisfactory a talk with her as one is apt to have. Filled with noisy exuberance & no reality. She was nevertheless refreshing & *un*changed (after not seeing her for eight years!) I had looked for stout dignity from numerous tales—but met old time lightness. She seemed to appreciate that you do your job in Washington a little bit better than anyone else.

Private Mother is weary. *Don't* tell Mrs. P[arish]. I am very sad to realize—She is practically without any come back—if you know what I mean—while I think some of it is in the natural course of events & years I am confident we can gain back much by a real rest. I am filled with misgivings about Aug! & the tax it may be—but have all plans made for Nov at the Arizona hot springs where the waters may do good & the rest certainly will.

Eleanor dearest you are bad never to say a word about yourself. Thank goodness the Burro Mts. abound in little birds & we hear the truth in all sorts of ways & know you were up much too soon & that all the children were under the weather & that your spring must have spelt some warmer season!![135]—& there, with a twinkle, you say you are "lazy"—Do try and find some peace at Campo.

'Twas wonderful beyond words to come back this time to a foot hold—a *home* of our own—after nine years of tramp life. The house is more comfy every day. The air heavy with honeysuckle & roses peeping in all the windows. A *grand* garden of all kinds of vegetables—& a sense of remote peace that you can turn the key on & use any old time in the future.[136] Bob is

---

134. Isabella's great aunt Julia Dinsmore reared her nieces Patty (Selmes) and Sally (Cutcheon) after their mother, Isabella Dinsmore Flandrau, died shortly after Sally was born. Patty called Julia "my own," often shortened to "Owny."
135. Possibly hell.
136. Peace that would be available—mentally—to them at anytime.

excellently well, for him & seems to have turned a critical corner (mentally) by getting out & going to Bisbee etc while I was away. He's relaxed & normal again & so happy in this place.

I've a dear little woman—helping me—Her husband is an Englishman—Prisoner in Germany—& she is her own & his support meantime—& speaks perfect French & German tho' she is American. I hope to gain a footing in French—for M & B. Everyone is bitterly up against it here abouts. All Silver men having to be in Columbus for $15.00 a month & their families left with *no* means of support. *It's outrageous.* Doctors who are needed and all.[137] Bless you dearest of all.

Ever yrs.

Isabella

Tell Anna Martha & I brought a setting [138] of pheasant eggs with us & hope soon for a lot of ring necked pheasants such as they have in the zoo—to go with our peacocks.

Hug Mary Newbold for us. It's grand to think of the third! Love to Franklin.

If Eleanor was flattered by Isabella passing along Alice's compliment, she did not show it. She granted that Alice was a brilliant hostess; many Washingtonians were attracted to her parties for the "sophisticated political debate that took place there."[139] But she thought her cousin was shallow. Alice as yet had no children, and none of the concerns they bring. Both Eleanor and Isabella believed that responsibility and overcoming difficulties gave people strength and taught them compassion. All three women, however, were intensely interested in the political problems of the day.

Hyde Park on Hudson   June 21st [1916]
Isabella dearest

It was a real disappointment that you couldn't come East but I did not have much hope that you would for I know how much is always on your shoulders. I do hope the little lady you have to help you with the children

---

137. Isabella complains that local men have been drafted at low wages to patrol the Mexican border. Eventually 150,000 National Guardsmen would come to relieve them. http://www.az.ngb.army.mil/Museum/aznghistory.htm.

138. All the eggs incubated by a fowl at one time. One could buy them to put under another fowl to hatch. *Webster's Dictionary*, 1923

139. Cordery, "Alice Longworth Roosevelt," *ER Encyclopedia*, 319.

will continue to prove all you could wish & take responsibility off you & I am more than happy to hear Bob's trip to Bisbee did him so much good.

Ethel [Roosevelt Derby] told me you had seen Alice. Of course she isn't a bit changed & it is always entertaining to see her but now that I am older & have my own values fixed a little I can only say what little I saw of her life gave me a feeling of dreariness & waste. Her house is charming, her entertainment delightful. She's a born hostess & has an extraordinary mind but as for real friendship & what it means she hasn't a conception of any depth in any feeling or so it seems. Life seems to be one long pursuit of pleasure & excitement & rather little real happiness either given or taken on the way, the "bluebird" always to be searched for in some new & novel way. I sometimes think that the lives of many burdens are not really to be pitied for at least they live deeply & from their sorrows spring up flowers but an empty life is really dreadful!

And this brings me to Cousin Susie [Parish] who looked really ill when I saw her in May & from all accounts she is no better, has not been to Orange & is now gone to Narragansett. I am so sorry your Mother seems weary & I fear August if it is to be [spent with] Cousin Susie will be no rest.

Where do you plan going in Arizona next Nov? We saw Bishop Atwood[140] the other day, who spoke most warmly of you. He urged us to go to him for a day if we are in your part of the country next autumn but we can have no plans as yet. I long to see you however & shall go somewhere to accomplish that if possible! All goes very serenely with us now, our winter after Feb. 1st was rather hectic beginning with Franklin being ill for nearly a month with a dreadful throat & ending off with Elliott getting the same germ while I was ill and being laid up with a trained nurse for a month & it has left his kidneys slightly affected so his diet is still rather restricted however he is really quite well.

The baby (named John Aspinwall) for Franklin's uncle thrives & I still nurse him & hope to continue till we get back from Campo. We are off on the 29th & Franklin goes up with us for a week. Margaret & her baby come July 8th for a month while Hall goes to Plattsburgh. Just now, I wish we had conscription for I feel sure if we really go in to Mexico it means many men who ought to stay at home will go & many who should go won't do so![141] I rather think before long the Silver situation will be repeated in a good many

---

140. Rt. Rev. Julius Atwood, the Episcopalian missionary bishop of Arizona, would open a tubercular sanatorium in Tucson in 1918.

141. At the time of Eleanor's letter, the U.S. was indeed already in Mexico, with the previously mentioned 6,000 troops. Meyer et al., *Course of Mexican History*, 521.

towns.[142] I hope daily that Austria will crumble, the Russian drive seems so successful. You knew Sir Cecil lost his brother, didn't you? What do you hear from Hector?

Pauline & Grenville [Merrill] motored over to lunch last Sunday & both seemed so well, it was a real pleasure. They seemed to like the house & I wish you could see it for I think you & Bob would like it. The big room is comfortable & restful & looks lived in all ready & I look forward to the autumn & big fires in it with much pleasurable anticipation.

Anna is growing such a big girl & in many ways a real help. James at present drives me crazy by being unable to remember any rule 5 minutes. I tell him to dress & 20 minutes later find him absorbed in the "Graphics" not having even begun & so on ad infinitum! However, he's dear & will come out of this phase I know. Elliott & the babies are too young to have any personal responsibilities & I'm thankful.

Love to Bob & kiss Martha & Buzz & Mrs. Selmes & a heartfull to you always dear.

> Devotedly
>
> E.R.

Isabella's life was very full, and she could not write as often as she would have wished. Time would pass. Then, to make amends, she would answer at length. Lapses in Eleanor's correspondence occurred from time to time, too. But each woman counted on the patience and understanding of the other.

Isabella here describes her life as "humdrum," even though the Mexican situation had provided considerable excitement. Bob was having a hard time, unable to take part in the war his brother was fighting. But he had rallied to deal with the border problems. Bob organized a civil defense network, sending away for Springfield rifles and investing in road repair. The men of the community drafted an emergency plan to use the large, well-built Burro Mountain homestead as a defensive position in case of attack. Bob, meanwhile, devised a system of rifle-shot signals whereby households discovering danger could signal to one another.[143]

Despite protestations that old age and rural living had made her uninteresting, Isabella was enjoying another visit from Dan Barney, the young poet

---

142. Politically motivated violence did occur sporadically in the border towns, but no subsequent attack approximated the magnitude of Pancho Villa's March 9, 1916 raid on Columbus.
143. Miller, *Isabella Greenway*, 84.

she had met in Maine two years earlier, who had been much taken by Isabella. He could provide both intellectual stimulation and reassurance that Isabella had lost none of her youthful charm.

The children, now ten and eight years old, were another constant source of amusement.

Burro Mountain Homestead   November 2, 1916
Tyrone, New Mexico

Eleanor mine, Thus do I presume! Franklin & all the babes must grant me this long distance privilege. How constantly I have thought of you these shocking number of weeks you will never know—all the evils of being an old woman of the mountains has held my pen spell bound; self conscious, & wondering if there were anything in our humdrum copper, cattle & domestic world worth sending across the continent—& all the while I've been fairly famished for a scrap of your news. I look at Anna, James & Elliot on my long table of specially beloveds & realize they have advanced feet since then. When may I have their last [picture]? You are ever before me as you *are*—& more strongly with the years—& more inspiring if possible.

Bob's was a wretched summer—weak and *alarming* & out of it he has sprung (with this cool weather & no further explanation) to being fitter than in ages. He went with Col T. R. from Albuquerque thro' Arizona for four or five days—saw Bronson [Cutting] & any no. of old friends & returned from it all as stimulated as you can imagine. We take considerable time daily to bury Wilson & kill Germans & you can be sure the trip with the Col has not influenced that.

We border folk do feel more keenly than can be expressed the bungling of Mexican affairs[144]—& the frightful resulting personal trajedies on U. S. soil. Do you realize that for six weeks (before they sent the troops) we had to organize a local army & agree to take in local women & children in case of danger. We had 53 armed men & signals & finally the Grant Co. Sheriff announced his intention of putting a resident Sheriff with us!! he stopped [stayed] 2 mo[nth]s. The children weren't allowed a 100 ft. off & the hills rang with shots of armed Mexicans drifting around with no explanation of existance.[145]

144. The "bungling" might mean President Wilson's decision not to invade Mexico with a large enough force to guarantee border security.
145. Although gunfire ringing in the hills had to have been terrifying, the danger subsided more quickly than many had feared. What accounted for the lack of more organized Columbus-style attacks? If Pancho Villa's goal in attacking Columbus had been to lure

Many tried to move us into the hospital & Bob in a truly Bob way announced from his back during severe pleurisy which rendered him quite helpless "Yes I think you & the children *should* go—Of course *I* won't budge on account of the moral effect on the neighborhood." This is all very old news—tho it will doubtless repeat at once were the troops [to be] removed. So far none [no Mexicans] at Deming have been discovered at anything resembling manoevers—& all the funerals have been the result of self-injuries from becoming familiar or too familiar with their guns!

I *am* so distressed over this last trial for Mrs. Parish.[146] Can it be that it will throw any light on the root of the trouble? or that she will find her way back to any sort of health. I pray so. *What* a gloomy outlook. You and yours the only bright spots for them both.

Dan Barney is one of us. So pleasantly so. A *young* man of rare consideration & a mature lighter touch. He brings much that is grateful [appreciated] of a lyric & studious world to us plodding cattle copper folk. It sounds almost like a foreign language. His book of verses come out next month.

I am teaching M & B from 9 till 3 & then sitting up nights to prepare for the following day! We leave no course untouched & are embracing the world at large & they seem to enjoy it as much as I do. 4 & 5 grade work respectively. Martha develops *so* rapidly—& so blessedly—a female to her fingertips with a love of adventure—a singular (Scotch) streak of being practical & provident & then again utterly (American!!) regardless careless & forever in the clouds.

Near & far *depend* instinctively on Bobbie.[147] Long may it be so—& he is in no way dazzled by Martha's more nimble imagination. Tell Anna they are trapping for a living. Bobbie is saving his to go to [boarding] school on—& Martha skins all the squirrels chipmonks etc, never scratching an eyelash & tans the hides. They get 10 [cents] for squirrel/ 5 for skunks & weasels & have made $3.75 this month & keep 15 traps going. Good night

the U.S. into Mexico, then General Pershing's expedition arguably satisfied that goal and no further attacks were needed (see notes to Isabella's Spring 1916 letter). Why was there not more random Mexican violence directed toward U.S. citizens? A possible reason is that Mexicans living near the border feared the periodic arrival of revolutionary soldiers and wanted to escape to America rather than attack it. "It is axiomatic that war elicits not only the worst in man but often psychotic behavior in otherwise normal human beings.... In northern Mexico tens of thousands of rural Mexicans joined their middle class and wealthy counterparts in seeking the security of the United States." Meyer et al., *Course of Mexican History*, 532, 533.

146. Susie Parish had to have surgery for an abscess on the rectum.

147. From an early age, Bobbie helped on the Homestead. By the time he was twelve, he was able to brand and inoculate a small herd of calves. Miller, *Isabella Greenway*, 104.

dear Eleanor. When Mother comes I might go East. I *do* long to [go now] but am not sure of the 4 days between Martha & me.[148] Meantime I love you as never before. Ever yrs. Isabella

Love to Franklin & the children. Bob's love too. We're all sitting so cozily & sleepily by our turquoise studded mantel.[149] Do you ever have a peaceful evening?

Eleanor was staying at Campobello Island an extra month, due to a severe outbreak of polio (infantile paralysis) in the northeastern United States.[150] This was forty years before the development of the polio vaccine, and the devastating disease killed many victims and crippled many more. Although children were particularly susceptible, adults could also contract the illness.

While Eleanor could be very tender hearted toward friends and family in real trouble, she had less and less patience with Susie Parish, whose health problems Eleanor attributed to her cousin's overdependence on sleeping pills.

Finally she brought the children down to Hyde Park, leaving them with Sara in her newly enlarged house, while Eleanor joined Franklin in Washington. Mostly, though, Franklin was traveling to campaign for Democrats in a presidential election year.

Eleanor was interested in Isabella's assessment of Mexico's threat, and promised to use her growing influence in Washington to bring her friend's concerns to the attention of the War Department. As events would prove, Isabella's worries were well founded. A growing political partnership would bind the two friends ever closer together over the next twenty years.

Hyde Park on Hudson   Nov. 13 [1916]
Dearest dear Isabella

How very negligent in the letter-writing way have I been! But you've been almost daily in my thoughts in spite of it & I can't tell you how glad I was to get your letter. I am so sorry Bob had a bad summer—bad for him & I know hard for you but it is a pleasure to think of him about again & as to Martha & Buzz your description made me long to see them at once. Do come East soon

148. It was four days' train travel from New Mexico to Washington, D.C. Isabella could not leave Martha, because it would take Isabella too long to get back to her if she got sick. When Patty arrived she would be able to take over and free Isabella to travel.

149. Initials of the Ferguson family members were inlaid with turquoise nuggets in the mantel at the Homestead.

150. 27,000 Americans were affected. New York had 19,000 cases, 2,448 of them fatal. Ward, *A First-Class Temperament*, 317.

& next summer do plan to bring them out at Campo for a month. I can't bear to have Anna & James not with them during these years.

We had a family photograph taken in the big room a week ago & I will send it later. You would not know the house here, we all love the big room & I think it is very homelike & for the chicks it is now ideal. They are staying till after Xmas here as I've got a very good public school teacher for them so they keep up & we are so crowded in A. Bye's house that we didn't want a long season.[151]

I was much interested in what you said of conditions before the troops went to the border & in the condition & occupations of those now at Deming & I will pass on the information to the War Department! Sometimes I wonder if we ever will develop a little German efficiency!

I have had a fairly peaceful autumn with only one trip to Washington as Franklin was so busy campaigning he was more out of Washington than in it. I've had many quiet evenings this summer & since the infantile paralysis kept us a month later than we expected at Campo I really did much reading & worked hard over the chicks all day. Anna is going to be capable & dependable I think & James already devours books & I think will have a quick & interesting mind. Elliott is just very lovable & sensitive & stormy & the 2 babies very soft & adorable.

I will get Dan Barney's poems. Is he staying with you now or living near? Have you read "Mr. Britling Sees It Through"?[152] I like it & will send it to you if you care to have it.

I saw Auntie Bye in New York last week & she looked so much better & walked with far more ease. I see Cousin Susie [Parish] whenever I go to N.Y. but so far my longest visit has been 15 minutes. *Private*—the root of all her trouble lay in her taking Eudonal for years & lately veronal.[153] The small abscess or fistula in the rectum cannot have been very serious for she recovered very rapidly from the operation but there was some poison from it & the other habit undermined her health & I think her character. She seems to have

---

151. Eleanor stayed in the newly remodeled house at Hyde Park with the children that autumn, joining Franklin in Washington only once, as he was out of town most of the time campaigning.

152. H. G. Wells, *Mr. Britling Sees It Through* (New York: Macmillan Company, 1916) was a bestseller and one of the first books available in the U. S. that described the English perspective on World War I.

153. Veronal (the trademark name for barbital) was used as a sleeping aid. http://www.merriam-webster.com/medical/veronal.

had an obsession about sleep & still has it, tells me she has not had a good night if she sleeps less than ten hours.

I feel her chance of ever being other than an invalid is slight unless she gets over this "idée fixe." The doctors found no sign of any malignant trouble & she has a marvellous constitution, even Cousin Henry [Parish] feels as I do now I believe. If only she had something necessary to do, it is pitiful & if ever you are tired & your cares weigh heavily upon you just think how immeasurably worse that would be, it really is a help!

I am off to Washington to-morrow so goodnight my dearest, love to Bob & to Martha & Buzz & if you don't come to see us we will of course go to see you.

> Always devotedly,
> Eleanor

Isabella's six years in New Mexico had alternated between debilitating hot summers and winter rounds of colds and flu. During the last six weeks of 1916, the whole household was ill, including the governess, the cook, and the houseboy. Isabella felt as if she were running a hospital: "I shut my eyes & see trays and hot water bottles and pills . . . "[154]

By Christmas, though, everyone had recovered enough for the Fergusons to enjoy a good time with many neighbors who managed to reach the Homestead through deep snow.

Burro Mountain Homestead, Tyrone   [Jan. 1917]
New Mexico

My very dearest Eleanor—Such an Xmas as we have had—there never was the like in the Burros or two small hearts—& I guess twenty five other small hearts. We'd a terrific blizzard. Sixteen grownups from Tyrone reached us by having their motors pulled by teams [of horses]. In the afternoon we sent the wagon & collected 25 small children living in this cañon. A real Santa Claus just paralyzed them with joy—& when, out of his sack, after all the presents, jumped two New Zealand hares! our cup was full to overflowing!!—& all the while I said to myself—if only Eleanor's might be with ours. I pray some kind future may bring them together.

The first thing in the morning—Martha & Bobbie found these lovely handkerchiefs in their stockings & they were *so* pleased. Out of the blur of

154. IG to Olivia Cutting, [December 1916], FC.

grownup friends you stand very distinct—& "Aunt Eleanor" is very real to them & a place is always waiting for Anna & James.

Martha has already dived into the Celtic Tales[155] & Captain J. Smith (their favorite hero!) while she recuperated one afternoon from too much sliding [sledding]. They will give great pleasure. Here on the mt. top where we do settle to all sorts of happy reading. Bob will write you how much he looks forward to the "Reminiscences of War Times." It looks intensely interesting. I hope to find time for it, too.

Am I to thank you for this very enchanting table set of linen with a blue border.[156] It is most of all acceptable & we'll be using it for aye [forever]. I never saw anything like it or anything more appropriate for our table. I love sitting down to anything that means Eleanor to me. It doesn't take material reminders but they endear this "painful kingdom of time & space" no end.

Here we were all sick for weeks with grippe & unable to do any of the things we enjoy before Xmas & sent the merest greetings to Anna & her Brothers in Honey. But you'll understand. Bob was dressed for Xmas (I staggered up several days before) & now he's coming on pretty fairly.

I'm so hoping to go East for a few weeks after Mother comes—but can't plan—can only board a train at some moment when all is smooth. I want to go to you for two or three days wherever you are if you can have me conveniently. Fully appreciating how your every moment is planned ahead but longing to live under the same roof with you—& just know you are coming & going—& maybe I can walk to school with Anna &—well it is very lovely to even think of—& you'll hear quick enough if the chance comes.

Good heavens I'm not going to forget to tell you that your handkerchiefs came just in the nick of time to replenish an emptied box! I'd none left in the world—& if I do go East it will be largely because I have some again! & such beauties. Bless you my dearest of all—over & over—& hug you near.

Ever Yr Devoted

Isabella

155. Louey Chisolm, *Celtic Tales Told to the Children*. London: T.C. & E.C. Jack; New York: E. Dutton & Co., 1910. These are not cheerful stories. One character moans a "mournful strain, her heartstrings broke, and she fell at the feet of her dead husband, and there did she die, and by his side was she buried" (41). But they also offer insight into happy marriages: when Grania is depressed and wants to have a feast for the whole family, her husband "because of the love he bore Grania, granted her wish, and for a year they were making ready for the great feast" (105).

156. Possibly Eleanor had ordered the linens sent from a store and they arrived without a note to say who had sent them. Isabella knew, however, they were likely to be from Eleanor.

Poor Dan [Barney] had 3 weeks' jaundice while here. He was so dear & we miss him endlessly—think of my pleasure when he handed me his book [of poetry] & I learned for the first time he'd dedicated it to me. I hope you will like them.

Love to Franklin. I wish I knew what he thought about *so* many things these days.

Patty's arrival, along with a new governess, gave Isabella the chance to get away. In late January, she left with the Walter Douglases, in their private railroad car, for New York City, where she embarked on a whirlwind of activity.

During a week in Washington, on March 3 she and Eleanor sat in the visitors' gallery, observing the final session of Congress until nearly two in the morning. Despite Germany's resumption of unrestricted submarine warfare on February 1, and despite the infamous "Zimmerman telegram," the House adjourned without taking any action on the war. [157]

On April 6, 1917, however, soon after Isabella's return home, the United States declared war on Germany.

The war gave Eleanor Roosevelt the opportunity to discontinue unrewarding activities like paying social calls, and to do something more constructive. She learned how to drive, thinking she might join the new Red Cross Motor Corps. [158] She helped organize the Red Cross canteen, which operated in Union Station in Washington, D.C., where women made and handed out sandwiches and coffee to troops passing through. Eleanor worked two or three shifts a week, distributing free wool provided by the Navy League, collecting the knitted articles, and knitting more or less constantly herself. [159] She also visited the wounded at the Naval Hospital and at St. Elizabeth's, where "shell-shocked" patients were housed. [160]

157. On March 1, Wilson announced that the United States had intercepted a German message to Mexico (the "Zimmerman telegram") promising the return of Arizona, New Mexico, and Texas in exchange for Mexico's support in the war. http://www.historymatters.gmu.edu/d/4938/

158. Florence Jaffray "Daisy" Harriman organized the Red Cross Motor Corps. Roosevelt, *This is My Story*, 185. Eleanor longed to go overseas, like her cousin Ted's wife, Eleanor Butler Roosevelt, but felt she should not on account of her children. Ibid., 197.

159. Typically, Eleanor, who would knit in meetings and in public places for the rest of her life, observed: "Even if your life seemed to call you away from where you could render some kind of direct service, you could be knitting all the time." Ibid., 188.

160. Cook, *Eleanor Roosevelt*, I, 215.

Isabella's uncle, Frank Cutcheon, was offered a staff job with General John Pershing, commander of the American Expeditionary Force (AEF) overseas. Isabella traveled East in October 1917 to confer with Frank about her financial affairs, before his departure. This gave her a chance to see John Greenway, who was in New York preparing to go overseas in November 1917 as a major in the Engineer Officers Reserve Corps. Isabella's chaperone, Margaret Douglas, permitted them one carriage ride alone around Central Park, the only known time they broke their promise to Bob.

Eleanor, meanwhile, had bought Christmas gifts for Isabella from needy orphans and old folks. Isabella was most interested. It would eventually lead her to found a crafts and furniture-making program for disabled vets.

Back in New Mexico, Isabella also took up war work. At the request of the governor's wife, she organized the state's Woman's Auxiliary of the Council of Defense for Grant and Luna counties, instructing women in economizing, planting and canning—what Isabella called "potato patriotism." She also started a Red Cross chapter in Tyrone. During the summer, Isabella organized a massive fund-raising fair at their homestead that drew 450 people. Of course, she still had to care for Bob, who was worsening, and to teach the children.

Burro Mountain Homestead, Tyrone   [Jan 3, 1918]
Eleanor my dearest

You & Santa Claus were very naughty & certainly stole a march[161] on us. We had removed our names from his list "until the war ends" & here we are the glad enjoyers of such lovely things. My portfolio shall be cherished as everything is that pertains to you from a thought to a tangible keepsake—& the frame is really very very pretty—& what an admirable way to help out— we'd like to get in touch with the way of getting the work done by them (the old & orphans?)[162]

Bob & I had a good laugh (as maybe you did too!) over the choice of modern heros—in the book you sent Martha & Bobbie. Emerson says "Those who live to the future must always appear selfish"!—Certainly this can pertain only to intellectuals!—& then he goes on—"Character—needs perspective

---

161. Meaning, to to get ahead of by stealth; gain an advantage on. *The New Shorter Oxford English Dictionary.*

162. She seems to want to know more about a program that sold items made by disadvantaged people.

as a great building."—"We have seen many counterfeits—but we are born believers in great men."—"I should think myself very unhappy in my associates if I could not credit [believe] the best things in History."[163]

[And] this last, dearest, brings me to you—I'll let you wonder why!—but don't be saying to yourself "What can have happened to Isabella that she can sit down to quotations from Emerson thro' times like these?" —It's an outrage. You doubtless dashing to give some canteen soup to soldiers—or wool to knitters—with every moment mapped for the next six months. Well, I promise you, I'm not wholly idle!!

It was as well that I came [back home] when I did—Bob was on the verge of a breakdown—& and has had a very wretched time with pleurisy. Is mending very slowly—& is pathetically weak. I believe it will be a very long pull back to even a little strength—but we are all in good shape to help him & every day proves the perfection of our situation to cope with the problem—the days are filled with children's voices—sunshine—blue hills—open books—firelight—& privacy from the hourly invasions peculiar to small towns but plenty of blessed thoughtful friends who come occasionally.

[And] the days—no one [day] is long enough; what with teaching & small nursing efforts—& it is always sustaining to *know* where one's job is—All this because I know you care—& the world at large is beyond words—these days anyway. Of course we can hardly wait to see what resulting reforms this investigation[164] will bring about—?

My heart ful[l] of love always—If you can find time to do one more blessed thing for some one—address an envelope to Bob sometimes with little more than a word in it. I'll always take my share of the thought[165] & letters are his whole pleasure. But only a *line*.

Please give my love to Franklin and hugs no end to Anna—the boys can't know who we are even—but we feel they are our best.

Isn't Uncle's chance [to work with Pershing] *splendid*? He was so appreciative of your many efforts to get him to drive [to take a drive with you][166]—&

163. Eleanor's gift to the Ferguson children of a book of "modern heroes" prompted Isabella to quote Emerson on the nature of greatness. Her three quotes are from his essay "Character" (1844). See, for example, *Essays by Ralph Waldo Emerson*. New York: Harper Collins, 1981.

164. The editors do not know to what investigation Isabella refers.

165. i.e., I'll know you are thinking about me.

166. When automobiles were relatively new, taking a drive was considered a form of recreation.

enjoyed tea [with you] finally—& was loud in his praises—E[lizabeth] Hoyt also thought you were indeed good to ask her. Bless you 1000 times.

> Yr. loving
>
> Isabella

Mother sounds [as if she's] mending splendidly.

Even while the country was at war, Eleanor knew that Isabella would still share her small personal sorrows—the departure from Washington of Cecil Spring Rice,[167] the "witty old British Ambassador,"[168] and his wife who had been close friends of the Roosevelt family; and the death of Cyril Martineau, after a long battle against tuberculosis.

2131 R Street[169] [Washington, DC]   Jan. 11 [1918]

Dearest Isabella,

Just a line to thank you for your letter & say I will write Bob next week after your Mother has been here & I will give him what gossip I can. When I ask Mr. Henry Adams how he feels about things he says "I'm only glad I'm not responsible for them"! We are all feeling very sad over the Spring Rice's sudden departure. Governments are not kind, are they? & again Mr. Adams [says] "Jews are trumps"[170] just now!

I feel very sad for poor Muriel [Martineau], her husband died on the 8th & her cable is heart broken. He managed in spite of endless operations & suffering to make their life a living joy & I am very thankful she has the baby girl to take her constant care & attention.

My dearest love to you one & all.

> Devotedly,
>
> E.R.

167. Spring-Rice was abruptly recalled by his government, perhaps because the British wanted someone who could work more closely with President Woodrow Wilson. Spring-Rice was a close friend of Theodore Roosevelt, who had been very critical of Wilson's war policy. Willert, *Washington & Other Memories*, 106.
168. Roosevelt, *This is My Story*.
169. Eleanor's Auntie Bye's house, where the FDRs stayed when they first came to Washington, was too small for a family of seven, so they rented a "pleasant" house with a small garden in the back. Ibid., 184.
170. Rufus Daniel Isaacs, who succeeded Spring-Rice, was Jewish. Eventually, Isaacs was elevated to Earl of Reading. http://www.1911encyclopedia.org/Rufus_Daniel_Isaacs_ Reading. People of Eleanor's age and social status made anti-Semitic remarks impersonally and casually, according to ER biographer Blanche Wiesen Cook. Cook, *Eleanor Roosevelt*, I, 390.

The war inspired Eleanor to a frenzy of activity. Caroline Phillips wrote Isabella: "Eleanor works all day and half the night . . . I used to make mild suggestions that she might sometimes take one hour out of the 24 to come and sit with me in the garden, but she merely looked at me as though I were wildly insane and said it was impossible." [171]

Eleanor did not even see much of Franklin. Her war work made it impossible for her to go with Franklin to the parties he always enjoyed. Sometimes he took Eleanor's social secretary, Lucy Mercer. Perhaps when Eleanor wrote below, "one must work and not think," she may have been referring to more than the tragedy of war.

ER's brother Hall, along with his cousin Quentin Roosevelt, TR's youngest son, enlisted as aviators in July 1917.

Even though Eleanor worried that Isabella was doing too much, she did not hesitate to ask her to do one thing more.

2131 R Street [Washington, DC]   March 2nd [1918]
My dearest Isabella,

Such a lovely box of flowers from you, were they meant for our wedding [anniversary] day, if so a thousand thanks for your constant remembrance as well as for the flowers.

Bob's letter troubled me mightily about you, it sounded as though you must have such a lot on your shoulders but of course you wouldn't say so even if you were nearly dead & I only ask that before you are quite done up you get on a train & come East or wire me to come out & help! In the meantime I'm going to give a letter to a very charming young French woman & her officer husband to you & I know if it isn't quite impossible you'll let them spend a day with you. They are going to the camp at Deming in the near future on an inspection trip & expect to be there a few days only. Of course if this is just more than you can manage tell them so frankly & they'll understand for they are really nice. The name is Coustivan.

The children are all well & life goes on fairly smoothly but I seem to acquire more work daily & I now never see my friends except at dinner.

Poor Caroline [Phillips] has had a horrid time. William [Phillips] has had some minor operation (hemorrhoids) I gather from her reticence & is still in

171. Miller, *Isabella Greenway*, 91–92.

the hospital & the baby had eczema so she had to have a wet nurse.[172] The latter is a success however which is a comfort & the baby is thriving again.

The news these days does seem discouraging, doesn't it? However one must work and not think. Margaret is going to Lake Charles[,] Louisiana on the 9th to see Hall & he seems happy now & is flying daily.

   Devoted love always.

    E.R.

Isabella continued to hope that the Roosevelt children might come some time to visit. Martha and Bobbie lived very solitary lives, out in the country, with no school. And, of course, Isabella wanted her best friend's children to be friends with her own children.

Burro Mountain Homestead   March 12, 1918
Tyrone, New Mexico
Eleanor mine!

Not at all—those flowers were the most ordinary week day greeting. No garden of flowers would be an adequate Good morning for you!

Don't you have a worry about me. No woman I know these days has as healthy an existence! I am fully so. We're making the household change—giving up old Louis[173]—& praying that you are going to make our summer happy with Anna, James & a "Miss [Blanche] Spring."

We are looking forward keenly to the pleasure of the charming French lady & husband—& will try to get our mail oftener[174] for fear of missing them. Anyone you send means *such a pleasant touch from the outside.* This winter I've not communicated with [been in the town of] Deming. But Bob is strong enough now to want & enjoy a little diversion.

If in the course of your circulations you hear of a *reliable* French woman who would care to come out here to me next autumn for one year—to talk & teach French with the children I would like to know of her. It would of course be a great advantage if she could teach incidentally first year Latin but that doesn't count if she is good at the other & *nice*. Cheery principally—this is only "in case" you stumble on some one. I have some other lines out—so

---

172. Presumably the baby was thought to be allergic to the mother's milk, and it was hoped she might improve with the milk of another woman.

173. An employee who may have joined the army?

174. Probably mail was not delivered to the Ferguson house because it was so far from town. Consequently, they had to go into the post office to pick it up.

don't worry. Before they go to schools, I'd like a good French foundation—&
will pay what is reasonable—but know very little about such matters. Maybe
you can tell me.

A world—all springy—with columbine, marigolds & hollyhocks starting
forth—a very world of love.

> Ever yr. Devoted
> Isabella

Again & again Mother tells us in glowing terms of you. I never tire of hearing. Belle Eckles [was] recently in Washington for two days[,] called you up
but found you out. She didn't know her address ahead[175] so I couldn't write
you [to go see her].

When she learned that Eleanor was not planning to go to Campobello
as usual, Isabella renewed her plea for Anna and James's company over the
summer, reassuring the Roosevelts that the children would be in no danger of
contracting tuberculosis from Bob.

Burro Mountain Homestead   [late spring 1918]
Tyrone, New Mexico
Eleanor darling

Ever since asking you to write Bob I've felt as guilty as I deserved—while you
would have felt *so* fully repaid for the time & effort that must have been hard to
find—could you have seen Bob's real pleasure in receiving it. He was delighted—
& it just came at a time when he was having a long tedious pull up—from such
a sinking point—& to take his friends hands held out has helped no end.

He gains steadily & I feel confident will be on his feet by spring.

Its warmed some very innermost corners of my heart to have Mother's news
of you. She enjoyed every moment & every one & most of all yours & Franklin's
special dearness—& says "Anna & James are the *most* attractive natural companionable children I have seen & [are] far in away [far and away] the most fun."

Will you take the following very seriously? Bob, Mother & I are wondering *so hopefully*—if you & Franklin would consider sending Anna & James
out to us for the summer or a portion of it—with Miss [Blanche] Spring—or
anyone you feel understands them & would help keep them well. It would
spell *heaven* for us—& (with nothing unexpected) might do them good.

175. i.e., she didn't know where she would be staying before she went.

You must understand it would mean stopping on the other side of the house from Bob—Possibly putting the boys in a tent house—& Bob has everything separate—china glass spoons forks etc—& no one ever goes into his bathroom & if they should come I'll have everything of his washed in separate vessels (a matter that the Drs have not thought necessary)—but we'd play on the safe side.

The life is primitive but that's what they would enjoy—& if Mother is here we'll try to go on some *not remote* camping trip—& let the children do the cooking etc—with some cowboys who are good at that sort of thing—& I'm sure you agree with me that a certain amount of bedmaking etc is good for children—! I only dare make such a selfish suggestion on hearing you aren't going to Campobello.

Our children ride every day & take entire charge & care of their ponies—very docile creatures. There would be nothing but untold joy connected with such a visit for each member of this household & not one *scrap* of trouble. So in considering this, you'll realize I speak the truth—it's only whether you feel it might be feasible or do them any good.

I'd never be able to tell you what such a chance to have ours [our children] together would mean!!—or how I long to come to know my goddaughter.

I don't believe Miss Spring would find it irksome—or anyone else you might send.

Dear—you'll think it over at your leisure—there is no hurry whatever—& a decision at the last moment would not ruffle us in any way—but don't turn it down at once!

What is there in Franklin's running for Gov[176]—Could he give up the interest of his present position for another—except begrudgingly—

& just here comes your second wonderful letter to Bob![177] I'll send this anyway—because we can't take "no" so lightly—& remember always that the greatest thing that could ever happen to Martha & Bobbie would be to have your two—& they need them sorely—they are such a solitary two—tho' full of fun all the while—& we are powerless to alter this lonely upbringing.

Maybe later when the summer begins to take form you can consider it more favorably.

176. This is an unfounded rumor. Franklin would not run for governor of New York until 1928.

177. Eleanor wrote to Bob, answering Isabella's March 12, 1918 letter that first invited the Roosevelt children to visit. She declined, as she was planning to have the children stay at Hyde Park that summer.

Poor Lady Spring Rice,[178] her married years have been a "seat of war"—in such numberless illness'—I thought her utterly broken & a different woman—& one prays—the little boy will get strong. Alfred Noyes[179] wrote such a nice verse in his [Spring Rice's] memory. That letter of Theodate Popes[180] to her Mother about the sinking of the Lusitania will follow to you. Cousin Helen Houghton has it. You mentioned wishing to see it ages ago! It's perfectly marvellous to share lessons [teaching responsibilities] with Mother! We're installing a "couple" shortly—so don't have misgivings about our staff.

> Hugs & hearts full of love
> Isabella

Theodore Roosevelt had written from the Dakotas after the deaths of his wife and mother: "Black care rarely sits behind a rider whose pace is fast enough."[181] Eleanor, too, recognized that work blotted out all kinds of unwelcome information. She helped Addie Daniels, the wife of her husband's boss, to organize the Navy Red Cross.[182] Her work with the soldiers made the once-shy woman more comfortable with people she did not ordinarily meet. Even people Eleanor had encountered in New Mexico came to wartime Washington.

2131 R Street [Washington, DC]   [April 2, 1918]
Isabella dearest

Two letters from you, such joy & such tardy answering but I can only say the days are full. I've been more than glad these past days of the big German offensive not to have much time for thought. It's been a very anxious time. General [Leonard] Wood[183] has been here & Franklin has been fearfully depressed by what he tells. Hopeless incompetency seems to surround us in high places & yet the *men* who go are fine. I know that for I see train

---

178. Cecil Spring Rice died on February 14, 1918. Evidently, Lady Spring Rice's son had been frequently ill, too.

179. English poet best known for "The Highwayman."

180. Theodate (Effie) Brooks Pope (1867–1946) was on the *Lusitania* when it was torpedoed in 1915. She fainted while in the water and was found floating across an oar. The crew revived her. She later held séances to try to contact the spirits of friends on board who were lost. http://www.rmslusitania.info/pages/saloon_class/pope_theodate.html

181. Roosevelt, *Ranch Life and the Hunting Trail*, 59.

182. Cook, *Eleanor Roosevelt*, I, 215.

183. Leonard Wood (1860–1927) who, with Theodore Roosevelt, organized the 1st Volunteer Cavalry regiment, popularly known as the Rough Riders, was the U. S. Army chief of staff, 1910–1914.

load after train load go to ports of embarkation & it is a liberal education in the American soldier! My heart aches much of the time though. Mrs. Stone (whom I last knew as Mrs. Cooley) appeared at the canteen on Monday & it seemed a far cry from Cat Canyon.

I am so more than sorry not to have seen Belle Eckles. Tell her another time she must leave word where she is. I would so have loved to see her.

I fear my French officer & his wife may never get to Deming as I heard they were side tracked in Texas.

Did you know Sheffield [Cowles] was to be allowed in the officers training camp in spite of his youth [age twenty]? Just a few of them are going & evade the rule apparently & A. Bye is much relieved.[184]

Indeed I'm fearfully tempted to take Anna & James out to you myself this summer for a bit but I've so much work on my hands I don't know if I'd have the right to go this year. We'll surely come the summer the war is over & perhaps this year! At last the Navy Dept. is getting organized for real Red Cross work & we're getting the women in the Dept. connected with it & it's a lot of work, sewing & surgical dressings etc.

Franklin is certainly not going to run for Governor. It has been suggested but he could not leave the Dept. during the war for anything but a destroyer! His one hope now is that he may get abroad as he feels there is much he could do over there.

Alice [Longworth] has been here twice in two days & to ask if I want her to work anywhere & I'm going to try to get her interested, it is a pity so much energy should go to waste!

Anna & James have celebrated their Easter holidays by having their tonsils out just one week apart & both seem very flourishing.

We went on Sunday to the [National] Cathedral to hear the Archbishop of York preach & I think I never heard a finer sermon. Simple & clear, but high minded & fine, just what his face led you to hope he would say. I have not yet met Mr. Readings but they dine here the 18th.

Pauline [Merrill] was here for a week with Mrs. [illegible] it was nice to see her. I hope they will both come & stay here sometime this month.

Cousin Susie [Parish] writes she is home in New York & better but will not be able to give up bromides[185] entirely for another year!

My love to Bob & your Mother the chicks, & a heartfull to you always my

---

184. She thinks that, as an officer, he would have a better chance of surviving the war.
185. Bromides were sedatives, often used as sleeping pills in the nineteenth century.

dear, you mean so much to me how I wish often & often that only happiness might lie along your path but that never is the lot of the really fine people.

Devotedly always,

E.R.

Franklin sailed for Europe on July 9 to inspect U.S. naval forces. The children had gone to their grandmother at Hyde Park, where they were learning French with a governess. Eleanor stayed in Washington for the rest of July, working harder than ever, raising money for projects like a recreational center for wounded men who needed physical therapy. She also learned how to drive and how to swim. Then she joined her children in Hyde Park for the month of August.[186]

A number of Eleanor's relatives were fighting in Europe. Her cousin Quentin, TR's youngest, was shot down and killed by anti-aircraft fire on July 14 behind enemy lines. He was twenty years old.

Isabella was anxious for John Greenway, who was among the first Americans to see action. As an engineer, he helped design the trenches at Cantigny, at the second battle of the Marne, and at Belleau Wood. Greenway was promoted to full colonel and was later awarded a Distinguished Service Cross, for bravery under fire, and the French Croix de Guerre. Eventually, he received a brevet promotion to brigadier general.[187]

In June 1918, Isabella was drafted by the governor to head New Mexico's Women's Land Army, building on her earlier work for the state Women's Council of Defense. Isabella was responsible for organization, publicity, financing, and housing women who took over the farm work left by men who had gone to war. She joined them in cutting hay, harvesting corn, putting up silage,[188] and filling over one hundred railroad carloads of apples.[189] She had been out in the fields for several months and unable to answer Eleanor's last letter.

2131 R Street [Washington, DC]   July 28th [1918]

Dearest Isabella

It's ages since I wrote & I do want news of you if you have a moment to write. You were all too dear to want me [to come visit you in New Mexico]

186. Cook, *Eleanor Roosevelt*, I, 225.

187. Miller, *Isabella Greenway*, 92, 97–98.

188. Silage is "fodder for winter use, cut, compressed, and preserved by its own fermentation in an airtight chamber, as a silo." *Webster's Collegiate Dictionary*, 1953.

189. Miller, *Isabella Greenway*, 93–97.

with the chicks this year but I knew Franklin hoped to go over [to Europe] sometime & could make no plans & since he's been gone I've been alone down here working on the canteen as we have been short handed & the work very heavy. I expect now to go home [to Hyde Park] on Wednesday but I really think a summer of French governess & quiet was necessary this year.

I dined with Alice [Longworth] last night & she says the family have been wonderful about Quentin. He was instantly killed by 2 bullet holes in the head they have heard through Spain so he did not suffer & it is a glorious way to die but I know A. Edith & Ethel [Derby] are suffering.

Sheffield is back at Quantico after 10 days leave & working in a machine gun battery in the overseas depot & he expects to go the end of August but of course he doesn't know. Auntie Bye is in N.Y. just now with her doctor but returns the end of the week. She was miserable before she left & the strain is fearful for her but she keeps cheerful all the time with Sheffield in the most wonderful way.

Do you know where Dave Goodrich is now & do you hear anything from Jack Greenway? I've often thought as he is in the engineers he must have had some pretty thrilling experiences.

I have seen Mr. Freylinghuysen[190] twice & it was nice to hear of you. He dined here the other night & was very nice. Gen. Bridges has gone abroad & so he can't be very busy now but I've been so busy I haven't had time to see much of anyone. The Readings have sailed too for a few weeks & a number of the other Englishmen.

I expect Franklin back sometime in Sept. but of course the date is uncertain & I shan't come back here till Sept. 24th when I bring James & Elliott for school.

I hope I shall see Pauline [Merrill] while I am at home. I'm afraid having a new baby was rather a shock after such a long time!

Much love dearest & kiss Martha & Buzz for me & give Bob & your Mother lots of love also.

   Devotedly,
    Eleanor

190. The Freylinghuysens were an old Massachusetts and New Jersey family.

Part Four

Heartbreak and Happiness in Postwar America

On September 12 Franklin, returning from Europe, cabled for Eleanor to meet his ship in New York with an ambulance. The 1918 influenza epidemic[1] was sweeping across the world, and he had contracted double pneumonia and influenza.

While Franklin was in bed, Eleanor began to unpack his suitcase. She found there a bundle of love letters from Lucy Mercer. For two years, Franklin had frequently been seen with Lucy at social gatherings, even dinner parties. Eleanor, who was often out of town with the children, had tried to think it was reasonable for her husband and her social secretary to be often in each other's company. But Eleanor later said, "I did not believe in knowing things. . ."[2] Eleanor offered him a divorce, but the scandal would have ruined his political career. When they told Sara about the situation, she threatened to stop her financial support if Franklin left Eleanor. It was her money that made his political career possible.[3] Eleanor was deeply hurt, but she did not confide her pain in letters. After a silence of almost a year, she referred to her anguish only indirectly, even to Isabella. When Isabella did learn about FDR's infidelity, her son later said, she was never again able to regard Franklin in quite the same way.[4]

The Great War ended on November 11, 1918. John Greenway was mustered out before the end of the year, and proudly sent Isabella his letter of commendation from Pershing's chief of staff. Greenway visited Theodore Roosevelt on January 4, 1919, just two days before the former president died.

1. The influenza pandemic of 1918–1919 killed between 20 and 40 million people. A fifth of the world's population was infected. An estimated 675,000 Americans died of influenza during those years, ten times as many as in the war. Of the American soldiers who died in Europe, only half were war casualties; the other half were influenza victims. http://virus.stanford.edu/uda/
2. Cook, *Eleanor Roosevelt*, I, 217–20, 224.
3. Ward, *A First-Class Temperament*, 413; Cook, *Eleanor Roosevelt*, I, 227–32.
4. Ward, *A First-Class Temperament*, 614.

Eleanor was on the high seas when she learned of her uncle Theodore's death. Franklin, who wanted to make amends, had obtained permission for Eleanor to accompany him to inspect the dismantling of Navy installations in Europe, even though official policy prohibited wives from accompanying their husbands abroad. The trip helped the couple reconnect and rediscover shared goals as they toured the battlefields and planned for postwar reconstruction.[5]

The Roosevelts returned to the States on the same ship as President and Mrs. Woodrow Wilson, who had been at the Paris Peace Conference. Wilson had worked hard to insert into the Treaty of Versailles a provision for a League of Nations. But the United States would have to ratify the treaty, and Wilson had done little to convince the Republican-dominated Senate to embrace it.

After an absence of two months, Eleanor devoted herself for a time to domestic affairs, spending more time with the children and reorganizing her household. After almost a year, she finally found time to write to Isabella.

Hyde Park on the Hudson   July 11, 1919
Dearest Isabella

Strange though it may seem I've been getting news of you now again though not through any letters on your part or on mine! Bishop Atwood gave me my last news & was so full of admiration for you dear & of course you know I always like that. I've just been spending two days with Auntie Bye & she was saying she thought you had some idea before long of sending Bobby to school. If he comes East & if you can ever let me have him for the whole or part of any holiday do remember that I always have room for him & we will do our best to make him happy. James will go to Groton a year from this autumn I think.

This past year has rather got the better of me it has been so full of all kinds of things that I still have a breathless, hunted feeling[6] about it though for the moment I am leading an idle if at times a somewhat trying life!

You probably heard that all the children had "flu" last December & Elliott [and Franklin had] double pneumonia so he & Franklin both have been through quite a siege but all the chicks were pretty well before Franklin & I

---

5. Ward, *A First-Class Temperament*, 418–19; Cook, *Eleanor Roosevelt*, I, 232–33.
6. Virtually every biographer of Eleanor Roosevelt quotes these haunting but obscure words. Her sense of being "hunted" may have come from trying to escape her knowledge of Franklin's affair. Additionally, after feeling unloved as a child, then delighting in her husband's attention, Eleanor might well have felt "breathless" beneath the crushing weight of her discovery of Franklin's infidelity.

sailed Jan. 2nd. I hated to go but I was afraid to let Franklin go without me as I know the climate & many discomforts might be hard for him after pneumonia in October.

I must own the interest of seeing even a little was a great temptation.[7] It proved for me even more interesting than I had expected for we were able to motor from Paris to Boulogne through the northern part of France over which the British & French had fought & refought for four years. I do not think one can quite realize [the devastation] without seeing [it]. Bourlon Wood[8] with its few bare sticks[9] to mark what once had been gave one an even more ghostly feeling than the shelled & ruined towns.

The sea of mud on every side also must be seen to be fully realized & what the men who fought there lived through is inconceivable. We had 2 young American officers with us who had been brigaded with the British at the taking of the St. Quentin canal[10] & as we went by they could describe it all & it seemed a very wonderful feat for the cut is some 60 feet deep, very steep & just mud from top to bottom & they had to slide down & cross & climb up in the face of the German machine gun fire!

I saw much of Muriel [Martineau] in London & she had not aged at all & her little boys are sweet. Her baby girl still had eczema badly which complaint they do not seem to treat very successfully in England but she is nearly well now. I stayed with her for a few days while Franklin went to Brussels & down to Cobbutz to see the Mariuis [—] they would not give me a pass for the Rhine so I rejoined Franklin in Paris.

Ted & Kermit were both in Paris & I like Kermit & Belle so much. He is very anxious to get out to see you. Munro was also in Paris, behaving too dreadfully & as you have doubtless heard he proceeded to do the same when he got home & is now in Bloomingdale's.[11] I suppose he will soon be out again but I confess to rather a hopeless feeling as to the future unless they can send him where he must work hard physically as well as mentally.

7. i.e., I admit that I was interested in seeing at least a little of the aftermath of war.
8. Part of the battle of the Hindenburg Line, September 29–October 2, 1918, that proved to be a turning point in the war.
9. Lime trees in the area, though shattered by shell-fire, have since been nursed back to health and now form part of the memorial to the Canadian forces that captured a dominating hill.
10. Canals were German defensive barriers. http://www.awm.gov.au/units/event_147.asp.
11. Bloomingdale Hospital, a mental asylum, originally part of New York Hospital, moved in 1894 from New York City to White Plains, N.Y. Now known as New York Hospital-Westchester Division. Munro may have been suffering from alcoholism.

I saw Corinne [Alsop] at Farmington & she is worlds better & the 3 younger children are sweet though they do not look as strong as one would expect. Little Joe was away for a day so I missed him but Joe & Corinne came to dine in the evening. Joe has done everything for A. Corinne in a business way this past year & Teddy [Robinson] has been quite useless though he is supposedly scouring the country for a job.

Auntie Bye herself is wonderful in her courage & patience & still keeps her interest in everything but it breaks your heart to see anyone suffer as she does. They say she is stronger but her rheumatism is much worse & she cannot move without its being agony. She uses a rolling chair, gets down [comes downstairs] at one and goes up again at 8:30 & I think guests for more than 24 hours would exhaust her, in fact, she said she had asked no one which will show you how she feels. She is very thin & her face is entirely without color.

We brought Sheffield back with us & he is again in college & just now cruising up the coast with 5 others & a cook in a chartered schooner which none of them seem to know much about sailing! I think he is a fine boy if he only isn't spoiled, he is surprisingly young in spots & old in others & as yet his values of life are fairly muddled but I think he'll turn out all right.

How are Bob & Martha & Bobby & you yourself & how & where is your Mother? I was so distressed to hear of Miss Dinsmore's accident.[12]

I am now commuting between Washington & here but I hope Franklin arrives today for ten days & then I take the three younger children to Fairhaven for a little sea bathing & once settled I shall leave them & go back to Washington & go fetch them about Aug. 17th. Anna & James stay here with Mama as they prefer it to any other place & are thriving. All are well though Elliott had his adenoids out for the 2nd time two weeks ago. He always looks thin & pale but in spite of his illness last winter he did very well at school. Anna is young in her ways still, but she has a very sweet nature & will be a fine girl I hope.

Thank Bob for his long letter & tell him I will write him very soon.

Dearest love to you Isabella dear, though I don't write my feelings never change.

> Devotedly ever,
> Eleanor R.

---

12. Patty, while visiting Julia Dinsmore, had accidentally run over her aunt with a car. The ground was soft and no bones were broken, but Julia was eighty-six years old and the accident put her in bed for a month. Miller, *Isabella Greenway*, 100.

In the summer of 1919, Isabella, who had not left New Mexico for eighteen months, rented a cottage in Santa Barbara, California. She needed rest after her arduous Land Army work. At the same time she was looking for a place to put the children in school, now that they were approaching their teens.

Away in California, she had not answered Eleanor's letter. Eleanor wrote again, hoping to pick up their neglected correspondence.

Henderson House[13]   Sept. 16 [1919]
Mohawk Herkimer Co. NY
Isabella dearest,

I've just written Bob a long letter but I want to send you just a line to tell you what a joy it was to hear your news from Auntie Corinne. Oh! My dear, it is so long since I've seen or heard from you & I know I am worse even than you are about writing but somehow you mean more to me every year & your life & the way you have faced it & all you do & are doing has meant so much to me in example & inspiration. Someday when much lies behind us both & we have time to be together & talk again there is going to be real joy for both of us I hope.

Franklin hopes to go on a shooting trip in Newfoundland between Oct. 15th & Nov. 1st & I was wondering if you couldn't break away & come to Washington to me for that time? Franklin would feel dreadfully to miss you so you might come a little before but it would be lovely to be together for a while & we might take a jaunt to New York & Farmington together. Your godchild is growing very tall & I think you will like her. She will be a fine girl I hope & life is pure joy to her now!

This was just to say I love you & must come to an end as A. Corinne is entertaining most of Jordanville[14] for tea & I must go down & do what I can! A heart full of love to you always.

    Devotedly
      Eleanor

After her return from the coast, Isabella plunged once again into running the household and overseeing the children's education. Her workday began at

13. At one time the Roosevelt family owned Henderson House, built in 1833 by Harriett Douglas Cruger, ancestor of Helen Roosevelt Robinson. http://herkimer.nygenweb.net/warren/gelstoncastle.html.

14. Jordanville is near Mohawk, between Albany and Syracuse, in upstate New York.

6:30 and ended when she tumbled into bed: "I sometimes lie down, I never sit down," she said.[15]

Isabella was contrite for not having written in well over a year. In a somewhat garbled note, she attempted to re-establish the old intimacy by asking Eleanor to look after the children in the event of Isabella's death.

Burro Mountain Homestead, Tyrone   October 7 1919
Eleanor darling

I'd stop [writing] entirely if I didn't know you were there [for me] & [in order] to show you my faith thro' the silences, [you should know that] I never start over our bad roads that I don't say to Marie [Ballet] (she who teaches M & B) "remember if any thing happens to me Martha & Bobbie are to go to Mrs. Franklin Roosevelt for half of *every* year"!!!

Dear soul there's nothing from cooking to house painting that hasn't taken me from my desk lately. This is a forerunner—a real letter goes tonight. If you could imagine how sorely you tempt me to go onto you—or what it would mean! I just wired[16] to say how sorry I am it is impossible—as I'll explain in detail.

All the love of a life time with compound interest.

    Yr. devoted
       Isabella

We have three trains a week so [the] next [letter] may be a day or two in catching up.

Like many elite families of the time, the Roosevelts and the Fergusons planned to send their children to boarding school. That time was fast approaching for Anna Roosevelt and Martha Ferguson, who were now thirteen years old.

Bob's elder brother, Ronald Ferguson, complicated matters by suggesting that Bobbie should be his heir (he had no children). He insisted, however, that Bobbie would have to be educated in Great Britain, if he were going to take over a Scottish estate. Bob regarded this as a demand for the "total surrender of my entire family," [17] and refused the offer.

From Santa Barbara, Isabella had taken the children to Los Angeles for Bobbie to have his tonsils removed. Isabella's merry description of a week

15. Miller, *Isabella Greenway*, 102.
16. Missing.
17. RHMF to IG, May 9, 1919, FC.

spent in a hotel while Bobbie was recovering is testimony to her remarkable ability to enjoy life, even under trying circumstances. While there, she and the children read a book about Abraham Lincoln, whose determination to be of public service Isabella greatly admired.

Back in New Mexico, eleven-year-old Bobbie demonstrated that his unorthodox schooling had taught him to be independent. He rode his horse twenty miles to Silver City, by himself.

Burro Mountain Homestead, Tyrone   October 15 1919
Eleanor dearest—

My silences are inexcusable—but somehow I know you understand. At least [you should understand] that every day strengthens my adoration of you—& [you are as much] a part of my existance as the sun shining—& what an inspiring part you are far too modest to ever guess—

I would have gone to you had it been possible. How I longed to—You would find it hard to believe what the temptation was—Eleanor dearest—nothing means, in life, just what seeing you does—As I look back you almost represent the milestones—the times I have been with you—& it never occurs to me that we will not, one of these day—be near each other & able to share all the 100 little things that do come to spell the sum total.

I didn't come because it is almost impossible to leave the place when the children & Miss [Marie] Ballet are here—unless Mother is too—for reasons that you can readily imagine—from holding the cook on the Mt top—to keeping peace between the children & Miss B who they do tease unmercifully—& then we spent our whole holiday margin [savings] in our trip to the coast. Everything costs so infernally these days & Bobbie's operation (we had his tonsils out) rather brought us down to bedrock—with our income unchanged—& cost[s] mounting so steadily we have been wonderfully fortunate in having Homesteaded when we did. For now we have all that's best in farm produce without limit for the children as we could not have had we still been renting & buying.

Eleanor I simply crave to see your children—& when you say that James is in Groton[18] my heart sort of stops short. Is it possible. Dear, how did it feel to leave him?—& as for Anna—I just feel shy in thinking of her loveliness—because I saw it all coming when in Washington—& Martha is ever so impatient to see her—but a little shy.

18. His father's preparatory school.

We just had such a lovely note from my old teacher Miss Chapin[19] sending Martha the schedule of school work for this year. She has told me that Martha could even live with her & go to school if I couldn't be East at the time. Wasn't that very wonderful? Martha being the first grandchild of the school. I'd love to talk to you about the future—in fact I must before long.

For the next year, & maybe the next, I don't believe either of the children are suffering by staying at home. Were we to leave Bob until it is an absolute necessity I always feel that the children would have failed in their first duty. For, after all, Bob is their first problem & they must help make his years possible—while they can—& I don't believe that any life could be healthier for them until they are 14 or 15—Do you?

Private What an outpouring—Ronald somewhat took my breath away by announcing his desire to have Bobbie begin his life in Scotland at once!! because he proposed leaving his property only to a British subject—Thanks to Col T. R.[,] Bob is as stanch an American as I am—& as determined Bobbie shall be brought up one. Bob plans to meet Ronald next May in Washington (I am somewhat disgusted that R. & Nelly[20] don't stop off here)—but it's all quite typical.[21] So maybe you'll let me go to you then? May I perhaps, or at any rate, be near you—& see as much of Anna as possible. Bob might not be able to go but I believe he will on sheer determination.

Santa Barbara was a great success. We all grew fat & happy & forgot our worries & had lots of happy times with all sorts & ages. Bobbie is a new person after having his tonsils out—& we did have such a fine time together recuperating in the top of a hotel in Los Angeles—where for a week we stayed in one room reading the Child's History of Great Americans—a thing we should all do from time to time!!

It's the best week I've had in years—when one read that Lincoln said he might be defeated for the legislature 5 or 6 times but would win eventually & having to finally borrow $200 to buy clothes & then walked a hundred miles to serve! What tissue paper most of us are—not you—my dear—but the rest of us.

19. Maria Bowin Chapin founded a private school for girls in New York City. It opened in 1901 with seven teachers and seventy-eight students; Isabella was one of the first pupils. *Time Magazine* obit, March 19, 1934.
20. Sir Ronald and his wife, Lady Helen.
21. Ronald seems never to have visited New Mexico.

By the way, young Mr. and Mrs Houghtling (can't spell—was a Delano)[22] talked glowingly of you & he said Franklin must in all natural course of events end in the White House.

This must stop—but now that I have the habit you may be deluged. Martha & I drove Bob over to Silver so he could organize the memorial campaign for the Col.[23]—& here we are 9:30 P. M. in Silver City writing you in a wholesale grocer shop—with 20 miles ahead of us to drive. Bobbie having ridden his horse to town to be shod [get horseshoes]. We have a 50 ft. swimming pool in our courtyard & count on Anna & James coming to us soon for a summer.

My heart full of love. The best I have is always yours—& I depend on you as on no one.

    Yr devoted

        Isabella

Although Bob's elder brother Ronald and his wife never seemed able to make the trip to New Mexico to see Bob, they nonetheless were planning to visit Washington, D.C. Isabella considered meeting them there.

The U. S. Senate had refused to ratify the Treaty of Versailles without changes, or "reservations," to the League of Nations provisions. Wilson, who believed that he would not be able to get the other signatories to agree to changes, decided to appeal the subject to the American people through an extended speaking trip. The trip exhausted him and his health broke down. Wilson suffered a stroke in early October 1919, and remained largely incapacitated for many months. The Wilsons did very little entertaining at the White House during his illness. An exception was made, however, for the King and Queen of the Belgians, with whom Wilson and his wife Edith had become good friends in Paris earlier that year.

Eleanor's war work was finished, but the crisis in her marriage prompted her to seek satisfaction through more work outside her home. She did not mention to Isabella that she met in early October with women's organizations trying to improve working conditions for women, possibly because she did not yet know what role she would be taking.[24]

22. Fred Delano's son-in-law, James L. Houghteling. Ward to editors, March 6, 2007.
23. Raising money to build a memorial to Theodore Roosevelt, who died January 6, 1919.
24. Cook, *Eleanor Roosevelt*, I, 258.

Eleanor was enjoying her children more, too. The older ones were becoming good companions, and she was learning to be closer to her younger children than she had been to her first babies.

2131 R Street, Washington, DC[25]   Oct. 26, [1919]
My dearest Isabella,

I must get this off before coal strikes, railroad strikes etc[26] make it impossible to communicate! Excuse the paper[27] but I ordered new pads weeks ago & they have never come.

Your two letters were joy. I was just hungry for a bit of you & have read & reread every word you wrote. I'm sorry for Ronald & Lady Helen's sake that they did not plan to go to you but I am so glad they are going to oblige you to come here. Of course if you don't stay with me I should be most unhappy & I want every spare moment you have. I can take in Bob too if you think he could sleep in a very cold sun parlor & use the children's bathroom! Alice [Longworth] would love to have him I know however & make him far more comfortable.

Is there any truth in the rumor which we heard that Ronald was to be the next ambassador here? Lord Grey[28] dined with us the other night & was too pathetic about his eyes, he can see but it all looks like a bad photograph. Dr. Wilmer[29] thinks however he may have found the cause in a tooth & if it should turn out to be so, his trip to America would be worthwhile.

25. The house belonging to Anna Cowles (ER's Auntie Bye) was too small for the Roosevelts' large family, and in 1917 they had moved into a rented house, which Eleanor described as "pleasant." Roosevelt, *This is My Story*, 184.
26. The end of the war brought labor unrest as the country tried to absorb all the returning soldiers. In 1919 and 1920 "more than four million workers participated in 2,665 strikes." Cook, *Eleanor Roosevelt*, I, 237.
27. Lined yellow paper.
28. Sir Edward Grey (1862–1933) served as ambassador to Washington from Great Britain, 1919–1920. http://www.answers.com/topic/edward-grey-1st-viscount-grey-of-fallodon. He sought treatment at Johns Hopkins for his poor eyesight. Cooper, *Breaking the Heart of the World*, 220.
29. William H. Wilmer, the first director of the Johns Hopkins Department of Ophthalmology, had a distinguished career at Georgetown University and a flourishing private practice in the nation's capital before coming to Hopkins in 1925. He was considered among the preeminent ophthalmologists of his day, treating presidents, Supreme Court justices, and senators.

The town is agog over the Belgian King & Queen's arrival to-morrow night & I am hoping the children get a glimpse of him for he did behave so finely[30] but Franklin's being away makes it hard for me to arrange. They [official Washingtonians] are only having dinners, no big reception so I don't suppose I shall see them either. Franklin made a speech at the American Legion meeting in N.Y. where the king & prince were guests so he saw him before leaving.

I don't see how I could have said James was at Groton he goes next September & that will be soon enough as he's only twelve in Dec.[31] I know it will be a dreadful blow on him & I shall always expect things to happen to him! The football season is on now & I fear the games are more important than his lessons as he has made the junior team. So far he's only had a knee & head kicked & no serious results but I'll be glad when the season is over without broken bones! Even Elliott at 9 plays but it isn't quite as strenuous with him as yet.

How I wish Bobby could teach them both to shoot & trap animals. We must come out in a year or two & set up tents beside you & spend a whole summer! When you come in May I want to talk it over and oh! So many other things. I need your help & advice in so many ways, for I never want anyone as I want you.

Anna is really getting very lovely in many ways, her love of the country & animals is a very pronounced trait & she has decided to take an agricultural course when she finishes school as she prefers to know how to earn her living on a farm! Franklin Jr. & John are such a delightful pair & I'm so glad to be bringing them back next week. Franklin went in to the New Brunswick woods a week ago & will I hope meet me at Hyde Park Nov. 3rd & we will all return together the 5th. I hope he gets 2 moose but above all I hope he gets a much needed rest.

I am so glad you decided to bring Bobby up an American, aside from everything else the future of properties in England seems very dubious![32]

30. Albert I displayed strong leadership during World War I, commanding the Belgian army to resist the German invasion and leading his troops in the final Allied offensive. His wife, Elizabeth, was daughter of the Duke of Bavaria. http://www.famousbelgians.net/albert1.htm.

31. Because of her critical mother, Eleanor was very sensitive and apt to be defensive when she thought a misunderstanding might expose her to censure.

32. The 1909 Finance Act increased taxation on all land revenues and triggered a sell-off of farmland and estates. After the First World War, an estimated eight million acres in Britain changed hands, far more than at any other time in history. http://www.pbs.org/wgbh/masterpiece/cazalets/society.html

Amid a world of people who are having fearful domestic [household management] trials, I seem to be sailing along peacefully, having acquired on my return from England last summer a complete darky household,[33] but I have not yet succeeded in crawling out of the interminable "drives" which are going on. The latest I am really interested in is the "Women's Roosevelt Memorial Ass'n."[34]

I'm trying to wind up the Navy Red Cross rather unsuccessfully for I am promptly being involved in trying to get rest rooms for the girls established in the Department with a woman doctor in charge! Sometimes I wish I could disappear & lead a hermit's life for a year with only my husband & children & real friends to think about.

Miss [Marie] Ballet sounds so nice but I'm glad the children tease her, that sounds like mine! I quite see why you can't leave & I do hope your Mother will be out with you soon. How is she? I wrote her from Henderson but haven't heard anything from her since.

I spent a night with Cousin Henry [Parish] this autumn & he has Elizabeth Hall with him but Cousin Susie is at Dr. Riggs Sanitarium[35] in Stockbridge. He seems to think her better & I hope she is, though her letters do not seem to me to be much changed. Of course, I think she proves your rule, one should learn young to have duties & bear responsibilities & I don't think you'll ever regret keeping Martha & Buzz at the Homestead till they are 14 or 15, aside from the wonderful physical start it gives them, feeling a duty to Bob is fine. I sometimes wonder if Cousin Susie ever had to consider anyone before herself, now she can't help it & is not to blame.

No one less resembles tissue paper than you do. I know no one, least of all myself, who could have done what you've done with your life so far & I'm

33. This was unusual at the time, when most domestic servants were white. Eleanor said she was influenced by her admiration for Julia Loving, Isabella's "Mammy." Roosevelt, *This is My Story*, 220. Geoffrey Ward thinks it is more likely she was intimidated by giving orders to white servants. Ward to editors, March 6, 2007. Many years later, Eleanor was rebuked by an African American friend for using the term "darky." ER apologized, saying she thought it was a term of affection, and promised never to use it again.

34. The Women's Roosevelt Memorial Association was founded in 1919 by an act of the New York State Assembly. It later joined with the Roosevelt Memorial Association, chartered by an act of Congress in 1920, successor to an unofficial Permanent Memorial National Committee started by friends and family after TR's death in January 1919. Today it is known as the Theodore Roosevelt Association. http://theodoreroosevelt.org/TR%20Web%20Book/TR_CD_to_HTML713.html

35. Austen Riggs Sanitarium, established in 1919, now the Austen Riggs Center in Stockbridge, Massachusetts.

sure you have made Bobby a fit follower of the old frontier stock! I know you hated the tonsil operation for it is horrid but I'm glad you already see a real improvement in Bobby.

Give him our love & tell him that Anna, James, Elliott & Franklin Jr. can all sympathize with him. Give Martha our love too & tell her Anna & I often talk about her & wonder if she likes the things we do!

My love to Bob & to you dearest Isabella more than I can ever tell you.

Devotedly,

Eleanor

Although heading the Women's Land Army had taught Isabella executive skills and how to work with many different sorts of people, her first actual experience with politics was serving on the Grant County Board of Education with her friend Belle Eckles. Isabella wrote Eleanor on school board letterhead, complaining that she had no other stationery. But, perhaps she wanted to let Eleanor know that her friend in the country was also doing interesting things in politics.

Musing on a photo of the Roosevelt family, Isabella observed once again that people who faced troubles were actually fortunate, because they developed skills and confidence.

Bob, who suddenly rallied from his illness, went to Santa Barbara to look into schools for the children, who were now thirteen and twelve. He also wanted to prove to himself that he could travel there to visit them. Isabella was glad to see him taking an interest in life. She was also glad, after a busy Christmas season, to have some time alone with the children.

Bob considered buying a cottage in Santa Barbara, but Isabella suggested that they build their own house. This idea had the added benefit of giving Bob something to work on.

Grant County Board of Education   January 6, 1920
Silver City NM
Isabel Lancaster Eckles, President
Mrs. R. F. Stovall, Vice president
Mrs. T. W. Holland, Secretary
Mrs. Robert Munro-Ferguson
Mrs. Holmes Maddox
(If I could spell I wouldn't mind using this imposing paper—we're high & dry for any)

Eleanor mine—

You & yours have been the real delight of my Xmas. I've carried the photograph from table to table; from room to room—& it seems but yesterday that I stood alongside in the white taffeta & saw you step over the border[36]—& now dear I simply can't say the pride that wells up with the tears when I try to tell you the admiration there is for the way you have carried yourself & the grand old success you've made—as no one else I know—& who feels regret for those to whom trouble comes early?[37] I[t] makes [the] most of us.

I have only one regret about the photograph. It looks alarmingly like the ones of families that end up in the White House—& that I'm not sure I would wish for any one I loved. As for Anna—I *feast* my eyes on her in unbelief & happiness because she is in such large part *you*. James is too handsome for words. Elliot looks such a dear gentle person (a misleading way they have in photographs!!) & John & Franklin are adorable & look perfect mischiefs! As for you dear it's almost a passable photograph—but nothing much of Franklin.

I'm about to enjoy Sec Lane's[38] little book & mighty glad we have it.

Please take hold of something *very tight* & be prepared even then to fall over when you hear that Bob with Hector is sojourning in Santa Barbara— Marry a Scotchman & live long enough & he'll give you a surprise. I think the fact that Belle Breckinridge (Dave [Goodrich]'s sister for whom Bob was trustee for so long) is there with her family has something to do with it. But I am just a[s] thrilled as tho it were Martha's debut & hoping he'll have no end of fun & plenty of rejuvenating shocks!!—after *ten* years without budging— It's like suddenly finding yourself adrift in the South Seas after picking your way thro ice bergs for years from a mental point of view.

Here we are slightly snowed in & are revelling in the remoteness of Siberia! as far as interruptions go & the heaven of wandering about as care free as visitors. Looking with stern disapproval on the dust & disorder but doing nothing about it. We were all in [exhausted] before they left[,] what with Xmas[,] Hector (a vague factor in any household)[,] a visiting Australian & [only] one old cook ("beyond the realm of human desire." We have to get them there or they can't stand our loneliness)—& always outsiders [other guests] to meals.

Well dear its lovely to read & look out the window & write to you!! Long may it last.

36. An allusion to Eleanor's wedding in which Isabella was a bridesmaid.
37. Both Eleanor's parents had died before she was ten.
38. Woodrow Wilson's secretary of interior, Franklin Lane.

You'll be shocked to hear that you[r] Xmas gift is *just* starting [has just been mailed]. You can imagine the limits of shopping in Silver City & only just now have I seen what I think you could use & that's rather handsome. I hope you'll think so. I'm glad I waited because its rather unusual. As for Anna—her Godmother will send her a token around Easter. Again when she finds something. I've given up sending things just to be sending.

The napkins are exquisite—there's a sort of separate corner for you in the linen closet nowadays—& its very sacred.

Ronald writes more & more & I'm ready to wager that Nelly will take him home via Suez.[39] What putty he is in her hands—we're all willing to meet him any where any time.

In any case I must see you in 1920—upon that my plans shall hinge. Its an imposition to write so at length to one so busy! Just skip it all—& remember I love you more dearly with every year.

    Yr devoted

      Isabella

Mother, at last, is getting a rest & a cure at French Lick.[40] She wrote the other day "Everything by the name of Roosevelt is either having a baby or writing a book."[41] Since you have paused in the first line dear, I scan the reviews for your book!

Give Franklin my love & tell him I know him to be handsomer than the photograph.

In her post-Christmas letter, Eleanor, as usual, mingles family news and political speculation.

The League of Nations would be one of the issues in the 1920 election. On November 19, 1919, the U.S. Senate voted on the ratification of the Treaty

---

39. Ronald and Helen ("Nelly") Munro-Ferguson were in Australia, where Ronald was governor general. Bob and Isabella hoped Ronald and Helen would go from Australia to California, then to New Mexico, on their way back to Scotland. But here Lady Helen is presumed to have prefered traveling in the opposite direction—from Australia to Great Britain via the Suez Canal in Egypt.

40. Mineral spring resort in Indiana.

41. Kermit Roosevelt and his wife, Belle, had their second child, Joe, in January 1918, and their third child, also Belle, in November 1919. Ted Roosevelt and his wife, Eleanor, had their fourth child, Quentin II, also in November 1919. Archie Roosevelt and his wife, Grace, had their first child, Archie, Jr., in February 1918 and their second child, Theodora, in June 1919. Theodore Roosevelt, who wrote more than thirty-five books in his lifetime, published his last volume, *The Great Adventure*, in 1918. Kermit published a memoir about his service in World War I, *War in the Garden of Eden*, in 1919.

of Versailles. Henry Cabot Lodge and a number of other senators insisted, however, on certain "reservations" that would protect American sovereignty. Wilson refused to consider any changes. Although Eleanor would later be at the forefront of efforts to establish the United Nations, at this time she was merely regretful. Postwar domestic problems loomed larger, as did the question of who would be the Republican presidential candidate.

Although neither woman was overtly religious, Eleanor recommended to Isabella a book, *The Great Desire*, by Alexander Black.[42] The cover was embossed with a large question mark, as if to ask, "What IS our great desire?"[43]

2131 R Street, Washington, DC   Jan. 11 [1920]
Isabella dearest,

So many thanks to you & Bob for the book & your Xmas thought of us.

We thought of you all & hoped you had a happy day. We indulged in two trees[,] at least the same one lighted twice, Xmas eve for 30 men from the Naval Hospital & Xmas day [for] all the family. Lord Grey, Sir William Tyrrel[44] & Ronald Campbell lunched here & the children had the tree with their presents after lunch. We were sorry to see Lord Grey & Sir William go. I fear it may mean a change in your plans or will you still come here in the spring?[45] I was surprised to hear that Hector was with you. Your hands must be pretty full but after all it is better so.

I saw poor cousin Susie [Parish] just before New Year's in New York & it was very sad. After 3 months with Dr. Riggs she has returned taking no interest in life, dreading the lightest care or even the thought of seeing a friend. The root of it all is that she cares for no one sufficiently to forget herself & it is hard to undo even for her own good the habit of years. I am sorry for her

42. New York: Harper & Brothers Publishers, 1919. William Dean Howells, reviewing the book for the *New York Times*, October 12, 1919, found it unsurpassed "for literary novelty and for constancy to a high ideal of life and the poetry and truth and beauty of it."

43. According to one of the book's characters, "There is but one desire that has held men and goaded men from the beginning . . . It is the desire to find God." Later, though, we find: "The most we can expect from any glare that lights up the spaces of life is that those who will look shall see things as they are! My father uttered the cry—for Light!" The most telling and saddest sentiment expressed, taking into account the century following the book's publication, is: "Perhaps light enough would unify the desires of the world." Black, *The Great Desire*, 390 and 380, respectively.

44. Lord Grey's aide, without whose help the visually impaired Grey would not have been able to work.

45. Apparently, they had hoped Ronald would come to Washington for consultations with Lord Grey.

& for Cousin Henry who blames himself now & yet I doubt if he could have done any differently, she was a spoiled child & a spoiled woman & never was forced to sink her own feelings in anyone else's good.

You'll be interested to hear that the rumor is Ted Roosevelt may be run by the G.O.P. for Governor next fall. Alice [Longworth] says she is quite happy about politics & Mr. Lodge[46] is the greatest man in the country. I can't say I entirely share her feeling, though, I wish the President had been more willing to accept reservations still I do wish we could have had the League. I want it behind us & a free mind for all the domestic problems.

Now all men of the parties are busy discussing presidential possibilities. What do the people in your part of the world think of Mr. Hoover.[47] He's the only man I know who has first hand knowledge of European questions & great organizing ability & understands business & not only from the capitalistic point of view but also from the workers' standpoint.

Have you read a novel "The Great Desire"? It is worth while & I'll send it if you haven't it.

Did you know Hall & Margaret had a baby girl about six weeks ago? She is to be named Eleanor & I feel much flattered.

Franklin sends you both much love. There are some things I want to write about but I simply haven't time & must wait till we meet! I saw Pauline [Merrill], Grenville, the children & new house when in New York. All very happy & the house delightful, the baby a darling. Munro [Monroe Robinson] has gone back to Dorothy. Helen is having a pretty hard time with Teddy [Robinson]. She is a wonder but he is beyond her managing & I think in time even her love & respect must be forfeit! He does nothing, is very gay & says he gave up everything to go in the army,[48] cares for nothing but politics & so has found nothing to interest him the past 2 years!

All my chicks except John are getting over the chicken pox, I wish he had had it but of course he will wait till all the others are well. Jr. Franklin had his tonsils out about a month ago & is just over one old fashioned cold & sore throat which is distressing when we thought the cause was removed! James is probably going to have his appendix out on the 19th as he had an attack the

---

46. Henry Cabot Lodge, Republican senator from Massachusetts, chairman of the Senate Foreign Affairs Committee, and leader of the group who opposed the League of Nations.

47. Herbert Hoover, who at that time had not announced his party affiliation. Cook, *Eleanor Roosevelt*, I, 276.

48. Evidently, Teddy Robinson thinks that he sacrificed to go into the army, and now feels entitled to do just as he pleases.

doctors advise doing it between times[49] when they say it doesn't amount to anything. Of course I don't like it, but I am not telling him till the day so he won't be nervous & there is no use making much of such things, is there?

Much, much love to you all, especially to you dear.

Devotedly,

E.R.

On February 4, 1920, Eleanor lost yet another of her close kin—her young aunt, Edith ("Pussie") Hall Morgan,[50] who perished in a house fire, along with her two daughters, fourteen and ten years of age. Eleanor considered Pussie, who had played a large part in the motherless Eleanor's adolescence, as one of the seven people who had shaped her life. Stoic though she was, Eleanor always regarded Pussie's death as "one of those horrors I can hardly bear to think of."[51]

New York at the time was "enveloped in a blizzard," but Eleanor had striven mightily to help Pussie's husband cope with the funeral arrangements.[52] According to Eleanor biographer Blanche Cook, Eleanor took away from the experience a recognition of the satisfaction that she earned from being needed and being able to take charge of situations.[53]

Although Eleanor was beginning to explore her own political interests, she also continued to support her husband's career. The Republicans now controlled the Senate, and the Naval Affairs Committee planned to investigate the Navy's wartime activities, including the preparedness issue and an ill-advised plan to use enlisted men as decoys to entrap homosexuals in Newport.

2131 R Street, Washington, DC   Feb. 10, [1920]

Dearest Isabella

Here it is Feb. 10th & your letter[54] unanswered & I haven't yet had the courage to tell you that the charming Indian vase arrived broken in many pieces. I was so sorry especially after seeing Auntie Bye's & I know you will

---

49. After one attack and before another can occur.

50. Edith Hall Morgan, younger sister of ER's mother, was only eleven years older than Eleanor and had been a society belle. ER thought Pussie could have been "something useful professionally," but she "did not have to." Betty Boyd Caroli, "Edith Hall Morgan," *ER Encyclopedia*, 168. She had separated from her husband, William Forbes Morgan.

51. Roosevelt, *This is My Story*, 228.

52. Ibid., 228–29.

53. Cook, *Eleanor Roosevelt*, I, 264.

54. Missing.

be disappointed but the Express is so careless these days. A thousand thanks anyway dear for thinking of us. Franklin made me tell you as he said you should go after the Express Co! I wonder if you ever got intact some little jars of guava from Florida which we ordered for you?

I'm glad you liked the photograph but it is awful of Franklin! He went on last Saturday to speak in Brooklyn N.Y. (one place was the Colony Club[55] with Ogden Mills[56] & it was such a funny contrast & I went also & took James to spend three weeks with Mama where there is not the temptation there is at home to do things one shouldn't do after an appendicitis operation!)

Monday night I spent with Auntie Bye & she moves less & less & looked to me frailer though Uncle Will insists she is stronger. Courage like hers is wonderfully inspiring, one couldn't be a coward over minor trials after seeing her. She was so pleased to have your letter & the photo of Martha & Bobby. Martha is going to be a beauty & look like you. How I wish we knew her & could see you all more! Sheffield was home, so big & handsome & dear but not very settled yet, still in the stormy period!

I got back here Tuesday night & Wednesday got the tragic news of Pussie Morgan's death with her two little girls smothered by smoke when their home in 9th St. burned. I went back at once as Maude Gray & I were the only members of the family who could help Forbes [Morgan]. Tissie Mortimer[57] is abroad & I was sorry for she had seen more of the poor little boy[58] than anyone. If it were not for the horror I would feel sure that Pussie was happier than she's ever been here, she could not meet an every day existence but she had some lovely qualities & was always groping for spiritual truth. Forbes, whom she had divorced, had a deep affection for her & loved the children & often went to see them but no one could live with her.

Isn't it strange world tragedies on every side in life & death & yet so much kindness, goodness, & helpfulness that one knows it must all be for some worth while end. Now we are home again & taking a week off to gather ourselves together again.

55. The city's most exclusive and prestigious private women's social club. http://www. thecityreview.com/ues/parkave/colonyc.html.
56. Ogden Mills was president of the New York State Tax Association and treasurer of the Republican County Committee of New York. He would later be very critical of FDR's New Deal policies. The Colony Club was something of a Democratic stronghold; Mills would have been out of place there.
57. Elizabeth Hall ("Tissie") Mortimer was another aunt of Eleanor's, and sister of the deceased Pussie. Cook, *Eleanor Roosevelt*, I, 151–52.
58. Pussie's son, William, Jr., had been away at boarding school.

Auntie Corinne is becoming an inveterate public speaker & it seems to agree with her.

I hear as a *secret* that William Phillips has been offered the Netherlands & accepted & they are on their way home to pick up children etc & depart again. I am so glad for he deserved it.

I do hope Ronald comes home this way but I hear he is going by Suez & coming here later. Is it true?

I must stop but in closing let me say that I am entirely decided that we must meet in 1920, even if I can't make it till after the Nov. elections! I rather hope we retire to private life for a time at least!

Much, much love dear I'm so glad you've had a little rest & hope you will not work too hard even when Bob is home again. When is that to be? Tell Bobby I loved his letter & am going to write him soon.

> Ever your devoted
> Eleanor

The Navy Dept. is now being investigated by the Senate but so far Franklin hasn't been called.

Isabella did come East in 1920, but to deal with an emergency. Patty, who had been staying at the Burro Mountain Homestead while Bob and Hector were in Santa Barbara, became ill. She and Isabella hurriedly left on the next train east, "through shrieking sandstorms," to New York. A distraught Isabella wired John Greenway: "Mother making splendid fight for life. There is hope. Help us with your thoughts."[59]

147 East 36th Street New York, NY   [April 1920]
Eleanor darling,

It's good to know I'm even this near to you! Bless you & how I count on its being nearer-*much* & before long.

You'll be distressed to hear that Mother has been ill for several weeks—with a tedious jaundice which refused to be shaken. So I came to N.Y. with her & for 48 hours we have been trying to get at the root of the evil—& I believe we'll be there in a few days—& able to start on a quicker remedy—we've just arrived.

As soon as I know our plans (from the Drs) you shall hear—because my dearest & most determined wish is to see you & Anna & the whole family—there is nothing to say at this moment.

59. Miller, *Isabella Greenway*, 103.

I just hate to have you bothering over Hector. It's just not *worth* it (& I'd appreciate it if you'll destroy this!) I told him just how difficult it was for you to put up anyone. Most of all a man & generally discouraged him—& as I've not seen him since arrival, don't know the outcome.[60]

There is so much to say writing is tantalizing beyond measure. Uncle will mail this in Washington tomorrow & it carries a heart full of love & a hug as big as the world & Mother sends her love.

> Devotedly,
> Isabella

Of course you know Mrs. Parish has measles!! Let us know if there is a chance of seeing you here.

I have read & reread your last letters in amazed admiration—as ever.

Diagnosed with "soft gallstones," Patty slowly but steadily improved over the next three weeks.[61] Isabella, rejoicing in her mother's recovery, was made even happier by hearing that Eleanor planned to come up to New York for the express purpose of seeing her.[62] Isabella may also have visited Eleanor in Washington.

Refreshed by seeing each other, the women parted again. Isabella returned to New Mexico, and Eleanor went to Campobello with her children. Franklin went to the Democratic National Convention in San Francisco. There he seconded the nomination of New York governor Alfred E. Smith. Smith, William Gibbs McAdoo (Woodrow Wilson's treasury secretary and son-in-law), and the reactionary Attorney General A. Mitchell Palmer deadlocked in a three-way race.

Finally, on the forty-fourth ballot, the Democrats selected a compromise candidate, Ohio governor James M. Cox. Cox chose Franklin Roosevelt as his running mate.[63]

Eleanor professed to be not "much excited" by Franklin's nomination, perhaps because it was clear the Democrats' chances in 1920 were doomed. As TR's niece, Eleanor had originally been a Republican, but she had by now come to believe the Democrats were the more progressive party.[64] Other TR

---

60. Evidently, after visiting with the Fergusons, Hector had gone East. Perhaps he had assumed he could stay with his old friends, the Roosevelts.
61. Miller, *Isabella Greenway*, 103.
62. IG to RHMF, April 25, 1920, FC.
63. Cook, *Eleanor Roosevelt*, I, 271–72.
64. Ibid., 274.

progressive Republicans, like John Greenway, were equally disenchanted, and joined the Democrats around this time.

Isabella followed the political situation closely, at least when she was not planning for a drastic change in her own life: within a few months, she would take up residence in Santa Barbara for nine months of the year, so that the children could attend school for the first time in their lives.

Burro Mountain Homestead, Tyrone   July 16, 1920
New Mexico
Eleanor darling—

Its no end thrilling to think what you & Franklin may have a hand in for the benefit of this country. Dear, were I to write truly you couldn't believe a word of it because of your predominating characteristic of innate modesty. Every one in this remote countryside knows of you from my overflowing admiration & when the news came [of Franklin's nomination] the whole neighborhood called up to offer congratulations—I wish I knew more of Cox—but I will probably hear soon. The things I read about him sounded all to the good but were written to be such so it was hard to judge.

I must quote from two letters I had today. The first from Mother at Henderson[65] where, by the way she says "all here who I have talked to are *so* nice about Franklin's nomination." She goes on to describe the three ringed circus existence of unintelligent amusement that apparently prevails & ends [her letter,] "Darling, I am glad you are mine. You & Eleanor, tho different in type, are what I prefer." [66]

In a letter from John Greenway—in connection with his disgust of the Republican party control which lies in the National Committee & the Senate—he says "I know Franklin is to be depended on" and "Can't you see the pride of his splendid wife."

The most of the news has gone to Anna.[67] Bless her. I wonder if she really does care to receive letters from her stodgy old Godmother? We are blissfully believing a small house can be better built [in Santa Barbara] without us & hope we can move in in mid Sept when school begins. [And] here the range is ridden daily. Some tutoring managed & much swimming & we imagine a 1000 things about when Aunty Pauline [Merrill] & [her daughter] Pauline

65. The home of Corinne Robinson, TR's sister. Although Corinne was a Republican, she was still happy for Franklin.
66. Patty Selmes is at a house party and finds the other guests disagreeably frivolous.
67. Isabella has been writing separately to Anna, her fourteen-year-old goddaughter.

& Grenville are one of us!! Cant you see Pauline Sen[ior?]—beginning the housework at six thirty?[68]

I can but look back a bit [69]—& wonder at the steady progress that has been yours. It gives one a great sense of accumulative might & I believe one of your strongest policies is that you are ever *prepared* for reverses. How I hope my beloved mother will go to your dream island [Campobello]. She sounds so much better & the world is so right again for me. Bob sends his love & I send you the utmost love of yr devoted

> Isabella

I have thought of you *so* much I can't remember if I wrote since Washington.[70]

In the past, Isabella had apologized for letting too much time slip by without writing; now she apologized for bothering a busy friend. But Isabella had been busy, too—preoccupied with moving to Santa Barbara; tutoring the children, who would be enrolling in school that fall; and putting up itinerant cowboys. The Homestead had expanded to include a herd of cattle.

Burro Mountain Homestead   July 29, 1920
Tyrone, New Mexico
Eleanor darling

Its a shame to bother you with a detail like this but the Express people have been following up several of my lost or smashed shipments & you'd do us a great favor by signing this claim & mailing it to the address on the enclosed envelope.

Dear, I think of you so constantly & how you are doubtless throwing yourself into the campaign—& what a strenuous affair this summer will be. If I dont hear a word from you I'll understand *absolutely* & it would be a great comfort to think that if you had an inspiration to write me a line you will, instead, stretch out with a good book—& *if its very good* give me its name. I hope Mother will be a comfort to you as well as a guest—& I feel sure she will & I envy you both.

---

68. The Fergusons are expecting a visit of Pauline and Grenville Merrill, with their daughter, to the Fergusons at the Homestead. "Aunty" was an honorific title children used for friends of their parents. The elder Pauline was an Astor by birth, and Isabella was probably amused by the thought of her doing housework.
69. i.e., I can't help looking back a bit.
70. This suggests that Isabella did visit Eleanor in Washington, D.C.

Bob is telling me I must go to Santa Barbara & see if our cottage is materializing but I just hate leaving—we are so deep in tutoring & examinations etc.

We've just had a round up—of "strays" on the range. I wish the [Roosevelt] children had been here—they would have enjoyed the cow punchers—a unique set—& alas! not many of the real ones left. It was very strenuous— Every bed full & having to take turns at the dinner table while the extras [cowboys] held the herd[71]—& then a big storm after all the cows were gathered—but they went right on cutting them out [separating the ones that had to be branded] etc—I dont see how Bobbie will stand school!! & I'm homesick already.

All my love always. Anna is my first "Good morning" by my mirror always—& you & the family are on my sewing table—never far away you see. It was so lovely to see you this spring. I cherish & relive every moment.

> Yr devoted
> Isabella

The next year and a half would be a tumultuous time for the two women; exactly 17 months would elapse before the two friends corresponded again.

On August 26, 1920, the Nineteenth Amendment was ratified, granting women all over America the right to vote in the November election.

In September, Eleanor joined FDR's campaign. At first she had little to do, other than read what the newspapers had to say and look at Franklin with wifely admiration.[72] Soon FDR's strategist, Louis Howe, began consulting Eleanor and tutoring her in the art of cultivating the press.[73]

Harding and Coolidge handily beat Cox and Roosevelt, and FDR returned to his law practice. Determined to make some money, he also joined a Wall Street bond company, the Fidelity & Deposit Company, in charge of their New England branch. But it was unsatisfying work. Franklin brought in new clients to both businesses, through his extensive contacts, while he continued to speak with civic groups.

Eleanor began doing political work of her own, joining the Women's City Club and the League of Women Voters, where she made new friends.[74] Esther Lape,[75] world peace and national health care activist, and her life-partner,

---

71. Kept the cattle herded together so they would not disperse.
72. Cook, *Eleanor Roosevelt*, I, 278–82.
73. Ibid., 283–84.
74. Ibid., 287–301.
75. Kristie Miller, "Esther Everett Lape," *Eleanor Roosevelt Encyclopedia*, 301–304.

attorney Elizabeth Read, worked closely with Eleanor on a variety of progressive political projects. Marion Dickerman and her lifelong companion, Nancy Cook, also became Eleanor's close friends, as well as business partners in the Val-Kil Industries and Todhunter School.[76] From time to time, Eleanor and her allies combined forces with FDR and Louis Howe to plan political strategy.[77]

Isabella, meanwhile, took the children to California. Martha, fourteen, attended a girls' day school in Santa Barbara, while Bobbie, twelve, boarded at the nearby Cate School. The nine-month separation was hard on the Fergusons. Bob and Isabella had agreed that Isabella should go with the children to California, but Bob felt useless and depressed. He frequently wrote critical letters to Isabella, until she concluded that they must not spend another year apart. She and Bob were reunited when Isabella and the children returned to the ranch over the summer of 1921. At the same time, Bob's health continued to worsen.[78]

A Senate Committee report that summer criticized the Navy Department's use of entrapment during FDR's tenure as assistant secretary to discover homosexuals in the service; it accused Navy Secretary Daniels and Roosevelt of exhibiting "an utter lack of moral perspective."[79] Franklin worked for two weeks at damage control, denying he had authorized the "revolting methods" used to identify targeted individuals.[80]

He arrived at Campobello "exhausted and depressed," but determined to have a good time with a house full of friends. On August 10, after working hard with the family to extinguish a brush fire, Franklin cooled off with a swim in a pond, followed by a plunge into the freezing cold Bay of Fundy. Feeling chilled, he went to bed. The next morning, he awoke with a fever and a great deal of pain. The following day, he lost the ability to walk or to move his legs.

The first doctor to examine Franklin suspected he had a blood clot. For three weeks, Franklin's condition worsened, as Eleanor nursed him around the clock. Finally, on August 25, he was diagnosed with polio. In mid-September, he was moved secretly—Louis Howe, who always believed FDR would be

76. See description of Val-Kil Industries in introduction before letter of August 22, 1927. Eleanor Roosevelt, Dickerman, and Cook purchased the Todhunter School in 1927. Kenneth S. Davis, "Marion Dickerman," ibid. 134–36.
77. Cook, *Eleanore Roosevelt*, I, 302.
78. Miller, *Isabella Greenway*, 107.
79. Ward, *A First-Class Temperment*, 571–72.
80. Cook, *Eleanor Roosevelt*, I, 307.

president, was determined to keep the news out of the press—to New York's Presbyterian Hospital, where he remained until Christmas.[81]

Now both Eleanor and Isabella were coping with invalid husbands. Isabella was the first to break the long silence. Once she knew Eleanor shared some of her own hard-won perspective, Isabella allowed herself unusual freedom in expressing her thoughts and feelings.

In the fall of 1921, Isabella and Bob took Martha and Bobbie back to California, and, leaving Patty to supervise the children, returned together to the Homestead. As Bob's health grew steadily worse, Isabella took over more and more of the responsibility for running the ranch. His doctor had diagnosed Bob with a kidney condition, warning that he was now a much sicker man than previously. Bob observed sardonically to Eleanor that he had been sick for "quite a considerable time," but hoped to "thumb-nose" the doctor by living at least until the spring.[82]

To pass the time in the evenings, Isabella was trying her hand at writing a play. She casually mentioned that she could use Franklin's help, probably in order to make him feel useful and loved, despite his new handicap.

Tyrone, New Mexico   Dec 29, 1921
Eleanor mine

I hope you have not felt one hundredth as badly about my not writing you as I have about it. Dearest its nothing more than a disease with me—& the harder I love someone the more difficult it is to write. I can't explain or excuse it. I can only ask your forgiveness & one more chance because life without it & you would indeed seem impossible & the curious part of it all is that I believe I can truly say that hardly an *hour* goes by in this many months especially since Franklin's illness that I haven't thought of you *adoringly* & prayed for you, too—& simply *craved* to see you. Well I shall just beg you to send me a little line of forgiveness & hope that 1922 will prove me a worthier friend.

Mother always tells me what Mrs. Parish says of Franklin so I do keep in touch—& the last sounded so hopeful & splendid. I wonder if I have misinterpreted in that it read as tho' he were improving steady & with greater hope of ultimate recovery?

Every inch of the last long & dreadful months stands amazingly vivid before me—as you do in your superb courage & determination. Dearest its

81. Ibid., 302–311.
82. Miller, *Isabella Greenway*, 109.

an inspiration to see it all as I do constantly—& let me say what I believe you'll understand.

When great difficulties come to us in extreme youth we stagger along creditably because we are unable to see the whole truth & have abundant strength. When distress comes to us in older age we face up to it steadily & splendidly partly thro' resignation & a sense of finish. When it comes to us at yours & my ages—I believe it is the hardest of all tests because ours are the years when clear perception has come & with it the intense desire to live while we may. I wonder if you know what I mean—It is above all hard to mark time at our ages—no matter what spiritual interpretation we try to attach to the cause.

I simply long to talk to you—for the selfish knowledge of the good it would do me as much as anything else.

[And] now, assuming you do care to hear I'll write our little news. Mother has played the role of Grandmother as becomingly as all the other parts that have come to her in life—& is loved by all Martha's & Bobbie's friends & has taken the children off of me this winter—so I could dive in & straighten out affairs here where we find ourselves ranching in deadly earnest. Bob had a trying autumn & is confined to his room except once in a while when he wanders out on a horse on a mild day or comes into a meal. He's *better* than he was—& goes with us to the coast on Jan. 6—for 2 or 3 months.

You'd have died of laughter over my efforts to run a ranch. I fired everyone & have what thoroughly pleases me as a personnel—a sturdy old Farmer & a young cowboy. Bob isn't crazy about the latter but I cant see that it is his inefficiency![83] Then 10 men came to *stop* with us & help remove their cattle off our 22 sq miles of fenced range & (*suffering in all spots*) I stayed in the saddle from 6:30 AM till 6 PM day after day—housekeeping consisted in making beds when the men washed up for supper. I wouldn't have missed it for words—& really am now absorbed in the future of our *tiny* start [our little ranch]. I cant yet tell a steer from a heifer unless it is turned upside down for me!

Then I fetched the children home for Xmas—as Santa Barbara offers poor amusement for their ages & they *longed* for home.

By the way—just as we were leaving Santa B—two packages came from you—& I asked Mother to keep them.[84] So you'll hear later. I bought in Los Angeles a small volume of Emerson's Essays for you—because I wanted you

---

83. Possibly she is hinting that Bob was jealous, or pretended to be.

84. When Isabella went to Santa Barbara to get the children, she saw packages from Eleanor, but may not have wanted to take them back to New Mexico on the train. So she left them with Patty, who was staying in Santa Barbara, and planned to open them on her return.

to have it *from me*—& in a small form that is of no value[85] because I hope you may care for them as I do & use them. They have meant more to me than any influence almost in this world—& I attribute most that has spelt happiness to their interpretation of life.

Mother defies [illegible] old New Englander [Emerson]—the children make continual fun of him. All of which proves—that he is almost my daily bread! One forgets about him & it is a mistake—as his philosophy is modern & advanced beyond any I know—& applies today.

I wish always Anna & Martha might be together. What are you going to do with Anna next winter? M will be 16 & needs the East. We dont know what we are going to do—as it is such a fierce distance to put between us & them. I'd like to know what boarding school has done for James? I am still without a formed opinion about boy's boarding schools as *fitters* for real life—& am inclined to think that day schools with a little family life are more normal—if we had the character to give children in their homes![86] It is a problem isn't it. Bobbie loves his & is doing finely—was second in the school out of 40 boys—last fortnight.

Martha is simply the sweetest of mortals & eternally full of fun.

Please give Franklin my love & tell him in odd moments *very odd*—I'm writing a play & while I can handle the first two acts which are in the west I can't do anything with the third in London—& would he mind just taking the London act off my hands? I don't mind a bit what he does with the characters in fact their future is a terrible responsibility to me now.

Has he read "Dangerous Ages"?[87] Dont fail to let me know.

God bless you dearest Eleanor—I do feel so much happier now I've broken the nightmare silence on my part—& dont ever feel you must write.

Yr devoted—*utterly devoted*—

Isabella

In April 1922, Patty Selmes endured a siege of influenza, complicated by a weak heart. For the next four months, Isabella stayed with her alternately delirious and unconscious mother in the Santa Barbara hospital, musing on their close relationship.

85. In other words, not a first edition. Almost surely *Emerson's Essays*, edited by Arthur Hobson Quinn. New York: Charles Scribner's Sons, 1920. This edition is a small volume, about 4 inches by 7 inches.
86. She means "If our characters were good enough to serve as a model."
87. Rose Macaulay, *Dangerous Ages*. New York: Boni and Liveright, 1921.

Cottage Hospital May 5, 1922
Eleanor my *dearest*—

A perfect craving to see you comes over me—at times—a longing all the time—So much so I know it must result in a glimpse soon.

Mother *sleeps*—in the land of dreams—& utter exhaustion from which she comes out for moments to ask vaguely where she is & what has happened—& we are all in the land of *good hope* with justification owing to her *miraculous* rally—tho the balance must necessarily remain a delicate one for days.

I mailed yesterday—rather an overflow of detail to Mrs. Robinson & asked her to give it to you & Mrs. Parish. I wrote it hoping it would give you all a picture of Mother's illness—& her surroundings of love & care—the things that (never mind how little) do comfort—I am *so* sorry for Mrs. R.

Having sent her that letter I won't go into any more detail with you—but think, [you can imagine] with what an overflowing heart I hope & plan for her convalescence—to [ensure] stronger & more serene years than have been hers—for a long time—the sense of crushing calamities was almost insurmountable as she lay in the shadow—We slipped in & out of that valley—so many times, hand in hand—[88]

If Eleanor responded to Isabella's anguished letter, her answer has been lost. Patty recovered slowly. But then, Martha and Bobbie contracted whooping cough (pertussis) in July. After the children were well enough to travel, the family returned to New Mexico at the end of the summer for a short visit before the start of school.

Eleanor, hearing of Isabella's troubles, wrote to offer sympathy and support. She and Franklin had been preoccupied with trying to adapt to his disability. Franklin, wearing heavy braces on his legs, toiled day after day to walk a quarter mile down the Hyde Park driveway. Eleanor was "not sanguine" about his chances for recovery, but said nothing about her misgivings, either to Franklin or to Isabella. She and Franklin's key political advisor, Louis Howe, were determined, however, not to treat Franklin like an invalid, and they continued to plan for his political future.[89]

88. Second page missing.
89. Ward, *A First-Class Temperament*, 616–17; 647–48.

Westport Point, Mass. [90]   [September 1922]
Isabella dearest,

I've just heard from cousin Susie of the children's whooping cough and I am sorry for it's such a long, distressful thing, but now you are back in Tyrone they will soon pick up. My three oldest ones had it together some years ago and I remember well its horrors! I am glad you are home however and glad Mrs. Selmes is out of the hospital and well enough for you to have her. Cousin Susie tells me she is begging you to send Martha to her for next winter and she wants me to tell you that I will help her and do all I can for Martha. It hardly seems necessary for I know that you know that already and if at any time cousin Susie wants to send her to us for a few days she can always share Anna's room which is large, quite comfortable for two. Somehow I doubt you [will] let Martha come, but should you do so won't you let me please—so that she and Anna go out in the afternoons together and do the same things?

I brought the little boys [91] here Aug. 20th to picnic in a most primitive house on the sand. I went back for one week and now I've been here for a week and I take them down Saturday and meet Mama and Anna and James at the steamer Sunday or Monday. It will be really exciting to see what changes the summer has made in them.

Franklin is well, but the walking even with crutches is a slow process.

Pauline and Grenville lunched with us at Hyde Park ten days ago and she was so funny about her stay in Newport with Cousin Susie. She says seldom in the vale of tears does one see anyone so completely satisfied with their life and surroundings & it's quite true! [92]

Love to Bob and our love and sympathy to the "whoopers."

    Ever lovingly,

      E.R.

[Ferguson Family Papers]

In the fall of 1922, Bob accompanied the family back to Santa Barbara, grumbling that "They don't trust me alone in the sticks." [93] But two weeks after their return, on October 3, Bob Ferguson collapsed with sudden kidney

90. Louis Howe had a beach house at Westport Point. Eleanor and Franklin were frequent visitors.
91. Franklin, Jr. and John.
92. Eleanor seems to be saying that Susie, usually so discontented, is laughably happy and smug at fashionable Newport, Rhode Island.
93. RHMF to Frank Cutcheon, January 17, 1922, FC.

failure. He had finally lost his long battle with tuberculosis. He died the following night in fourteen-year-old Bobbie's arms, with Isabella and Martha by
his side. "Bob, you have made me very happy," Isabella said lovingly, as he
slipped away.[94]

Isabella wired Eleanor at once. Eleanor sorrowed not only for her friend's
bereavement but also for the loss of her own childhood friend, and for the
long, painful condition that had sapped his strength and spirit. It was, as she
said, the end of a chapter.

49 East 65th St.   Oct. 4th [1922]

Isabella my dearest,

Your telegram only reached me today and I've been wishing every minute
since that I was with you or could meet the [children] [&] you somewhere.
I'm glad the end came quickly for Bob and that you had all been able to have
a little time together at the Homestead. He was a devoted, loyal friend and I
always felt time and distance made no difference in his feelings for his friends.
How I wish we could all have met again. When you come to my age and
chapters begin to close in life I suppose there must always be some regrets that
that future is at an end. We count so much on the future without realizing it.
However we must all think of Bob, the old Bob we all loved, over the strain
and stress of bodily ailment, able to be at peace and full of strength again.

How much you have been through dearest, I must confess that I wanted
to start at once and meet you in Chicago but cousin Susie firmly told me
how much I would get in the way and common sense came to my rescue and
yours! But you Martha and Bobbie are so much in my thoughts, also your
mother and I wonder if perhaps she will wake now with a longing to help you
all three. If only I could feel free to fly out to you, it's the one thing I long to
do but I've succeeded in involving myself in so many things which it seems
hard to have not to speak of a slightly complicated household! Franklin is
now in Boston but returns in a week for a few days here then to Hyde Park
again. The children and I are here for school during the week and up at Hyde
Park for week ends until mama comes down after Thanksgiving.

I know you have grieved for Ethel and Dick in their sorrow, it seems so
fearfully hard when they have done so much for little Dick[95] and have him go
just when they felt he was really getting strong. I'm sure they are wonderful

94. Miller, *Isabella Greenway*, 108–111.
95. Richard Derby, Jr., 1914–22, died at age 8 of septicemia. http://www.theodoreroosevelt.
   org/life/familytree/Ethel.htm.

about it for they are so fine and so happy in each other. I enclose a little note for Mrs. Selmes—when she is better and you are a little settled again I'm going to ask you to do two things for me, but not till later in the winter!

My heart full of love, and I hate my pen for being so inadequate—but you know without words I think what I feel always for you and yours.

Ever yours,
Eleanor
[Ferguson Family Papers]

Isabella took Bob's body back to the farm in Boone, Kentucky, to be buried in the family plot. Then she rejoined the children in California.[96] In her first letter to Eleanor following Bob's death, she provides a hint of her extremely complex feelings.

Mission Ridge Road   Dec. 2, 1922
Santa Barbara, California
Oh my beloved Eleanor—

With you one doesn't begin—One just goes on—& *you* are the wonderful friend who has made that possible in the face of my inexplicable *silence*. I have never known anything like it—& hope I may never know again the anguish & mortification that has been mine—over these ages—while I have loved & thought of you—(adored & cherished you would be truer) & have said never a word—

There is no excuse—the waters seem to have closed over my head—while you seem forever capable of striding ahead always in the pace that circumstances call for—my admiration knows no limit—May I someday profit by your example—

Your dear friend Bob—has found rest—& it is as tho my husband, brother, Father, & sick boy had left our hours desolate. No words can describe the emptiness after all these years—during which his spirit of progress—his desires & care for us—filled life's least nook & cranny—& spelt the motive for our whole beings. Could there be a greater tribute to the going of an invalid of thirteen years.

I find myself yearning to tell his friends of [his] stronger years [about] the glory & triumph of those that followed—feeling it a very selfishness—to carry their inspiration to myself. You know something of his uncomplaining

96. After Bob's death, Isabella had little reason to go back to the Homestead in New Mexico. The center of her life shifted to Santa Barbara.

courage & I take comfort in the fact—& I hope you'll feel the true satisfaction of knowing what you did for him from time to time—Lifting & sharing his burden in so many blessed & thoughtful ways. He loved & admired you so—Your inability to fail or weaken went without saying—& he wanted your influence with our children as I do.

We were confident Bob was recovering from this particular crisis—so his going was a great shock—tho' now I am realizing it was as he would have wished it in no parting—no wasting—& it is as it should be at the end of thirteen years of miraculous *life* when there was no hope of any.

You'll be good enough to believe I helped Bob to longer years. It was inevitable that my abundant strength should be shared thus—but it seems as nothing in the balance with what he did & gave us—We'll talk of it someday Eleanor—It can but live thro all time as all good does. Martha is staggering back—the strain having told in many ways. Bobbie has had an easier time at school with fewer associations.[97] He told me Daddy had told him that "no matter what happens one must go on with the rest of the world" & he's building on that as are M & I. Believing it absolutely—Our eighteen years— (since we honeymooned together) are but a chapter to close but a book to live with—Precious beyond measure in its completeness.

I wish I could give you any idea of Bob's vigorous enjoyment these past two years— when he did so *many* things with the children & me. I would [wish I could] make a picture that would give you the kind of satisfaction it does me—

Plans have not come yet—about next winter for a multitude of reasons. Where is Anna going? & when? Martha could be ready [for college] in the autumn of 1924—if she stays here. I fear a change would lose a year for her—& she is very earnest & anxious about it. Anything you could tell me about Vassar or Bryn Mawr[,] & Miss Chapin's[98] method of preparing for them would mean a lot. I am somewhat overcome at having a daughter bent on college—but admire her for it & want to help her to it.

Give Franklin my love—I think of him so often.

The enclosed is a photograph of an 8 ft !! portrait that a friend of ours painted of Bobbie & gave us. Bob *loved* it—& it is absolutely *like* [Bobbie] & like his boyhood in New Mexico.

97. Bobbie was at boarding school, where there were no mementoes of Bob.
98. Anna was at Miss Chapin's school.

What wouldn't I give if you were sitting right here. I'd never let you go—Never again. Just this word with you has somehow made you mine again. Eleanor it would help so if I might compare your notes with mine. One doesn't stand still in the thirties [99] tho' I used to think one had one foot in the grave by then.

Yr wholly devoted

Isabella

Isabella does not appear to have been a churchgoer, and Eleanor's letters are practically mute on the subject of religious beliefs. Here, though, Isabella implies that she is sustained in this grieving time by her faith. She wonders if her similarly challenged friend does not also rely on a higher power.

Mission Ridge Road, Santa Barbara   Dec. 10, 1922
California
Eleanor dearest

I had this enclosed scrap [100] that you may see I am not the utterly faithless creature I seem [in forgetting to send the photograph in the previous letter]. I have been rereading many of your letters. What a volume of friendship is there—& how I cherish it. You say something in one of them [101] that I would like to talk to you of. It has to do with standing alone—& leaning—& I wonder if in your heart of hearts you do not believe that he marches happily who goes hand in hand with his faith. Oh Eleanor—I wish I knew much of your thinking.

Yr devoted

Isabella

[with picture] I failed to enclose this in the other letter. Hope you like it as we do—the sunshine of New Mexico is in the original.

[on back of picture] Robert M. Ferguson August 1922

Eleanor responded to Isabella in a letter that is missing.

In Isabella's next letter, she gives evidence that the strain has been telling on her. However, she makes light of her physical problems, referring casually to having had severe eyestrain around Christmastime, and only well into the

99. Isabella was thirty-six.
100. Possibly the following note.
101. The editors are unable to identify such a letter.

letter mentioning that she was suffering from chicken pox, an illness that can be severe in adulthood.

John Greenway, who had been waiting for Isabella for almost twelve years, discreetly waited for another three months after Bob's death, and then went to see Isabella in California. Isabella loved John, but with teenaged children and an invalid mother to consider, she hesitated before committing to marry him. This letter also suggests that Isabella may have been reluctant to pledge herself too soon to another life-long relationship. She expresses her willingness to consider divorce in cases of incompatibility.

By March, Isabella had agreed to an engagement, but she wanted to keep it secret so soon after Bob's death. Meanwhile, she was careful to assure Eleanor, who had known Bob Ferguson since childhood, that she had loved and appreciated him.

Isabella planned to take the children to visit the Cutcheons on Long Island in July, when she hoped to be able to see Eleanor as well.

Mission Ridge Road   [June 2 1923]
Santa Barbara, California

Eleanor mine—when I think of life—*my life*—I think of *you*—& as I review these last years—I realize that I have failed you utterly—tho' you have all the while, inspired me—to all that's best—I worship you ever more over the years—& believe I know somewhat what these last have meant for you.

When you are mentioned I say "There is probably the greatest woman of this generation"—& it doesn't seem yesterday that we were snuggled in a bed at Mrs. D [Corinne] Robinson's at Orange [NJ]—discussing your marriage—I remember every least detail of it.[102]

Thank God there is a prospect of my seeing you this summer—we hope to reach Locust Valley (Aunty's) about July 10th—the idea being that an insight into the lives of the east may partially make up to Martha for finishing school here.[103] Bobbie says "Of course I don't doubt that this is the right thing to do for Martha but how are you & I going to stand it?"!! Just tell us your whereabouts & we'll make it ours & be as little trouble to you as ever we can—maybe Anna & James could stop with us at Aunty's.

Mother (*for you only*—Mrs. Parish finds it so hard to understand—& my heart aches for her)—is a crumpled little invalid. Living as a miracle—After

102. See ER to IG, October 24, 1904.
103. This could mean that Isabella hoped a little exposure to an Eastern environment would help Martha adapt to an Eastern college later.

losing [declining in health] out here rapidly—I took her the first of May to the Homestead with a nurse—& a friend of Bobbie's who was convalescing from pneumonia—She is unquestionably *gaining* again—& a touch of her old vigor is in her letters & my heart is full of hope—

We all adore that place—& the poor family [Martha and Bobbie] are facing the fact that I am bent on being a *rancher*!

Appropos of your letter[104] about Hall—I hoped so he would turn up [in Santa Barbara] & wrote Martha in my absence, to receive him & try to persuade him to stay with her—but he's never come. I kept this amazing article on marriage[105] as a social failure for you. I haven't constructive theories to offer—as yet but find it *im*possible to believe that good Providence meant man or woman to block his or her natural productive fulfillment for good & service—by remaining tied to incessant incompatibility. Oh I wish so I knew what you really thought.

Having just nursed Bobbie thro chicken pox *I* am now enjoying a thorough case of it. Martha was told by the Dr that grown ups never had it & says her point is now proved—"That you've never grown up"! Do your children talk to you that way—Couldn't we have a Kodak of Anna—Martha's hair gets up[106] upon occasion now, & we have House parties—this house is known as the Yale Club—all Bobbie's friends centering here[107]—but *all* when we meet—& my heart full of love meantime.

At one period this winter (when my eyes were on strike) I employed a secretary & have vague memories of having tried to thank you thro her for a most wonderful Xmas—that warmed our hearts when we needed it. I hope my memory has not played me false.

If by any chance you are due a respite won't you join us here (till June 24th) or at the Homestead & take a little rest & then we can go East together. Maybe the children would come. Having no idea when Eastern schools close.

> Yr ever adoring
>
> Isabella

How I miss Bob. Since I can remember the whole of our lives have centered about him—the adjustment now, back to an active life—or I might say back into the world's life—seems at times insurmountable. No one ever

104. Missing.
105. Missing.
106. Young girls wore their long hair loose, or "down." It was a mark of maturity when a young woman began to pin her hair up on her head.
107. Bobbie did go to Yale in 1925; perhaps his friends were hoping to as well.

endeared himself to his small family as Bob did—& he'll come back to us in the mysterious way that is life's all unhampered.[108] I could but smile a little as I read Mrs. Anna [Bye]'s letter telling me that you as well as every one else (Helen etc) felt we should go to Scotland.[109]

Hector is engaged [to be married] I hear from the *outside* [not from Hector].

Isabella never made the trip East. Her mother's health worsened, and she died on July 17. Isabella took Patty back to Boone, her second visit to the hilltop graveyard in less than a year. The two women had been unusually close, even for mother and daughter; it seemed to Isabella that she and Patty had had "a perfect relationship." She expressed her grief to John: "Still I cannot believe that my Mummy is left in the hilltop graveyard. Such a sense of despair comes."[110]

Once again, Eleanor wrote to say that she shared Isabella's loss, for Patty's friendship with Eleanor's cousin Susie had drawn the two girls close in the first place.

49 E. 65th St.   July 18 [1923]
New York City
My dearest Isabella,

My heart has been full for you all day. There is a real sense of personal loss, for I loved your mother very, very dearly and she is one of the few older people with whom there was no age difference. She knew the world and human nature and had a broadness and sympathy which couldn't but make better those she came in contact with—after her long fight and yours for her, it seems doubly hard she couldn't have won back to a few years of happiness with you all. I think it must seem to you that you have few bulwarks left dear, and I wish I were near you now. You will miss, as we all do, the one who has filled your thoughts and heart for so long but if there is any consolation it must come to you for you have been for so long the whole joy and all that

---

108. Perhaps she means that Bob will remain with them in memory as he was before he became ill.

109. Isabella's friends apparently thought she should go to see Bob's family and stay connected with them. Maybe her "smile" indicates that Eleanor knew Isabella had other plans involving John Greenway.

110. Miller, *Isabella Greenway*, 116.

anyone could be to your mother. Dearest, none of this says what I want it to say, I've always loved you and Mrs. Selmes ever since we first met and so many of my thoughts have gone to you both, during the long periods when we've been separated, that I have always felt you very near and close to my heart and life and I do want to feel that you count on me and will ask everything of me and know that to do even a little thing for you dear would be a joy—my love to Martha and Bobby. This second great sorrow will come very hard to them, but they will help you.

A heart full of love,

Eleanor

[Ferguson Family Papers]

After her mother's funeral, Isabella went with the children to New York for an extended visit. Isabella saw Eleanor often. Isabella observed that she was "deep in politics, speech-making all over the state" and predicted to John that Eleanor would "end in Congress." [111]

Eleanor belonged to a small network that worked primarily through the New York State Democratic Committee. She raised money, edited newsletters, moderated panels, and learned, painfully, to make effective speeches.

Meanwhile, Franklin was managing the presidential nomination campaign of New York governor Al Smith. [112] Despite these accomplishments, the Roosevelts were struggling with Franklin's paralysis. "The weight of the tragedy of this house almost suffocates me at times," Isabella wrote John. "But Eleanor carries her head high and is a great woman and will go the whole distance of life triumphantly." [113]

As their wedding date approached, John confessed to Isabella, "It's like the last days of fighting after the Armistice was signed . . . I've fought so long for you." [114] On November 4, 1923, Isabella Selmes Ferguson married John Greenway in a small ceremony in Santa Barbara, with only family and a few old friends present. The couple honeymooned at the Grand Canyon, then settled in John's home in Warren, Arizona. They were planning to move to Ajo, Arizona, in the southwest part of the state, where John had opened a new copper mine. Isabella began to design another house. In January 1924, she became pregnant.

111. IG to John C. Greenway, August 5, 1923, GC.
112. Smith did not win the 1924 Democratic presidential nomination.
113. Miller, *Isabella Greenway*, 117–18.
114. Ibid., 119–20.

Mrs. John C. Greenway   May 9, 1924
Warren, Arizona
Eleanor darling

My love flows out & out to you—as undam[m]ed as the Colorado River itself—tho' you'd never guess it. Today as yesterday & the day before John says "When is Eleanor coming" or "Let's get dear Eleanor here."

I faintly lead him to believe that there is a chance this summer when the whole Franklin Roosevelt family considered [will consider] a Western tour to educate their children. How about it, dearest. I believe we could make Franklin very comfortable in a bedroom on the ground floor—& plenty of people to help him. Just remember that the doors are open wide for you—& Franklin & the children—& that if by chance, you can't come maybe Anna or Anna & James could drop in—& we could see something of the S. West.[115]

Our plans are partially in the air in that we—hold your breath—are expecting a *baby* in late Sept.—& a good deal depends too whether Martha passes her exams for Bryn Mawr—but we mean to be about the west together—we four—& it would mean so much if you were to be—I know how busy you are—Maybe Anna will tell me.

What particularly interests me is how Franklin is managing Smith's [pre-convention] campaign & you—as one of the heads of the Democratic women voters—get round their objections to him from a "wet" point of view.[116]

I was interested in Franklin's message—that was in "Time" [magazine] as to previous scandals in Republican administrations etc.[117]

But I do think the public has wearied dreadfully of it all—from too much investigation in the papers.[118]

115. Anna did go west in July to visit Martha and the Greenways in Arizona. She joined them on a visit to John Greenway's new copper mine in Ajo. Anna enjoyed riding and camping out under the stars. Roosevelt, *Mother and Daughter*, 33.

116. Smith favored the repeal of Prohibition, i.e. was "wet." Southern Democrats and women in general tended to favor Prohibition.

117. Franklin Roosevelt composed a short paragraph to be read at the annual Jefferson Day dinner of the National Democratic Club in New York City, accusing the Republican party of a half century of scandal: the impeachment of Andrew Johnson; scandals in the Grant, Hayes and Arthur administrations; graft in the McKinley War Department; the dishonesty of Taft's secretary of the interior; and recent corruption in the Harding administration. It was reprinted in *Time*, April 21, 1924.

118. Isabella refers to investigation into the Teapot Dome scandal. Although referring specifically to an oil field on public land in Wyoming, "Teapot Dome" is shorthand for the government corruption scandal that tainted President Warren G. Harding's administration.

You & Franklin would have enjoyed Martha's letter after travelling in the dining car with Mr. McAdoo.[119] "We entered the dining car just as Mr. McAdoo finished his dinner. He arose & standing in the middle of the aisle said with a flourish to the waiters 'Well, good night boys' and taking a toothpick walked out. Imagine how I felt when Bobbie, finishing his dinner stood up & said to the waiters 'Well good night boys' & walk[ed] out with a tooth pick to everyone's amusement."

Eleanor we dearly love our Xmas-wedding present even if we did wait till 4th of July to tell you. They are *most* beautiful—& I not only use them & cherish them here but take them along in my suitcase to Ajo—to enhance our long wooden table[120]—& bring them back & see that they are most carefully laundered. They are just like you *too* dear—& fill my eye with sentiment every time I sit before one.

Life has held its breath & I've basked in a happiness that I find hard to believe—while the miracle of it all is John's wonderful joy—& now that we have hopes of a baby—the very world seems turned to magic. Martha is as happy as can be & planning its upbringing quite independently of us—!— Even thinks it might spend part of the winter with her in Bryn Mawr!

I picture you & yours & life as it must tumble over itself for you these days—& my admiration & confidence know no limit.

  Yr ever adoring
   Isabella

John would join me I know in love—were he here. A letter from you would be beyond words welcome.

In recognition of her leadership among women politicians, Eleanor Roosevelt was named chair of the women's platform committee for the Democratic National Convention.[121] She arranged for two extra tickets so that John and Isabella could take the Ferguson children to the convention at Madison Square Garden in New York City, June 24–July 9, 1924.

119. William Gibbs McAdoo and Al Smith were top contenders for the Democratic presidential nomination in 1924. McAdoo had been secretary of the treasury for Woodrow Wilson, married Wilson's daughter Eleanor (Nell), and was an unsuccessful candidate for the Democratic nomination for president in 1920. http://bioguide.congress.gov/scripts/biodisplay.pl?index=M000293

120. Their Ajo house was still under construction. The Greenways may have been renting a dwelling, or "camping out" in the new house.

121. Cook, *Eleanor Roosevelt*, I, 346.

Mission Ridge Road, Santa Barbara   June 11, 1924
California
Eleanor darling

What a magic politician you are. It never occurred to me that there would be but the remotest chance of getting seats—when your prompt wire came. I forwarded the $200.00 right away & doubtless John will be calling for them soon after the 20th. He & Bobbie arrive NY then—Martha & I on the 25th (college exams hold us here).—It's a great relief to me to have the Dr. say I can go in reasonable safety if I stay quiet at the other end. We'll be in the Plaza Hotel & I pray you will use my room as a haven whenever you are reeling with exhaustion & can escape the turmoil. John goes as an alternate [delegate] from Arizona & has two seats—these others we wanted for the children's education—my indulgence!

You would have been so proud of Martha. She left the only school she attended with flying colors. They wholeheartedly gave her every honor & the children's applause just melted me as nothing else ever will.

Your letter hasn't caught up with me yet.[122]

All lovingly,
Isabella

With intense interest do I for the first time try to look deep into *your* Democratic party to which John has gone after supporting Col R for 22 years.

FDR earned a national reputation at the convention when his nominating speech for Al Smith inspired the crowd to cheer for more than an hour.[123]

John Greenway looked as though he might have a political future, himself. Arizona had nominated him as a "favorite son" vice-presidential candidate; Minnesota, where he had started in mining, seconded the nomination. McAdoo and Smith deadlocked and after 103 ballots, the convention compromised on a Wall-Street lawyer, John W. Davis. That summer, several newspapers touted Greenway as a gubernatorial candidate.[124]

Eleanor continued to work for the Women's Division of the Democratic party. "I'm only being active again til you can be again," she assured Franklin. "It isn't such a great desire on my part to serve the world."[125] She gleefully joined Smith's campaign for re-election as New York governor—against Republican

122. ER may have said in her wire that a letter was on the way. If so, it is missing.
123. Cook, *Eleanor Roosevelt*, I, 351.
124. Miller, *Isabella Greenway*, 123.
125. Ward, *A First-Class Temperament*, 688.

nominee Theodore Roosevelt, Jr., her own first cousin. She toured the state in a car topped with a papier-maché teapot emitting real steam, to suggest TR Jr.'s ties to the Teapot Dome scandal.[126] Isabella was appalled. "Do you think E[leanor] has lost her mind?" she asked John.[127]

Eleanor took time out to send a congratulatory telegram to Isabella on the birth of a son, John Selmes Greenway (called Jack), on October 11, 1924. It was, coincidentally, Eleanor's fortieth birthday.

Syracuse, New York   October 13, 1924
     Telegram
     Congratulations and best love to you all so happy for you Isabella dearest
               Eleanor Roosevelt

This telegram marks the first surviving communication from Eleanor in over a year. The stress of dealing with Franklin's polio and building a new life may account for some slowing of the correspondence.

Just as Eleanor's letters resume, Isabella's letters seem to stop. She, too, would be going through a time of trials.

In any case, Eleanor now included both John and Isabella in her political network.

49 East 65th Street   Jan 14 [1925]
Dearest Isabella and John,
     This will introduce to you Sidney Sherwood who is going out to Arizona to work for Mr. Douglas.[128] He is one of our great friends & I know you will both like him so do all you can for him for our sake.
          Always devotedly,
               Eleanor Roosevelt

During the spring of 1925 Isabella collapsed with what later proved to be thyroid deficiency. She spent ninety-eight days in bed, taking iodine. Baby Jack was a great consolation, as John traveled a great deal on business. He was planning, however, to retire from the Calumet and Arizona Mining Company

---

126. Ted was later cleared of any involvement. Cook, *Eleanor Roosevelt*, I, 352; Ward, *A First-Class Temperament*, 684.
127. IG to John C. Greenway, October 20, 1924, GC.
128. This could have been either Isabella's old friend Walter Douglas or Walter's nephew, Arizona congressman Lewis Douglas.

in order to have time for other projects, including politics. Calls for him to run for governor increased.

Meanwhile, Eleanor was taking a break from campaigning. She tried to make more time for her children, filling in for Franklin on outdoor excursions.

Hyde Park on Hudson   July 5 [1925]

Isabella dearest,

It was a relief to get your telegram[129] but I fear you have been through some terrible times.

I was so happy to hear that you were better & I do hope you will be East next autumn.

How has Martha come through her first year at Bryn Mawr? I heard her room mate Sylvia Brewster did not like college & wondered if it would affect Martha. Has Bobby passed for Yale?

I took Anna to the Geneva Experiment Station (our state agricultural experiment station) last Tuesday & left her & so far have heard no word of how it is working out. I hope she enjoys her six weeks there but of course when you've done no work it is hard to start again.[130] James & Elliott left for the [illegible] ranch on Tuesday also & all there will join me at Campobello about Aug. 22nd. I am taking the little boys on a motor camping trip, starting next Tuesday & reaching Campo the 14th & staying with them till Aug. 5th when I come back to Franklin [and stay with him at Hyde Park] till I can get Anna at Geneva.[131]

Cousin Susie [Parish] & Henry sailed for Europe last week & I hope they have a perfect time. Mrs. Parsons went with them & they will not lack for Americans I know as it seems that everyone is going over!

Write me if you have a minute & feel up to it & tell me about the baby & remember I love [you] always.

> Devotedly
>> Eleanor

My love to John.

That fall, John began suffering from gall bladder problems. Despite Isabella's extreme reluctance, he agreed to his doctors' recommendations that

---

129. Missing.
130. She may mean that, since this is Anna's first job, it will be hard for her.
131. i.e., until it is time to pick up Anna at the Experiment Station in Geneva.

he undergo an operation. In early January 1926, Isabella accompanied him to New York for the surgery.

Isabella was overwhelmed with feelings of foreboding. Operations, she feared, risked "surprises and horrors beyond remotest conception." [132] No one seemed to understand her misgivings about what was supposed to be a simple operation. Tragically her fears were well founded. At first, the operation appeared to have been successful. After a week had passed, Isabella left John's side for the first time to have lunch with her uncle. Then they received a frantic call at the restaurant. A blood clot had broken loose and lodged in John's lung. On January 19, John died in Isabella's arms. They had been married two years, two months, and two weeks.

Isabella boarded a train to take John's body back to Arizona. Jack was still in Arizona with his nurse, and Bobbie would have to return to Yale, but Martha went with her. She had not adapted well, and she would not return to college.

Eleanor was planning to go to Florida with Franklin for his annual hydrotherapy session to treat the effects of the polio. She ached for her friend's loss and tried to console her with assurances of their lasting friendship.

49 East 65th Street, New York City   Jan. 23 [1926]
Isabella darling

Here are six editorial pages [133] with Bishop Atwood's appreciation [134] & the editorial, both of which are very fine I think.

You are so constantly in my thoughts dear, & I wish I were with you but I know John's friends will enfold you with love for him & for you & you will soon have Jack but remember if ever you & Martha really want me I can come for I love you oh! so dearly & long to help even though I know no one can—though we've been apart so much I always feel as though we'd travelled the last twenty-two years very closely & I hope dear that what remains to us here on earth we may hold even more closely for I need you & the inspiration you are more than you can know.

    All my love
      Eleanor
Love to Martha

132. Isabella Greenway Journal, January 7, 1926, GC.
133. Missing.
134. Presumably the sermon at John's memorial service in New York. Atwood had officiated at Isabella and John's wedding.

Knowing that her letter would not have reached Isabella by the time she arrived in Arizona, Eleanor sent a telegram, too.

Telegram New York NY   Jan. 26 1926
To Ajo Arizona

I am thinking of you constantly hope the long trip has not been too hard for you all wish I could be near you tomorrow but my thoughts will be there all my love and Anna's to Martha.

Eleanor Roosevelt

Isabella could not retreat into mourning. Not only did her toddler son Jack need her, but, Bob, now eighteen, suddenly needed her, as well. In Pittsburgh in early April with the Yale polo team, he had contracted scarlet fever,[135] which affected his lungs. The doctors operated to relieve the pressure, leaving a huge gash in his back. Isabella raced out to Pittsburgh on a train, and nursed him back to health. Four months later, Bobbie was well enough to join the family for a trip to Scotland to reconnect with the Ferguson relatives.[136]

Eleanor, meanwhile, was busy writing articles on "issues of war and peace" for the *Women's Democratic News*.[137]

Willowbud Farm, Marion[138]   July 26 [1926]
Massachusetts
Isabella darling,

I saw Auntie Corinne yesterday at Newport & she told me you were back on Long Island & might sail the 31st. I am so glad Bobby is better & that you may get off. I've tried to get to Pittsburgh but it has been a little hectic here. If by chance you don't sail before Aug. 3rd let Martha telephone my N.Y. house Rhin[ebeck] 7428 as I'll be there the 3rd of August & would love a glimpse of you all.

Dearest, I want to put my arms around you & hold you tight. I know how hard, how unreal much of life must seem, just living through is not an easy thing to do & you've had so much of it in your short life but if it helps at all

---

135. Scarlet fever is caused by a streptococcus bacterial infection. Toxins from the bacteria produce a scarlet-colored rash. http://www.kidshealth.org/parent/infections/bacterial_viral/scarlet_fever.html.
136. Miller, *Isabella Greenway*, 139–40.
137. Cook, *Eleanor Roosevelt*, I, 364.
138. Possibly Willow Bend (now a golf course).

to know that there are people who love you & need you & think of you very constantly just remember that you mean more to me than I could ever tell you & in ways that you don't even know.

I met Anna yesterday & she & Curtis[139] have had a wonderful trip & look very well & very happy. James is hard at work in Canada but returns to civilization on Aug. 15th. I think Franklin is improving under Dr. McDonald & Elliott & the little boys are having a pleasant summer I think. So all is well with us & here we stay more or less steadily till Sept. 10th.

Do write me your plans & if there is anything at anytime I can do in N.Y. let me know. Dear love to Martha & a heartfull to you dearest.

> As ever
>
> Eleanor R.

Eleanor and Isabella were pre-eminently practical women who rose to meet the trials that beset them both—early loss of parents, invalid husbands, frighteningly ill children, and their own health crises. But from time to time the difficulties they had to face inspired philosophical musing.

Hyde Park on the Hudson, N.Y.   Jan 1, 1927
Isabella dearest

The basket has its place already in my room & I shall use it constantly & think of you. We all love the picture of Jackie & he looks a handsome, healthy manly little chap, worth living for dear, such good material to help you carry on in John's spirit. I wonder if we can look back & follow the doings of this world if, what really matters to us is not that the spirit in which we strove should live—the works are so often less than we had hoped & dreamed—but the spirit in which all work is undertaken is what fundamentally affects the final achievement—perhaps generations later.[140]

I was so happy to get Martha's letter & to hear that Bobby is much better & she herself so well. I'm so thankful you have Martha.

Anna expects her baby in late March & I think she is very happy about it. I confess to dreading it more than I ever dreaded it for myself but I

---

139. Anna Roosevelt married New York stockbroker Curtis Dall in 1926. They would have two children, Anna Eleanor and Curtis.

140. Eleanor's complicated rhetoric makes this hard to understand. She says that what really matters is the spirit in which we strive, which may have its final effect in works accomplished generations later.

wouldn't tell anyone but you! I shall go south to Warm Springs, Georgia[141] with Franklin about Feb. 12th & home by March 5th as Anna is coming home for the event.

We are at present entertaining or rather chaperoning 16 of James & Elliott's friends over the weekend & they are all loudly singing in an adjoining room, rather nice but distracting.

Much, much love dearest. My thoughts are with you so much & I long to see you.

> Devotedly,
> Eleanor

Like Eleanor, Isabella sought to overcome adversity by engaging in worthwhile projects. She had the means. John Greenway's will had left her $2 million (worth about $22 million in 2005.) She lobbied the Arizona legislature to commission a statue of John Greenway to represent Arizona in Statuary Hall at the U. S. Capitol in Washington, D.C.[142] Then she hired Gutzon Borglum, later the sculptor of Mount Rushmore, to create the statue.

Since both her husbands had been veterans, Isabella also wanted to do something for the thousands of tubercular veterans who settled in Arizona seeking, like Bob, to prolong their lives. She founded a small factory known as the Arizona Hut,[143] where men could make furniture and novelty items, and their wives could do needlework as a means of supplementing their small pensions. She spent more time in Tucson, where there were greater opportunities. Eventually she built a house and moved there permanently.

Isabella also followed through on a plan she had conceived with John to buy a ranch in northern Arizona. She purchased the Quarter Circle Double X Ranch, six miles west of Williams, Arizona, near the Grand Canyon, where she could escape the suffocating summer heat of southern Arizona.[144]

141. A resort where Franklin spent many weeks each year doing therapy in the warm waters to try to regain function in his legs. He believed that if he was going to have a career in politics, he must be able to walk again. Ward, *A First-Class Temperament*, 700–705. He was haunted by his memory of the stricken President Woodrow Wilson in a wheelchair in 1920. Link, *Papers of Woodrow Wilson*, v. 65, 521 n. 1.

142. Greenway was not necessarily an obvious choice for this honor, but Isabella joined with John's Rough Rider comrades and mining executives to carry the day.

143. A "hut" was what the World War I Doughboys called a place where they could retreat from the trenches for a rest.

144. Miller, *Isabella Greenway*, 142–46.

At the same time, Eleanor, together with a few friends, started the Val-Kil furniture factory near Hyde Park, hoping to induce farm families to remain in the community by providing a second source of income.

Hyde Park, NY   Aug. 22 [1927]

Isabella dearest,

I saw this ridiculous bag the other day & thought some of your women [145] might find it saleable. It can be made in different colors & is washable & people seem to like it.

You all sound busy & healthy & I love to hear of Jack sleeping in your room. [146] Of course you've done a wonderful thing in acquiring the ranch but so few people could have put it through. [147] You always do things which no one else could do however & I feel you are going to get people together & solve this question of the tubercular war veterans as no one else could have done. Let me know if ever I can do anything for you in N.Y. My own particular tubercular war veteran [148] in H.P. [Hyde Park] hasn't been out of bed for over a year but tells me he hopes to get to Arizona!

The little boys & I had an amusing jaunt to Detroit & Niagara Falls & I stopped for tea at Henderson when I was motoring back & saw A. Corinne [Robinson] & Corinne Heber [.] A. Corinne has been very miserable I fear bad news from Monroe [Robinson] tho' she said nothing, Corinne Alsop looks well & is painting & has sold an article to McCall for $350. [149] Isn't that grand?

Much, much love dearest, don't get too tired.
          Devotedly
               Eleanor

By 1928, Eleanor Roosevelt had become a major political force. In July, after Smith was nominated to run for president at the Democratic National Convention in Houston, she was invited to direct the Women's Advisory

145. Perhaps the women who sold the veterans' items.
146. Since we have no letter referring to Jack's sleeping in her room, this suggests there was a letter that is missing.
147. Eleanor, financially dependent on her mother-in-law, may have been in awe of Isabella's ability to buy a large ranch in a far-off locale.
148. Eleanor had apparently befriended a local man with TB.
149. It is hardly surprising that the mother of future columnists Joe and Stewart Alsop was earning substantial sums for her writing.

Committee of the Democratic National Committee, assisting his campaign.[150] In October, Smith and John J. Raskob, the Democratic national chairman, asked Eleanor to help them persuade FDR to run for governor of New York. She did so, but kept her distance from his campaign. Already her position as a female political leader was causing some controversy in New York.[151]

Isabella, too, was moving into politics. Her work with the veterans had brought her visibility, and in 1928 she was named Arizona's Democratic National Committeewoman, a member of the organization in which Eleanor was taking a leadership role.

Isabella was also approached to run as a candidate for either the governorship or the state senate. She seriously considered both offers, but was ultimately deterred by the prospect of trying to straddle both wings of the divided Arizona Democratic party.[152]

Now, Isabella and Eleanor had a political relationship, in addition to their friendship. Eleanor dictated an official letter to Isabella requesting information about organizing women in Arizona for Smith. At the bottom, she scrawled an affectionate handwritten note.

Democratic National Committee   August 2, 1928
New York City
My dear Mrs. Greeenway:
   Mr. Fred W. Johnson, who is in charge of the office in Salt Lake City, has asked that you refer all the information which I have asked for direct to him and he will send it to me.

Everything for the states for which he is responsible is to be handled through his office, and he is going to set up in every state a group of women to help in the organizing work.

Please provide him with all the information possible, as we are anxious to know as much as we can about what the [Democratic] women are doing.

Mr. Johnson's address is New House Hotel, Salt Lake City, Utah.

      Very sincerely yours,
         Eleanor Roosevelt
         (Mrs. Franklin D. Roosevelt)

150. Cook, *Eleanor Roosevelt*, I, 365–66.
151. Ibid., 368–77.
152. Miller, *Isabella Greenway*, 149–51.

[by hand] Isabella dearest, I'm thinking so much of you, but too busy to write.

      Love always.

        ER

Arizona was planning to form, in addition to the traditional Democratic state organization, new "Smith-Robinson Clubs"[153] to attract crossover votes from anyone not wishing to identify as a Democrat.

Isabella assured Eleanor that the two organizations would be able to work together.

Telegram
Williams, Arizona   September 15, 1928
To Mrs. Franklin D Roosevelt, Democratic Committee Headquarters
1775 Broadway, New York City

Rest assured with primaries[154] out of the way state will be properly organized in two lines working together as follows Smith Robinson clubs and Democratic state organization stop.

        Isabella Greenway

A few days later, Isabella wired again with reassurance that, despite some factional disturbances, her plan was working.

Telegram
Williams, Arizona,   September 20, 1928
To Mrs. Franklin D Roosevelt, 1775 Broadway, New York City

Kindly wire if possible whether Mrs. Robinson coming with Senator Robinson and where stop organization supporting Smith [Smith-Robinson Clubs] going forward splendidly throughout state amongst the men and women stop clubs now working with central committees and believe can now disregard all unfortunate internal state conflicts which reached headquarters stop you can expect good report soon

        Isabella Greenway

Isabella traveled throughout the state, speaking in a different town practically every night.

153. Senator Joseph Taylor Robinson of Arkansas was Smith's running-mate.
154. Isabella refers here to primaries for local offices.

Perhaps a little defensive because of Eleanor's new political prominence, Isabella continued to stress that she knew the local situation better than national campaign workers. Then as now, people in the East were apt to underestimate the vast distances between towns in the West.

To Mrs. Franklin D Roosevelt   October 10, 1928
Democratic Committee Headquarters
1775 Broadway, New York City
PERSONAL
 Dear Eleanor:

We did receive your maps—such humorous documents—we think of having them framed!! But never you mind[,] we understand, thru the very fact they were forthcoming, that you people at Headquarters are right on the job.

As far as covering the State, as they designate, they are wholly impracticable from a point of view of time, distance, and roads; and sizes of towns—some of the places designated are practically nothing more than two red [fire?] station houses, and while it is splendid, indeed, if we could devote real time to places of this size, I do not believe it could be done. Nor do they tie into the meetings of local candidates, etc.

Tomorrow night I am starting out and speaking in a different town all but four nights until the first of November, taking with me somebody whose name I have not yet learned from Headquarters, who will help me. The women are organizing as never before, and the enthusiasm is on a high pitch.

In case it is of any use to Headquarters for publicity, I send you a copy of my speech,[155] written primarily with the object of drawing back into the fold our anti-catholic democrats and our prohibitionist women. It is very simple, but it has proven effective.

Senator Robinson's visit was met with splendid response, and he helped enormously. I do not believe you progress more rapidly or more hel[p]fully [elsewhere] than we are [progressing] in this State, but, like every State, the unknown give and take between the two Parties in silent vote is beyond any prophesy.

  Much devotion,
    Isabella
IG: hec[156]

155. Not reprinted here
156. Isabella's secretary, Howard E. Caffrey, who had originally worked in that capacity for John Greenway.

P.S.

For your information my tentative itinerary is as follows:

October

10th Night— Winslow

11th Night— Prescott

12th Noon—Tucson

13th Night— Tucson—visit Casa Grande

14th Sunday— Tucson

15th All Day—Douglas

16th All Day—Bisbee

17th All Day—Thatcher

18th All Day—Miami —visit Clifton & Morenci

19th All Day—Globe

20th to 28th Home, trips from—Flagstaff, Prescott & other northern Arizona points.

29th Kingman

30th to Nov. 6th Phoenix, Ajo, Yuma & intermediate

Phoenix has already been covered twice, and in the bigger towns the women's organizations are having weekly meetings right up to election.

Eleanor soothed her friend's feelings by continuing to ask for her support. In the following letter she requests help for a woman who seems to be afraid that she might lose her job if it were known she was supporting the Democrats. Eleanor and Isabella would work together more easily as Isabella grew more confident of her abilities.

Democratic National Committee   Oct. 16, 1928

New York City

Dear Isabella:

The maps we sent you were nothing but suggestions and I knew that when they were done by people who had never been in that country they would have to be revised[157] by those in the states, if used at all! However, you know best how to plan, and I wish you the best of luck.

157. Eleanor says that since the maps were done by people who had never been in Arizona, they would have to be revised.

I am sorry to say that the speech did not come out [arrive here] but I am very anxious to have it, also a photograph of yourself to go with it for publicity purposes.[158]

I am enclosing to you a letter because I think you could help better than anybody else. Can't you get somebody to send word to the people at Dawson [159] that they can vote as they please without fear of losing their jobs?

> Affectionately,
> Eleanor Roosevelt

Isabella, who seems to have felt insecure because of Eleanor's exalted position in the party, wrote to make sure Eleanor knew how hard she was working, as she drove back and forth over a large state with few roads.

Isabella was fighting an uphill battle. Smith's greatest liability would prove to be his Catholic religious beliefs.

To Mrs. Franklin D Roosevelt   October 24, 1928
Democratic Committee Headquarters
1775 Broadway, New York City
Dearest Eleanor;

My wire yesterday to Mr. Arthur Curtis Janes is, I believe, our strongest method of approach to the Phelps Dodge Companies. He is one of their directors, working for Al Smith.

I don't believe the people will lose their jobs by declaring their politics, but I know they feel they may. I doubt if any open statement will be forthcoming, as Walter Douglas [160] is stoutly supporting Mr. Hoover, and a declaration of this kind might admit the tendency of politics in connection with employment.[161]

I have written Mrs. Wright, who made this complaint, as per the enclosed copy of letter.[162]

---

158. Evidently ER had not received a speech she was hoping Isabella had sent. Isabella would not send a picture, though. Having been a beauty in her youth, she was extremely reluctant to send out photos of herself in middle age. Eventually she commissioned a flattering pencil sketch that could be used for publicity.

159. The Phelps Dodge Company, of which Isabella was a big stockholder through her inheritance from John, had a coal-mine in Dawson, New Mexico.

160. Douglas was the Phelps Dodge general manager.

161. Isabella seems to be saying to Eleanor that she does know a director supporting Smith who might help.

162. The letter is not included.

Martha is planning to buy a stretcher to take me out of Arizona the day after election, and charge it to the Democratic party. We motor [drive] hundreds of miles daily, speaking once or twice, and there never has been a campaign like it; and the women are organized 100% thruout the State.

If Governor Smith does not carry Arizona, I believe it will be based on religious prejudice.

> Very sincerely,
> IG: hec

Al Smith lost the presidency. He was defeated in Arizona and failed by a wide margin to carry his home state of New York. Franklin Roosevelt, on the other hand, easily won the race to succeed Smith as governor. The Roosevelts moved back to Albany, this time into the governor's mansion. Eleanor was helpful to Franklin, but did not give up her own political pursuits.[163]

Eleanor Roosevelt had been working for U.S. entrance into the World Court, starting in 1923. The House of Representatives had voted for U.S. participation, and now Eleanor was leading "a woman's crusade to achieve Senate approval." She believed membership in the Court was a necessary first step toward international peace.[164] Knowing that Isabella had great influence in the Arizona Democratic party, Eleanor asked her to lobby Arizona's senators about the issue.

Isabella's work in reorganizing the Democratic party and campaigning in 1928 had been effective: all the local Democrats won election.

Isabella was again approached to become a candidate for governor in 1930. One Arizonan even lobbied FDR to persuade Isabella to run. She modestly declined, saying that her appreciation of the compliment was "as profound as if I deserved it." But she kept her options open, writing of Arizona's successes to national leaders. Part of the reason she declined to run for office was because she doubted that women would vote for a widow with a four-year-old child. She continued to work at the grass-roots level, recruiting more women to the Democratic party, and looking toward future elections.[165]

The day before Eleanor wrote the following letter, the stock market crashed. At first, few people foresaw the consequences.

163. Cook, *Eleanor Roosevelt*, I, 382.
164. Ibid., 346.
165. Miller, *Isabella Greenway*, 154, 157–58.

The American Foundation[166]   October 30, 1929
New York City
Dear Isabella:

Would you feel able to ask Senator Ashurst[167] and Senator Hayden[168] the following questions:

Do you approve the World Court protocol accepting the Senate reservations of 1926 and embodying Mr. Root's formula for the operation of the fifth reservation? [169]

How do you now think you would vote upon the protocol when it comes to the Senate?

In your letters to the senators you might want to remind them that the protocol has already been signed by 50 of the 54 member nations of the Court, including all the large nations, and the signatures of the other 4 are expected very soon.

I don't write the Arizona senators myself because I don't know them personally and because I think they would be more likely to reply to you.

Of course no public use whatever will be made of any replies that you receive. I want the information just to know what the chances of the present World court measure are in the Senate.

[by hand] How about the [Arizona] Governorship [for you]? Did you have a happy summer & are you coming East soon? I long to see you. All my love.
                    Eleanor R.
Did you know Cousin Susie [Parish] had broken her arm?

Her thank-you letter for Isabella's Christmas present allowed Eleanor to turn for a moment to the family concerns that had dominated their correspondence in earlier times.

166. The American Foundation was a private organization that supported U.S. participation in the World Court. For over thirty years it was directed by Eleanor's friend Esther Lape.
167. Henry Fountain Ashurst (1874–1962), Democratic senator from Arizona from 1912, when it was granted statehood, until 1941.
168. Carl Hayden (1877–1972) became the longest-serving member of the U.S. Congress. A Democrat, he served as U.S. Representative, 1912–1926, and U.S. Senator, 1927–1969.
169. The U.S. Senate, which had voted against joining the League of Nations in 1920, was still grappling with issues related to the League, especially membership in the World Court.

Executive Mansion, Albany, NY   Jan. 15, 1930
Isabella dearest

The bag with all its nice toilet requisites [cosmetics and bath items] is a joy to a constantly moving person like myself but the sight of your handwriting was nicest & gave me a warm feeling around my heart.

This of course comes to thank you dear for your thought & to wish you a happy New Year, but also to ask if you are coming East soon? I long to see you, couldn't you plan to spend from Wed. to Sunday here & bring Jackie? There is plenty of play space for him.

How is Martha? Is she still heart whole & fancy free? Is Bobby well & getting on well?

Anna expects another baby the first part of April & Curt has had an anxious time in his firm but they are very happy & the new home is charming, so even if they have to be a little careful for a few years it won't hurt them, perhaps it will be good in the long run.

James plans to be married in Brookline, Mass. on June 4th. Is there a chance of your being here? Also, do you think you will be on the ranch next summer? If so, I really may take F. Jr. to you & leave him a little longer than I can stay away in a campaign summer.

The Republicans are suddenly handing Franklin his water power bill on a plate & I can't help being suspicious that there is a "nigger in the wood pile" [170] [a hidden motive]—tho' we haven't found it yet!

Much, much love dear Isabella, I love you always
        Devotedly,
                Eleanor

The deepening depression caused a drastic drop in the sales of Arizona Hut veterans' furniture. Isabella kept buying furniture, trying to soften the economic blow. Finally, someone asked if she planned to equip a hotel with all the furniture she was accumulating. She did. The Arizona Inn opened on December 18, 1930.

Isabella also helped Charles W. Gilpin, who had been John Greenway's military chauffeur in France, by investing with him in G & G Airlines, a small commuter operation.[171]

170. The modern reader needs to remember that phrases such as this were in common usage, and did not indicate the kind of animus that such words convey today.
171. Isabella operated G & G Airlines, which made flights between Arizona, California, and Mexico, until 1934, during a very competitive time in the airline industry. Holmstrom, "Isabella Greenway," 15.

Eleanor's Val-Kil plant weathered the depression without laying off even one of its thirty workers.[172]

Women in the workforce experienced great discrimination during the depression. The federal government and sixty percent of all companies refused to hire married women, arguing that men, as heads of households, needed the jobs more. Eleanor, who believed there was opportunity enough for all, fought for women's right to work. [173]

Eleanor also continued her work with the American Foundation. While earlier she had merely asked Isabella to lobby Arizona's senators on the issue, now she asked for a statement from Isabella herself, testimony to her Arizona friend's growing political influence.

The American Foundation   Feb. 3, 1930
New York City
Dear Isabella:

Can you send me a few lines expressing your own point of view on the World Court situation or briefly expressing your hope that the Senate will speedily ratify the three World Court protocols that were signed on December 9 last?

The American Foundation would like to issue your statement with a number of others from every state in the Union, shortly *after* the President has sent the protocols to the Senate, which may be in the not distant future. Until that time no public use will be made of anything you send me.

The kind of statement I have in mind has already been given by two or three people whom you know. They are quoted on the attached slip.[174] It is a few lines like these that would help us. I hope you will send them.

      Affectionately,
        ER

Young Bob Ferguson, now twenty-two, had gone to Northern Rhodesia (present-day Zambia) for a year to learn the mining business. Isabella planned to go East with Jack, meet up with Martha, who was then living in New York City, and then go on to pay Bob a long visit in Africa. Her friend Olivia Cutting James[175] reasoned that a trip to Rhodesia might actually be restful for

---

172. It would close in 1936, when ER and her partners in the enterprise experienced a rift in their friendship.
173. Cook, *Eleanor Roosevelt*, I, 419–21.
174. Missing.
175. Olivia Cutting had married Henry James, the son of philosopher William James, in 1917.

Isabella, since it was "one of the few places (as yet) you have neither mines, hotels, houses, ranches or airplane lines of your own to look after." [176] Eleanor hoped that Isabella would come East via Albany, but she did not.

Executive Mansion, Albany, NY   Feb. 27 [1931]
Dearest Isabella,

Martha tells me you are all going to Africa in April which means you must come East & I wonder if you couldn't plan to bring Jackie & his nurse here on your way as of course, once [you are] in New York [City] I will never pry you loose! I'll be here steadily from April 1st -13th & every Wednesday to Sunday evening after that. Do come if you can for I long to see you & I can find plenty for Jackie to do I feel sure.

Martha looked sweet last Tuesday afternoon at Cousin Susie [Parish]'s musical & she is coming to lunch with Anna & Bishop Atwood next Tuesday. I wish I saw her more often but the young must be busy about their own business, mustn't they? You must be proud of her for the fineness that shines in her face.

Anna is looking better & I think their financial difficulties will gradually smooth themselves out. She is wonderful with Curt & the children & so much wiser than I could have been at her age!

What do you hear from Bobby? I envy you your trip for we seem pretty well tied to this state but then it is good to have a job & [it] means so much to Franklin.

A world of love to you always.
     Devotedly,
       Eleanor
Don't bother to write just wire if we may hope to see you.

Isabella returned from Africa in October and plunged into the minutiae of her many interests: everything from the inventory of bed sheets at the Arizona Inn to the Arizona governor's commission on the copper tariff. Her known friendship with Eleanor meant that anyone trying to reach the head of the Democratic women's organization was likely to go through Isabella.

176. Miller, *Isabella Greenway*, 167.

Tucson, Arizona nd [1931]

Eleanor dearest

The plates are from *Mrs. Smith*—& the *baskets* especially woven for you from desert shrubs & presented by *Mrs. McDonald.*

If a letter comes thro to me I shall see that these ladies receive it (their address is over in the Phoenix file) but I have told them how grateful I know you are.

   Lovingly—& still gasping for breath since we circled the world.

    Isabella

Part Five

FDR and the New Deal

Franklin D. Roosevelt's political ascent continued during his term as governor of New York. In 1931, he began making plans to run for president. Eleanor reached out to Isabella to help achieve his goal.

Eleanor asked Isabella, as Arizona's representative on the Democratic National Committee (DNC), to make certain her vote would be counted in an upcoming meeting, as many on the DNC opposed FDR's candidacy.

Eleanor also wanted Isabella to confer with Mary (Molly) Dewson,[1] who had organized women for Franklin Roosevelt's second race for governor in 1930, and who was now rounding up support for FDR's presidential candidacy.

At the same time, Eleanor made every effort to keep a note of warmth in her business letter.

Executive Mansion, Albany, NY   [n.d.—late 1931]
Dearest Isabella:

If you are not going to the National Committee meeting, do you think you could send your proxy to Miss Marbury? She is trying to collect some before the time arrives. Also if you know of any other national committee-woman not going to the meeting, would you suggest that they let her have their proxies?

Molly Dewson, a great friend of mine[,] is going to stop and see a number of people on her way out and back to California to talk the situation [FDR's presidential campaign] over and I will be terribly grateful if you could see her for a little while. She will send you a wire when she finds out the time she will be there.

[by hand] How I long to see you! I love you very dearly.

Eleanor

---

1. Mary "Molly" Dewson was a reformer recruited by ER to organize Democratic women for Smith in 1928. She went on to work in a similar capacity for FDR's gubernatorial and presidential races.

As the depression wore on, and it became obvious that Hoover could not be re-elected, intense competition arose for the Democratic nomination. Al Smith had not declared he was running, but he was suspected of trying to block Roosevelt by arranging for his ally, Jouette Shouse, to be named chairman of the Democratic executive committee.[2] From time to time, Franklin, as well as Eleanor, wrote Isabella to discuss strategy.

In this letter, Eleanor describes Franklin's and her own position on prohibition, explaining how they differ from the stand Smith had taken in the 1928 campaign.

She also began sounding out Isabella on the possibility of Arizona's delegates to the upcoming Democratic National Convention pledging in advance to support FDR. Arizona at the time did not hold a presidential primary election.

Executive Mansion, Albany, NY   January 23, 1932
Dear Isabella:

Molly Dewson has come back and tells me of her meeting with you. She says that you did not realize that the [Democratic] National Committee was not in complete sympathy with Franklin's candidacy.[3]

I think Mr. Shouse personally likes Franklin but his bread and butter depends on Mr. Raskob.[4] Mr. Roskob's greatest interest is in the wet and dry question. You, of course, are familiar with Franklin's position on that. I think you saw his original statement, which was that he doubted if there could ever be a repeal of the amendment, but he thought there could be an amendment to the amendment, as there had been in so many other cases, which would make the present amendment inoperative and allow of legislation which would cure some of the present evils of prohibition.

Exactly what this legislation shall be, I think he is still considering. They are always discussing it and he may by this time have some more definite plan, but I do not think anyone as yet is entirely certain of the type of legislation which will have to be passed.

My own ideas are much as they were when last we talked. I do not like the evils of prohibition but nobody as yet has suggested to me a plan which really precludes the return of the salon [saloon?] or the return of the power of the

2. Miller, *Isabella Greenway*, 169.
3. Historian Richard Oulahan puts it more strongly: "The National committee was directed by [Roosevelt's] sworn enemies." Oulahan, *The Man Who*, 45.
4. John J. Raskob, Smith's 1928 campaign manager, was trying to round up support, including Shouse's, for Smith in 1932.

brewery and distilling interests, and I still feel that they were more powerful in the control of government than is even the bootlegger today. Therefore, I am not able to work with any enthusiasm for any particular change at present, though I am quite willing to see some really good change come about.

This is just for your information, as it does not really make much difference what I think in the present political situation!

Have you decided anything as to Mr. Adams[5] and your attitude towards him? We are tremendously interested in who is really going to control the Arizona situation. Do write me as to your ideas on the possibility of getting the Arizona delegates elected for Franklin.

[by hand] Darling, all this is official, willy nilly I am doing some work at headquarters. I hope all is well with Jackie? Doesn't Elliott seem young to be married[6] & off to Florida on a honeymoon [?] She's sweet & I want to have you see them both soon. Anna's husband is hard hit financially but she is a brick & they are now living in our N.Y. house. Do come East soon. I love you always more & more.

> Devotedly
> Eleanor

Although Isabella was excited to be working for Franklin, she once again insisted, possibly with some irritation, that she knew best how to do things in Arizona. Arizona delegates historically had not committed themselves to particular candidates prior to the national conventions. In light of this tradition, Isabella argued that it would be difficult to force Arizona delegates to pledge their votes to Franklin.

If they waited for Arizona Democrats to organize on their own, they would be more willing to support Franklin than if Isabella tried to push them. She assured Eleanor that people were already beginning to organize spontaneously for Roosevelt, and that FDR strategist Jim Farley[7] had been in touch with Tucson newspaper editor Bill Mathews.[8]

5. C. E. Addams, chairman of the Arizona Democratic committee, was contending with Isabella's male counterpart, national committeeman Wirt Bowman, for control of the Democratic campaign in Arizona.
6. Elliott was twenty-one. On January 16, 1932, he married Elizabeth Donner; the couple divorced in 1933. Elliott would eventually marry five times.
7. James Farley worked closely with ER and the Women's Division to help FDR win his narrow victory in 1928, his landslide in 1930, and his nomination and election to the presidency in 1932.
8. Bill Mathews was editor of the *Arizona Daily Star*.

Isabella also explained that the head of the Arizona Democratic party wished to remain neutral until the party had nominated a candidate. She did not believe, however, he was opposed to Franklin.

Franklin's best move, she suggested, would be to make friends with Arizona's lone congressman, Lewis Douglas, who had not yet endorsed a candidate for president.

Despite her optimistic assessment, Isabella encloses an editorial expressing some of the negative reactions to FDR's candidacy.

February 4, 1932

Eleanor darling:

You and Miss Dueson [Dewson] may think that we are not crystalizing our efforts out here; but I can assure you they [our efforts for Franklin] are not out of our minds a moment, and our moves have been, I think, of such diplomatic nature that I can now say we have achieved the goal through waiting and letting those who might not have *followed* us to Franklin, now be in a position to *lead* us to Franklin.

To have the group wire Mr. Farley that did yesterday, from Phoenix, asking that they might start a Roosevelt Club, is the heart of the situation.[9] I mean the group in which Mr. Joyner and Mrs. French's names were, and refer to the wire that Mr. Farley sent [*Arizona Daily Star* editor] Mr. Mathews.[10]

That group are in the so-called machine that support Governor Hunt, and are the undeniable organized force in this state. They are most active when following their own initiative, and by waiting on our club problem [waiting until they asked to form a Roosevelt club] we have achieved that. The clubs are now generally under way, I understand there is one [a club] of seven hundred [members] up in Winslow, Navajo County, and Santa Cruz County is starting [one] shortly, etc.

Mr. Addams, Democratic State Chairman, came to see me a few days ago. *IMPORTANT*: You are alright as far as he is concerned; but I do not believe he will make any active indication of this for the present, as he apparently feels that his position of Democratic State Chairman necessitates neutrality in action on the presidential issue.

9. A group of prominent Democrats had recently wired Roosevelt strategist James Farley, asking to start a Roosevelt club. Isabella believes this proves her point that she can get people to commit to FDR, if she lets them do it on their own.

10. Presumably, Isabella learned about prominent Democrats French and Joyner making contact with Farley from her friend Bill Mathews, to whom Farley sent a wire.

This [is enough] of this—I believe Mr. James Douglas, father of our only congressman, Lewis Douglas, and brother of Walter Douglas, is the only prominent man that I can hear of, against Franklin and actively for Richey. He [James Douglas] is an eratic, opinionated person, whose influence will probably take no form of leadership.

Lewis Douglas, his son, has expressed himself for no one, or against anyone that I have heard. I wrote Franklin and Mr. House [Shouse?] some time ago how much it would mean to Arizona if Lewis could meet Franklin and become his friend. I am writing at this time again [soon] to ask that Lewis go and see Franklin.

SUMMARY: I do not see how you can improve Franklin's outlook in this State further than the above mentioned contact with Lewis. The clubs are beginning to form everywhere and are inspired from within the community which is healthy and fortunate. The delegates are being, I believe, chosen wholly with Franklin in view from what I can learn.

Arizona has but once, that I know of, sent an instructed delegation [a delegation pledged to a candidate], so a move to than [that] end would be very harmful, and create immediate antagonism.—I have already had emphatic protests from people who thought I might attempt this.—Everything indicates the delegates will be 100% for Franklin. I can hear nothing to the contrary.

Realizing you want me to be only honest with you in this earnest fight, and send you all that might help, I feel that this enclosed Editorial[11] is a sample of general feeling that is creeping in. Take it for what it is worth, and let me quote, in line with this, what Mr. Jim Douglas wrote me—"He weaves and wobbles and doesn't stay put."[12]

Eleanor respected Isabella's knowledge of Arizona politics, but she was also determined that Franklin should go into the Democratic convention in Chicago with the strongest possible support. At that time, a presidential nomination required two-thirds of the delegates' votes. In spite of Isabella's insistence that it would be unwise to push for an instructed delegation, Eleanor made another (ultimately successful) attempt to persuade her, this time appealing to Isabella's unique position in Arizona politics.

11. Not included here.

12. Ward believes this is what Isabella privately thought, too, especially after the Lucy Mercer affair. Ward to editors, March 6, 2007. The second page of Isabella's letter is missing.

49 East 65th Street, NY   April 12, 1932
Isabella dear:

There is a great deal of excitement around here because they are most anxious to have the Arizona delegation an instructed delegation, and they are afraid there is no man strong enough to get it through, so they have asked me to write you and urge that you do whatever you can to bring this about.

It is wonderful to have all the men saying such wonderful things about [you] but it does result in every body laying [bearing] down on you! I shall be awfully interested to see whether you think you can get an instructed delegation or not.

I never thought you and I would be urged on on every hand in a political way but we certainly have seen many changes in our respective lives!

I can hardly wait to see you and have a good chance to talk.

      Much love,
         Eleanor

Despite the demands of the campaign, Eleanor still had the responsibility of her two younger sons, who were living at home during their vacations from boarding school. Johnny was sixteen and Franklin was not quite eighteen. Eleanor hoped that Johnny could spend the summer at Isabella's ranch. Isabella welcomed him, together with his friend Laurence Rockefeller. One day the boys went to get their mail from the Post Office in the little town of Williams. When they told the post mistress they were Johnny Roosevelt and Laurence Rockefeller, she reportedly exclaimed, "Yes, and I am the Queen of Romania."[13]

Executive Mansion, Albany, NY   [late Spring 1932]
Isabella dear:

I never seem to get around to writing so forgive this typewritten note. Franklin said he talked with you the other night and was so pleased to have a word with you. You do not know how I love to get the chance of hearing your voice.

In the meantime I am wondering if you would be willing this summer to let your head man on the ranch take Johnny on as a hand from early in

13. Ruth McCormick Tankersley to Kristie Miller, interview, 1997. Following this tradition, Isabella's son Jack would later host a high-school classmate's son. Jack had been at Andover with George Herbert Walker Bush. Bush's son, George W., worked as a cowhand on the Quarter Circle Double X Ranch for a summer in the 1960s when he was in his teens. Tom Miller to Kristie Miller, 2004.

August until early in September sometime? We would like to send him somewhere where he felt he had a regular job to do and was on a business basis, and where his treatment was exactly the same as the other cowboys.

He has had a little bit too much of Groton and his Grandmother and the things that money mean and I think standing on his own two feet is a very necessary experience for a time this summer.

Please be entirely frank with me if your man does not want to do a thing of this kind and I would be glad if you can suggest to me any other place where we might get him taken on. We would be quite willing to pay for him, only we would not want him to know. He does not want to be in the same place with Franklin, Jr., as Franklin, Jr. rather lords it over him so we are trying to do the same thing with Franklin, Jr. but somewhere else. If you have any suggestions to make as to a place for him, I would be very grateful.

I hate to bother you but think your advice would be better than any other I could get.

> A world of love dearest,
> Eleanor

Eventually, Isabella persuaded the Democratic state central committee to pledge Arizona's delegates to Franklin. At the Democratic National Convention in Chicago in June 1932, Isabella Greenway made the first seconding speech for her friend of almost thirty years, Franklin D. Roosevelt. The balloting that followed was nerve-wracking. Roosevelt had more delegates than anyone else, but not nearly enough for nomination. Texas congressman and Speaker of the House John Nance Garner was gaining on him.

After the third ballot, the convention adjourned for eleven hours. FDR's supporters raced around to find more votes. Santa Barbara newspaper editor Tom Storke, a California delegate, later wrote that a number of petitioners lobbied him in an attempt to switch California's support from Garner. Isabella Greenway was the "most insistent visitor" they had, he later recalled. "Her tearful pleas" finally convinced Storke to meet with Jim Farley, FDR's campaign manager. During the next four hours, the California delegation caucused and switched to Roosevelt.[14] Later, *Time* magazine identified Isabella as having "had a large hand in engineering" the crucial California switch that put Franklin over the top.[15]

14. Miller, *Isabella Greenway*, 176–79.
15. *Time*, August 21, 1933: 8.

Isabella worked actively on the campaign, and even spent her own money to further Franklin's interests in Arizona.

Johnny Roosevelt had returned from his summer on the ranch, and now Franklin and Eleanor planned a visit themselves, as part of their campaign through the West in September.

49 East 65th Street, New York, NY   Sept. 6 [1932]

Darling Isabella

Of course I know & understand & I hate you to have to spend so much in Arizona. You will be as glad as I will be when this campaign [ends] from the financial as well as personal point of view.

John had such a good time & I am so glad you liked him. He's so different from F. Jr. but has capabilities in his own way when certain things are either overcome or outgrown!

I am looking forward to the 25th. I get to Winslow by air about 6 p.m. & imagine I can get a train or a motor over to you.

    A world of love,

      E.R.

Franklin and Eleanor stopped off in Williams in late September for a rally at Isabella's ranch. There, FDR finally met Lewis Douglas. Eleanor and Isabella stole a few moments together amid the tumult of a celebratory rodeo.

Executive Mansion, Albany, NY   October 21 [1932]

Isabella dearest

I have wanted ever since we left you to write & tell you how much we appreciated all you did for us but time is very full these days & here we are on another trip & I'm just sitting down to write!

It fills me with pride to see you in your own surroundings & realize how people love & respect you & how wonderful you are with your own children & with all the other young things (& older ones for the matter of that) who come under your influence. It is an inspiration just to know you & what you mean to me I never could tell you dear but it was a joy to be with you & sometime let's have more than a minute together!

Franklin is very confident of success but I never am sure beforehand! Anyhow he is enjoying the campaign & thriving on it!

I spent the night with Cousin Susie [Parish] last week & she is becoming a little more philosophical about the [economic] depression & I think Cousin Henry is happier!

Will you tell Martha & Bobby for us how grateful we all are for all they did to make the day such a grand success & thank Bobby especially for me because of the delightful way in which he made me feel that midnight drives were really a pleasure!

Everyone sends their love to you & yours & all of mine you have.

> Devotedly,
> Eleanor

Please wire me the name & address of your friend who has the adopted children. I want a story from her for "Babies."[16] ER

On November 8, 1932, Franklin D. Roosevelt was elected thirty-second president of the United States, a feat that no one would have considered possible after he was stricken by polio eleven years earlier. "The struggle to walk again . . . toughened Roosevelt," wrote Garry Wills.[17] His disability made him sensitive to the impression he made on others. He won more than 57% of the popular vote.

Eleanor's correspondence with Isabella after the election gives no hint of her enormous misgivings about her new role as First Lady. With typical understatement, she admitted later that she was not "pleased at the prospect." Eleanor enjoyed earning money, and doing the things that interested her. She feared that Franklin's election would make her a prisoner in the White House.[18]

Executive Mansion, Albany, NY   Nov. 14, 1932
Isabella darling,

Many thanks for your telegram[19] to us both on the election. It was a great & glorious victory but such an endorsement means great responsibility too & redoubles work for the programme which it approves. Also many thanks for all your trouble about the school, the boy is ill again & can go nowhere sad to say & I wired the school on hearing this morning.[20]

16. ER was editing a new magazine of advice for mothers called *Babies—Just Babies*.
17. Wills, *Certain Trumpets*, 26.
18. Roosevelt, *This I Remember*, 74.
19. Missing.
20. One of the countless sad cases that ER was constantly taking up and enlisting her friends to help solve, it sounds as though the boy had TB, Isabella got him admitted to a school in Arizona, but he was now too ill to travel.

I hope to see Martha next week.

Franklin goes to Warm Springs on the 17th & I go down on the 25th to stay till the 6th. You couldn't come with Jackie? We could put you in the hotel or in Mama's cottage near ours & we could have you with us for all meals & what a lovely peaceful time we would have. There is swimming & riding & golf & tennis & lovely walks & I long to see you, can't you manage it? The Southern [Railroad] has a station near us.

> A world of love,
> Eleanor

The Roosevelts' victory had been expensive, and Isabella made a contribution.

Executive Mansion, Albany   December 1, 1932
Isabella Dearest:

Many, many thanks for the check which I have turned over to the Campaign Committee.

You were a dear, and both Franklin and I deeply appreciate it.

> Ever so much love,
> Eleanor Roosevelt

FDR wired Isabella on February 24 that he intended to name Lewis Douglas his director of the budget. Isabella promptly resigned as national committeewoman and announced her intention to run for Arizona's vacant congressional seat.[21] Franklin's appointment of Douglas, clearing the way for Isabella to campaign, may have been a way of acknowledging her help with his nomination; it may also have been a way to ensure support for his programs in the new Congress.

For Isabella and Eleanor, though, personal concerns were always mingled with the political. Soon after Franklin's inauguration on March 4, 1933, Eleanor sought Isabella's help with a family matter.

Elliott Roosevelt, now twenty-two, was looking for a job. He had been working in an advertising partnership that, during the depression, "was not earning enough to support three men and their families," he later wrote. In addition, there were strains in his marriage. He decided to try his luck in the

---

21. Arizona still had a small population, and had only one member in the U.S. House of Representatives. A congress member who represents an entire state is said to be "at-large."

West, where he had spent happy times as a teenager. Leaving his young wife, Betty, with his parents, Elliott drove to Tucson.[22]

Isabella, with her usual enthusiasm for Eleanor's children, soon found a job for Elliott. "Have decided to develop Indian Hot Springs with Aunt Isabella," he wired his mother.[23] Eleanor expressed her gratitude in a telegram of good wishes on Isabella's birthday.

Telegram   March 22, 1933

Many many happy returns of the day a heartful of thanks for all you are doing for Elliott so happy that he is going in to your development of the Springs much love Eleanor

In the middle of her congressional campaign, Isabella took time off to make arrangements for her daughter Martha's marriage on June 28 to Charles "Chuck" Breasted.[24] Although Isabella and Eleanor were extremely busy, Eleanor hoped they would be able to spend a little time together when Eleanor was in the West.

Telegram   May 29, 1933

Planning to go Fort Worth June fifth would you care to meet me there for the night or would you like me to spend a few hours in Tucson or would you like to meet me in Los Angeles know you are busy with wedding so will come wherever you are many many thanks for all you have done much love Eleanor

Eleanor also hoped the trip West would help her resolve a family crisis. She was beginning to suspect that Elliott's separation from Betty was going to be permanent.[25] The following flurry of telegrams suggests that Eleanor, who was already planning to be in the area, had decided to meet Elliott in Tucson and to hold a family conference on the matter.

22. Roosevelt and Brough, *Rendezvous with Destiny*, 38–66 passim.
23. Elliott Roosevelt to ER, March 22, 1933, FDRL.
24. Chuck was the son of Dr. James H. Breasted, whose University of Chicago team of archeologists had unearthed Tut-ankh-amen's tomb nine years earlier.
25. Roosevelt and Brough, *Rendezvous with Destiny*, 38–66 passim; Elliott Roosevelt to ER, FDR Children, Box 19/f. 2, FDRL.

Telegram   June 1, 1933

Would be grateful if you can make arrangements on my behalf to meet all family in Tucson will arrive by plane Monday afternoon June fifth five fourteen weather permitting leave for Los Angeles Tuesday afternoon five fifteen prefer to have meeting Monday evening if possible will you notify Elliott I haven't his address much love Eleanor

Telegram
Tucson, Arizona   June 1, 1933
Mrs. Franklin D. Roosevelt, The White House

Understand Elliott in process of telephoning you now from Sacramento unless I hear from you to the contrary I shall carry out your wishes regarding family meeting Tucson Monday night as you suggest will keep you in close touch possibly joining you at El Paso dearest love and gratitude that Martha and Charles may have the joy of seeing you Isabella

While Isabella was looking out for Eleanor's son in Arizona, Eleanor was planning to entertain Isabella's daughter in Washington.

Day Letter   June 2, 1933

Elliott did telephone me saying he would be willing to see me. He asked me not to see mother [probably Sara Roosevelt] till afterwards, but I insisted if I did not see her I would write just what I had said to him. Will abide by your decision as to whether it is better to have mother in Tucson or not. I have had no wires from Elliott yet. I shall go to Tucson in any case and if you let them know that I will be there then I will feel that I have done my share. Am seeing Martha and Charles this afternoon.[26]

　　　　Much love to you.
　　　　Eleanor Roosevelt

Telegram   June 3, 1933

Plane reaches Douglas four ten will be delighted to see you but do not do anything which makes life more difficult for you will certainly do anything

---

26. Isabella had intended to keep the wedding private. But when Martha and Chuck were visiting the White House, Anna came into the sun parlor where Eleanor was speaking with some women reporters. Anna asked her mother where Martha and Chuck were. The reporters asked who Chuck might be, and ER answered that he was the man engaged to Martha Ferguson.

you want on Tuesday but must leave by five fourteen plane for Los Angeles much love am thrilled to have Martha stay over weekend Eleanor

The meeting with Elliott did not lead to reconciliation with his wife. The couple divorced and, six weeks later, on July 22, 1933, he married Ruth Josephine Goggins. Elliott was the first White House offspring to seek a divorce.

As Isabella campaigned for Congress, she appealed to Eleanor for help in lobbying to preserve the veterans' benefits. Congress had given FDR extraordinary powers to slash government expenditures in an attempt to balance the budget. Some 90% of the veterans in Tucson were drawing disability pay, and these benefits were now threatened. Isabella had to walk a fine line between representing the interests of her constituents and remaining on good terms with her friend, the president.

Eleanor, however, supported Isabella's position, joining her in protesting the Economy Act.[27] While Isabella protested the Act's effect on veterans,[28] Eleanor was concerned about cuts that affected women.[29]

Telegram
Tucson, Arizona   June 14, 1933
To Mrs. Franklin Roosevelt, The White House

Eleanor dear everything seems to be pending tonight in relation to the veterans and I can only pray that the information we tried to assemble though Ryckman etc will seem convincing enough to necessitate the care of those under the presumptive clause and Spanish War veterans.[30] You know from our talk that all I have contributed is in the sincere belief that Franklins goal is justice and that he has been ill advised in this human equation love Isabella

27. Within a week of his inauguration, FDR sent to Congress, and Congress immediately passed, the Economy Act, an attempt to balance the federal budget by a 15% cut in government employees' salaries and veterans' pensions. Ortiz, "The New Deal for Veterans," 415–38.

28. Isabella was largely successful in getting the veterans' pensions restored. IG to George Senner, April 25, 1934, GC.

29. ER especially deplored the decision to lay off married women employed by the federal government. She was not able to get her husband to reverse his position on the marital status clause. Cook, *Eleanor Roosevelt*, II, 73–74.

30. Isabella feared that FDR's budget policies would cut benefits for Spanish-American War veterans covered by the "presumptive clause" that allowed "a reasonable length of time to elapse in the development of certain types of diseases—such as tuberculosis—in granting that these diseases are in fact the result of the veterans' service during the war." *Arizona Daily Star*, March 17, 1933; and *Star* clipping, undated, Box 61/ f.736, GC.

While Eleanor and Isabella collaborated on policy issues, they still counted on each other for personal favors.

Tucson, Arizona   June 14, 1933
Dear Eleanor,

Two children (one of them the son of a particular friend of mine) & the other a most popular girl in Tucson—are just starting on an educational tour East—under the auspices of the Fox-Chandler vacation trip. It is their great desire to present to you—a greeting—& I am writing this letter introducing Delia Carillo & Edgar Goyette—in the hopes that you will still be in Washington & able to give the children this great privilege. I have suggested this letter be sent in advance to Miss Thompson.[31] These children won this trip by being voted the most popular two in Tucson.

With them is another very good friend of mine Captain Russel B. Fairgrieve who has a very remarkable & successful boys school out here. They will be in Washington June 26 & 27. New Willard Hotel.

> Ever gratefully,
> Isabella

Arizona had become a solidly Democratic state, so the primary on August 7, in which Isabella faced two male opponents, was decisive. She won handily, and campaigned little before the special election on October 3. Anticipating her election, she planned to go to Washington on October 10.

Telegram
Tucson, Arizona   September 27, 1933
Mrs. Franklin D. Roosevelt, The White House

Lovely visit with Elliott who seems happy full of plans and much work. Writing details. Dear friends of mine have insisted I urge you to accept invitation Tournament of Roses January First Pasadena national hookup etc. I explained [to them the] probability [that] Christmas holidays [with] your children [would] make [it] impossible. Whatever you decide [I] suggest [you give a] painstaking answer [on] account [of the] prevailing disappointment [of the] political organization [in] southern California [caused by] your inability

---

31. Malvina Thompson (Scheider) (1893–1953), nicknamed "Tommy," ER's "trusted assistant, secretary, traveling companion, gatekeeper, and dear friend." http://www.nps.gov/archive/elro/glossary/thompson-malvina.htm.

[to] appear [during] your last visit. Dearest love. Hope [there is a] possibility [to] see you for a moment after October tenth. Isabella

Eleanor was unable to oblige Isabella in this instance. But, nonetheless, she invited Isabella to stay with her at the White House.

As expected, Isabella won the general election handily, and she and Jack left at once by train for Washington. Arizona's new representative was eager to obtain funding for public works, which, as she had earlier wired Franklin, were the "only relief for desperate unemployment."[32]

Telegram   [n.d. 1933]
Deeply grieved out of question to leave Washington during the holidays boys home until January tenth and expect winter to be too busy to prevent [permit] my going very far away unless some family reason made it imperative stop will you be in Washington after October tenth if so we count on your staying with us much much love Eleanor

In spite of her close friendship with the Roosevelts, Isabella planned to maintain her independence by staying at a hotel. Because of her challenge to FDR's Economy Act, she realized there might be other times at which they would differ politically. She also may not have wanted to be perceived as too much under the Roosevelts' influence. However, on the day after Isabella arrived in Washington, she dropped by the White House to greet Eleanor on her forty-ninth birthday.[33]

Telegram
Mrs. Roosevelt, White House   October 9, 1933
Your invitation warms our hearts dearest but we know you will understand that if Jack and I go to the Willard[34] it is because we don't want to be a nuisance will count on all chances to see you love Isabella

Elliott Roosevelt was not the only young man looking for work during the depression. A mother, Eleanor Harris Krause, had petitioned Eleanor to find employment for her son, adding that she knew many other families were

32. IG to FDR, September 26, 1933, GC.
33. *Chicago Tribune*, October 12, 1933: 21.
34. Washington's historic hotel at 14ᵗʰ Street and Pennsylvania Avenue, two blocks from the White House, founded in 1847.

facing the same difficulties. Eleanor promised to write Isabella "to see if she can help in any way to give your boy a helping hand."[35]

She enclosed Mrs. Krause's letter[36] when she wrote next to Isabella:

The White House   November 27, 1933
Dearest Isabella,

Do you remember this boy and is there anything you can do to help him? Possibly Lewis Douglass might be willing to do something.

  Affectionately,
    Eleanor

Once Isabella was living in the same town as Eleanor, there were more opportunities to meet, and thus less need to write. Eleanor often walked her dog over to the Willard Hotel; Isabella often lunched and dined at the White House. The two women corresponded chiefly to make dates with each other and to exchange items of interest.

This note suggests that Isabella spent the Christmas holiday in New York, presumably with the Cutcheons. She may have seen Eleanor in Washington before she left, and they hoped to meet again in New York.

The White House, Washington   Dec. 26 [1933]
Isabella darling

Such a merry note of color & it did add to a happy Xmas to have your card with your gifts. It was so good to see you!

I missed so much not having Anna here but all those here seemed to have a happy time.

I'm going to NY next Monday to try to see both Cousin Henry & Susie [Parish]. The latter is ill again & he wants to see me for a few minutes alone so I am going to try & fly over in time for lunch. If I manage it[,] may I drop in on you around four? Telephone St.G-6848 & the maid will tell me.

  Many thanks again dear & much love always.
    Eleanor

By the beginning of the New Year, the two women were both back in Washington. Isabella was sworn in as Arizona's sole U.S. Representative on

35. ER to Mrs. Eleanor Harris Krause, November 27, 1933, FDRL.
36. Not included here.

January 3, 1934, along with eight other new House members. Eleanor Roosevelt was in the gallery, knitting as usual. Isabella turned to smile as she was sworn in and raised her hand in salute to the president's wife, whose knitting needles finally stopped as she gazed down upon the scene.[37]

The two women, reunited in the same city at last, prepared to enjoy each other's company.

The White House   January 13, 1934
Dear Isabella:

I have been asked by the Junior League of Washington to attend their ball, which they call the "Wear Something New" ball. They remind me that you and Mary [Harriman Rumsey] organized the first Junior League performance[38] some thirty odd years ago. Don't you think it would be fun if we could dig up some pictures of that period and have something made so that we would look as nearly like we did then as possible?

Much love.

    Affectionately,

        Eleanor

After the success of Johnny's stay the previous summer, Isabella, in a letter that is missing, expressed her hope that all the Roosevelts would make the Quarter Circle Double X Ranch their summer White House. Eleanor responded gracefully, without committing herself.

The White House, Washington   February 12, 1934
Dearest Isabella,

I wish we were going to make our summer home in Arizona if it would mean seeing a lot of you!

    Affectionately,

        ER

Anna Pennybacker,[39] a prominent Texas Democrat who worked closely with ER, had written to Eleanor asking her to contact Isabella about speaking

37. Miller, *Isabella Greenway*, 202.
38. In New York.
39. Clubwoman, woman suffrage advocate, author, and lecturer (1861–1938).

at Chautauqua.[40] Pennybacker wanted an "outstanding man or woman." "[W]e must draw the people," she explained, to raise money so the institute could continue to exist.[41] Eleanor forwarded her letter to Isabella.

The White House   March 19, 1934
Dear Isabella:
    Would you consider going to Chautauqua for Mrs. Pennybacker?
        Affectionately,
            Eleanor

Understandably, legislative matters were among the highest priorities for both women. Isabella had a particular interest in aviation bills, and sent Eleanor a copy of HR 9241, asking her to get Franklin's support for it. This note was written on the bill.

[House of Representatives]   April 19, 1934
    Mr. Meades [Mead's][42] aviation bill. This could be achieved easily I believe if it was know[n] to have Administration approval. The *Senate* are looking with greater favor on this than [on] the Mr. Kellar Black bills I am told.

Isabella surprised the pundits when she took issue with some of Franklin Roosevelt's policies. In her maiden speech in the House, she continued her opposition to the administration's Economy Act. Later on in her congressional career, she would be the only House Democrat to vote against a bill authorizing the Army to carry airmail, citing her expertise as an airline owner.

On the other hand, Isabella wholeheartedly supported a measure that would fund a project of Eleanor's to build a furniture factory in Reedsville, West Virginia[43] to give employment to homesteaders. It was an issue close to both their hearts. Isabella had homesteaded and both women had founded furniture factories.

40. The Chautauqua Institution in Chautauqua, N.Y. was founded in 1874 on the belief that everyone "has a right to be all that he can be—to know all that he can know." http://www.ciweb.org/about-chautauqua/

41. Anna Pennybacker to ER, March 8, 1934, FDRL

42. New York representative James Michael Mead (1919–1938).

43. AKA "Arthurdale"—"a rural experiment in living that would be economically self-contained and agriculturally self-sufficient." Cook, *Eleanor Roosevelt*, II, 133.

Eleanor and Isabella continued to work together on other issues. Here Isabella forwards to Eleanor a letter from a Civil Works Administration [44] worker, showing how effective that program had been in alleviating hardship.

House of Representatives   April 21, 1934

Eleanor dear:

This enclosed letter [45] is, to my mind, a beautiful piece of English literature, in achieving such a vivid picture. I almost feel as though we ought to have it published, but, good heavens, don't even read it unless it happens to interest you. I do feel, though, it is an almost historical piece of publicity for the C. W. A. I am keeping it for the campaign and speeches.

    Sincerely,

        Isabella Greenway

[handwritten ps] I send this because I would not have you miss it & am trying to get it published in our effort to help the Harry Hopkins fund. [46]

Isabella also depended on Eleanor to present important ideas to the president. On the floor beside Franklin's bedside table lay a small basket into which Eleanor regularly left memos, letters, and reports that she wanted Franklin to see. [47]

House of Representatives   [April 1934]

Dearest Eleanor

Here's Mr. Lempke's [48] letter [not included here]. If Franklin can hold this ever increasing Farm Union Bloc—built around this bill—by investigating

---

44. Part of FDR's New Deal program, the Civil Works Administration was established by executive order in November, 1933 "to provide work for some four million unemployed over the winter months." It was a temporary agency to provide jobs during the winter months and ceased operation in March 1934. http://xroads.virginia.edu/~MA02/volpe/newdeal/timeline_text.html.

45. Not included here.

46. Harry Hopkins was one of the architects of the New Deal relief programs, first as administrator for the Civil Works Administration (CWA), and then for its successor, the Works Progress Administration (WPA). He had responsibility for finding employment for 3.5 million people. During the early days of World War II, his reports to FDR led to the passage of the Lend-Lease bill in 1941. http://www.library.georgetown.edu/dept/speccoll/hopbio.htm. When the CWA ended in March 1934, it was replaced by state relief organizations. *New York Times*, March 20, 1934: 2. It sounds as if Isabella planned to contribute to a fund to keep the state relief organizations going.

47. Goodwin, *No Ordinary Time*, 15.

48. North Dakota congressman William Lemke and North Dakota senator Lynn Frazier were sponsors of the Frazier-Lemke bill intended to reduce the hardship experienced by

the facts they claim as necessitating this inflationary measure it might *save* a complete break.

The *northwestern* Congressmen are being *bombarded*. I am relieved to know how you are handling this.

Devotedly

Isabella

Just as Eleanor knew Isabella would support federal aid for housing in West Virginia, Isabella knew Eleanor would approve of aid for housing in Arizona. Although both women were well off financially, circumstances were such that neither one had enjoyed homes of their own for more than a few years, here and there.

House of Representatives   April 23, 1934

Dearest Eleanor:

The last paragraph of this, Secretary Ickes' report [not included here] on Arizona's Rural Homes, will interest you.

Devotedly,

Isabella

Much of a Congress member's life is spent responding to constituent requests. Isabella, who employed a large staff at her own expense, was exceptionally good at this. Eleanor sometimes asked for help with petitions that came to her at the White House, such as the request mentioned in the following letter, which seems to have been from a job seeker in Arizona.

Isabella's letter, although addressed to Eleanor's secretary, closes with a personal note to Eleanor. It is written on House of Representatives stationery, but she may have been writing from Arizona during the August recess.

The letter also mentions Eleanor's daughter, Anna, Isabella's goddaughter. Anna had separated from Curtis Dall and was living with their two children

Depression-era farmers. The legislation proposed, among other things, to liberalize the bankruptcy law to permit continued possession of farms even after mortgage default. The specific letter referred to by Isabella focused on a related proposal by which the federal government would "refinance existing farm indebtedness" by issuing "Federal Reserve Notes." William Lemke to Isabella Greenway, April 21, 1934. This specific idea did not prevail, but the bankruptcy modifications of Lemke and Frazier were passed and signed into law by President Roosevelt. The U.S. Supreme Court held the law unconstitutional in 1935. Undaunted, Lemke and Frazier rewrote the act, which Congress passed as modified. Appealed to the Supreme Court a second time, the Frazier-Lemke Act was held constitutional. Papke, "Rhetoric and Retrenchment," 871, 883–88.

in the White House, while she waited for a divorce. She planned to marry John Boettinger, a *Chicago Tribune* reporter.

On July 30, Boettinger attacked Isabella in print, writing that Arizona had been a prime beneficiary of the New Deal, "getting back in easy money more than 36 times" what Arizonans had paid in taxes. This largess was due to the "wily, solitary woman" who represented them in Congress; Isabella had "gotten more for her state than any man in the whole Congress."[49] Isabella probably understood that to keep his job, Anna's fiancé had to go along with the conservative editorial policy of Robert R. McCormick, once referred to as "the greatest mind of the 14th century."[50]

House of Representatives   August 3, 1934
Washington, D. C.
My dear Mrs. Scheider:[51]

In connection with the request for help you sent me from Mrs. Winston, I have taken the matter up with Miss Warner,[52] Administrator of Welfare Work in Phoenix, and Miss Reid, Chairman of Women's Division of Welfare Work, Phoenix, and have written to Mrs. Winston suggesting that she keep in touch with both of them. I am not sending you copies of the letters realizing how heavy your correspondence is.

Very sincerely yours,

Isabella Greenway

[handwritten below] I was so sorry not to see you those last days in Washington when the waters veritable [veritably] closed over my head in *heat*, dentists, office, & house hunting. We had a lovely visit with Anna & she looked so *well*. My love to you.

Isabella sometimes asked Eleanor to approach Franklin with her projects, including a currency program supported by the governor of Arizona. Eleanor, in turn, felt free to approach Isabella for help with things that were troubling Franklin.

Eleanor responded to Isabella's request on White House stationery, but seems to have been writing from Warm Springs.

---

49. *Chicago Tribune*, July 30, 1934.
50. http://www.bookrags.com/biography/robert-rutherford-mccormick.
51. Malvina Thompson "Tommy" Scheider.
52. Florence Warner, secretary of the Emergency Relief Administration in Arizona.

Eleanor Roosevelt, 1902. *47962538, FDR Presidential Library.*

Eleanor Roosevelt, Franklin Roosevelt, Isabella Ferguson, Scotland, 1905. *Eleanor_fdr_isabella_1905_scotland.tif, Ferguson Family.*

Eleanor Roosevelt, Robert Ferguson, Isabella Ferguson, Scotland, 1905. *FDR Presidential Library.*

Isabella Selmes, ca. 1903. *AZinn_120905-2.tif.*

Isabella Ferguson, 1905. *AZinn_120905-2.tif, Ferguson Family.*

Eleanor, Franklin, James, and Anna Roosevelt, ca. 1908. *4796;882, FDR Presidential Library.*

Robert Harry Munro-Ferguson, sketch by Isabella Ferguson, 1908. *AZ_Inn_061208-8. jpg, Ferguson Family.*

Isabella Ferguson and Julia (Mammy) Loving at Locust Valley, 1908. *GC, MS311/f. 3029H, AHS.*

Eleanor and Franklin at Campobello, 1910. *7337(3), FDR Presidential Library.*

Eleanor Roosevelt, 1911. *7794 (206), FDR
Presidential Library.*

Self-portrait by Isabella Ferguson, 1913.
FDR Presidential Library.

Martha and Bobbie Ferguson, ca. 1916. *Ferguson Family.*

Eleanor and Franklin with their children and Franklin's mother, Sara, 1919. *47962024, FDR Presidential Library.*

John C. Greenway, ca. 1912.
GC, MS311/f. 3032V, AHS.

Eleanor and Anna Roosevelt, 1925. *8191(542), FDR Presidential Library.*

Franklin D. Roosevelt, Eleanor Roosevelt, Isabella Greenway, and Senator Thomas Walsh at the Greenway ranch near Williams, Arizona, September 28, 1932. *Port. #72119, AHS.*

Eleanor Roosevelt campaigning for Isabella
Greenway, Douglas, Arizona, June 5, 1933.
GC, MS311/f. 3057G, AHS.

Eleanor Roosevelt, 1933. *57247(42),
FDR Presidential Library.*

Congresswoman Isabella
Greenway. *GC, MS311/f.
3030I, AHS.*

Isabella and Harry King. *GC, MS311/f. 3031, AHS.*

Eleanor Roosevelt, 1951. *54260, FDR Presidential Library.*

The White House   [Nov. 15, 1934]

Dearest Isabella:

I took your letter[53] and the plan from the Governor into Franklin and he at once set it by for careful looking over and finding out if there was any way constitutionally under which a state could issue scrip.[54]

Thank you ever so much for your dear letter which caught up with me here. I am having a grand time riding and swimming and getting generally full of health.

Franklin wants to know if by any chance you really are a financial backer of an organization called America First?[55] It is doing much the same type of thing that the Liberty League is doing and apparently is causing a great deal of trouble. Some one is spreading the report that you are the financial angel. Having heard a number of such reports spread on various other occasions, I doubt if this is accurate, but I would be glad to have my doubts confirmed.

[by hand] Dearest I love you & want you in Washington soon.

    Devotedly

    Eleanor

Isabella was writing to Eleanor on the same day. The letter above and the following letter crossed in the mail.

Isabella faced another election just thirteen months after her first one. This time she could run on her record, and on Roosevelt's record. But continued unemployment in Arizona and across the country plagued her campaign. In one town she was hung in effigy, along with Secretary of the Interior Harold

---

53. Missing.

54. Scrip, a substitute for legal currency, was issued by towns (Henderson, Ky.), counties (Monmouth County, N.J.), and states (Iowa) during the monetary crisis in 1933–34. FDR's Secretary of the Treasury, William H. Woodin, briefly considered a plan for national scrip; other countries, including Germany, Colombia, and Canada, did issue scrip. *Chicago Tribune,* January 28, 1934: 25; *New York Times,* March 9, 1933: 2; October 2, 1933: 1; March 7, 1934: 32; May 6, 1934: N-2; December 23, 1934: E-7. Isabella urged that Arizona be allowed to experiment as well. Two years later, she would enlist FDR's help in trying to pass a bill authorizing the District of Columbia to issue scrip. IG to FDR, June 6, 1936, Box 33/f. 419, GC.

55. This letter is puzzling. As Ayres et al. write, "In 1940, FDR's opponents organized the America First Committee to keep the nation 'neutral' by defeating Lend-Lease," a program to supply England with war materiel. *American Passages,* 901. The date of this letter was added in brackets by the Arizona Historical Society. Isabella's answer is clearly dated 1934, so the supposed date of ER's letter must be right. Ward thinks America First "must have been an anti-New Deal splinter group, like the Liberty League she mentions." Ward to editors, March 6, 2007.

Ickes, and Arizona's new governor, B. B. Moeur. Nevertheless, Isabella won re-election easily. Eleanor apparently telegraphed her congratulations,[56] prompting an effusive reply.

Isabella more fully describes the creative new project that she hopes Eleanor will present for her to Franklin. Isabella wanted assurance that Arizona would not lose federal aid if it experimented with a scrip plan.

[Tucson]   November Fifteenth, 1934
Eleanor Dearest:

To be like yourself is to be the most extraordinary of beings and no mere mortal at all—and it was just like you to send the wire wishing me well in my foolhardy endeavor to be allied with the useful.

Again elected, I am off on that devastating course through which one occasionally emerges to see ones traditional soul, on a far horizon, clean and sweet as of old, waving an echoing hand of memory at the all engulfing confusion and poison of the "ever present."

It's a great challenge! No one knows as well (or ever will) as you. To come through, friends with oneself, is perhaps the lonely goal that is the way of wisdom.

How happy you must be about Mrs. O'Day's[57] election. You should be able to count on some substantial comfort therefrom. I look forward very much to meeting her.

At last there is one good movie of you, voting in Poughkeepsie. It gave me a great thrill.

The plan proposed by letter as Arizona's only means to help herself has every element of unsoundness except as a national program that might enable us to continue to spend as we must and pay as we go. The eternal process of begging for P. W. A.[58] with Mr. Ickes and pleading with Mr. Hopkins in

---

56. Missing.
57. Caroline Goodwin O'Day (1869?–1943), one of ER's group of social activists in New York in the 1920s. Like IG, O'Day helped in FDR's 1932 campaign, and was helped in turn by the Roosevelts when she ran for Congress in 1934. http://www.nps.gov/archive/elro/what-is-vk/q-and-a/oday-caroline.htm.
58. On June 16, 1933, the final day of the "Hundred Days Session," Congress passed the National Industrial Recovery Act establishing the Public Works Administration (PWA). http://xroads.virginia.edu/~MA02/volpe/newdeal/timeline_text.html. Several billion dollars were budgeted to be spent on construction of public works to provide employment and revive American industry. "Between July 1933 and March 1939, the PWA funded the construction of more than 34,000 projects." http://www.nps.gov/elro/glossary/pwa.htm.

behalf of the helpless, whose breaking spirit threatens the national health, is unfair to them and to us, having the identical purpose.

The states' administrations require new nerve and need encouragement and backing—drastic, even if risky, self-help measures that will eliminate relief and create work. I believe all they need is a fight talk and the certainty that federal aid will not desert them if any scheme tried fails and that their efforts are interpreted in their true light of trying to help the federal Administration.

[by hand] Good night dear—this is just one of the daily 400 letters— Don't carry it in the basket that catches up with you at 3 AM—but let it find a fireplace—& know I love you dearly.

     Isabella

The next letter answers ER's November 15 letter. At this time, Eleanor is with Franklin in Warm Springs, Georgia, for Thanksgiving.

Here Isabella continues to discuss the scrip plan she had previously proposed to Franklin. She appreciated his appearing to give the matter serious consideration.

Eleanor evidently hoped that Isabella could attend what was probably the Parishes' fiftieth wedding anniversary. Isabella also wished very much that she could go, to celebrate a last link with her mother, but she was swamped in the office. Her son Jack later observed about his mother, "Everybody who wanted somebody to go and trace out their lost veteran's pension, they spread the word how good she was and she got thirty referrals."[59]

Tucson, Arizona   November 27, 1934
Dearest Eleanor:

To know you are riding and swimming gives *me* a new lease on life.

Franklin is so fine to give his real concern to Arizona's possible plan of paying as she goes and contributing to the Federal aid.

The scheme will never be pronounced sound as a state move by bankers, etc., and probably with good reason, but as a national means of carrying a work program with current taxation it is meeting with serious encouragement.

I never heard of "America first", but have a vague memory that Mrs. Hearst started something in behalf of Franklin in October '32 called "America Incorporated" and we all contributed ten dollars. Its wonderful what we hear about ourselves, isn't it?

59. Miller, *Isabella Greenway*, 230.

If only Cousin Susie [Parish] had been married on December 19th instead of December 13, I'd be there. I long to go, but have so much to do before leaving; its almost impossible but I'll try. I just can't bear to miss it—on account of so much, especially "Mummy".

All devotion,
[AHS cc][60]

Because Isabella was an innkeeper, as well as a member of Congress, Eleanor had recommended that a friend of hers stay at the Arizona Inn. Evidently, the friend found the accommodations too expensive; other hotels were equally out of her range. Eleanor protested in a telegram:

The White House   October 18, 1934[61]
You must think my friends are all millionaires is there no place in Tucson that is fairly reasonable? Much love Eleanor

Isabella impulsively offered her own house, quite forgetting that she had already rented it out. To make amends, she offered to put Eleanor's friend up at the Inn at no cost.

Telegram   December 29, 1934
Terribly sorry that since inviting Mrs. Huntington to stop with me in Tucson in October I closed the house and have since rented it will she honor us by being my guest at the Arizona Inn stop am sending her a telegram your care today Mr Howard manager will be so delighted meet and care for her every possible way dearest love Isabella Greenway

After her re-election in November 1934 to a second term, Isabella continued to collaborate with Eleanor on legislative issues vital to them both.

3147 P Street N.W., Washington, D. C.   March 25, [1935]
Dearest-
When you can I'd be grateful to talk over some things important to us both—It's *not a rush* matter & yet not one we can afford to neglect.

Devotedly, Isabella

60. AHS, carbon copy.
61. This letter has been presented out of sequence in order to combine it with the letter that follows, for better understanding.

After a grueling session, Isabella got away in August of 1935 for her first real vacation in over three years. She was proud of her accomplishments, among them her success in obtaining federal funding to pave "every foot of Route 66 across the State" of Arizona. Her efforts also contributed to the creation of sixty Civilian Conservation Corps (CCC) camps in Arizona. Congress would not reconvene until January 1936.[62]

Telegram   Nov. 15, 1935

Elizabeth Lindsey[63] and I decided at lunch today we must know something of your plans and whereabouts how are you and when do you come back and have you the same house please wire stop our dearest love Eleanor Roosevelt

Isabella Greenway was back in Washington by February 19, 1936. On that day, she and Eleanor met with Russian women who headed factories that made soap, cosmetics, and perfume. Eleanor reported in her syndicated newspaper column, "My Day," that Isabella got a laugh at the First Lady's expense when she begged the Russian women not to believe that she and Eleanor represented American women's use of cosmetics: "I feel quite sure that if Mrs. Roosevelt began to do one eyebrow she would go out forgetting to do the other!"[64]

On March 22, 1936, her fiftieth birthday, Isabella Greenway announced her decision to retire from Congress. She had tried hard to respond to a deluge of constituent requests. As her son Jack later remarked, she was completely exhausted. Isabella also wanted to spend more time with her Uncle

---

62. Miller, *Isabella Greenway*, 226.
63. Elizabeth Sherman Hoyt Lindsay gained distinction as "A landscape architect in New York, an official of the American Red Cross in France during the First World War, and later, as wife of the British Ambassador, Sir Ronald Lindsay, to Constantinople, Rome and Washington." James, ed., *Letters of Elizabeth Sherman Lindsay*. "ER appreciated Lady Lindsay's 'keen,' occasionally 'wicked' sense of humor." Cook, *Eleanor Roosevelt*, II, 73. Isabella called her "Lillybub," and took a house behind the British Embassy during her second session in Congress in order to be near her.
64. "My Day," February 20, 1936. Eleanor Roosevelt's syndicated newspaper column was published six days a week, from 1935 to 1962. The only interruption was when her husband died, and even then she missed only four days. The column allowed Eleanor to reach millions of Americans with her views on social and political issues, current and historical events, and her private and public life. http://www.pbs.org/wgbh/amex/eleanor/sfeature/myday.html. By 1938, "My Day" ran in sixty-two newspapers with a total readership of more than 4 million. Alf Pratte, "'My Day,'" *ER Encyclopedia*, 354–5. The "My Day" columns are archived at http://www.gwu.edu/~erpapers/

Frank Cutcheon, who had been like a father to her and was now in ill health. Meanwhile, she would serve out her term until January 1, 1937.

Although Isabella would no longer be a part of the political scene, Eleanor cherished their continued closeness.

The White House   April 11 [1936]
Dearest Isabella,

Just a line to thank you for your wire[65] & tell you all is going well in Seattle.[66] I am going back on Saturday & will be home on the 25th.

I hope all goes well with Martha & the baby.[67] Write me & tell me all about them.

I often think what fun we all had at lunch with you that day. You are a wonderful person Isabella & you give so much happiness to so many people.

A world of love dear & best wishes to Martha.

Devotedly, Eleanor

Although Isabella worked hard for the rest of her term, she was thinking wistfully about returning to Arizona. As she wrote to her Aunt Mary Selmes, Isabella could hardly wait to be "home with a right to stay there."[68] Eleanor, however, had no intention of letting Isabella stay idle.

[The White House]   June 27, 1936
Dearest Isabella,

This is just a note to tell you that a girl who went to our school,[69] Jane Holmes, has been ill and is now living at Sonoita [Arizona]. I thought if you were in that vicinity and had a moment that you might call on her.

Affectionately, Eleanor

[FDRL cc][70]

65. Missing.
66. ER's daughter Anna began working as a writer after her divorce from Curtis Dall, a career she continued after her second marriage to journalist John Boettiger in 1936. Anna and John worked on the *Seattle Post-Intelligencer* until 1943, when Boettiger went into the military and Anna returned to the White House as her father's confidential assistant.
67. David Breasted (b. 1935).
68. IG to Mary Selmes, May 30, 1936, GC.
69. Probably the Todhunter School, a small private girls school in New York City, which ER and two friends bought in 1927. Eleanor resigned as assistant principal in 1933, when she became First Lady, but continued a close association with the school for several more years. *ER Encyclopedia*, 515–17.
70. Franklin D. Roosevelt Presidential Library, carbon copy.

Retirement gave Isabella a chance to get to know her two grandchildren, one each from Bob[71] and Martha. She took an apartment in New York, on 840 Park Avenue, three blocks from Martha's family and two blocks from Bob's. Eleanor herself had a hideaway, a third-floor walk-up in Greenwich Village.[72] The two friends met each other at times in New York, even while Isabella was still in Congress and maintained her Washington D.C. residence. Sometimes they had to resort to a go-between, as in this telegram from Eleanor's secretary conveying a message to the first lady from Isabella.

Telegram
2222 Wyoming Avenue, Washington DC   October 6, 1936
From Mollie Somerville[73]

Mrs. Greenway in DC received Mrs. Roosevelt's invitation to dine NY tonight [just] as she boarded [her] train. She is staying over [in New York] tomorrow [so] if [it is] agreeable [to] Mrs. Roosevelt [Mrs. Greenway will] see her then

FDRL cc

Isabella Greenway officially left Congress in January 1937. Despite wanting to spend more time with her family, Isabella could not completely abandon the interests that had motivated her for so long. In early February, she visited Washington, "in an unofficial capacity," to lobby for the renewal of the tariff on copper. Her friends in Congress gave her a gratifyingly warm welcome, and she stayed at the White House for several days, contradicting gossip that her retirement was due to a breach with the Roosevelts.[74] Isabella wrote to a friend that staying with Eleanor "with no politics in the picture was an unspeakable joy and relief."[75]

But she still counted on Eleanor, as Eleanor counted on her. Over the following nine months, Isabella urged Eleanor, among others, to help Belle Eckles, Isabella's old friend from New Mexico, whom Eleanor also knew. However, finding work for a middle-aged woman during the depression would not be easy.

71. IG's son Bob Ferguson married Frances, the daughter of Judge Learned Hand, in November 1933. Their daughter Frances ("Patty") Ferguson was born in 1935.
72. Eleanor rented the apartment from her close friends Esther Lape and Elizabeth Read.
73. Mollie Somerville was an aide and friend of ER. See Somerville, *Eleanor Roosevelt As I Knew Her*.
74. *Arizona Daily Star*, February 14, 1937.
75. IG to Mayela McKinney, February 18, 1937, Box 3/f. 33, GC.

Telegram   March 1, 1937

Bell Eckles at Willard Hotel leaves for New Mexico tonight. Realizing she will not let you know I am doing so in case you want to see her. She does not know I have telegraphed you. Congressman Jack Dempsey will be in touch with her. Much love Isabella

Eleanor had been too busy to see her, as Eleanor informed Isabella in a telegram asking for the return of a loaned book.

Telegram   March 3, 1937

Can you mail me special delivery today copy of autobiography I gave you to read? Sorry couldn't see Belle Eckles as time was jammed full. Much love Eleanor Roosevelt

FDRL cc

Isabella later received a letter from Eleanor's secretary asking Isabella to suggest what else Eleanor might do for their old friend, adding that Miss Eckles was too old for the Foreign Service exam.[76] Isabella would continue to ask Eleanor for help in finding employment for Eckles.

Although Isabella did not hesitate to ask Eleanor for help in personal matters, she evidently steered clear of policy issues. In the following letter, Eleanor, referring to a missing letter of Isabella's, assures Isabella that divisive issues would never intrude on their friendship.

During her time in Congress, Isabella had participated in Eleanor's biweekly "air our minds" luncheons, which also included Secretary of Labor Frances Perkins; Elizabeth Lindsay, the wife of the British Ambassador to the U.S.; and, before her untimely death, Mary Harriman Rumsey, chairman of the Consumers' Advisory Board.[77] Even after Isabella left Washington, Eleanor tried to pull her back to join them.

76. FDRL, carbon copy.
77. The Consumers' Advisory Board of the National Recovery Administration (NRA) brought together economists and clubwomen to represent consumers' interests when the NRA fair practices codes were being written. Cook, *Eleanor Roosevelt*, II, 73. Rumsey died on December 18, 1934, from injuries after a fall while fox hunting. "Mary Harriman Rumsey," *ER Encyclopedia*, 470.

The White House   April 12 [1937]

Isabella dearest

Your letter[78] was so like you, of course dear nothing will ever interfere with our real feelings for we understand motives & even if we don't agree on questions we always trust each other's motives.

Could we have an "air your mind" lunch on Good Friday or should it be after the British Embassy [function] on Elizabeth's account?

      Much, much love

         ER

Is Martha still here?

Isabella accepted an invitation from the Roosevelts to a party on May 28, and Eleanor asked Isabella to stay with them. Eleanor often invited people to stay with her, whose feelings were subsequently hurt when they realized that the busy First Lady had little time to spare for socializing.

[The White House]   May 18, 1937

Dearest Isabella:

I see that you are coming to the newspaper dance[79] so won't you come that afternoon and spend the weekend? It will give me a chance to see you again and I will be a little more free than I was the last time.

      Much love,

         Eleanor

FDRL cc

Isabella was keeping busy herself. All through her first year after leaving Congress, she traveled back and forth between New York, Washington, and Boston. Frank Cutcheon was ill, and she spent time with him in New York, as well as with her grandchildren. Every other week she visited Jack, who was now twelve, and had started at the Fay School in Southborough, Massachusetts, just outside of Boston. The boys' school provided a transition between home and larger boarding schools.[80] Isabella did not go West except

---

78. Missing.

79. A dinner given by Eleanor and Franklin for the Washington press corps. The Roosevelts rehearsed the newsmen and their wives in the Virginia Reel the night before ER wrote this letter. *New York Times*, May 18, 1937.

80. IG to Bess Casey, February 19, 1937, Box 3/f. 34, GC.

when Jack was on vacation, as she had a "terror of putting four days' train travel" between herself and her son in the event of an emergency."[81]

Isabella was prepared to go to considerable lengths to snatch whatever time her busy friend could spare.

840 Park Avenue, New York   May 21, 1937
Dearest Eleanor,

Yours is such a blessed & generous invitation. I hardly know how to tell you how lovely I think it is—& that all sorts of factors make it necessary that I return Friday midnight for prize day in Southborough & the western start—with Jack.

Would there be a chance of seeing you anytime Friday—before the dance?

I really had accepted the dance with little idea of being there but now I know there is a chance of seeing you I'll go right down. Thursday *or* Friday—if you haven't more than five minutes to spare—& if you haven't that I'll understand perfectly.

     Lovingly,
          Isabella
FDRL

Eleanor, like Isabella, was willing to carve time out of her hectic schedule to make time to visit.

Telegram   May 24, 1937

Please come Thursday. Let me know time of arrival so car can meet you. Love Eleanor

Sometimes, though, they just could not manage to get together.

The White House   Nov. 10, 1937
Isabella dear:

We missed you very much but we did not have an "air your mind" luncheon as Elizabeth Lindsey and I were the only ones who could be there.

When do you get back? I am most anxious to see you. Perhaps we could get together in New York if you can not come to Washington soon for the night

81. IG to Mayela McKinney, February 18, 1937, Box 3/f. 33, GC.

and luncheon. I will not be in Washington for any length of time until the sixth of December, but I will be in New York before that.

> Much love to you,
> Eleanor

Meanwhile, Isabella continued to explore employment opportunities for her old friend Belle Eckles.

Telegram   December 6, 1937

Have just learned of opening in WPA[82] for state director woman's work in New Mexico. Could anyone serve the public better than Belle Eckles and I know how truly she needs the opportunity after several idle years due to political juggling and treachery. It's good to live in the world with you and one of these days I'm going to see you. Love Isabella

Eleanor offered to try, but she reminded Isabella of the limits of a First Lady's influence.

[The White House]   December 8, 1937

Dearest Isabella:

I had already written Mrs. Woodward[83] and Mr. Hopkins in behalf of Nancy Lane. I will write Mrs. Woodward about Belle Eckles, saying if they don't give it to Nancy Lane, that Belle is really better fitted. However, Nancy Lane has congressional and senatorial endorsements.

I do hope you are coming Saturday. If not, do let me see you very soon.

> Much love,
> Eleanor

FDRL cc

Now that she could no longer see Eleanor as often as she liked, Isabella became quite sentimental about her friend, especially when ER published her memoir, *This is My Story*, in 1937. Isabella appreciated more than most how fine a line Eleanor had walked between discretion and candor.

---

82. The Works Progress Administration was a federal agency created in 1935 to provide jobs. "At its height in 1936, the WPA employed 25% of the nation's entire workforce." Ayres et al., *American Passages*, 876.

83. Ellen Sullivan Woodward was "administrator of New Deal women's relief programs." Martha Swain, "Ellen Sullivan Woodward," *ER Encyclopedia*, 582.

Tucson, Arizona   December 19, 1937

Eleanor *my* dearest—& for the moment *no* one else's. There's almost every topic to write you about—& I am allowing myself the delight of forgetting the other 399 daily letters that will accompany this into your privacy. I need to feel I have you all to myself & the desire is *so* great I have no difficulty in creating the illusion—that it is possible.

First this book of Your Story—as you call it—you have in your own way (great in its kind honesty) found such a perfect middle path for *narrative* that I am amazed at each page and incident. You tip toe, you run, you march & you stride between fundamental causes & interesting happenings. Your good taste & sense of fairness prevail beyond an inference.

The measure of experience is, inevitably, built upon some bitterness—but your example (for thoughtful between the line readers) of translating bitterness to triumph thro interpretation—will help many a person.

Your wisdom is unconfused, & clean—& seems to come from a heart alert, like a child's, with gratitude. To have recaptured that quality (or sustained it thro 50 years) is one of the few unconscious tributes to your self that appease those of us who would like to shout across the frontiers.[84]

AHS cc

During her time in Congress, Isabella had worked closely with Harry O. King. As deputy administrator for the National Recovery Administration,[85] King was responsible for drawing up the copper code production guidelines that would enable the copper mines to re-open and give employment to Arizonans. His marriage had ended in divorce, and he hoped to marry Isabella, a fact she denied publicly. Eleanor must have known the truth, when she asked about his children.

The White House   Dec. 30 [1937]
Isabella dearest

You couldn't have sent me anything I would find more useful than this set of trays for my mail. A world of thanks for your letter too. I think of you so often & sometime I hope to see you. Are you coming down here soon?

84. Isabella says here that the wisdom in the book is an unconscious tribute Eleanor has paid to herself, and that it pleases those like Isabella who would like to shout out Eleanor's praises. The rest of this letter is missing.
85. "[T]he NRA encouraged representatives of business and labor to create codes of 'fair practice' designed to stabilize the economy through planning and cooperation." Ayres et al., *American Passages*, 871.

We had a scare about Franklin Jr. & Ethel [Roosevelt]but they were lucky children & came through with very slight injuries.[86]

How is Jackie & how are Martha & Chuck & the babies & Bob and his family to say nothing of the young Kings? We must meet soon so I can catch up.

A world of love to you dear always,
>   Devotedly,
>   Eleanor

Isabella was still keenly interested in Eleanor's children, too.

Telegram   January 6, 1938

Overjoyed Anna and John [Boettinger, Anna's second husband] can come Tucson. Of course can take care of them in either rooms or cottage. Remaining here myself and cannot tell you how lovely it will be to see them. Will the children be along? Love Isabella

Isabella's and Eleanor's lives diverged more and more after Isabella left Congress. Eleanor's activities as First Lady increased after Franklin was elected to a second term, especially her civil rights activism.[87]

Isabella, herself, was often on the road between New York, Tucson, and her ranch outside Williams, Arizona, to such an extent that her manager wrote, "Your wire was welcome news . . . for the deduction it gave us that you were still here among us mortals on earth." Isabella missed the sense of purpose being in Congress had given her, but she was glad to be able to ask friends to drop in on her in New York, to go out to dinner and take in a play.[88]

Eleanor, though extremely busy, still made an effort to stay in touch.

The White House   Feb. 24, 1938
Dearest Isabella:

I am so anxious to see you. I wonder if we could meet somewhere at 11:15 and roam around together and then lunch with Mama, on Tuesday, March 1?

86. One of FDR Jr.'s five wives was Ethel du Pont [Roosevelt]. It sounds as though they had been in a car accident.
87. Black, "Eleanor Roosevelt," 441.
88. Miller, *Isabella Greenway*, 238–89.

I will be here until Sunday night and after that at 20 East 11th Street. Tel [illegible]

        Affectionately

           Eleanor

Isabella took on a few small political projects, and she counted on Eleanor for support. The American Arbitration Association, founded in 1926, came to play an important role in commerce, not only in the United States but also overseas.

New York NY   April 22[,] 1938

Telegram

In case letter sent by messenger misses you[89] I am wiring to ask if you could lunch on May 24 at the Waldorf and present the medal awarded by the American Arbitration Association to Juan Trippe[90] in connection with international good will[.] The association asked me to extend this invitation and hope that you may come and to tell you how truly they would appreciate it. Love Isabella

[Accompanied by letter to Isabella Greenway from Frances Kellor[91] with a design for the medal, April 21, 1938]

As had been their habit for many, many years, Isabella and Eleanor continued to help each other give relief to unfortunate individuals.

840 Park Avenue, New York   May 18, 1938

Dearest Eleanor:-

In the excitement of yesterday's exciting luncheon I forgot to talk to you about Miss [Mary] Blanchard's hospital bill, about which you wrote me.[92] It is a bill owing to the hospital in Tucson, which is in the process of complete re-financing. It is a non-profit institution, but at this moment it is being completely reorganized and I, who hold merely the titular position of President, have no idea how this particular bill could be handled.

---

89. Missing.
90. Juan Trippe was president of Pan American Airways. In the *New York Times* articles reporting the event, there is no mention of ER among those paying tribute to Trippe.
91. Frances Kellor (1873–1952) was a pioneering sociologist and an eminent authority on arbitration, who earned a law degree from Cornell Law School in 1897. This letter is not included here.
92. Missing.

I wrote to the Executive Committee and explained the tragic circumstances surrounding Miss Blanchard's death and her gallant fight to meet all her obligations, with the hope that it would be possible to wipe this sum off any unpaid record of Miss Blanchard's. I have not had time to hear yet what can be done but will let you know just as soon as I do.

> Ever devotedly,
> Isabella

At least in this instance, Isabella was able to oblige Eleanor. The following letter enclosed a letter from Robert C. Baker,[93] from the Tucson branch of the Works Progress Administration, who wrote that he had contacted the hospital superintendent, who agreed to clear Miss Blanchard's record.[94] It would be hard to imagine a clearer example of the power of political connections: the First Lady contacts a former Congress member; the former Congress member contacts a well-placed federal official; the federal official contacts the person who can solve the problem; the problem is solved.

840 Park Avenue, New York   May 28, 1938
Eleanor dearest-

This explains the clearing—of the record of indebtedness of poor little Miss Blanchard. If only more of us could have records of courage—like hers.

A heart full of love to Anna when you see her—& may the summer find its harvest for you—dearest.

> Isabella

Eleanor spent the summer of 1938 mainly at Hyde Park, enjoying what, for her, was a relaxing vacation. Her youngest son, John, was married in June to Anne Lindsay Clark. Anna and her family came for a visit. Eleanor did some writing: in addition to her regular "My Day" column, she prepared two years of earlier columns for publication, and wrote several articles.

With European democracies crumbling, Eleanor had turned hopefully to a growing youth movement at home, and she agreed to address the second World Youth Congress at nearby Vassar College.[95]

93. Not included here.
94. Robert C. Baker to IG, May 20, 1938, FDRL.
95. Cook, *Eleanor Roosevelt*, II, 509–11, 516.

June 7, 1938

Dearest Isabella,

Thank you so much for taking care of the hospital charges for Mary Blanchard.

Anna and John and the children arrive on the 10th and I am overjoyed at the prospect of seeing them. They stay until the 20th. It seems a very short time but I am grateful for as much time as I can have with them.

I plan to stay at Hyde Park all summer and hope for some peace and quiet.

Devotedly,

[Eleanor]

cc. FDRL

Isabella spent the summer on her Arizona ranch. When she returned to New York in the fall, she began remodeling a brownstone house at 132 E. 92nd Street, as she tried to make up her mind whether to marry Harry King.[96] Back on the East coast, she tried to reach Eleanor by phone. Eleanor was chagrined to have missed her, and proposed a meeting in New York.

[The White House]   Oct. 13, 1938

Dear Isabella:

I wish they had let me know when you called up last night. I would have loved to hear your voice. Elizabeth [Lady Lindsay] had been in to tea and we talked about you and she told me of seeing you.

I am so anxious to see you and so annoyed to have missed your call. Will you be in New York City for some time now? If so, I will try to make a date next time I go up, in November.

Much love, dear.

Affectionately,

[Eleanor]

cc. FDRL

Eleanor did a great deal during the depression to ensure that women journalists were able to keep their jobs. The Gridiron Club, "an organization of elite journalists," held annual all-male banquets that featured skits satirizing current political topics. The president traditionally attended these dinners. Eleanor responded by instituting the popular "Gridiron Widows" parties held

96. Miller, *Isabella Greenway*, 239.

"in the White House for women journalists and officials, including Secretary of Labor Frances Perkins, who were excluded from the Gridiron dinners."[97]

[The White House]   November 16, 1938
Isabella dear:

I know a formal invitation is going to you for the annual Gridiron Widows' Party on December 17. I do hope you can come down.

Of course you are to spend the night with us and it will be a great joy to have you.

>   Much love always,
>   Eleanor
> FDRL cc

In 1938, Jack enrolled at the Phillips Academy in Andover, Massachusetts. Isabella had even fewer demands on her time. She had undertaken some small jobs, such as remodeling the Inn and serving on committees. But she obviously waited for her much busier friend to suggest meetings when she could spare the time.

Warm Springs, Georgia   Nov. 24 [1938]
Dearest Isabella,

I do look forward to your coming & hope we'll have a chance for a talk as well as a good party.

Sometime gather any old friends you think would like to see me together & I'll come on for a reunion. I think it would be interesting if all of us could say to what life had taught them were the real truths!

I hope you are having a happy Thanksgiving & my love to all your family with devotion & admiration to you always, dearest of friends.

>   ER

Eleanor wrote the following letter to Isabella the day before Isabella was married for the third time, to Harry O. King, at the brownstone on East 92nd Street in New York City.[98] She did not remove John Greenway's ring, but wore Harry's next to it. Meanwhile, Eleanor was preoccupied with the lives and losses of her children, including Hall, for whom she always felt a maternal responsibility.

---

97. Bonnie Brennan, "Frances Perkins," *ER Encyclopedia*, 579.
98. Even before they were married, Harry and Isabella remodeled two brownstones on E. 92nd
    Street, between Park and Lexington, gutting the insides and re-facing the outsides. They

20 East 11th Street, New York City   April 21 [1939]

Isabella dearest,

Your wire[99] just reached me & many, many thanks. I always count on your thoughts.

I left Seattle Wed. night & got in last night in time to meet Hall at the airport this morning. We go to Boston tonight & the Ramsy boy's funeral on Sunday. It was a bad shock to Hall & I dread seeing Margaret to-morrow but Danny was a born adventurer. It is sad to lose a young life & all its promises.

Anna & John & the new baby are all settled at home & well & happy. How are Martha & her youngest?[100]

    Much, much love to you dear,

      E.R.

That summer, Isabella was frequently in the West, checking up on the Inn, her drought-stricken ranch, and her aging aunt, Sally Cutcheon, who lived in Santa Barbara.

In this letter Eleanor implores Isabella to help find work for a young man whose case reached the First Lady through the office of his congressman. The country was still in the grip of the depression.

Hyde Park   July 12, 1939

Dearest Isabella:

I am sending you this letter, in fact the whole file, with my answer to Congressman Keller.[101] I have no idea whether you would know of any work at present which could be obtained for this boy with his experience and pluck, but if you do know of a job he might go down by himself and then if he makes good he could send for his father and mother.

Much love, dear, and I hope you are having a nice summer. I have no idea where you are but imagine you must now be at the ranch.

    Affectionately,

      Eleanor

FDRL cc

---

would live there after they were married. Kristie Miller interview with Saranne Neuman, March 10, 1998.

99. Missing.

100. Charles and Martha Breasted would have four children: David (1935), Macomb "Mac" (1939), Isabella (1941), and Sarah Grace (1946).

101. Kent E. Keller, Democrat, U.S. Representative from Illinois, 1931–1941. http://bioguide.congress.gov/scripts/biodisplay.pl?index=k000056

Part Six
World War II and After —
Eleanor and Isabella on the National Scene

*O*n September 1, 1939, Germany invaded Poland, launching Europe into World War II. At the time of the following letter, the seriousness of the war might not have been apparent to Isabella, although later it certainly would be. In the letter Isabella may be referring to an anniversary dinner to be hosted by *The Nation* on May 1 at the Hotel Astor in New York City. The magazine was planning to give its 1940 award to Eleanor Roosevelt.[1]

132 E. 92nd Street New York, NY   March 2, 1940
Eleanor darling—

What an honor to be asked as one of *your allowed* guests. I'm just overwhelmed—& so distressed that plans to go West (on a business & [Jack's] school holiday trip) mean I can't accept—You can't imagine what a thrill I get—when I think—of all you have builded & are building—& the fact I was to be included on your professional invitation!!! Dear I am so truly sorry—& your loveliness in asking me—means ever so much—I understood so much when you said "Gentlemen is it not a little hard to advise young people to a policy of expediency rather than one of ideals"[2]

> All devotedly
> Isabella

Eleanor routinely worked until midnight, exhausting her long-suffering secretaries. But even with all she had to do, she remembered Isabella's birthday.

Telegram   March 22, 1940

A world of love and many happy returns of the day Isabella dear from your devoted Eleanor

    cc. FDRL

1. *New York Times*, May 1, 1940.
2. ER thinks young people should be advised to be idealistic.

The spring of 1940 was very difficult for Eleanor. The United States was gearing up to deal with the war in Europe. Even though the increased spending would finally bring an end to the depression, Eleanor feared that the social reforms she had worked for over the last seven years would be swept away, and her own usefulness would be at an end.[3] Perhaps Isabella realized how her friend might be feeling. She responded to Eleanor's birthday telegram with this reassuringly appreciative letter.

132 E. 92nd Street New York,   NY April 20, 1940
Eleanor darling

Across the wide world came your birthday message—What a part you have played in those personal milestones & all the "Days of My Years"[4]— between—& so many others—You have blessed this world beyond the limit of measure—& I only hope your consciousness pauses long enough to reap the harvest of realizing your own fulfillment.

Thank you for the telegram—which made me so happy.

Imagine my joy (after all these years of talking) to have a chance to be *working*— on the Employment problem with a *nonpolitical* organization[5]—the chances are it will come to naught—but it's very satisfying meantime.

We had such fun with Martha Chuck & the boys—on the Easter holiday.

All devotedly with a hug & a kiss.

& everything cozy & heartwarming that could defy this grim world.

                              Isabella

Eleanor responded by return of post, something she often did. This may be why Isabella seldom wrote—she knew Eleanor would feel obliged to reply.

[The White House]   April 23, 1940
Isabella dear:

I was perfectly delighted to get your letter and so glad you are working on the unemployment situation. It was dear of you to write, and I do hope this

---

3. Goodwin, *No Ordinary Time*, 81.
4. Isabella is referring to the well-known verse 10 in Psalm 90 which begins: "The days of our years are threescore years and ten. . . ," meaning the whole of a human life.
5. It is unclear to what organization Isabella refers.

spring, when I am in New York, I may have a chance to see you. In all the visits I have made this past winter, I haven't had a single free minute.

> Affectionately,
>> [Eleanor]

cc. FDRL

Likewise, on a visit to Washington later that spring, Isabella refrained from calling her friend. It was a particularly hectic time. The Nazi invasion of Belgium and Holland had taken place in May. Then, on June 10, Italy entered the war on the side of Germany. The Germans were poised to enter Paris. Isabella must have felt that this was an inopportune moment to ask for a meeting. She had, however, seen Franklin, Jr.

The Carlton, Washington, DC   [June 1940]
Eleanor darling

I love you too much to call you—on my unplanned visits here—It makes me unhappy not to pay my respects—but when I picture the reality of your hours & your efforts to make it possible (against all odds) to give me the selfish pleasure of seeing you —I just can't do it. This is to tell you I love you 1000 ways—send you a hug & a kiss & I know you understand it is to save you.

> Lovingly—dearest
>> Isabella

I never saw Franklin Jr. looking so wonderfully well & handsome.
Just starting to NY & shortly West. Don't bother to answer.

Eleanor reassured Isabella that she would have made time for a visit. Their friendship of almost forty years was still very precious to her.

[The White House]   June 13, 1940
Dearest Isabella:

I am so distressed not to have known you were here. Please do let me know. I so love to see you and it has been such a long time.

> Much love always.
>> [Eleanor]

cc. FDRL

The Democrats, reluctant to abandon a proven leader when Europe was at war, nominated Franklin D. Roosevelt for an unprecedented third term. The Republicans nominated Wendell Willkie, a Wall Street lawyer and utilities executive with no prior experience in government. Isabella believed that Willkie might yet succeed, where Franklin had not, in alleviating unemployment. These events prompted the hardest letter Isabella ever wrote to Eleanor: explaining why she would be supporting Wendell Willkie, and not Franklin, for president.

Quarter Circle Double X Ranch   August 19, 1940
Williams, AZ
Eleanor dearest

Here comes another chapter & one I don't like the experience of—I haven't a doubt that some of the publicity (for which I am in no way responsible to date) has reached you about my support of Willkie—& that you have wondered why you have not heard from me—

For too many reasons to inflict on you—I made my mind up before the Democratic convention that I couldn't endorse a third term. I didn't really believe, right up to the last moment that it would come about.

In addition to that you know my overwhelming conviction that more and different programs could & should be followed thro about employment.

After meeting a stone wall of rebuff in many & constant efforts in various departments of Government, including that in which you & Franklin gave me such real help—at the Department of Commerce last year—I became entirely disheartened.

I went to see Mr. Willkie in Colorado Springs[6] & have his statement of his program in behalf of re-employment. It has elements that to date have not been tried in which I believe there is hope.

You & I (I think) have much the same realistic sense of the pitfalls & precariousness of the human equation in all things including Government—but I know we keep on trying and hoping.

How I love & admire you—you know—There was enough to read between the lines of your convention speech to convince me that you were not instrumental in initiating the third term policy—& your statement (a while ago) that to date "we have bought the time to think"—is I believe one of the great truths of this period. It is in the hope that further constructive efforts can be

6. After he won the Republican nomination, Willkie met in Colorado Springs with leading Republican strategists and potential Democratic backers.

forced thro that I am going to join those Democrats working for Willkie who feel as I do.

You would I know do what I am doing if you felt as I do.

I feel very confident that my participation will be kept to impersonal issues & that our lifelong family relations will be safeguarded to the best of my ability. I am prepared however for the fact that in a political campaign others will not respect or help in keeping the whole on the plane it belongs.

A heart full of love always—& an understanding that surpasses all words—& will survive in spite of everything.

> Devotedly,
> Isabella

Eleanor responded promptly, clearly believing that her friend was mistaken, but trying to be large-minded. However, Eleanor's use of the inflammatory word "fascist" to refer to Willkie revealed how upset she was by Isabella's desertion. Eleanor confided to her close friend Lorena Hickok, "I'm a bit weary of having her reasoning always so pure but I know she thinks she is doing the right thing."[7]

[The White House]   August 22, 1940

Isabella dear:

I had not seen any publicity, and as far as I know, the New York papers have not carried anything about your visit to Mr. Willkie, nor your support of him, as yet.

I am, of course, sorry to have you openly on the other side, but I realize that you have to do whatever you think is right.

It is a little difficult, however, for me to understand, with your knowledge of Congress, why you think that Mr. Willkie can accomplish the things which he promises. Also, it is hard for me to believe that knowing his record as you must have read his testimony as a utility head, how you can feel safe in his future attitude toward labor and social reform.

As to the third term, I never have felt very strongly about that and I think that Franklin felt more strongly about the traditional part of it than I did. I do not think he made up his mind as to what he thought he ought to do until he really found that he was being nominated. I think he always had a feeling that if the situation in the world was really serious, he ought to do whatever the convention decided.

---

7. Lash, *Eleanor and Franklin*, 478.

I feel they nominated him purely because he probably knows more about world conditions than anyone else, and might therefore be more useful to the country. I never asked him what his decision was going to be up to the time of the convention, because I felt that it was such a serious one, that only the person involved should make it, and he should make it with no urging one way or the other from anybody else. After all the rest of us carry no responsibility.

You may well know that I would not look forward to four years more in the White House with joy but at the present moment, what any one likes or dislikes does not seem very important.

I should view Mr. Willkie's election with apprehension for the things I care about, but of course, I should consider if he were elected, that all of us had to hope that he would prove to be a successful President and that we would give him the support which any President must have in the next few years. I am afraid I would watch with considerable apprehension for fascist tendencies in him and in the group which nominated him.

I felt I had to say this to you so you would understand what my feeling is, but of course, as far as I am concerned political differences never make any difference in one's own personal feelings.

Every good wish to you and yours.

    Devotedly,

        [Eleanor]

cc. FDRL

Franklin Roosevelt won re-election easily. Eleanor, true to her word, did not let the incident mar her friendship with Isabella, sending Christmas presents as usual. Isabella, taking her cue from Eleanor, thanked her friend effusively. She also warned Eleanor that Julia "Mammy" Loving, might presume on her old friendship with Eleanor to ask favors. Isabella assured Eleanor that Loving was being well looked after in her old age.

132 E. 92nd Street New York, NY   January 7, 1941
Dearest Eleanor—

How like your sweet & generous self. Here we are one & all—receiving again the blessings of your great thoughtfulness—& such delectable goodies as I have[,] & Frances & Bob[,] [8] & Jack's ties were under the Xmas tree.

---

8. Isabella's son Bob Ferguson had married Frances Hand, daughter of Judge Learned Hand, in November 1933.

It was—as ever—lovely of you & incomprehensible to me how you ever manage—& sustain the heart warming flow & expression of friendship over the years as they have come to you.

I was sorry to miss your call—Jack & I had gone south to get the better of his cold.

If you should receive a note from old Mammy—just ignore it—She's awfully old & strange & dramatic. She mentioned in her last letter planning to write to you about a pension. We see her constantly & are in touch with her Doctor & have cared for her always—Mother having left her a very substantial sum—& she receives pensions from Aunty [Sally] Cutcheon & Martha & Bob & me.

She's been slipping rather rapidly lately & is very pitiful—A photo of you is always on her table. I'm sorry to bother you about this but just wanted to warn you in case you did hear—not to heed it.

May the New Year bring peace out of anguish [the war]—& may you have the comfort of your unfailing efforts in behalf of greater good.

> With devoted affection & love
> Isabella

Eleanor replied to Isabella's warm letter with an invitation to lunch.

[The White House]   Jan. 13, 1941

Dearest Isabella:

I was so glad to get your letter and am so anxious to see you. I am going to be in New York City on the 17th and would love it if you could lunch with me at the Cosmopolitan Club, 122 East 66th Street, at one o'clock that day.

> Affectionately,
> [Eleanor]

cc. FDRL

Fearing that the war would sooner or later involve the United States, Congress had passed, and Roosevelt had signed, America's first peacetime conscription law, requiring men between the ages of twenty-one and thirty to register with their local draft boards. The draft began in October 1940.

Isabella wanted to do something constructive for the preparedness effort. The American Women's Voluntary Services, established in January 1940, recruited women volunteers throughout the country to supplement national defense. Isabella joined the AWVS in 1941, serving as chairman of the board.

By that time, AWVS had 13,000 members. The organization trained women in fire fighting, air-raid precaution, radio code, first aid, convoy driving, and motor mechanics. It also furnished personnel to the armed services, police and fire departments, and draft and rationing boards.[9]

In this letter, Isabella refers to the deep divisions between Americans over the extent to which the United States ought to participate in the war.

132 E. 92nd Street New York, NY   July 14, 1941

Dearest Eleanor,

Every one interested in the American Women's Volunteer Services were so pleased & grateful to you for your kind & helpful comment in My Day.[10]

We do so want to cooperate with the mayor[11]—& become ever more useful in the Defense Program.

It is overwhelming & encouraging to realize the volunteer services pouring in nationally & locally. We are organized in 22 states—& the fire & police Departments seem so satisfied with the adequacy of the training in all the needed subjects.

Everyone seems so relieved & grateful to find a place to work where they can *unite*—on the common object of self reliance in Defense & not scrap with their best friends all day on the vast controversial issues consuming the energies of so many.

It's heartening & inspiring & this word of yours will help immeasurably, I know, & we are so grateful.

9. Miller, *Isabella Greenway*, 246–47.

10. In "My Day," July 11, 1941, Eleanor wrote: "I am so interested to read that Mrs. Greenway King is going to be chairman of the board of the American Woman's Voluntary Services. She has always shown great organizing ability for work of this kind and will do it very well and cooperate with the Mayor's Committee in every way." Other "My Day" columns that mention Isabella are February 20, 1936; March 19, 1936; May 5, 1936; October 7, 1936; February 14, 1937; February 15, 1937; May 28, 1937; December 24, 1953.

11. Mayor Fiorello La Guardia, who was the director of the Office of Civilian Defense within the Office for Emergency Management of the Executive Office of the President. This office was established by Executive Order 8757, May 20, 1941. *Federal Register*, v. 6, May 22, 1941, p. 2517. La Guardia had remained mayor of New York during this appointment, but in 1942, after the attack on Pearl Harbor, he was succeeded at the OCD by a full-time director. The OCD "had a broad mandate to enlist men, women and children as defense volunteers." Goodwin, *No Ordinary Time*, 279–80.

It was sad to be away this spring when you sent the lovely flowers[12]—but your thought has not faded.

> Ever with devoted affection,
> Isabella

Eleanor welcomed her friend's participation in the preparedness effort.

[The White House]   July 22, 1941

Dearest Isabella:

I was delighted to get your letter. I know you will do a grand job. Life seems very full for all of us these days.

> With my love,
> Devotedly,
> [Eleanor]

cc. FDRL

Franklin's mother, Sara Delano Roosevelt, and Eleanor's brother, Hall Roosevelt, died within three weeks of each other in September 1941.[13] Eleanor worked harder than ever that fall, as assistant director of the Office of Civilian Defense (OCD), in an attempt to numb her feelings of loss. It was the first paid government job ever held by a First Lady.[14]

The OCD mobilized the civilian population through the Citizens Defense Corps (CDC), which organized millions of volunteers to fight fires, provide first aid, and react to chemical attacks.[15] The similarity of the Citizens Defense Corps' mission to that of the AWVS meant that Isabella and Eleanor once again would have an opportunity to work closely together.

Although it is not clear from the following letter exactly what Isabella has requested, it appears from Eleanor's response that she may have asked for someone from the AWVS to coordinate with the CDC regional office.

12. Probably for Isabella's birthday on March 22.
13. Hall, who suffered from alcoholism like his father Elliott Roosevelt, died at age fifty.
14. Goodwin, *No Ordinary Time*, 279–80.
15. The Citizens Defense Corps has sometimes been inaccurately referred to as the Civil Defense Corps (a later government agency), but the former is the correct name. See *Federal Register*, v. 7, May 1, 1942, p. 3244. See also "Civilian Defense—Some Administrative and Legal Problems," pp. 844–59.

[The White House]   Oct. 7, 1941
Dearest Isabella:

Dr. Reinhart is one of the five on the volunteer participation committee for the [Citizens Defense] corps areas. They work with the regional director and there are not more than five in any corps area. However, I feel sure that Mrs. Stanhope Noxon[16] can in some way be tied in with the work of that regional office. I will take it up with Miss [Eloise] Davison who is in charge of women's participation, and find out what her suggestions might be.

I hope that you will be able to come down here for the meeting of the national women's organizations,[17] and if you do why don't you come and spend the night with us?

    Much love,
            [Eleanor]
    cc: FDRL

Isabella wanted Eleanor's admiration as well as her love. As she had done in the 1920s, Isabella wrote on letterhead stationery about the important work she was doing. She attached the AWVS mission statement and enclosed a letter from a woman who had asked the AWVS for help in organizing free transportation for New York servicemen and defense workers. Isabella indicates that it was just one of many such requests.

American Women's Voluntary Services, Inc.   October 10, 1941
1 E. 57th Street, New York, NY
Dearest Eleanor:

The attached[18] gives an idea of what the American Women's Voluntary Services has to offer. We have been given some wonderful assignments like this one from Mrs. [Anna M.] Rosenberg, and we are very pleased and happy over the results to date.

Of late quite a few other organizations have brought us some of their problems, and we have been able to help them out.

    Ever, with devoted affection,
            Isabella

16. Mrs. Stanhope Noxon was chairman of the AWVS regional office in San Francisco.
17. ER, as assistant director of the OCD, was convening 200 representatives of 67 national organizations of women for a conference on women's contributions toward preparedness. *New York Times*, November 9, 1941: 38.
18. Not included.

Isabella knew that a word from Eleanor would boost AWVS morale.

Telegram
New York, NY   October 11, 1941
To Mrs. Roosevelt, Care Mayor Rossi, City Hall, San Francisco
A word of commendation from you on tireless work of AWVS in San Francisco would mean everything to members and chairman Mrs. Stanhope Nixon [Noxon]. Gratefully Isabella Greenway King

Eleanor did not disappoint Isabella, apparently writing something appreciative about Mrs. Noxon's work.

Telegram
New York Airport, North Beach NY   October 13, 1941
To Mrs. Roosevelt, The White House
So grateful your letter[19] about Mrs. Nixon [Noxon] and particularly appreciate your dearness in invitation. Unable accept as will explain. Looking forward hear you [at] luncheon[20] today. Love. Isabelle[21]

Eleanor also commended Isabella for AWVS work.

[The White House]   Oct. 13, 1941
Dear Isabella:
I am glad to see the letter from Mrs. Rosenberg and am glad that you are reaping such splendid results from the work of the American Women's Voluntary Services.
Thank you for sending it on to me.
                Affectionately,
                        [Eleanor]
cc: FDRL

Turf battles had broken out among various women's volunteer organizations. Consequently, Isabella as chairman and Alice T. McLean, the executive director of the AWVS, met with Eleanor at the White House to coordinate

19. Missing.
20. The editors are unable to identify this event.
21. Telegraph company's typographical error.

AWVS activities with the OCD. Eleanor sent Isabella a copy of her memo to Mrs. McLean, summarizing their agreement.[22]

[The White House]   Oct. 21, 1941

Dearest Isabella:

I am enclosing a copy of a letter which I have just written to Mrs. McLean. I thought it would be well to send you this memo of my understanding of our conference here at the White House last week.

      Sincerely,

          [Eleanor]

cc: FDRL

Even before she had received Eleanor's letter, Isabella forwarded to Eleanor a copy of a memo summarizing Isabella's understanding of their meeting. She had originally sent the memo to Miss Davison, who was in charge of women's participation in the OCD.

1 E. 57th Street, New York, NY   October 22, 1941

Dear Eleanor

You were very generous & we are most appreciative—& glad to feel we may be a useful part of the official Defense program.

I wrote Miss Davison as enclosed with a memorandum of our memory of what we had understood.

      Ever aff'ly,

          Isabella

[Memorandum of understanding]

The Civilian Defense Volunteer Office [CDVO][23] will expect the cooperation of the American Women's Voluntary Services on the following basis: that they—

---

22. Missing.

23. "The majority of cities and towns have established a Civilian Defense Volunteer Office which is the one official center where all citizens wishing to participate in some phase of the war effort may register." Frost, "Cities and Towns Mobilize for War," 87. See also U.S. Office of Civilian Defense, "Civilian Defense Volunteer Office: What It Is; How It Is Set Up; What It Does; How To Organize It." http://digitallibrary.smu.edu/cul/gir/ww2/pdf/p0104.pdf.

1. Continue to Enroll Members:

    A comprehensive and classified list of AWVS enrollees to be supplied to the offices of Defense Councils.[24]

2. Continue to Train Members:

    It is of course understood that the courses given by the AWVS be kept up to standards of the CDVO.

3. Anticipate that hereafter assignments will clear more and more through the CDVO.

4. Wear their own uniform, and when on defense work the insignia of the CDVO as well, except in the case of air wardens or when specific technical assignments make it impractical.

It seems that Eleanor's and Isabella's understandings of the meeting differed somewhat. Eleanor wrote back to clarify the points of difference.

To avoid duplication of effort, Eleanor wanted AWVS volunteers to register with the appropriate local federal offices, telling those offices what work they were doing. She also wanted Isabella to send descriptions of the AWVS training courses, giving hours and fieldwork required. Finally, Eleanor explained that in some locales, such as Cleveland, pre-existing organizations had been authorized to enroll volunteers. She advised Isabella that the AWVS could not supercede them.

[The White House]   Oct. 31, 1941
Isabella:

Since I sent my letter to Mrs. McLean, a copy of which was sent to you and Mrs. Davie [Davison?], your letter has been brought to my attention.

On point number one, I hope it is understood between us that your enrollees, if our offices are not joined together, are to enroll as individuals in our office, simply giving the work which they are doing for you.

We think it important that they should at least know where the office is and go at once to enroll.

On point two, I understand that you have not as yet sent us your complete courses for training in any of your training groups for final approval. We will have to have a complete description of courses with hours that are required to

24. The state or local defense councils established to work with the OCD. By early 1941, thirty-five states had formed defense councils. http://arcweb.sos.state.or.us/exhibits/ww2/before/defense.htm.

cover each section of training, and the practical laboratory work that is done where such work is needed. I hope you will hurry these along as we want to approve them as quickly as possible.

We will of course, send you copies of pamphlets as they come out, covering courses which we think necessary which will make it easy for you to conform.

In Cleveland a difficulty seems to have arisen which may arise some where else. Mrs. Rohde [25] apparently in speaking to a meeting of the AWVS gave the impression that they were to be the only agency establishing volunteer offices. She did not know, of course, that if they were going to be a volunteer office they had to contact us. We naturally would have to clear with the local defense council through our regional director and the state Defense Council.

In Cleveland they had already organized a civilian defense state office under the State council of defense which was really a reorganization of the volunteer department of the welfare federation. This bureau has already expanded and has become a civilian defense volunteer office. In cases like this it is quite impossible to have you supercede a previously established bureau.

I think you should make an effort to cooperate as far as possible with these bureaus. If you prefer to set up a separate office and send your enrollees to enroll and consider yourself a separate organization that seems to me all right, but you can not become a civilian defense enrollment office where there is one already.

I have copied the second paragraph of a letter which shows you the confusion that arose out of the Cleveland meeting.

"This letter is a plea to you as Assistant Director of the Office of Civilian Defense to clarify the confusion here in Cleveland with regard to volunteer activities under the Defense Program. We are informed that this confusion exits elsewhere, as it does in Cleveland, because the American Women's Voluntary Services claims to have authority from Mayor LaGuardia to handle women's activities in Civilian Defense. We, on the other hand, have been recognized by the mayor of Cleveland and his appointed Director of Civilian Defense, Mr. Keith Wilson, as the 'committee in charge of volunteers' under the local Defense Council."

> Affectionately,
>
> [Eleanor]

cc: FDRL

25. Possibly Ruth Bryan Owen Rohde, the daughter of William Jennings Bryan. Rohde became the first woman elected to Congress from the Deep South (Florida, 1928–1932),

The Japanese attacked Pearl Harbor on December 7, 1941. The following day, President Roosevelt appeared at the Capitol, where he gave a short but furious speech asking Congress to declare war. Eleanor accompanied Franklin, but left immediately after his speech on an overnight trip to the West coast. Reports that California cities might be attacked next required her presence to supervise civil defense preparations.[26]

AWVS volunteers drove Eleanor around California. Eager to keep up morale among civilian defense workers, she evidently wrote Isabella an effusive letter of thanks. Isabella appreciated Eleanor's acknowledgement, as well as her suggestion that the AWVS might help the men who were patrolling the coastlines.

American Women's Voluntary Services   December 18, 1941
1 E. 57th Street, New York, NY
Dearest Eleanor:

It is amazing that you could find time to write this wonderful letter[27] from California. I appreciate it very much.

I hadn't known that our Motor Corps had offered its services in your official trip.

We are, I understand, already functioning in our Motor corps services, as you suggest, in many places with the councils of Civilian Defense.

Your suggestion in connection with the men on the water fronts, which was not to be shouted from the housetops, is, of course, splendid, and we are very glad to know of this opportunity to be useful.

       Ever so gratefully and with dearest love,
         Isabella

Isabella wanted Eleanor to meet with her and the AWVS, probably to accept a token of their appreciation. But less than two months after the attack on Pearl Harbor, Eleanor was too busy to accept. Once again, Isabella directed her letter to Eleanor's secretary, hopeful that it would finally find its way to Eleanor.

and the first woman chief of a diplomatic mission, serving as U.S. Minister to Denmark (1933–1936). Having married a Dane, she resigned her post, and returned to the U.S., where she lectured and served on various committees. She would later work in several capacities for the United Nations. Louise M. Young, "Ruth Bryan Owen Rhode," in Sicherman and Green, eds., *Notable American Women*, 591–93.

26. Goodwin, *No Ordinary Time*, 295.
27. Missing.

American Women's Voluntary Services   January 27, 1942
295 Madison Avenue, New York, NY
To Miss Malvina Thompson, Secretary to Mrs. Roosevelt
My dear Miss Thompson:

Thank you for your gracious wire which we one and all find very disappointing. The AWVS feels that Mrs. Roosevelt has been so cooperative and broad in her contributing interest that we are truly disappointed that we may not thank her in person.

So much that has been complicated is beginning to iron out into effective united service throughout the country that we are very happy.

If the occasion ever allows, will you tell Mrs. Roosevelt that her suggestion that we feed the Coast guard in our private homes when possible on their long watches is being put into practice. She would be interested to know that Lady Lindsay serves six meals in her house in Long Island during the twenty-four hours to these very men and it has become a general practice in California.

       Very sincerely yours, & with warm friendship [added by hand]
         Isabella Greenway King

Sure enough, Isabella's note reached Eleanor, who immediately replied.

[The White House]   January 30, 1942
Dear Isabella:

I have read your letter of January 27th to Miss Thompson and I so much appreciate the feelings you express on behalf of the AWVS.

Thank you for the information about what Lady Lindsey and others are doing for the Coast Guard men. This is grand.

       Affectionately,
         [Eleanor]
cc: FDRL

In spite of her responsibilities as a wartime first lady, Eleanor remembered Isabella's birthday. Isabella was touched by her thoughtfulness. The war had brought Isabella back to Washington, D.C. when Harry King accepted a "dollar a year" wartime job heading the copper division in the War Production Board. At first, Isabella Greenway King continued to work for the AWVS. She resigned at the beginning of 1943, when she found it too difficult to head a New York-based organization from Washington.[28]

28. Miller, *Isabella Greenway*, 249.

1815 Q Street NW   March 22, 1943
Eleanor dear

How remarkable—unbelievably so, you are & here's another proof—*flowers* on this the anniversary of my beloved Mother's special & only venture in parenthood.

She loved you so—as do I—& here's a heartful of thanksgiving for these flowers—& all the cherished experiences your friendship has lavished on my years.

> With devotion & love,
> Isabella

Their personal communication during the busy wartime years dwindled to Eleanor's annual birthday gift to Isabella and Isabella's heartfelt thanks.

132 E. 92 Street, New York   March 26, 1944
Eleanor dearest,

The whole house was permeated with the loveliness of your roses on my fifty-eighth birthday. They arrived with my breakfast tray & spelt something so sweet & forever-like & so it always is—when I think of you—which I do—a thousand times & a thousand ways—over all the days—& love you dearly.

Frances & Bob tell me Anna & John are coming to a party that a number of young people are giving in our house. The invitations are certainly *quaint*! I enclose a sample—& we would love it if you felt like coming for any moment you could spare. I know the chances are slim—but it certainly would make us happy to have a glimpse of you.

> Ever with devotion,
> Isabella

Jack Greenway had joined the Army Reserve Corps in 1942, and trained in Charlottesville, Virginia. While on leave, he sometimes visited Eleanor in the White House. The following year, he left Yale University to enroll in the Army.[29]

In addition to sending Isabella a 1944 Christmas present of nuts, Eleanor also wrote to Jack, who was being trained in cryptography in Texas.

29. Ibid., 250.

132 E. 92nd Street, New York   February 6, 1945

Eleanor darling—The *nuts* & I have been in a merry go round—but we have finally come face to face or mouth to mouth!—& I'm not as ungrateful as my silence would seem. Bless you now as always—the way in which you carry on in Xmas gifts & greetings to this now rather *large family*—is to me (& all of us) just one more proof that you are you & that no one ever has (& I don't believe ever will) measure up to you.

I spent Xmas with my Aunty [Sally] Cutcheon in California. She is a shut in—& we all felt that one of us, with her, would break her many lonely times since Uncle's death—& I only returned recently.

Jack was so truly pleased, amazed & touched with your note to him.

A heart full of love & infinite devotion always.

Isabella

Eleanor immediately scrawled on the bottom of Isabella's letter a reply, for her secretary to type up and mail off, asking Isabella if they could get together.

[The White House]   Feb. 10, 1945

Dearest Isabella:

I was so glad to hear from you and to know you are in New York City.

I would so love to see you and hope you can come to my apartment, #29 Washington Square West, on Thursday, the 15th, at four o'clock, for a really quiet hour.

Do come if you can.

Much love,

[Eleanor]

cc: FDRL

The really quiet hour, if it came, would have been one of the last for a while. Franklin Roosevelt died on April 12, 1945, in Warm Springs, Georgia, where he was sitting for a portrait by the well-known society artist Elizabeth Shoumatoff. Elizabeth had visited Isabella and Harry shortly before going to Georgia, and had told them, "I have a feeling that they think this may be his last portrait . . . . I must go and do it. It will be very interesting but . . . very difficult." [30]

30. Ibid., 252.

Within a week of Franklin's death, Eleanor had moved out of the White House. Two months later, she and Isabella lunched at the Biltmore Hotel in New York. Eleanor admitted to her old friend how hard it had been to have to leave so suddenly a place where she had lived for more than twelve years.

Eleanor soon found a new role for herself in the post-war world, helping guide the United Nations into being. President Harry Truman appointed her one of the first U.S. delegates. From 1946 to 1952, Eleanor oversaw the drafting and passage of the landmark Universal Declaration of Human Rights. According to biographer Allida Black, Eleanor's "seven year service to the U. N. was one of the most fulfilling assignments of her life." [31]

[Dictated draft]   [nd]
Dearest Isabella:

Many thanks for your heartening telegram.[32] I am so glad you thought the speech went well as I value your opinion.

I deplore the fact that we do not meet much more often. If I am again a delegate, I will be in NYC every week day after Oct. 14 so do come to lunch with me at the UN if I am there.

      Much love,
         [Eleanor]
cc: FDRL

Susie Parish died on July 9, 1950. Eleanor sent Isabella a few mementoes—possibly water colors of Isabella's that she had given the Parishes.

Val-Kill, Hyde Park, NY   Feb. 2, 1951
Dearest Isabella:

These are all I could find in Cousin Susie [Parish]'s New York house.

The Parish's could never find the water color you wanted in the [Parishes'] Orange [New Jersey] house, I am sorry to say. I thought you might like to have these. If you or your children do not want them, just destroy them.

      Much love,
        Eleanor Roosevelt

At age sixty-four, in 1950, Isabella's health began to decline. She was diagnosed with congestive heart failure. Her condition deteriorated over the next

31. Black, "Eleanor Roosevelt," 445.
32. Missing.

two years, and in November 1952 she suffered a heart attack. Eleanor was concerned, but apparently believed Isabella's health had improved, as she asked her to contact the Tucson newspaper editor with a query.

Dec. 18, 1952

Dearest Isabella:

C.R. Smith[33] told me you were ill and I was so glad to hear from Jack that you are better.

Could you ask Mr. [Bill] Mathews to advise the gentleman who wrote the following letter?

"First of all, my most grateful appreciation to you for your gracious offer to contact Arizona sources in my behalf relative to lining up potential employment contacts.

"After the grave news from our family physician the day before, I was feeling somewhat 'down in the boots' until I discussed the matter with you last Sunday. Incidentally, you are the only person I have discussed it with—because of rather obvious reasons. It will take some time to sell my home and dispose of my business. In the meanwhile, it would injure the latter if it became public knowledge that I was planning to move to Arizona.

"I am enclosing a dozen one-page profiles of myself which give in outline form, the salient facts about my work and background. If at all possible, I want to re-establish myself in Arizona in some type of work that will permit me to concentrate on writing—whether it be public relations, newspaper or advertising copy writing."

Affectionately,

[Eleanor]

cc. to Mr. Charles W. Pine, Providence RI

cc. FDRL

Isabella suffered another heart attack in the summer of 1953, while visiting the Ferguson children and grandchildren in New York. She returned to her beloved Tucson as soon as she could be moved. Eleanor, who had her own health challenges, wrote the last letter of their remarkable correspondence, almost forty-nine years after it had begun.

33. Possibly the longtime American Airlines president and aviation pioneer. Smith had close ties to many Democratic politicians, and would serve briefly in the cabinet of Lyndon B. Johnson. http://crsmithmuseum.org/AAhistory/AA_frameset.htm.

211 E. 62nd St.

New York 19, NY   October 9, 1953

Dearest Isabella:

My handwriting is so bad that I am not going to make you cope with it but I can't wait any longer to tell you how sorry I am to hear that you are ill and not able to see anyone. I do hope things are progressing even though slowly.

I would love to see you if the time ever comes when you will be near here and would want to see anyone. Our friendship is such an old one that time and distance have never made any difference and you know my thoughts will be constantly with you.

Much love,

Eleanor Roosevelt [signed in a very shaky hand]

On December 14, Isabella Greenway suffered a stroke from which she did not recover. She died four days later, on December 18, the twenty-third anniversary of the opening of the Arizona Inn. She was buried at the Dinsmore Farm.

Five years after Isabella's death, Eleanor Roosevelt visited Tucson and stayed at the Arizona Inn. "It seems strange," she wrote her close friend Lorena Hickok, "that she should have died and I should still be flourishing."[34]

Eleanor continued her work throughout the Eisenhower administration in the 1950s, urging the Democratic party to embrace the cause of racial justice. She, herself, served on the boards of the NAACP, CORE, and other civil rights organizations. She received death threats; the Ku Klux Klan put a bounty on her head.[35] In 1960, she supported John F. Kennedy, only after he embraced a civil rights agenda. As president, Kennedy appointed Eleanor Roosevelt to his Commission on the Status of Women.[36]

Eleanor died on November 7, 1962, of tuberculosis.[37]

34. Lash, *Eleanor and Franklin*, 478.
35. Black, "(Anna) Eleanor Roosevelt," in Gould, ed., *American First Ladies*, 445.
36. Ibid., 446.
37. Eleanor Roosevelt suffered from an acute form of miliary tuberculosis characterized by small lesions thought to resemble millet seeds (whence the name), disseminated throughout the body. Barron H. Lerner, "Final Diagnosis," *Washington Post*, February 8. 2000: Z.12.

Afterword

℧sabella Greenway characterized her half-century of correspondence with Eleanor Roosevelt as a "volume of friendship." [1] The arc of that friendship can be traced through these letters: it begins with two girls in their late teens snuggled in bed discussing Eleanor's decision to marry Franklin Roosevelt; it continues through a strong and satisfying political partnership; and it ends with Eleanor facing a "strange" world without her oldest friend. The letters take us back in time to the turn of the twentieth century. We see women shivering with cold as they march for the vote in 1913. We see wild ponies racing at sundown up a red, rocky canyon.

The letters also reveal darker aspects of that earlier time. References to disease and physical suffering abound. Tuberculosis [2] was then so widespread it was known as the "White Plague" (so-called because of the pallor of its victims). It touched both women closely: Isabella struggled with Bob's TB for fourteen years. One of the harshest consequences, especially for a couple not long married, would have been the impossibility of physical intimacy. Friends like Cyril Martineau and Bronson Cutting [3] also suffered from tuberculosis. Eleanor, herself, died of TB.

1. IG-ER, December 10, 1922, FC. Will biographers of the future ever have such a wealth of material about two intimate lives? Telephones threatened for a time to obliterate the record of everyday information such as these two women shared so naturally on paper. Now, however, the rise of indefinitely archived e-mails may provide rich resources in years to come.
2. Tuberculosis (abbreviated as TB for Tubercle Bacillus) is a deadly infectious disease caused by the bacterium Mycobacterium tuberculosis. The bacterium most commonly affects the lungs (pulmonary TB) but can also affect the central nervous system, lymphatic system, circulatory system, genitourinary system, bones and joints. Streptomycin, developed in 1946, was the first effective treatment. Drug-resistant strains and the emergence of AIDS have caused a resurgence of the disease. http://library.med.utah.edu/WebPath/TUTORIAL/MTB/MTB.html.
3. Cutting survived the disease, and was elected to the U.S. Senate. He died in an airplane crash.

Polio, or infantile paralysis, was common, too.[4] In 1916, five years before Franklin was stricken, Eleanor extended her stay in Canada in order to avoid an epidemic of polio sweeping through New England.

Absent effective drugs, prevention of disease was vitally important to Eleanor and Isabella's families. Their letters are full of references to the advisability of getting rest, gaining weight, and living or vacationing in presumably health-giving locales like the dry Southwest or the ocean shore.

Death, too, figures prominently in these letters. Child mortality was high in the early twentieth century.[5] Eleanor and Franklin lost a baby, as did Eleanor's brother and his wife. Her cousin Teddy Robinson and his wife Helen, mutual friends William and Caroline Phillips, and Isabella's Scottish neighbors in New Mexico—all saw their children die. At age nine, Eleanor and Isabella both lost their fathers. Eleanor had already lost her mother, and a younger brother died not long after their father. Isabella had only three years with Bob Ferguson before he contracted a fatal disease, and she spent just over two years with John Greenway before he, too, died.

Prior to the enactment of the New Deal Social Security Act (due, in part, to the efforts of Eleanor and Isabella) one's family was the only social safety net. Isabella's Uncle Frank, her mother, and Bob's brother all helped her cope with the effects of Bob's TB. Eleanor had her mother-in-law, Sara, to help her and the children when Franklin fell ill. A generation earlier, TR's sister Anna (Auntie Bye) had taken care of his little daughter, Alice, after Alice's mother died in childbirth. People depended on each other. Divorce was rare, even under trying circumstances. Of the scores of married couples described in the letters, only three of Eleanor and Isabella's contemporaries divorce.[6]

The letters show that families, at least elite families, sometimes behaved in ways that seem strange to us today. Children were often home-schooled by parents and governesses, then sent off in their early teens to boarding school. Parents, even mothers, often left their children, sometimes for months at a time, while they traveled for health, work, or pleasure. Wives took their

4. Poliomyelitis is a virally induced infectious disease, usually spread through contaminated water. One form, paralytic polio, causes muscle paralysis. When the chest muscles are affected, it may be fatal. It has been largely eliminated through vaccination, beginning in 1953. www.kidshealth.org/parent/infections/bacterial_viral/polio.html.

5. At the beginning of the twentieth century, approximately 100 infants out of 1000 died before the age of one year. By 1997, the infant mortality rate had declined by greater than 90% to just 7.2 per 1000 live births. http://www.cdc.gov/mmwr/preview/mmwrhtml/mm4838a2.htm.

6. Maude Waterbury, Harry King, Pussie Morgan.

children to cooler climes in the summer, leaving the husbands behind in the cities to work. People visited each other's homes for weeks at a time.

Eleanor belonged to one of the ruling families in America, part of what her journalist cousin Jospeh Alsop would call the "WASP Ascendancy." They were, he said, the class that owned things and ran things. Isabella's father had been a professional man and her mother was the daughter of a judge. Isabella herself married into the Scottish nobility.

These letters are studded with the names of the rich and the powerful. Their connections helped Eleanor Roosevelt and Isabella Greenway achieve what they did. But the letters also show that both women endeavored, all their lives, separately and together, to better the lot of the less fortunate and to include the excluded.

Eleanor Roosevelt, admired as the foremost American woman of the twentieth century, has been studied extensively. For many years, Isabella was virtually Eleanor's only correspondent. These letters reveal the private Eleanor before she became a public icon. In writing to Isabella, Eleanor describes in great detail her hopes, fears and plans for her six children. The letters show how much she depended on Sara Roosevelt, her mother-in-law, to help Eleanor as she tried to juggle the demands of a large brood of children and an ambitious husband.[7] The letters also show that Eleanor cultivated an astonishingly large number of friends.

Much has been made of Eleanor's rivalry with her cousin Alice Roosevelt Longworth. Alice had a tart tongue, and made some notoriously unkind remarks about Eleanor. But, according to Isabella, Alice was generous in her praise of Eleanor's work during the war. And ER's sharp criticisms of Alice in these letters show that Eleanor could give as good as she got.

A writer's style can reveal her personality. Eleanor comes across as girlishly enthusiastic in the early years, her letters sprinkled with exclamation points. Soon, though, her letters become more composed, in both senses of the word. It seems, from time to time, that Eleanor is writing for posterity. Even so, she is capable of dry humor and amused irony.[8]

Through these letters we discover another engaging personality, Isabella Selmes Ferguson Greenway King. She, too, proves to be worthy of our

---

7. Other sources, notably Blanche Wiesen Cook, Jan Pottker, and the Roosevelt children, interpret ER's behavior differently.

8. For example, her allusion to impending childbirth as "that entertainment," and her account of the concert pianist who would not be responsible for his singing if he was not accompanied by an Everett piano.

attention and admiration. Isabella shows her bravery, loyalty, and cheerful resilience as she struggles with hardship and loss. By creating lasting legacies to her husbands, she finds a path into political service. Isabella's legendary hospitality also comes through in these letters. Even when she was living in tents, she entertained houseguests. Eventually, she established an inn, which, in the early twenty-first century, is still being run by her descendants.[9] Isabella in her youth had trained as an artist, in the unlikely event that she never married and had to support herself by working. Her letters are full of visual details. Sometimes she illustrates them with quick sketches. She also makes use of dramatic dialogues, poetic comparisons, and humorous observations. Her irrepressible spirit bubbles over.[10]

Isabella Greenway and Eleanor Roosevelt became friends, and stayed friends, because of shared traits and interests. Both drew spiritual strength from the beauty of the natural world. Both, too, believed explicitly that suffering and trouble make people stronger and more empathic. They not only enjoyed helping others, but felt it was their duty and destiny to do so. That is why we remember them today.

Perhaps their sense of responsibility stemmed at least in part from both having been adult children of alcoholics, who often feel a need to take care of people.[11] Both women pushed Franklin to go further in his reforms than he, for political reasons, sometimes felt he was able to go. Their pressure undoubtedly gave him the support he needed for the reforms he did undertake.

Through their correspondence the two women derived much support and inspiration from each other. Clearly they loved each other deeply. Their terms of endearment may sound sexual to modern ears, but they were effusive about everything.[12] We can speculate about their private behavior; but in the end the letters fail to prove the existence or non-existence of a relationship more intense than profound friendship.

9. Isabella's granddaughter, Frances Ferguson Conroy Doar, and Isabella's great-grandson, Will Conroy.

10. For example, "A very sunny glistening world of love to you—laden with pines & junipers & cool breezes off the snowy mount[ain]."

11. For Eleanor, in particular, the foundation for friendship was often her ability to help. Journalist Martha Gellhorn had been very close to ER in the 1940s. But after Gellhorn married a wealthy man, she said ER "sort of vanish[ed] from my life." When Gellhorn asked what was the matter, Eleanor explained, "But darling, you're all right now. . . you don't need anything." Interview with Martha Gellhorn, February 20, 1980, pp. 28-29, FDRL.

12. For instance, Eleanor wrote that Isabella's gift of a rug brought Eleanor's daughter Anna "endless joy."

For millennia, a woman's life was deemed successful if she found a partner and reared their children well. That changed in the early-twentieth-century United States as women began to take up the world's work themselves. Eleanor Roosevelt and Isabella Greenway were among the pioneering women who entered the previously all-male realm of politics. Their correspondence is rich in examples of the emotional support, understanding, and appreciation that women have traditionally given each other. But it also offers an opportunity to see how women in the 1920s and 1930s worked to form a political network. They were able to achieve what they did, in part, because they had each other.

Appendix 1: The Children
Isabella's Children

1. Martha

Martha and Chuck Breasted settled in the Cutcheons' Locust Valley property on Long Island where Isabella and Bob Ferguson had been married. The Breasteds had four children: David (1935), Macomb, "Mac," (1939), Isabella (1941) and Sarah Grace (1946). Isabella built her last house, a spacious, two-story dwelling next door to the Arizona Inn, around 1950, as a home for Martha and her family, when the Breasteds moved to Tucson. Martha died in 1994.

2. Bobbie

Bob and Frances Ferguson lived for more than twenty years in the little brownstone "Bandbox" at 135 East 69th Street (now number 145), where they brought up their three children: Frances, always known as "Patty" (1935); Robert Harry Munro Ferguson, called "Bob" (1937); and Phyllis (1938). Patty married Frank Conroy, for many years head of the Writers Workshop at the University of Iowa. The couple had two children. After her divorce from Conroy, Patty married John Doar. She ran the Arizona Inn from 1995 to 2005, when her son Will Conroy took over.

3. Jack

Jack attended law school at the University of Arizona in Tucson. He became president of the Arizona Inn following Isabella's death in 1953, and continued until his death in 1995, but he was never a hands-on manager. He served as chairman of the Arizona Democratic party in the 1950s and 1960s, as well as Democratic national committeeman. He was also active in social and community causes.

Eleanor's Children

1. Anna

Anna married Curtis B. Dall in 1926. They had two children, Anna Eleanor (Seagraves) and Curtis (who later took the name Roosevelt). The Dalls divorced, and in 1935 Anna married John Boettinger, a journalist, with whom she worked professionally. In 1943, when John went into the army, Anna returned to the White House as her father's confidential assistant. Anna and John divorced in 1949. She married Dr. James A. Halstead in 1952 and worked in medical public relations. After ER's death, Anna worked for various organizations her mother had supported.

2. James

James founded an insurance company where he worked until 1937, when he left to serve as secretary to his father in the White House. He was a captain in the Marine Corps during World War II, leaving with the rank of brigadier general in the reserves. He continued in the insurance business until he was elected to Congress from California in 1954. He served for ten years, until 1965, when he served briefly as the United States representative to the United Nations Economic and Social Council. He was married four times.

3. Elliott

Elliott pursued a variety of interests in communications, business, and politics. He managed the Hearst radio chain in the 1930s. During World War II he was a bombardier in the U.S. Army, and also served as FDR's military attaché at conferences in Casablanca, Cairo, and Tehran. After the war, he turned to writing. He was ER's agent in serializing her second autobiography. He wrote memoirs and edited his father's letters. He later wrote three books of non-fiction and a mystery series in which his mother was a sleuth. He married five times.

4. Franklin, Jr.

Franklin, Jr. attended law school and served in the U.S. Navy in World War II, earning a Purple Heart and a Silver Star. He served as a U.S. representative from New York, 1949-1955. He ran unsuccessfully for several other offices, then took positions as under secretary of commerce in the Kennedy administration and as head of the Equal Employment Opportunity Commission under Lyndon B. Johnson. He worked in various business enterprises after that, and served as his mother's literary executor. Franklin, Jr. was married five times.

5. John

John served in the Navy in World War II. In 1952 he joined the Republican party in order to work for Dwight D. Eisenhower's presidential campaign. He lived in Hyde Park, near ER, until her death in 1962. He worked as a stock broker and served with several philanthropies. He married twice.

Eleanor Roosevelt and Isabella Greenway were among the first women in partisan politics. What effect did their extraordinary success and fame have on the lives of their children? It is impossible to tell. For a hundred years, people have been trying to find a connection between a woman who works and the success of her offspring. This is especially true if a woman's work is in the public eye. To date, there is no definitive evidence of any correlation, positive or negative.

Eleanor tended to blame herself for her children's many divorces. But whether the children's marital difficulties were due to their parents' own troubled relationship, Franklin's debilitating illness, or Eleanor's public prominence is an open question.

Although Isabella's and Eleanor's children had noteworthy careers, they never attained the phenomenal recognition that came to their mothers. The real question is how Isabella and Eleanor, themselves, came to achieve what they did. They both had seriously troubled childhoods, yet they accomplished a great deal. In the final analysis, the factors that lead to outstanding success are still as mysterious as they are rare.

Appendix 2: Genealogies

Theodore Roosevelt Branch

Genealogical Chart f

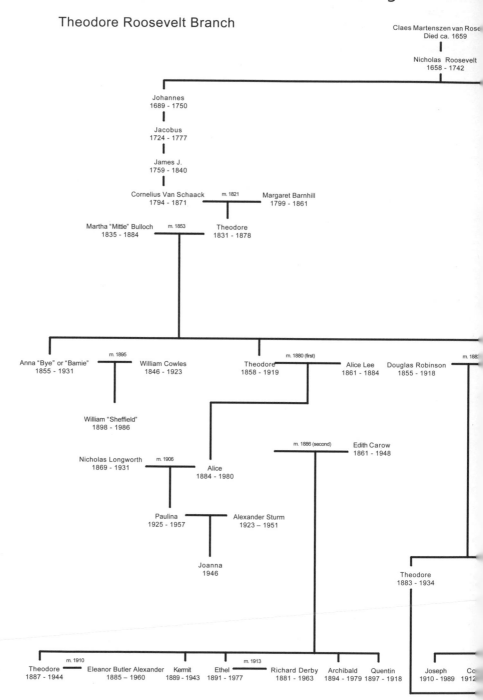

Claes Martenszen van Rose
Died ca. 1659

Nicholas Roosevelt
1658 - 1742

Johannes
1689 - 1750

Jacobus
1724 - 1777

James J.
1759 - 1840

Cornelius Van Schaack   m. 1821   Margaret Barnhill
1794 - 1871   1799 - 1861

Martha "Mittie" Bulloch   m. 1853   Theodore
1835 - 1884   1831 - 1878

Anna "Bye" or "Bamie"   m. 1895   William Cowles   Theodore   m. 1880 (first)   Alice Lee   Douglas Robinson   m. 188
1855 - 1931   1846 - 1923   1858 - 1919   1861 - 1884   1855 - 1918

William "Sheffield"
1898 - 1986

Nicholas Longworth   m. 1906   Alice
1869 - 1931   1884 - 1980

                                                              m. 1886 (second)   Edith Carow
                                                                                   1861 - 1948

Paulina   Alexander Sturm
1925 - 1957   1923 – 1951

Joanna
1946

Theodore
1883 - 1934

Theodore   m. 1910   Eleanor Butler Alexander   Kermit   Ethel   m. 1913   Richard Derby   Archibald   Quentin   Joseph   Co
1887 - 1944   1885 – 1960   1889 - 1943   1891 - 1977   1881 - 1963   1894 - 1979   1897 - 1918   1910 - 1989   1912

eanor Roosevelt

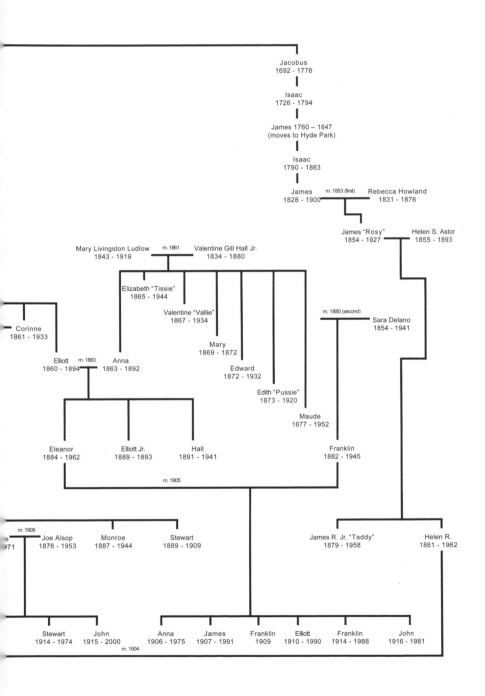

Jacobus
1692 - 1776

Isaac
1726 - 1794

James 1760 – 1847
(moves to Hyde Park)

Isaac
1790 - 1863

James   m. 1853 (first)   Rebecca Howland
1828 - 1900   1831 - 1876

James "Rosy"   Helen S. Astor
1854 - 1927   1855 - 1893

Mary Livingston Ludlow   m. 1861   Valentine Gill Hall Jr.
1843 - 1919   1834 - 1880

Elizabeth "Tissie"
1865 - 1944

Valentine "Vallie"
1867 - 1934

m. 1880 (second)

Sara Delano
1854 - 1941

Corinne
1861 - 1933

Mary
1869 - 1872

Elliott   m. 1883   Anna
1860 - 1894   1863 - 1892

Edward
1872 - 1932

Edith "Pussie"
1873 - 1920

Maude
1877 - 1952

Eleanor   Elliott Jr.   Hall   Franklin
1884 - 1962   1889 - 1893   1891 - 1941   1882 - 1945

m. 1905

m. 1909

Joe Alsop   Monroe   Stewart   James R. Jr. "Taddy"   Helen R.
1876 - 1953   1887 - 1944   1889 - 1909   1879 - 1958   1881 - 1962

71

Stewart   John   Anna   James   Franklin   Elliott   Franklin   John
1914 - 1974   1915 - 2000   1906 - 1975   1907 - 1991   1909   1910 - 1990   1914 - 1988   1916 - 1981

m. 1904

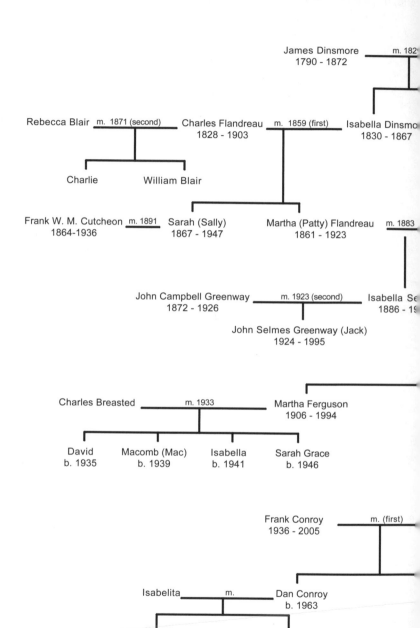

James Dinsmore
1790 - 1872   m. 182

Rebecca Blair   m. 1871 (second)   Charles Flandreau   m. 1859 (first)   Isabella Dinsmo
                                   1828 - 1903   1830 - 1867

Charlie   William Blair

Frank W. M. Cutcheon   m. 1891   Sarah (Sally)   Martha (Patty) Flandreau   m. 1883
1864-1936   1867 - 1947   1861 - 1923

John Campbell Greenway   m. 1923 (second)   Isabella Se
1872 - 1926   1886 - 19

John Selmes Greenway (Jack)
1924 - 1995

Charles Breasted   m. 1933   Martha Ferguson
                             1906 - 1994

David   Macomb (Mac)   Isabella   Sarah Grace
b. 1935   b. 1939   b. 1941   b. 1946

Frank Conroy   m. (first)
1936 - 2005

Isabelita   m.   Dan Conroy
                       b. 1963

Jonathan   (twins)   Nicholas
b. 2000   b. 2000

sabella Selmes Greenway King

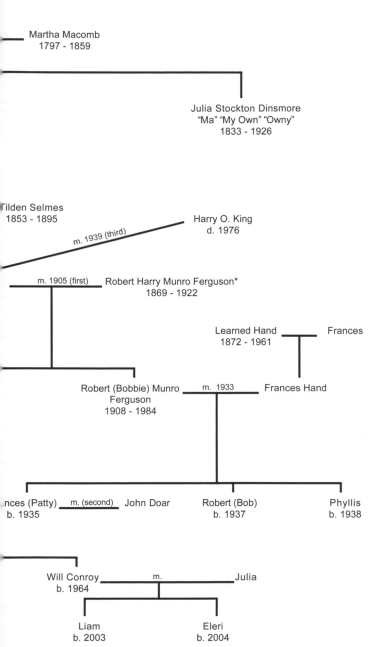

Martha Macomb
1797 - 1859

Julia Stockton Dinsmore
"Ma" "My Own" "Owny"
1833 - 1926

Tilden Selmes
1853 - 1895

Harry O. King
d. 1976

m. 1939 (third)

m. 1905 (first)   Robert Harry Munro Ferguson*
1869 - 1922

Learned Hand _____ Frances
1872 - 1961

Robert (Bobbie) Munro ___ m. 1933 ___ Frances Hand
Ferguson
1908 - 1984

nces (Patty) ___ m. (second) ___ John Doar   Robert (Bob)   Phyllis
b. 1935   b. 1937   b. 1938

Will Conroy _____ m. _____ Julia
b. 1964

Liam   Eleri
b. 2003   b. 2004

*See Ferguson Genealogical Chart

Genealogical Chart for Rober

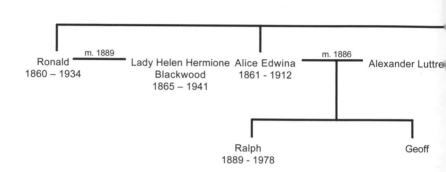

Robert Munro-Ferguson ___

Ronald
1860 – 1934
— m. 1889 —
Lady Helen Hermione
Blackwood
1865 – 1941

Alice Edwina
1861 - 1912
— m. 1886 —
Alexander Luttre

Ralph
1889 - 1978

Geoff

---

*In Scotland, Robert (or Bob) used the surname "Munro-Ferguson." In the U.S., he used "Munro Ferguson," unhyphenated.

**See Greenway Genealogical Chart for marriage and descendants.

*** Burke's Peerage & Gentry – The Authentic Guide to the UK and Ireland's Titled and Untitled Families (the online resource used for many dates on this chart) gives 1867 as Bob's date of birth. This year is suspect because it is also listed as the year of the birth of Bob's brother, Hector. 1869 is probably the correct year. The obituary in *The Scotsman* dated October 17, 1922, indicates Bob was 53 at the time of his death (October 3, 1922). Bob's granddaughter, Patty Doar, has advised the authors that her grandfather's birthday was in June. If both of these latter sources are correct, Bob would have to have been born in 1869.

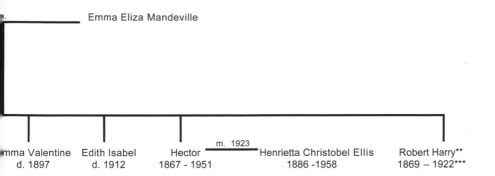

arry Munro-Ferguson*

Emma Eliza Mandeville

m. 1923

mma Valentine	Edith Isabel	Hector	Henrietta Christobel Ellis	Robert Harry**
d. 1897	d. 1912	1867 - 1951	1886 -1958	1869 – 1922***

Acknowledgments

$\mathcal{M}$any people had a hand in making Eleanor and Isabella's "volume of friendship" into a real book, and the editors want to thank them all.

Frances Ferguson "Patty" Doar and Will Conroy, Isabella's granddaughter and great-grandson, gave most generously of their time, energy, and fund of family lore. Just as the manuscript was going to press, they found three important ER letters in an old trunk and made heroic efforts to get them to us in time to be included. They also shared many family photos, carefully scanned by Armen Benneian.

Geoffrey Ward kindly supplied an expert's insight to locate many missing references. Mary Rothschild made important suggestions for organization. Ellen Twaddell read several drafts and gave guidance for revisions. Blanche Cook took precious time out of her own ongoing work on Eleanor Roosevelt to write the preface.

The staff of the Arizona Historical Society Manuscript Room and the staff of the Franklin D. Roosevelt Presidential Library worked hard to help us locate letters scattered throughout their vast collections. Archivist Alycia J. Vivona was especially helpful in explaining the Roosevelt family connections.

Cathy Callopy and Marty McDonald of the Dinsmore Homestead, as well as Allida Black and Christy Regenhardt of the Eleanor Roosevelt Papers Project at George Washington University answered several particularly challenging questions.

Author Tom Miller gave us the wonderful story about George W. Bush. Dianne Bret Harte and the Southwest Foundation lent moral and financial support.

Kristie is grateful to Sandy and Elyse Twaddell for the happy diversion of granddaughter Sarah. She thanks Stacy Cordery, Sara Day, Pat McNees, and Nell Minow, each of whom brought a writer's eye and a friend's sympathy to many obsessive discussions of this material. Special thanks go to her own dear friend of more than fifty years, Joanna Sturm. And thanks to her husband, T.L. Hawkins, for keeping the home fires burning.

Robert thanks Sarah McGinnis, Margaret McGinnis, Bill McGinnis, Elisabeth Bulloch, and Jeanne Hill. He is especially grateful to Carol McGinnis for enduring his preoccupation with life a hundred years ago. He also thanks Linda Clark for providing a refuge in Florida where portions of this book took form.

Both of us are grateful to Bruce Dinges for his faith in this project, his meticulous editing, and his patience when it turned out to be a far greater task than any of us imagined at the start.

Bibliography

ARTICLES AND BOOKS

Anderson, Mark Cronlund. *Pancho Villa's Revolution in Headlines.* Norman: University of Oklahoma Press, 2000.

Ayres, Edward L., Lewis L. Gould, David M. Oshinsky, and Jean R. Sonderlund. *American Passages: A History of the United States.* Orlando, Fla.: Harcourt College Publishers, 2000.

Beasley, Maurine, Holly Shulman, and Henry Beasley, eds. *The Eleanor Roosevelt [ER] Encyclopedia.* Westport, Conn.: Greenwood Press, 2001.

Black, Allida. "Eleanor Roosevelt," in Lewis L. Gould, ed. *American First Ladies: Their Lives and Their Legacy.* New York: Garland, 1996.

Caroli, Betty Boyd. *The Roosevelt Women.* New York: Basic Books, 1998.

"Civilian Defense—Some Administrative and Legal Problems," *Harvard Law Review* 55 (March 1942): 844–59.

Clements, Kendrick A. *The Presidency of Woodrow Wilson.* Lawrence: University Press of Kansas, 1992.

Cook, Blanche Weisen. *Eleanor Roosevelt, Volume I: 1884-1933; Volume II: 1933–1938.* New York: Viking, 1992, 1999.

Cooper, John Milton, Jr. *Breaking the Heart of the World.* New York and Cambridge: Cambridge University Press, 2001.

Cott, Nancy and Elizabeth H. Pleck, eds. *A Heritage of Her Own: Toward a New Social History of American Women.* New York: Simon & Schuster, 1979.

Cordery, Stacy A. *Alice Roosevelt Longworth: From White House Princess to Washington Power Broker.* New York: Viking, 2007.

Dalton, Kathleen. *Theodore Roosevelt: A Strenuous Life.* New York: Alfred A. Knopf, 2002.

Frost, Wladislava. "Cities and Towns Mobilize for War," *Amerian Sociological Review* 9 (February 1944): 85–89.

Goodwin, Doris Kearns. *No Ordinary Time: Franklin and Eleanor Roosevelt; The Home Front in World War II.* New York: Simon & Schuster, 1994.

Harvey, Paul, ed. *The Oxford Companion to English Literature.* 4th Edition. New York: Oxford University Press, 1967.

Herner, Charles. *The Arizona Rough Riders*. Reprint. Prescott, Ariz.: Sharlot Hall Museum Press, 1998.

Holmstrom, Betty. "Isabella Greenway and Gilpin Airlines." Unpublished manuscript. Greenway Collection, Arizona Historical Society, Tucson.

James, Olivia, ed. *The Letters of Elizabeth Sherman Lindsay, 1911–1954*. New York: Privately printed, 1960.

Katz, Friedrich. "Pancho Villa and the Attack on Columbus, New Mexico," *American Historical Review* 83 (1978): 102.

———. *The Secret War in Mexico: Europe, United States and the Mexican Revolution*. Chicago and London: University of Chicago Press, 1981.

Lash, Joseph P. *Eleanor and Franklin: The Story of Their Relationship*. New York: W. W. Norton & Co., 1973.

Link, Arthur S., ed. *The Papers of Woodrow Wilson. Volume 65: 1920*. Princeton: Princeton University Press, 1991.

Lowitt, Richard. *Bronson M. Cutting: Progressive Politician*. Albuquerque: University of New Mexico Press, 1992.

McCullough, David. *Mornings on Horseback*. New York: Simon & Schuster, 1981.

Meyer, Michael C., William L. Sherman, and Susan M. Deeds. *The Course of Mexican History*. 6th Editon. New York and London: Oxford University Press, 1999.

Miller, Candice. *The River of Doubt: Theodore Roosevelt's Darkest Journey*. New York: Doubleday, 2005.

Miller, Kristie. *Isabella Greenway: An Enterprising Woman*. Tucson: University of Arizona Press, 2004.

Morris, Edmund. *The Rise of Theodore Roosevelt*. New York: Coward, McCann & Geohegan, Inc., 1979.

———. *Theodore Rex*. New York: Random House, 2001.

Morris, Sylvia Jukes. *Edith Kermit Roosevelt: Portrait of a First Lady*. New York: Coward, McCann & Geoghegan, 1980.

The New Shorter Oxford English Dictionary on Historical Principles. Lesley Brown, ed. Volume 1. Oxford: Clarendon Press, 1993.

Ortiz, Stephen R. "The New Deal for Veterans: The Economy Act, the Veterans of Foreign Wars, and the Origins of New Deal Dissent," *The Journal of Military History* 70 (April 2006): 415–38.

Oulahan, Richard. *The Man Who . . .: 1932 Democratic National Convention*. New York: The Dial Press, 1971.

Papke, David Ray. "Rhetoric and Retrenchment: Agrarian Ideology and American Bankruptcy Law." *Missouri Law Review*. Fall 1989.

Pottker, Jan. *Sara and Eleanor: The Story of Sara Delano Roosevelt and Her Daughter-in-Law, Eleanor Roosevelt.* New York: St. Martin's Press, 2004.

Renehan, Edward. *The Lion's Pride: Theodore Roosevelt and His Family in Peace and War.* New York: Oxford University Press, 1998.

[Roosevelt, Eleanor.] *Mother and Daughter: The Letters of Anna and Eleanor Roosevelt.* New York: Fromm International, 1988.

———. *This I Remember.* New York: Harper & Brothers, 1949.

———. *This is My Story.* New York: Harper & Brothers, 1961.

Roosevelt, Elliott and James Brough. *A Rendezvous with Destiny: The Roosevelts of the White House.* New York: Putnam, 1975.

[Roosevelt, Theodore.] *Ranch Life and the Hunting Trail.* New York: The Century Co., 1888.

———. *Theodore Roosevelt: An Autobiography.* New York: Macmillan, 1913.

Sicherman, Barbara and Carol Hurd Green, eds. *Notable American Women: The Modern Period.* Cambridge, Mass.: The Belknap Press of Harvard University, 1980.

Somerville, Mollie. *Eleanor Roosevelt As I Knew Her.* Charlottesville: Howell Press, 1996.

Trager, James. *The People's Chronology.* New York: Henry Holt & Company, 1994.

Ward, Geoffrey C. *A First-Class Temperament: The Emergence of Franklin Roosevelt.* New York: Book of the Month Club, 1998.

Webster's New International Dictionary of the English Language. Springfield, Mass.: G & C Merriam Company, 1923.

Willert, Sir Arthur. *Washington & Other Memories.* Boston: Houghton Mifflin Company, 1972.

Wills, Garry. *Certain Trumpets: The Nature of Leadership.* New York: Simon & Schuster, 1994.

MANUSCRIPT COLLECTIONS

Eckles Papers. Fray Angélico Chávez History Library, Palace of the Governors (PG), Santa Fe. elibrary.unm.edu.

Ferguson Family Papers, private collection, Tucson, Arizona.

Greenway Papers, Arizona Historical Society (AHS), Tucson.
    Dinsmore Collection (DC)
    Ferguson Collection (FC)
    Greenway Collection (GC)

Eleanor Roosevelt Papers, Franklin D. Roosevelt Library (FDRL), Hyde Park, New York.

NEWSPAPERS AND PERIODICALS

Arizona Daily Star (Tucson)
Chicago Tribune
New York Times
Time
Town Topics (New York)
Wall Street Journal

Index

Index entries include page and note number, ie., 7n 32 = page 7, note 32.

174, 253, 254; illness of, 61; importance
of Isabella's friendship, xv, ix, 5, 7, 11,
19–20, 22–23, 37, 43, 54, 67, 106–107,
131–32, 148, 163–65, 244, 273, 277, 279,
281–82; interest in politics, 4, 31–32,
37, 39, 61, 133, 138, 287; and Isabella's
assistance to family, 227; and Isabella's
illness, 122; and Isabella's opposition
to FDR presidential re-election, x–xi,
261–62; and Isabella's relationship with
John Greenway, 85, 193, 273–74; life
in Albany, 40, 64; life in New York
City, 6, 46; life in Washington, D.C.,
70, 89, 134, 158, 247n 79; marriage of,
3–4; as Junior League member, 6n 27;
newspaper column by, 243, 253, 264n
10; and 1912 Democratic National
Convention, 46–47; opposes Economy
Act (1933), 230; personality of, 139;
political and social activism of, 30, 74n
151, 167, 170, 182, 196–98, 199–200,
203, 206, 215, 237, 240n 57, 258; political and social life of, 8, 29–30, 69–70,
72, 74, 91–93, 112, 133, 169; relationship
with Alice Roosevelt Longworth, 130,
135, 138, 281; relationship with Anna
Roosevelt Cowles, 10, 17 n70, 67, 70;
relationship with Ferguson children
85–86, 108, 116; relationship with Susan
Parish, 35n 33, 145, 170; relationship
with Theodore Roosevelt, 9–11, 78, 90;
role in Franklin's political life, 29–32,
34, 40, 67, 176, 182; self-education
of, 20–21, 39, 79, 92; sense of family duty, 110; servants of, 46, 91, 170;
shops for Isabella and children, 49,
60, 113–15; supports Arizona Inn, 242;
supports Isabella's political activities,
234, 240, 252; and TR's 1912 presidential campaign, 38, 40–41, 47, 61; and
threat from Mexican Revolution, 139,
143–44; travels of, 111, 161; views on
Prohibition, 219–20; views on women's
suffrage, 23, 57, 67; visits Isabella,

14–15, 24, 41-44, 45, 49, 92, 97,
99-103, 104-105, 109-13, 144, 147, 163,
165, 168, 179, 193, 197, 216, 227, 233,
241, 245, 247–49, 251–52, 255, 259, 263,
274; visits Tucson, 225, 228–30
Roosevelt, Eleanor (Hall Roosevelt's daughter), 175
Roosevelt, Eleanor Butler (Theodore
Roosevelt, Jr.'s wife), 24n 92, 147n 158,
172, 173n 41
Roosevelt, Elizabeth Donney, 220 n6
Roosevelt, Elliott (Eleanor's father), xiii n1,
111 1
Roosevelt, Elliott (Eleanor's son), 34, 110,
141, 171–72, 204, 232; activities of,
120-21; adult life of, 286; birth of, 26;
childhood of, 28–29, 32, 53, 123, 169,
140; education of, 158; and financial
assistance from Isabella, 227–28; illness
of, 84, 92, 136, 139, 160, 162; personality
of, 59, 61, 71, 79; in Tucson, 229, 231;
marriages of, 220, 230
Roosevelt, Emmett, 13
Roosevelt, Ethel (Theodore Roosevelt's
daughter). *See* Derby, Ethel Roosevelt
Roosevelt, Ethel du Pont (Franklin
Roosevelt, Jr.,'s wife), 251
Roosevelt, Franklin Delano, 163, 232, 247
n79; affair with Lucy Mercer, 151,
159 –60; as Assistant Secretary of
the Navy, 10n 43, 67, 68, 70, 72, 76,
83, 86, 91–93, 130, 156, 178, 183; as
campaign manager for Al Smith, 197;
at Campobello Island, 5, 16 –17, 48,
60, 73-79, 97, 99 –100, 121–22, 123n
87, 139; children of, 12, 14, 99, 286;
courtship of Eleanor, xvi, 1–2; and
disability from polio, 183–84, 187 –88,
196, 200, 202, 204–205, 280, 287;
death of, 274–75; education of, 122n
86; Eleanor's and Isabella's influence
on, 235–36, 238 –40, 282; Eleanor's role
in political career of, 29–30, 34; family
of, 8n 36, 9 –10, 15, 45n 66, 53, 60n 114,

The Arizona Historical Society, 2009